AFRIKAN BIBLE

THE AFRICAN SPIRITUAL BIBLE

Complied by Vincent Happy Mnisi

This Bible is composed of extracts from The Book of Enoch; The Kolbrin Bible and The Egyptian Book of the dead. I have not added or taken anything out of these books, I felt obliged to compile this Afrikan Bible and I pray that Africans can adopt their true religion of God. Overstanding that God lives in them making them virtually Gods too. Start to live your Godly purpose on Earth and stop praying for heaven when heaven is right here on Earth. Discover your Godly purpose now, because everyone is born with a divine spark in them discover your spark! Get Enlightened and start enjoying your life here on Earth…..Vincent Happy Mnisi

AFRIKAN BIBLE

Contents

Emancipation Lecture	Page 3
Romancathohellism	Page 29
The Book Of Enoch	Page 36
The Kolbrin Bible	Page 114
The Egyptian Book of the Dead	Page 416

Sunday 13th January 2018

Emancipation Lecture

AFRIKAN BIBLE

Good evening to you all and thank you you all for coming. I was born on the 29th of March 1970 it was at 5.30 on the morning of Easter Sunday in Soweto Zondi Two Johannesburg South Africa. I am very honored by everybody's presence here today as I try to break down the art of attaining African Enlightenment....

Firstly we must accept that the Christian way of life as false and that their belief systems created by the Roman Catholic Church to be false too. I will prove to you today that it was a European invention and was a means to of acquiring World Domination through religion.

It's time for Africa to wake up! I have been writing since 2010 with my first book being "Africa Must Unite" which was a rewrite of what I initially wrote down pen to paper after an incident that occurred in Grahamstown where I encountered a dark force that wanted my soul in 1992. It was after an arrest when some crazy stuff started happening around me as I found myself under attack from some demonic realm.

It was in the prison cell and time when I really acknowledged the presence of a Supreme God looking after me through my trials and tribulations. I have now learnt that I have an inner spirit that protects and guides me through my virtues life that I am very thankful for, Thanks God!

I recall seeing a holographic figure on the wall of the police cell of an Old Man sitting and I noticed that his skin was made of light, he had long white hair and a long beard too. He just stared at me and reached out to me and once he did that, I found the strength to beat the attack....

You all must be wondering what had got me into the Police cell in the first place. Right? I recall the arrest quite clearly even though it happened 23 years ago. I had long dreadlocks at that time student life smoking weed and selling weed too. Smoke weed Everyday!!!!

I believe my third eye opened up for the first time because all of a sudden I could tell and see the evilness of the gathering only to find out later that Grahamstown is a Stanistsic Town. I was shocked at the extent this attack went on for, I went berserk in the Police holding cell they had to sedate me and they institutionalised me.

I recall an awkward incident while under arrest, an African Police Officer was addressing somebody who never showed himself to me after I had demanded he show himself to me, as the Officer had addressed him as God and knowing me. I jumped on that statement demanding he show himself to me if he regarded himself as God on Earth. He never showed himself to me, but kept giving instructions to the Officer.

This made me really wonder what was happening to me? Some guy called God was giving instructions on how I should be incarcerated. I thought to myself "I am in some deep shit here" and it really felt like it. My mind was racing as I couldn't get my head around what was happening to me.

To cut a Long story short, My Mother praise my Mother got me out of this mental institution they had decided to admit me into, My brother had got hold of her and informed her of my situation and when she arrived because of her medical background informed me to stop taking any medication and informed the staff that they shouldn't feed me anything and that she was going to bring in home cooked meals. Clever Mum!!!.....I am very thankful to my mother, I wouldn't be standing here if it wasn't because of her naturing and tender loving care that will never end. Thanks Ma My Queen!!!..Why don't we all thank our mothers for the gift of life?....

I was released in my Mum's care and on our journey back to Cape Town I was still in haze from the overload of drugs but my Mum's food had worked magic and I began to regain myself. When we discuss the incident with my mother she tells me she was worried I might get a relapse or another attack. I told her I was just thinking how a weekend trip to Grahamstown turned out to last three weeks.

I was attending the AAA School of Advertising being sponsored by the ANC, my brother and I had a lovely one bedroomed flat on Long Street 408 Senator Park, it had the most amazing view of the Table Mountain.

My Girlfriend at that time Claudia Klaase who later became my Wife and the mother of my only child was overjoyed to see me and my Mother left me in her care. I picked up a pen and writing pad I began writing for three days none stop day and night I just could stop writing, I recall it was about the evils and the witchcraft of the Europeans.

Bless Claudia wherever she is now, because I recall her demanding I stop and eat something which she had to forced feed me oh bless her and thank you! I lost that transcript and wish I had kept it for future reference, As I have discovered lately that our brains are like computers and it has been filtering it in my books thus far.

In my first publication Africa Must Unite some white friends back in the UK found it radical and racist against them.

As The ANC had paid for my education in advertising, I felt obligated to help out in they 1995 Local Government Elections. I approached Hunt Lascaris TBWA by faxing them my CV, Faxing how things have changed? I enclosed a referral letter from the ANC, I even posted the originals keeping a copy of course….

I never heard from them for weeks, I recall spending days awaiting by phone and awaiting a letter of acknowledgement of having received my application. I decided to call them and enquire what was the hold up, only to be told that I wasn't even being considered for a position.

Knowing me I flipped on the phone and threatened the HR person on the phone with media exposure and just slammed the phone down. I decided to face this roadblock head on so I firstly cut my long dreadlocks and dressed as formally as I could master with my present wardrobe at that time. I was livered and angry that they were handling a Multi-Million Rand ANC advertising budget and they didn't want to employ me, I had to find out why? Not after I had enclosed a letter from the ANC Headquarters.

What happened at that office still stuns me to this very day when I think about it. As because of my resolute pragmatic approach I had encountered this problem head on, I left the office with a signed Letter of Appointment beginning tomorrow morning. This is when I first met Ken Modise who was then a Director in charge of the ANC account. He resigned on that day to make way for me. Thanks Ken, you were always a blessing even getting me a Job at Young and Rubicam Cape Town in 1997.

AMC Hunt Lascaris TBWA was an Inhouse Advertising/Marketing company in TBWA and operated as a separate entity from TBWA. I was placed under the Directorship of Lyn Mausenbaum a Jewish lady, I soon discovered that it was a Jewish Institution. I got to work on the ANC; SAB; EDS Computers and they Coca Cola accounts. I even helped them win loads of new accounts as I was always involved in pitches and presentations. I wonder why?...I was being used as a black face as I helped them win the Gauteng Housing Account beating Peter Vundla's pitch with HerdBoys in 1995.

I met Mandela, Zuma and Ramaphosa in 1995, I was shocked by Nelson Mandela because just before shaking his hand he stated "So you are Vincent Mnisi" as we shock hands I was amazed that he knew my name and just answered "yes Sir" he went on to say "You are doing a great job for us keep it up" and I replied "Thank you sir".

I was humbled and honoured and still brag about it every chance I get...like this one but after finding out how much he sold us out, I am not so honoured anymore I actually detest his name…..Just a little biography so you understand me.

Now to fast forward to the purpose of the Lecture "AFRICAN EMANCIPATION It's time for Africa to Awaken!!!, it's taken me over 48 years of my life to figure it out and discover the truth. I began digging the truth after watching and listening to Ex-Pastor Ray Hagin Sermons of Christianity on Youtube.

I began my own research and came across "The Roman Conspiracy to created Jesus Christ" and this had Professors; Doctors and renowned Authors who have identified the Bible to be an Algorithm of a book by Josepuish when he wrote about the life of Titus Flava The Great.

My research proved to me that the present Bible Text is nothing else but a mind controlling Propaganda machine and tool for the Roman Catholic Church and the Rothschild Family and the European Jewish tribe.

My research proved that the Roman Catholic Church created Jesus by allowing Cesare Borgia a son of a Pope to pose as Jesus. My research also proved that the

Jesus mystical virgin birth was stolen from the Mythical stories of Horus of Egypt and Yeshua Ben Pandira son of the Panther who lived one hundred and fifty years before they created Jesus, he was from Ethiopia. The dead sea scrolls describe him as the teacher of Righteousness.

I also discovered a funning thing I hadn't noticed in my 48 years of Christian life that most of the Bible is written by Saint Paul who was an ex-Roman Soldier who so happened to have some kind of Flashing lights talk to him after he had persecuted thousands of African Gnostic Christians. He claims that Jesus Christ confronted him, this is fifty years after Yeshua/Jesus was meant to have lived? If this doesn't not sound like another bases of a cult belief system? Then I don't know? It sounds like another John Smith in his book for the Mormons.

I have one question to ask devout Christians as I know they are plenty of you here, How can you believe the writings of Paul and his team of Scholars about the life of Jesus/Yeshua as though they lived with him 50 years after he had lived. I find this maneuver by the Roman Catholic Church quite cunny as they used the writings of Saint Paul as the foundings of the Christian Faith and a means to control Christianity.

The Bible in its present form has been doctored and it selected the Akerzarian Jews as God's chosen tribe writing in the Fake Zionist Jews into the Bible. I have always questioned myself and wondered why Jesus was born white, my extensive research led me to discover Yehusa of Ethiopia was actually born in a cave and had studied sorcery in Egypt and was killed by hanging in Israel by the Romans...Google it? "The True life of Yeshua Ben Pandira.

Look at this Map of Africa it's joined to the Middle East, as far as I am concerned there is no Middle East and that's North Africa. Everybody can see that right?

The gospels of Jesus Christ/Yeshua in King James Bible are a sophisticated pro-Roman multi-layered allegorical written text used a political tool to control the Christian World. I will now recite a view verses in the Bible which I must thank Lucia Pontsho Mathabo for highlighting these obvious and yet not so obvious contradictions written in the Bible. This Christian Bible you found so holy is not so holy after all after some closer inspection.

Psalms 92 V 15/Gen 18 V 25/Deut 32 V 4/ Rom 2 V 11/Ezek 18 V 25 states "God is Unjust and Partial" in Gen 9 V 25 and in Exodus 20 V 5 it states "God is the Author of Evil". In Rom 9 V 11/ Matt 13 V 12. In 2 Samuel 21 V 8; 9; 14 and also in Genesis 22 V 2 and also in Judges 11 V 300-32, 34-38 and 39 it states "God accepts Human Sacrifices. This just quoting three very contradictory ones they get worse.

"Slavery and oppression ordained" is in Genesis 9 v 25/ Leviticus 25 V 45,46 and also in Joel 3 V 8. Lying approved and sanctioned in Josh 2 V 4 to 6/James 2 V 25; Exodus 1 18 V 20/ 1 Kings 22 V 21 to 22. Robbery commanded in Exodus 3 V 21 to 22 and also in Exodus 13 V 135 to 136, I found these verses very contradictory to known Christian Values.

AFRIKAN BIBLE

Who ever rewrote the Bible definitely had a lot of guts because in Jer 32 V 27 they state "God is all Powerful" and go on to contradict it in Matt 19 V 26 were it states "God is not all powerful" WOW!!! Matthew had guts hay? I rest my case!!....

I will now refer you to a letter written by King Leopold to his Colonial Missionary venture in the Congo written in 1883, Google it please this is the age of information and it you are uninformed or ill-informed it's your fault. Information is key to self development.

Leopold states in his letter I quote " Reverends, Fathers and Dear compatriots The task that is given to you to fulfil is very delicate and requires much tact, You will go there to certainly to evangelize, but your evangelization must inspire above all Belgium's interests. Your principal objective in our mission in the Congo is never to teach the nigger to know God, this they know already....WOW!!!!...he was deep?

He went on to say " Keep watch and disinterest those savages from the riches that's plenty, Verse such as "My Riches await me in the kingdom of Heaven" "Happier are the poor because they will inherit their riches in heaven" Encourage them to love poverty with Verses like "It's difficult for the rich to enter the Kingdom of God" and teach they young to disrespect everything which may give them courage to confront us, I refer to they Mystic Systems and their war fetish protection which they pretend not to want to abandon and you must do everything in your power to make it disappear.

His ending took me back really giving me the psychological genius He goes on to instruct them " Your actions will be directed to the women and essentially the younger ones for they won't revolt when the recommendations of the Priest is in contradictory to their parents teachings.

The children have to learn to obey what the missionary father recommends who is their father of their soul....he was deep I must say!....I just wonder what the British Monarchy told their missionaries? It just makes you wonder doesn't it?

My research discovered loads I would like you all to Google the Christ used in the Russian Orthodox Church, Just google it now please and tell me what image do you see? Black Yeshua/Jesus right? This why the Roman Catholic split from the Orthodox Church in year 1054 because they wanted to create Jesus in their own image.

In 1090's the Roman Catholic Crusades began. This is after they had Cesare Borgia model for Leonardo Da Vinci essentially making him a God. You all must be wondering what happened to the those who knew the truth, they were burnt on the stake or had they heads chopped off.

They tried to burn any text that contradicted their Bible hence books such as the Kolbrin Bible had to be buried only to be resurrected now, I will quote from it later in the lecture it is a written translation from The Sixth Egyptian papyrus scrolls hence I have decided to compile the first African Bible along it's teachings of self belief and honoring the God in us first instead awaiting a God from the sky.

The Europeans wanted the future generations of Christians to be indoctrinated and only know their European Image of Christ. But behind closed doors or maybe not so closed because of this Picture of the two Popes talking under the Black madonna and child had me thinking and I think they did it intentionally too.

Europeans have used reverse psychology to have the world believe in their version of the European Jewish Blue Eyed and Blonde Jesus/Yeshua. I must admit that they used some very powerful spell because for 48 years of my life I believed that Yeshua AKA Jesus was a white Jew. Didn't you all? And I am quite sure they are some who still believe so, I hope to change your views and belief systems with this lecture too.

This fictional story of the white Jewish Jesus has led to the invasion of North Africa Palestine due the biblical story of them been led of Egypt by Moses was all made up and outrages. Look at what they are doing in Palestine now and they claim to be God's chosen tribe which God are they talking of here? They have used the Fake bible as a tool of colonising a nation of muslims, they have been building up for the biggest religious war between Muslims and Christians nations where they will spill loads of blood making it the bloodiest Nuclear third World War.

Yeshua was described as an Essene, they are portrayed as African people in the King James Bible they were brutally persecuted by Saint Paul and often feed to the Lions as source of entertainment.

Yeshua Ben Pandira was known as the Great Spiritual Master connected in particular with the power of speech of the words. He was accused of blasphemy was stoned and hanged on a tree. I will now sum up on my take on Christianity.

Christianity was devised and created to mislead us Africans from our natural beliefs systems of Ancestral Worship and African Spirituality. The Bible and Christianity is very confused because I do recall Jesus consulting with his Ancestors Moses and Isaiah double standards I must say? I really don't take the bible seriously anymore and I wouldn't use it in a court of law because it's all fiction.

Capitalism is usually assumed to have flowered around the same time as the age of European Enlightenment in the early 1800's. In fact the Catholic Church were instrumental in its inception by introducing rationalising economic life, it was the Catholics that put in place the preconditions of the Capitalism which certain tenets. Firstly was that the rule of law and bureaucracy for resolving disputes rationally when Ideas and patents were stolen. Educating and building a specialised labour force, the created Institutions that allow for transgenerational investment and sustained intellectual physical efforts together with the accumulation of long-term capital which encouraged the zest for new discoveries, enterprise, wealth creation and new business ventures.

All this was made possible by the Freedom for Enterprise Markets and Competition. Most Churches own nearly a third of all the land in the World.

Pope John Paul II once pointed out that the main cause of wealth is knowledge, science, know-how, discovery and human capital" Religious values attached to hard and good manual work was part of their propaganda to get Europe out of poverty in the late 1600's.

The Christian world is currently living under a spell that has been cast upon them with this fictional storyline of White Jewish Jesus who happens to love money and can't get enough of it. They constant rhetoric of tithing 10% of your earnings so that they can live like this and travel in Private Jets, I recall watching a televangelist programme sometime ago where this pastor in America got his congregation buy him a fifth plane.

I did a research on the wealth of all the churches and wondered why they couldn't stop world poverty and hunger overnight because they have the strength and power to do this. The Church of Jesus Christ of the Latter-Day is the wealthiest worth a whopping 40 billion dollars, second comes the Romans whom are worth 30 billion dollars; third comes The Church of England which is worth 7.8 billion dollars and then 4th is Opusi Dei which is worth 2.8 Billion. These Churches can solve world poverty with just 1% of their wealth.

Tithing has made Pastors rich and they congregations poor, the richest of them all is African Pastor Bishop Oyedepo who is worth 150 million dollars, Second place another African/American Pastor based in Ameirca Bishop TD Jakes who is worth 147 million dollars; Third place come in another African Pastor Pastor Chris Oyakholome who is worth 50 million dollars. Black Pastors siphoning money from their congregation in the name of this Fake White Jewish Jesus.

4th place spot is taken by a White man finally Benny Hinn who is worth 42 million dollars, 5th spot is taken by another African Pastor Adeboye who is worth 39 million dollars; 6th place is taken by Creflo Dollar who is worth 27 million; 7th place is taken by Pastor Kenneth Copeland who used to hold the number one spot is worth 25 million dollars sharing the number 7th spot is Billy Grahams. Prophet TB Joshua is worth 10 million dollars and finally Joseph Prince who is worth 5 million dollars all this money earned from book sales and other merchandise propagating the false Bible.

6 out of the 10 pastors I researched on are black pastors and they congregations comprise of mostly Black people. 4 out of the 10 are from Nigeria. The richest Churches are are situated in the USA, Vatican City and England.

The Christian world has to break away from funding the lavish lifestyles of these church leaders, I propose that Governments should take these Churches to task into actually spending all their hoarded monies into uplifting the communities that they serve in. I salute the Cameroonian President who shut down over 2000 churches overnight. Christianity is a cult developed by the Europeans to psychologically take over the world. This fictional Bible written by Paul and his team actually wrote in the Fake Khazarian Jews as their chosen tribe, I am actually ashamed of myself that I once believed in this Fake Bible what a pile of rubbish.

I will quote from my sixth book which was suppressed by Amazon "MY AFRICAN BLACK BOOK" "Capitalism is another system built to ensure that large corporations whose foundations can be traced back to slavery, colonisation, imperialism and Neo-Imperialism agendas will continue to own the world wealth which are in the hands and controlled by European run companies and establishments.

This Capitalistic world we live now is full of cheats, scoundrels, manipulative individuals and companies wanting in on the next big idea. They swamp on every latest innovation like bees do to honey. They break down products and recreate their own brands in-order to create competition which is at times unwarranted behavior causing loses for the innovators.

Capitalism is just pure evil thievery scheme worked up by the European Mentality is to discover Land that was already occupied by other Races and claim to invent products that were already invented by other Races here just a few examples of Black Inventor Excellence.

They even stole our Egyptian/Ethiopian Religions and sold it back to us packaged in their Fake Bible. The Venezuelan Crisis is another classic capitalist ploy, Imagine deposing an elected President and installing an unelected President shame on the European World. Venezuela, Syria and North Korea are the only countries without a Rothschild Usrary Reserve Bank hence the crisis. In Libya they created a Reserve Bank In Benghazi at the beginning of the Libyan Crisis, undermining the Libyan Currency. R.I.P Gaddafi he was one enlightened man you should all read his "Green Book" very deep indeed.

In a book "The Industrial Revolution of the Middle Ages by historian Jean Gimpel who wrote about the inventions of Mechanical Clocks, New Windmills, improvement to wagons and carts, eyeglasses, magnifying glasses, iron smelting and ironwork stone cutting and new architectural principle were refined all were inspired by capitalism which kinda makes it good but bad too because of the competitions it creates and what people will do to win is the question?. Look at these Black African American Brothers who made the first car before Henry Ford. Inventions are good by capitalism is bad because everyone want to capitalise on all new inventions and rebrand them....so be careful and always patent your inventions.

In my My African Black book I go on to state that "I propose that all companies should issue 20% shares to their Workforce in their annual profit sharing. My arguments is that workers contribute as much as the owners to make sure that their company remains profitable and hence should be rewarded profitably accordingly too.

Working and building another's person's dream at the current pay rate is economic slavery in disguise and now everybody in the world is out to get themselves on as much worthless paper-Money!!!

Which gets paid into a bank account, this money is then used by the Bankers to make more money while it sits in their bank accounts. This world is a Bankers paradise and they are the only ones profiting from everybody that is living.

Inflation is another made up fallacy and currencies can be controlled by the confidence in the currency as a means of exchange set by the internal forces and should never be influenced by outside forces. The London Currency Exchange centre needs to be put out of business, one question I would ask them what is in England in terms of mineral wealth that makes their currency so strong? I live there and I know that all their have is Coal and Scottish Oil.

Africa needs to set up their own African Reserve Bank without any Rothschild or private shares issued out. Shares must be issued to African states and its people. It should be run and controlled by the African Union, I do believe once we get our currencies away from the hands of the Rothschild family we have a better chance of survival in this Global economy.

European; American and Chinese economies are now heavily depended on their mineral rights that they have in Africa through their Multinational companies which are mainly controlled by graduates from one or more of these so called Secret Societies who appoint their graduates into Political, Business and Religious positions of power.

Our only economical hope from this abject poverty Africa finds itself in is African unity, Unity is strength which will liberate Africans to command respect from the World. We need to unite Politically; Economically; Socially and Culturally like it's never been done or attempted before. We Africans share one common theme and hold similar cultural values of Ubuntu and that should be the bases for out Unity.

Africa requires a new kind of leadership and all of you here are the future leaders of tomorrow. Never look down at your dreams because it's your intuition and your personal God alerting you of what is possible. It's time now to model your dreams within your chosen academic field as this capitalistic world is always looking for slaves to exploit and my advice is never be scared to change your mind and take a different path. Change is good.

The mounting crisis we now face and need to encounter head on is the current economic race being waged between China, USA and Europe utilizing African resources. If Africa does not unite our race will parish into the worst poverty unimaginable, we are already in Poverty as we are still being classified as the third world classes citizens.

It's known fact that the Rothschild Family have sponsored both sides of every war fought in Continental Europe and America. I also have some notions that they also sponsored other proxy wars in Africa too like they did with Cecil John Rhodes. They have been fueling the need for human carnage, from Napoleon times both sides of the war I wonder why? I found this picture rather interesting and odd, the current Catholic Pope kissing the hand of the Rothschilds.

They regard themselves as the Gods of the Earth, they wrote in the European Jews as the chosen tribe in their Fake Bible. Do you really believe some Europeans tribe originated from Palestine North Africa? There is no Middle East as far as I am concerned that's North Africa you can see that it's attached.

I will now quote from my fourth book Inspire Aspire for Assertiveness "Your purpose in life, you should have several which can be changed from time to time. One purpose everybody should have is making the world a better place.

May your lives be at peace and may it overflow with peace, love and pure awesomeness today and everyday of your life. May the Sun bring you new energy by day and may the Moon restore you by night. May the breeze blow new strength into your being. May you walk gently through the world and know it's beauty all the days of your life."

"God created humankind and gave them their rights to live their lives. With that right God gave humankind the power of discretion, which is the power to choose their own course of Action. Without discretion life is meaningless."

"A Good life is when you smile often, dream big, laugh a lot and realise how blessed you are for what you have. Let your dreams be bigger than your fears and your actions speak louder than your words. Enjoy your life, for life is for us to live the best at what we are great at, so self-discover what you are born to do and make mint."

"Learn to enjoy every minute of your life, be happy now don't wait for something outside yourself to make your happy in the future. Give so much time to the improvement of yourself that you have no time to criticise others, live in faith that the world is on your side for as long as you are true to the best that is in you."

"Revive your light manifest your dreams, realise your worth, the most important thing is to realise yourself worth. When you know your worth, you set standards for you. Don't be pushed by your problems, be led by your dreams."

"Once you connect with yourself it is impossible to be lonely or desperate for other peoples company. Be Happy like my name sake, Be Bright, Be You! The distance between your dreams and reality is called action…

Go forward in life with a twinkle in your eye and a smile on your face always with great strong purpose in your heart. I advice you all to watch David Icke's interview with Credo Mutwa he confirms that the Europeans used witchcraft to subue Africa, I must warn you it's six hours long.

I will end with a quote with a quote from my African Unity books Africa Must Unite and The United Countries of Africa Now!!!..."Africa Must Unite because of the common history and social conditions Africa's share, our societies have been more inclined to take for granted the Europeans desirable models, the thoughts as well as the artifacts of the dominant colonial culture. Artifacts indeed which we cannot do without such as Electricity; Cars; Telephones; Television; Western Music and European Literature etc. We can adopt all these but we will only become mimics if we do not adopt them fully conscious of our own History, Culture and Traditions." "Africa needs to establish its own think tanks and Social Institutions. Africa needs to cultivate upon our music and arts. African Hip Hop is making trends worldwide become creative, create yourself out of poverty by self discovery and selling yourself to the world".

"We must adopt a critical attitude both to what we have and what is brought to us. This should be a guiding principle in the selection of what we teach and how we teach it. African writers the creators of new Literature need to give us in this area of critical thinking."

"Our aims of teaching our youth should be to produce men and women who are both critical and creative. Our students should be encouraged to be thinkers and doers rather than accumulators of facts and received knowledge. It's time to start seeking knowledge from within. I am the future, we are the Future lets build a stable African society with any strive and want"

"This must be so if they are to be instrumental to the change that is needed. African Youth need communicate with each other and one African universal Language must be adopted by the African Union, which must be taught at every school in Africa. This Must be so if Africa aims to start working towards the realisation of a just and consequently stable African Society…..

African Spirituality is simple and does not require you to attend a church, you are the church. Firstly you have to overstand your heritage speak to your families from both sides Mother and Father get to know your family history and rediscover your true worth on earth. Always listen to that inner voice your intuition it's your Godly Spirit talking to you listen.

I will quote Emperor Haile Selassie I the last King of Ethiopia look at this picture of the English Queen Bowing down to him.

"Spirituality does not come from religion. It comes from our soul. We must stop confusing religion and spirituality. Religion is a set of rules, regulations and rituals created by humans, which was supposed to help people grow spiritually. Due to human imperfection religion has become corrupt, political, divisive and a tool for power struggle. Spirituality is not theology or ideology. It is simply a way of life, pure and original as was given by the Most High of Creation. Spirituality is a network linking us to the Most High, the universe and each other"……Haile Selassie I

"God is in all and He encompasses all...This is the secret of life: Man lives in God and God lives in man. This answers all questions"...Kolbrin Bible.

Those who turn away from the glorious jewel within to seek an outside god, a separate, unresponsive being, are looking for a mere trinket, while disregarding the priceless treasure already in their keeping"....Kolbrin Bible

Download it's for free now and get enlightened, deep I must say!!! hopefully resonates with your soul.....

"Man worships, not to make God greater, for this he cannot do, but to make himself greater. Nothing man can do can add to what God already has. Men conceive God as a Being having greatly magnified human qualities, as a kinglike Being greater than any king. Thus man falls into error...Kolbrin Bible

"Among earthly things man shall find nothing greater than himself. God is in all and He encompasses all. ...Kolbrin Bible

"A lifting hand is worth ten wagging tongues. Be a man of fortitude and courage. Prepare to fight, for Earth gives man but two choices: to struggle or perish. There is work to be done in the Garden of God, therefore cease useless performances and word-wasting discussions, go, pick up the hoe and tackle the task to hand"....Kolbrin Bible

"If a man would know Heaven, he must first know Earth. Man cannot understand Heaven until he understands Earth. He cannot understand God until he understands himself, and he cannot know love unless he has been loveless.

God is unknown but not unknowable. He is unseen but not unseeable. God is unheard but not unhearable. He is not understood but He is understandable. The goal of life is upstream, not downstream. Man must struggle against the current, not drift with the flow. A child is born knowing all God intended it to know, the rest it must discover for itself. Man does not live to increase the glory of God, this cannot be done, but to increase the glory of man"....Kolbrin Bible

"The purpose of all human life is a goal so glorious it surpasses all earthly understanding. We may visualise our individual goals as we will, it is ordained that we have this freedom. How close or how far we are from reality is of little consequence, what is, is. He who seeks a non-existent destination will, nevertheless, get somewhere. He who seeks not at all will get nowhere. Earthly life fulfils itself without attainment".....Kolbrin Bible

"Man sees glory by the reflected light of glory within him, he knows love by the love within himself. The sun is seen by the light of the sun and not by any light within man. Man sees the spirit by the light of the spirit, and not by any light within his mortal self. Only by the light of the spirit can the spirit of man be lit".....Kolbrin Bible

"I am the living consciousness within you, I am the knower. The things seen by the eye and the things smelt by the nose are received by me. The things heard and the things felt are registered by me.

I am the inner being causing all decisions to be made, though the tongue report back outside the things that I, the soul and the spirit, hold recorded. Everything done and undertaken, such as the working of the hands and movement of the legs, all are done in accordance with my command"….Kolbrin Bible

"Men reap as they sow and I am the Fertile Field which takes no part in the sowing or the reaping. Man is his own master and the lord of his own destiny. He cannot expect help from any great power, unless he himself expend effort to contact such power or be deserving of help. Everything a man is or becomes is the result of his own striving and efforts, or his lack of them. I made man to be a man",...Kolbrin Bible

"I am not influenced by the mere formal actions of men, or by empty sacrifice. Lighted lamps and candles, days of fasting and self-mortification by man cannot sway Me in his favour. I am not to be bribed, for I am God....Kolbrin Bible

I am the God Who ordained the Law, and nothing man can do will change it. My love alone mitigates the consequences of man's unredeemed wickedness."...Kolbrin Bible

"I am the Changeless One. Could a God of Love become a God of Vengeance? Revenge is something alien to Me. Therefore, is it reasonable that men should believe I could be one thing today and then because they fall into error become something else tomorrow? My nature is not as that of man. I AM as I AM......Kolbrin Bible

Thank you all for coming and listening to me tonight, I will now take your question? I will sign all bought copies afterwards thank you all!!!!Good Night!!!

Romancathohellism

The Roman Catholic Church created Jesus at the inception of Christianity into a formal religion at the Council of Nicaea by using mythical stories of Virgin Births from Egypt; Asia and South America. The Roman Catholic Church was formed in year 325 at the Council of Nicaea at their first post Apostical Ecumenical Council of the Christian community. Christianity began as a pagan and persecuted religion. It was illegal in the Roman Empire until Constantine gathered the different schools of thought of God to formulate one Religion.

The teachings of Jesus Christ of Nazareth came from their ancient pagan mystery schools and the Gospels of Jesus were written by a family of Caesars and their supporters, who left the World documents to prove that they fictionalised the stories of Jesus. The Gospels of Jesus Christ are a sophisticated pro-Roman multi-layered allegorical text used as a political tool to control the masses of that day and has evolved into as an accepted worldwide religion with more than one billion believers.

A number of Scholars and Professors have studied the bible, I recommend you to watch "The Roman Conspiracy to Create Christ" on Youtube. After careful inspections along with the works of Josephus on his biography of Titus Flava the Great on his military campaign in North Africa they couldn't help notice the similarities to the live of Jesus as described in the New Testament. This documentary proves that Jesus Christ nothing more than a fictional character cooked up by the Roman Catholic Church, they cooked up his disciples too.

The Roman Catholic Church in the 5th Century assumed both temporal and spiritual authority in Europe it had enormous influence on the developments of the art and culture of the Western World throughout the middles ages. Today its growth is concentrated in Africa, South America and Asia. The year 381 they held the "First Council of Constantinople, this council amended and ratified the Nicene Creed and resulting in the version of Christianity we have today in all Roman Catholic Churches and the Christian world.

In year 440 the Roman Catholic Church decided to appoint a Pope they own version of God on Earth by creating "The Holy Father" Pope Leo I was appointed the first ever Pope assuming the God on earth status.

In 451 at their Council of Chalcedon, at this council was the sign of institutionalised divisions within Christianity. In year 1054 the Great Schism was the formulation of the division and the Roman Catholic formally creating the European Jesus Christ image. The Church divided into Eastern and Western branches over theological, cultural, linguistic and ecclesiological disputes. This separation was the first Large-Scale division within Christendom.

In the 16th Century at the Council of Trent in 1545 became their centralising movement within Catholicism that enhanced the authority of of Rome. It was at this Council when the Protestant reformed and formed their own Church. They split was due to disputes over books that were included in the Old Testament which was the inclusion of the White Jewish Slavery story in Egypt which was to be foundation was to be the foundations of the formation of the Jewish Religion and the Zionist Jewish Religion.

Under the guise of Christianity the Papal Church has committed more crimes against humanity. Disregarding their maxim's and the spirit of the Gospel the Papal Church armed itself with the power of the sword during the Crusades they ravaged North Africa and main land Africa for centuries raping the woman and killing all the men hence Egyptian and Ethiopians today look mixed blooded.

Majority of practising Christians and practising Roman Catholic Priests and Bishops don't know or don't want to know about the true bloody history of the Papal Church of Rome the origin of Christianity. The true history of the Christian Faith has been hidden away from the eyes of the masse, through the rewriting of the history books.

"Roman Catholicism was born in blood, has wallowed in blood and has quenched it's thirst in blood, and it is in letter's of blood of the martyrs of Jesus" ....Baron De Ponnat 1940

The Roman Catholic Churches Crusades began in earnest in 1209 going on for over 20 years until 1229 with their Albigensian Crusades in Southern France. Roman Catholic Crusaders slaughtered approximately 200 000 citizens of Bezier, France on July 22 1209. Both Albigensian Christian and Catholics too were slain by the time the Roman Catholic Army finished their crusades in France almost the entire population of Southern France mostly Albigensian Christians had been exterminated.

The Catholic Crusades against the Albigensian's in Southern France from 1209-1229 under three Popes first being Pope Innocent III, Honorius and Gregory IX was one of the bloodiest tragedies in human history.

In the Year 1236 Roman Catholic Crusaders slaughtered 30 000 Jews in Anjou and Poitou regions of Western France in a severe wave of religious persecution.

In 1481 at the Direction from Rome the Roman Catholic Inquisitions began, authorising torture, burning and the slaughtering of hundreds of thousands of people during the Spanish Inquisition.

In 1540 the Roman Catholic Army killed 900 000 Waldensian Christians over a 30 years until 1570. In 1553 Roman Catholic backed English Queen Mary I burnt to death 300 men and women which included Bishops, Scholars and Protestant leaders in her attempt to bring back England under the yoke of the Vatican.

In 1572 the Saint Bartholomew's Day Massacre was when French Roman Catholic began killing Protestants in Paris from the night of August 24, they killed 18 000 protestants during the first three days of carnage.

From 1618 to 1648 the Roman Catholic Church waged a thirty years war instigated and orchestrated by the Jesuits Order in an attempt to exterminate all the Protestants in Europe, Killing half the populations of Europe killing millions. From 1641 the Jesuits became very instrumental in their global network of agents killing of Irish Protestants.

In 1685 the French Roman Catholic Soldiers slaughtered approximately 500 000 French Protestants Huguenots on the orders from King Louis of France. The Roman Catholic Church has always invested immensely in Wars and conquest of Lands in the name of the Pope.

When the Roman Catholic assumed and obtained the power to persecute bringing about the most ghastly part of human history. The total of numbers of Manichaeans, Arians, Priscillianists, Paulicians, Bogomiles, Hussites, Jews and Protestants killed is unknown. The victims were slaughtered and their wives and daughters raped. They sent all the women into convents to become sex slaves for the Catholic Priest.

In Bohemia in 1600 it had a population of 4 million people 80% of them Protestants. After the Hapsburg and the Jesuits had done their work only 800 000 citizens were left and all were Catholics.

In Austria, Hungary, Poland and even Italy they persecuted reformist especially those that pulled out of the Council of Churches. This Horror of the Catholic Inquisitions ordered and maintained by successive Popes from 500 years in which millions were killed constituting the most brutal beastly and devilish picture of human history.

The Pope sits in place of their fictitious Christ AKA Titus the Conqueror acting like God on earth. The Pope and the Catholic system is anti-God they mission in life is to mislead the public with the fictitious story of White Jewish Jesus who in real life was gay too. The Catholic system is Gay and has been propagating gayness by raping alter boys and boys in they care for centuries.

It has been reported that a 150 000 children were abused and killed in Government, Anglican and Roman Catholic run institutions in Canada from 1876 to 1996. Their wicked crimes against children history of sexual abuse is unspeakable.

My Research uncovered that in the 1920's approximately 10 000 women were sexulaly abuse in Ireland. From 1920 to 1996 500 000 children were taken from families, forced into Catholic institutions and sexually abused from 1930-1970. They also stole 300 000 babies from Spanish Roman Catholic in a BBC news report in the 70's. Thousands of children were reported to have been tortured and abused in Catholic Schools in Switzerland from 1930-1970.

In 1941 the Roman Catholic used Hitler, he was a Roman Catholic and had been Freemasonry trained too. Once stating "I learnt much from the Order of the Jesuits, until now there has never been anything more gandiso on the earth that the hierarchical organisation of the Catholic Church. I transferred much of this organization into my party"

20 000+ children have reported abuse from the Catholic Priest since 1945 in Netherlands, in the 1950's they abused hundreds of thousands of orphaned children spoils from the War creating care homes in Germany between 1950 and 1970. 4000 children have also been recorded to have been abused in Australia in the 1980's.

The Roman Catholic Church have been systematically abusing children in the Philippines too between 1980-2000 Pope John Paul II ignored the abuse reports and systematically sent accused paedophile Priests to South American Churches where they continued with their craft of abuse. They have continued with raping alter boys and nun's too. I read newspaper article this year were the Pope accepted it as a continuing problem in his Church.

In 1994 the massacre in Rwanda was created by the Roman Catholic Church and Nun's have been summoned to the International Criminal Courts.

In my extensive research I uncovered that the Rothschild Family are treated like they are God's on Earth and they are pictures of Pope Francis kissing the rings of the Rothschild. It's been said that they have direct descendants of Lucifer. The Rothschild's have been in bed with the Roman Catholic Church from 1500 writing in the White Jewish heritage in the bible.
I have come to the realisation and conclusion that the world and life we are all living is planned and controlled by the Jesuits Catholics, Freemasons, Illuminati and all Christian Societies misleading the world into believing into a returning Messiah who will lead them to heaven while heaven is here on earth now. The secret in all these so called secret societies is the fact of they made up the religion of Jesus Christ. Which the Catholics and the Rothschild Family want kept a secret of their wealth creation.

This white Jesus Story of him been born in Egypt and doing his works in Israel is a total fabricated story, they even gave us a clue when Pope Francis met outgoing Pope Benedict by meeting under the Black Madonna and Child google it?. This is also another Psychological warfare been played by the church on the Christian mind.

These scheming group of men and women who have set out to conquer the world by hook or crook succeeding everywhere they have gone. They infected the masses and left them in a deluded state of delusional belief system of Father, Son and the Holy spirit? Where is the female in this trinity confirming they gayness and wayward beliefs system.

The understanding of one's Spirituality has been capitalised upon by the springing up of Evangelistic Churches who have taken the Bible and made fortunes from it too. I wonder if they knew that Jesus is fictitious and will they all change they tunes once the truth comes out for all to see. But I don't think they will because last year's Forbes measured them to be all multi-millionaires from the word of Christ.

Once read an article written by a Catholic Bishop who stated that he thought Jesus was not coming back because the church and the world had lost its way. Their mission on earth is not save souls but to mislead them by turning men into women and women into men. They have been misleading the world from their true callings and of self actualisation by creating a capitalistic system which has been in place for thousands of years. It's now time to reexamine it's true intent and purpose and also who has the most to gain by perpetuating the lie and this religious beliefs systems.

The Roman Catholic Church had always used witchcraft and war as a means to subdue their oppositions putting in place a programme which has been in use for thousands of years. They have continued they murdering expeditions through America and England as they run every Intelligence agency in the West.

The world has been under a spell which has now been finally broken and it's time people realise that they have been lied to and misled for centuries amounting to thousands of years. This fictional story of the white Jewish Jesus has led to the invasion of North Africa Palestine due the biblical story of them been led of Egypt by Moses was all made up and outrages. Look at what they are doing in Palestine now and they claim to be God's chosen tribe which God are they talking of here? They have used the Fake bible as a tool of colonising a nation of muslims, they have been building up for the biggest religious war between Muslims and

Christians nations where they will spill loads of bloodiest Nuclear third World War.

The Book of Enoch

The History of the Book of Enoch

The book was thought to have been lost, for over 2,000 years, with many ancient sources referring to it, and even quoting parts, but no complete copies were known. Then in 1773, James Bruce brought three copies back from Ethiopia, having spent some years exploring the country. Enoch had two main reasons for writing his book. The first was because the Watchers instructed him to do it, (see section 15 at 81.5 and 81.6). The second reason; was to save his family from the flood. Enoch wrote his book, after his grandson Lamech was born, but before Noah was born. Noah is only named in the section that Methuselah wrote, (see section 10 at 107.3), and of course in his own section (section 11, The Book of Noah). So, there may still have been 40 - 80 years left before the flood, at the time when Enoch wrote his book. There is a long gap between the time of the flood and the time when Moses gave praise to Enoch in Genesis. Genesis dates from around 1400 BC, and forms part of the Torah (the first five books of the bible). In Genesis, there is Enoch's family; as named by him in this book, and a quick recap of some of Enoch's story.

It seems likely therefore, that copies of the Book of Enoch survived into Egyptian times, 3500 BC, and was known to Moses around 2,000 years later.

Moses presumably took a copy of the book with him when they all left Egypt, and he was no doubt pleased to see Enoch's prophecy fulfilled. The book probably existed mainly in Hebrew during the thousand years after the exodus. No Hebrew copies exist today, however, although there are some Hebrew passages quoted in some of the Aramaic fragments that survive from a few centuries BC. The appearance of the book in Ethiopia, is probably due to events in Jerusalem during the reign of King Manasseh of Judah, (695 - 642 BC), which are documented in the Bible, (2 Chronicles 33:1 - 20, and at 2 Kings 21:1 – 18).

King Manasseh was not of the Jewish faith, he erected alters to Baal and Asherah in Solomon's Temple. In Kings at 21:16, it says that so much innocent blood was shed that it filled Jerusalem from end to end. At this time, the religious establishment left the country, taking the Ark of the Covenant and all the important religious texts with them. After a number of years in Egypt, the refugees went further south, near to the source of the Nile, at Lake Tana in Ethiopia. The descendants of these people are the Falashas, who even today follow the form of Judaism that had been practiced in Israel only before 620 BC.

The Ethiopians translated The Book of Hanokh into Ge'ez, and had enough respect to look after it. Meanwhile, all Hebrew versions disappeared but a substantial part of the book had survived in Greek, and some parts in Aramaic, but until Scottish traveler, and freemason, James Bruce, returned from Ethiopia in 1773, with three manuscripts, no one in the west had ever seen the whole book. The two commonly available translations were done soon after this and the book was received with an embarrassed silence, for the most part, and not widely read. This book is based on a new translation published in 1978, which was produced as a result of research into a large number of the Ethiopian manuscripts and a review of all other surviving fragments.

1) THE BLESSING OF ENOCH

1.1 These are the words of the blessing of Enoch; according to which he blessed the chosen and righteous who must be present on the day of distress, which is appointed, for the removal of all the wicked and impious.

1.2 And Enoch began his story and said: -There was a righteous man whose eyes were opened by the Lord, and he saw a Holy vision in the Heavens, which the Angels showed to me. And I heard everything from them, and I understood what I saw: but not for this generation, but for a distant generation that will come.

1.3 Concerning the Chosen I spoke; and I uttered a parable concerning them: The Holy and Great One will come out of his dwelling.

1.4 And the Eternal God will tread from there upon Mount Sinai, and he will appear with his Host, and will appear in the strength of his power from Heaven.

1.5 And all will be afraid, and the Watchers will shake, and fear and great trembling will seize them, up to the ends of the earth.

1.6 And the high mountains will be shaken; and the high hills will be laid low and will melt like wax in a flame.

1.7 And the earth will sink, and everything that is on the earth will be destroyed, and there will be judgment upon all, and upon all the righteous.

1.8 But for the righteous: He will make peace, and He will keep safe the Chosen, and mercy will be upon them. They will all belong to God, and will prosper and be blessed, and the light of God will shine on them.

1.9 And behold! He comes with ten thousand Holy Ones; to execute judgment upon them and to destroy the impious, and to contend with all flesh concerning everything that the sinners and the impious have done and wrought against Him.

2) GOD'S LAWS

2.1 Contemplate all the events in the sky; how the lights in the sky do not change their courses, how each rises and sets in order, each at its proper time, and they do not transgress their law.
2.2 Consider the earth and understand from the work that is done upon it, from the beginning to the end, that no work of God changes as it becomes manifest.
2.3 Consider the summer and the winter; how the whole earth is full of water and the clouds and dew and rain rest upon it.
3.1 Contemplate and see how all the trees appear withered and all their leaves are stripped - with the exception of the fourteen trees, which are not stripped, which remain with the old leaves until the new come after two or three years.
4.1 And, again, contemplate the days of summer; how at its beginning the Sun is above it. You seek shelter and shade because of the heat of the Sun and the earth burns with scorching heat, and you cannot tread upon the earth or upon a rock, because of its heat.
5.1 Contemplate how the trees are covered with green leaves and bear fruit. And understand, in respect of everything, and perceive how He Who Lives Forever made all these things for you.
5.2 And how His works are before Him in each succeeding year, and all His works serve Him and do not change; but as God has decreed - so everything is done.
5.3 And consider how the seas and rivers together complete their tasks.
5.4 But you have not persevered in, nor observed, the Law of the Lord. But

you have transgressed and have spoken proud and hard words with your unclean mouth against his majesty. You hard of heart! You will not have peace!

5.5 And because of this you will curse your days, and the years of your life you will destroy. And the eternal curse will increase and you will not receive mercy.

5.6 In those days, you will transform your name into an eternal curse to all the righteous. And they will curse you sinners forever.

5.7 For the chosen; there will be light, joy, and peace, and they will inherit the earth. But for you, the impious, there will be a curse.

5.8 When wisdom is given to the chosen they will all live, and will not again do wrong, either through forgetfulness, or through pride. But those who possess wisdom will be humble.

5.9 They will not again do wrong, and they will not be judged in all the days of their life, and they will not die of wrath or anger. But they will complete the number of the days of their life. And their life will grow in peace, and the years of their joy will increase in gladness and eternal peace; all the days of their life.

3) REBELS AMONG THE WATCHERS

6.1 And it came to pass, when the sons of men had increased, that in those days there were born to them fair and beautiful daughters.
6.2 And the Angels, the sons of Heaven, saw them and desired them. And they said to one another: "Come, let us choose for ourselves wives, from the children of men, and let us beget, for ourselves, children."
6.3 And Semyaza, who was their leader, said to them: "I fear that you may not wish this deed to be done and that I alone will pay for this great sin."
6.4 And they all answered him, and said: "Let us all swear an oath, and bind one-another with curses, so not to alter this plan, but to carry out this plan effectively."
6.5 Then they all swore together and all bound one another with curses to it.
6.6 And they were, in all, two hundred and they came down on Ardis, which is the summit of Mount Hermon. And they called the mountain Hermon because on it they swore and bound one another with curses.
6.7 And these are the names of their leaders: Semyaza, who was their leader, Urakiba, Ramiel, Kokabiel, Tamiel, Ramiel, Daniel, Ezeqiel, Baraqiel, Asael, Armaros, Ananel, Zaqiel, Samsiel, Satael, Turiel, Yomiel, Araziel.
6.8 These are the leaders of the two hundred Angels and of all the others with them.
7.1 And they took wives for themselves and everyone chose for himself one each. And they began to go into them and were promiscuous with them. And they taught them charms and spells, and they showed them the cutting of roots and trees.
7.2 And they became pregnant and bore large giants. And their height was three thousand cubits.
7.3 These devoured all the toil of men; until men were unable to sustain them.
7.4 And the giants turned against them in order to devour men.
7.5 And they began to sin against birds, and against animals, and against reptiles, and against fish, and they devoured one another's flesh, and drank the blood from it.
7.6 Then the Earth complained about the lawless ones.

8.1 And Azazel taught men to make swords, and daggers, and shields, and breastplates. And he showed them the things after these, and the art of making them; bracelets, and ornaments, and the art of making up the eyes, and of beautifying the eyelids, and the most precious stones, and all kinds of coloured dyes. And the world was changed.

8.2 And there was great impiety, and much fornication, and they went astray, and all their ways became corrupt.

8.3 Amezarak taught all those who cast spells and cut roots, Armaros the release of spells, and Baraqiel astrologers, and Kokabiel portents, and Tamiel taught astrology, and Asradel taught the path of the Moon.

8.4 And at the destruction of men they cried out; and their voices reached Heaven.

9.1 And then Michael, Gabriel, Suriel and Uriel, looked down from Heaven and saw the mass of blood that was being shed on the earth and all the iniquity that was being done on the earth.

9.2 And they said to one another: "Let the devastated Earth cry out with the sound of their cries, up to the Gate of Heaven.

9.3 And now to you, Oh Holy Ones of Heaven, the souls of men complain, saying: "Bring our complaint before the Most High."

9.4 And they said to their Lord, the King: "Lord of Lords, God of Gods, King of Kings! Your glorious throne endures for all the generations of the world, and blessed and praised!

9.5 You have made everything, and power over everything is yours. And everything is uncovered, and open, in front of you, and you see everything, and there is nothing that can be hidden from you.

9.6 See then what Azazel has done; how he has taught all iniquity on the earth and revealed the eternal secrets that are made in Heaven.

9.7 And Semyaza has made known spells, he to whom you gave authority to rule over those who are with him.

9.8 And they went into the daughters of men together, lay with those women, became unclean, and revealed to them these sins.

9.9 And the women bore giants, and thereby the whole Earth has been filled with blood and iniquity.

9.10 And now behold the souls which have died cry out and complain unto the Gate of Heaven, and their lament has ascended, and they cannot go out in the face of the iniquity which is being committed on the earth.

9.11 And you know everything, before it happens, and you know this, and what concerns each of them. But you say nothing to us. What ought we to do with them, about this?"

10.1 And then the Most High, the Great and Holy One, spoke and sent Arsyalalyur to the son of Lamech, and said to him:

10.2 "Say to him in my name; hide yourself! And reveal to him the end, which is coming, because the whole earth will be destroyed. A deluge is about to come on all the earth; and all that is in it will be destroyed.

10.3 And now teach him so that he may escape and his offspring may survive for the whole Earth."

10.4 And further the Lord said to Raphael: "Bind Azazel by his hands and his feet and throw him into the darkness. And split open the desert, which is in Dudael, and throw him there.

10.5 And throw on him jagged and sharp stones and cover him with darkness. And let him stay there forever. And cover his face so that he may not see the light.

10.6 And so that, on the Great Day of Judgment, he may be hurled into the fire.

10.7 And restore the Earth which the Angels have ruined. And announce the restoration of the Earth. For I shall restore the Earth so that not all the sons of men shall be destroyed because of the knowledge which the Watchers made known and taught to their sons.

10.8 And the whole Earth has been ruined by the teaching of the works of Azazel; and against him write: ALL SIN."

10.9 And the Lord said to Gabriel: "Proceed against the bastards, and the reprobates, and against the sons of the fornicators. And destroy the sons of the fornicators, and the sons of the Watchers, from amongst men. And send them out, and send them against one another, and let them destroy themselves in battle; for they will not have length of days.

10.10 And they will petition you, but the petitioners will gain nothing in respect of them, for they hope for eternal life, and that each of them will live life for five hundred years."

10.11 And the Lord said to Michael: "Go, inform Semyaza, and the others with him, who have associated with the women to corrupt themselves with them in all their uncleanness.

10.12 When all their sons kill each other, and when they see the destruction of their loved ones, bind them for seventy generations, under the hills of the earth, until the day of their judgment and of their consummation, until the judgment, which is for all eternity, is accomplished.

10.13 And in those days, they will lead them to the Abyss of Fire; in torment, and in prison they will be shut up for all eternity.

10.14 And then Semyaza will be burnt, and from then on destroyed with them; together they will be bound until the end of all generations.

10.15 And destroy all the souls of lust, and the sons of the Watchers, for they have wronged men.

10.16 Destroy all wrong from the face of the Earth and every evil work will cease.

10.17 And now all the righteous will be humble, and will live until they beget thousands. And all the days of their youth, and their sabbaths, they will fulfill in peace.

10.18 And in those days the whole earth will be tilled in righteousness and all of it will be planted with trees; and it will be filled with blessing.

10.19 And all the pleasant trees they will plant on it and they will plant on it vines. And the vine that is planted on it will produce fruit in abundance; and every seed that is sown on it, each measure will produce a thousand, and each measure of olives will produce ten baths of oil.

10.20 And you cleanse the Earth from all wrong, and from all iniquity, and from all sin, and from all impiety, and from all the uncleanness which is brought about on the earth.

10.21 And all the sons of men shall be righteous, and all the nations shall serve and bless me and all shall worship me.

10.22 And the Earth will be cleansed from all corruption, and from all sin, and from all wrath, and from all torment; and I will not again send a flood upon it, for all generations, forever.

11.1 And in those days, I will open the Storehouses of Blessing, which are in Heaven, so that I may send them down upon the Earth, upon the work, and upon the toil, of the sons of men.

11.2 Peace and truth will be united, for all the days of eternity, and for all the generations of eternity.

12.1 And then Enoch disappeared and none of the sons of men knew where he was hidden, where he was, or what had happened.

12.2 And all his doings were with the Holy Ones, and with the Watchers, in his days.

12.3 And I Enoch, was blessing the Great Lord and the King of Eternity. And behold, the Watchers called to me - Enoch the scribe - and said to me:

12.4 "Enoch, scribe of righteousness. Go and inform the Watchers of Heaven, who have left the High Heaven and the Holy Eternal Place, and have corrupted themselves with women, and have done as the sons of men do and have taken wives for themselves, and have become completely corrupt on the earth.

12.5 They will have on Earth, neither peace, nor forgiveness of sin, for they will not rejoice in their sons.

12.6 The slaughter of their beloved ones they will see; and over the destruction of their sons they will lament and petition forever. But they will have neither mercy nor peace."

13.1 And Enoch went and said to Azazel: "You will not have peace. A severe sentence has come out against you that you should be bound.

13.2 And you will have neither rest nor mercy, nor the granting of any petitions, because of the wrong which you have taught, and because of all the works of blasphemy and wrong and sin which you have shown to the
sons of men."

13.3 And then I went and spoke to them all together, and they were all afraid; fear and trembling seized them.

13.4 And they asked me to write out for them the record of a petition, so that they might receive forgiveness, and to take a record of their petition up to the Lord in Heaven.

13.5 For they were not able, from then on, to speak, and they did not raise their eyes to Heaven, out of shame for the sins, for which they had been Condemned.

13.6 And then I wrote out the record of their petition, and their supplication in regard to their spirits, and the deeds of each one of them, and in regard to what they asked; that they should obtain absolution and forbearance.

13.7 And I went and sat down by the waters of Dan, in Dan, which is southwest of Hermon; and I read out the record of their petition, until I fell asleep.

13.8 And behold a dream came to me, and visions fell upon me, and I saw a vision of wrath; that I should speak to the sons of Heaven and reprove them.

13.9 And I woke up and went to them, and they were all sitting gathered together as they mourned, in Ubelseyael, which is between Lebanon and Senir, with their faces covered.

13.10 And I spoke in front of them all; the visions that I had seen in my sleep, and I began to speak these words to reprove the Watchers of Heaven.

14.1 This book is the word of righteousness, and of reproof, for the Watchers who are from Eternity; as the Holy and Great One commanded in that vision.

14.2 I saw in my sleep what I will now tell, with the tongue of flesh, and with my breath, which the Great One has given men in the mouth, so that they might speak with it, and understand with the heart.

14.3 As He has created, and appointed, men to understand the word of knowledge, so He created and appointed me to reprove the Watchers, the sons of Heaven.

14.4 And I wrote out your petition, but in my vision, thus it appeared, that your petition would not be granted to you, for all the days of eternity; and complete judgment has been decreed against you, and you will not have peace.

14.5 And from now on, you will not ascend into Heaven, for all eternity, and it has been decreed that you will be bound on Earth for all the days of eternity.

14.6 And before this, you will have seen the destruction of your beloved sons, and you will not be able to enjoy them, but they will fall before you by the sword.

14.7 And your petition will not be granted in respect of them or in respect of yourselves. And while you weep and supplicate you do not speak a single word from the writings which I have written.

14.8 And the vision appeared to me, as follows: -Behold; clouds called me in the vision, and mist called me. And the path of the stars, and flashes of lightning, hastened me and drove me. And in the vision winds caused me to fly, and hastened me, and lifted me up into the sky.

14.9 And I proceeded until I came near a wall which was made of hailstones, and a tongue of fire surrounded it, and it began to make me afraid.

14.10 And I went into the tongue of fire and came near to a large house, which was built of hailstones, and the wall of that house was like a mosaic of hailstones and its floor was snow.
14.11 Its roof was like the path of the stars and flashes of lightning, and among them was fiery cherubim, and their sky was like water.
14.12 And there was a fire burning around its wall and its door was ablaze with fire.
14.13 And I went into that house, and it was as hot as fire and as cold as snow, and there was neither pleasure nor life in it. Fear covered me and trembling took hold of me.
14.14 And as I was shaking and trembling, I fell on my face.
14.15 And I saw in the vision, and behold, another house which was larger than the former and all its doors were open before me, and it was built of a tongue of fire.
14.16 And in everything, it so excelled in glory and splendor and size, so that I am unable to describe to you its glory and its size.
14.17 And its floor was fire, and above lightning and the path of the stars, and its roof also was a burning fire.
14.18 And I looked, and I saw in it, a high throne, and its appearance was like ice, and its surrounds like the shining Sun and the sound of cherubim.
14.19 And from underneath the high throne there flowed out rivers of fire so that it was impossible to look at it.
14.20 And He who is Great in Glory sat upon it, and his raiment was brighter than the Sun, and whiter than any snow.
14.21 And no Angel could enter, and at the appearance of the face of Him who is Honoured and Praised, no creature of flesh could look.
14.22 A sea of fire burnt around Him, and a great fire stood in front of Him, and none of those around Him came near to Him. Ten thousand times ten thousand stood before Him but He needed no Holy Council.
14.23 And the Holy Ones who were near to Him did not leave by night or day and did not depart from Him.
14.24 And until then I had a covering on my face, as I trembled. And the Lord called me with his own mouth, and said to me: "Come here, Enoch, to my Holy Word."
14.25 And He lifted me up and brought me near to the door. And I looked, with my face down.

15.1 And He answered me, and said to me with His voice: "Hear! Do not be afraid, Enoch, you righteous man, and scribe of righteousness. Come here and hear my voice.

15.2 And go say to the Watchers of Heaven, who sent you to petition on their behalf: You ought to petition on behalf of men, not men on behalf of You.

15.3 Why have you left the High, Holy and Eternal Heaven, and lain with women, and become unclean with the daughters of men, and taken wives for yourselves, and done as the sons of the earth, and begotten giant sons?

15.4 And you were spiritual, Holy, living an eternal life, but you became unclean upon the women, and begot children through the blood of flesh, and lusted after the blood of men, and produced flesh and blood, as they do, who die and are destroyed.

15.5 And for this reason I give men wives; so that they might sow seed in them, and so that children might be born by them, so that deeds might be done on the Earth.

15.6 But you, formerly, were spiritual, living an eternal, immortal life, for all the generations of the world.

15.7 For this reason I did not arrange wives for you; because the dwelling of the spiritual ones is in Heaven

15.8 And now, the giants who were born from body and flesh will be called Evil Spirits on the Earth, and on the Earth will be their dwelling.

15.9 And evil spirits came out from their flesh, because from above they were created, from the Holy Watchers was their origin and first foundation. Evil spirits they will be on Earth and 'Spirits of the Evil Ones' they will be called.

15.10 And the dwelling of the Spirits of Heaven is Heaven, but the dwelling of the spirits of the Earth, who were born on the Earth, is Earth.

15.11 And the spirits of the giants do wrong, are corrupt, attack, fight, break on the Earth, and cause sorrow. And they eat no food, do not thirst, and are not observed.

15.12 And these spirits will rise against the sons of men, and against the women, because they came out of them during the days of slaughter and destruction.

16.1 And the death of the giants, wherever the spirits have gone out from their bodies, their flesh will be destroyed, before the Judgment. Thus they will be destroyed until the Day of the Great Consummation is accomplished, upon the Great Age, upon the Watchers and the impious ones."

16.2 And now to the Watchers, who sent you to petition on their behalf, who were formerly in Heaven:

16.3 "You were in Heaven but its secrets had not yet been revealed to you; and a worthless mystery you knew. This you made known to women, in the hardness of your hearts. And through this mystery the women and the men cause evil to increase on the Earth."

16.4 Say to them therefore: "You will not have peace."

17.1 And they took me to a place where they were like burning fire, and, when they wished, they made themselves look like men.

17.2 And they led me to a place of storm, and to a mountain, the tip of whose summit reached to Heaven.

17.3 And I saw lighted places, and thunder in the outermost ends, in its depths a bow of fire, and arrows and their quivers, and a sword of fire, and all the flashes of lightning.

17.4 And they took me to the Water of Life, as it is called, and to the Fire of the West, which receives every setting of the Sun.

17.5 And I came to a river of fire, whose fire flows like water, and pours out into the Great Sea, which is towards the west.

17.6 And I saw all the great rivers, and I reached the Great Darkness, and went where all flesh walks.

17.7 And I saw the Mountains of the Darkness of Winter and the place where the water of all the deeps pours out.

17.8 And I saw the mouths of all the rivers of the Earth, and the mouth of the deep.

18.1 And I saw the storehouses of all the winds, and I saw how with them He has adorned all creation, and I saw the foundations of the Earth.

18.2 And I saw the cornerstone of the Earth. And I saw the four winds which support the Earth and the sky.

18.3 And I saw how the winds stretch out the height of Heaven, and how they position themselves between Heaven and Earth; they are the Pillars of Heaven.

18.4 And I saw the winds which turn the sky and cause the disc of the Sun and all the stars to set.

18.5 And I saw the winds on the Earth which support the clouds and I saw the paths of the Angels. I saw at the end of the Earth; the firmament of Heaven above.

18.6 And I went towards the south, and it was burning day and night, where there were seven mountains of precious stones, three towards the east and three towards the south.

18.7 And those towards the east were of coloured stone, and one was of pearl, and one of healing stone; and those towards the south, of red stone.

18.8 And the middle one reached to Heaven, like the throne of the Lord, of stibium, and the top of the throne was of sapphire.

18.9 And I saw a burning fire, and what was in all the mountains.

18.10 And I saw a place there, beyond the great earth; there the waters gathered together.

18.11 And I saw a deep chasm of the earth, with pillars of heavenly fire, and I saw among them fiery pillars of Heaven, which were falling, and as regards both height and depth, they were immeasurable.

18.12 And beyond this chasm, I saw a place, and it had neither the sky above it, nor the foundation of earth below it; there was no water on it, and no birds, but it was a desert place.

18.13 And a terrible thing I saw there, seven stars, like great burning mountains.

18.14 And like a spirit questioning me, the Angel said: "This is the place of the end of Heaven and Earth; this is the prison for the Stars of Heaven and the Host of Heaven.

18.15 And the stars which roll over the fire, these are the ones which transgressed the command of the Lord, from the beginning of their rising, because they did not come out at their proper times.

18.16 And He was angry with them, and bound them until the time of the consummation of their sin, in the Year of Mystery."

19.1 And Uriel said to me: "The spirits of the Angels who were promiscuous with women will stand here; and they, assuming many forms, made men unclean and will lead men astray so that they sacrifice to demons as gods. And they will stand there until the great judgment day, on which they will be judged, so that an end will be made of them.

19.2 And their wives, having led astray the Angels of Heaven, will become peaceful."

19.3 And I, Enoch, alone saw the sight, the ends of everything; and no man has seen what I have seen.

20.1 And these are the names of the Holy Angels who keep watch.

20.2 Uriel, one of the Holy Angels; namely the Holy Angel of the Spirits of Men.

20.4 Raguel, one of the Holy Angels; who takes vengeance on the world, and on the lights.

20.5 Michael, one of the Holy Angels, namely the one put in charge of the best part of humankind, in charge of the nation.

20.6 Saraqael, one of the Holy Angels; who is in charge of the spirits of men who cause the spirits to sin.

20.7 Gabriel, one of the Holy Angels, who is in charge of the Serpents, and the Garden, and the Cherubim.

21.1 And I went round to a place where nothing was made.

21.2 And I saw a terrible thing, neither the High Heaven nor the firm ground, but a desert place, prepared and terrible.

21.3 And there, I saw seven Stars of Heaven, bound on it together, like great mountains, and burning like fire.

21.4 Then I said: "For what sin have they been bound, and why have they been thrown here?"

21.5 And Uriel, one of the Holy Angels, who was with me and led me, spoke to me and said: "Enoch, about whom do you ask? About whom do you inquire, ask, and care?

21.6 These are some of the stars which transgressed the command of the Lord Most High, and they have been bound here until ten thousand ages are completed; the number of days of their sin."

21.7 And from there I went to another place, more terrible than this. And I saw a terrible thing: there was a great fire there, which burnt and blazed. And the place had a cleft reaching into the abyss, full of great pillars of fire, which were made to fall; neither its extent nor its size could I see, nor could I see its source.

21.8 Then I said: "How terrible this place is, and how painful to look at!"

21.9 Then Uriel, one of the Holy Angels, who was with me, answered me. He answered me and said to me: "Enoch, why do you have such fear and terror because of this terrible place, and before this pain?"

21.10 And he said to me: "This place is the prison of the Angels, and there they will be held for ever."

22.1 And from there, I went to another place, and he showed me in the west a large and high mountain, and a hard rock, and four beautiful places.

22.2 And inside, it was deep, wide, and very smooth. How smooth is that which rolls, and deep and dark to look at!

22.3 Then Raphael, one of the Holy Angels who was with me, answered me, and said to me: "These beautiful places are there so that the spirits, the souls of the dead, might be gathered into them. For them they were created; so that here they might gather the souls of the sons of men.

22.4 And these places they made, where they will keep them until the Day of Judgment, and until their appointed time, and that appointed time will be long, until the great judgment comes upon them.

22.5 And I saw the spirits of the sons of men who were dead and their voices reached Heaven and complained.

22.6 Then I asked Raphael, the Angel who was with me, and said to him: "Whose is this spirit, whose voice thus reaches Heaven and complains?"

22.7 And he answered me, and said to me, saying: "This spirit is the one that came out of Abel, whom Cain, his brother, killed. And he will complain about him until his offspring are destroyed from the face of the Earth, and from amongst the offspring of men, his offspring perish."

22.8 Then I asked about him, and about judgment on all, and I said: "Why is one separated from another?"

22.9 And he answered me, and said to me: "These three places where made, in order that they might separate the spirits of the dead. And thus the souls of the righteous have been separated; this is the spring of water, and on it the light.

22.10 Likewise, a place has been created for sinners, when they die, and are buried in the earth, and judgment has not come upon them during their life.

22.11 And here their souls will be separated for this great torment, until the Great Day of Judgment and Punishment and Torment for those who curse, forever, and of vengeance on their souls. And there he will bind them forever. Verily, He is, from the beginning of the world.

22.12 And thus a place has been separated for the souls of those who complain, and give information about their destruction, about when they were killed, in the days of the sinners.

22.13 Thus a place has been created, for the souls of men who are not righteous, but sinners, accomplished in wrongdoing, and with the wrongdoers will be their lot. But their souls will not be killed on the day of judgment, nor will they rise from here."

22.14 Then I blessed the Lord of Glory, and said: "Blessed be my Lord, the Lord of Glory and Righteousness, who rules everything forever."

23.1 And from there I went to another place, towards the west, to the ends of the Earth.

23.2 And I saw a fire that burnt and ran, without resting or ceasing from running, by day or by night, but continued in exactly the same way.

23.3 And I asked saying: "What is this which has no rest?"

23.4 Then Raguel, one of the Holy Angels, who was with me, answered me, and said to me: "This burning fire, whose course you saw towards the west, is the fire of all the Lights of Heaven."

24.1 And from there I went to another place of the Earth and he showed me a mountain of fire that blazed day and night.

24.2 And I went towards it and saw seven magnificent mountains. And all were different from one another, and precious and beautiful stones, and all were precious, and their appearance glorious, and their form was beautiful. Three towards the east one fixed firmly on another and three towards the south one on another, and deep and rugged valleys, no one of which was near another.

24.3 And there was a seventh mountain, in the middle of these, and in their height they were all like the seat of a throne and fragrant trees surrounded it.

24.4 And there was among them a tree such as which I have never smelt, and none of them, or any others, were like it. It smells more fragrant than any fragrance, and its leaves, and its flowers, and its wood never wither. Its fruit is good, and its fruit is like bunches of dates on a palm.

24.5 And then I said: "Behold, this beautiful tree! Beautiful to look at, and pleasant are its leaves, and its fruit very delightful in appearance."

24.6 And then Michael, one of the Holy and Honoured Angels, who was with me, and was in charge of them,

25.1 answered me and said to me: "Enoch, why do you ask me about the fragrance of this tree, and why do you inquire to learn?"

25.2 Then I, Enoch, answered him saying: "I wish to learn about everything, but especially about this tree."

25.3 And he answered me, saying: "This high mountain, which you saw, whose summit is like the Throne of the Lord, is the throne where the Holy and Great One, the Lord of Glory, the Eternal King, will sit, when he comes down to visit the Earth for good.

25.4 And this beautiful and fragrant tree, and no creature of flesh has authority to touch it until the great judgment, when he will take vengeance on all and bring everything to a consummation forever, this will be given to the righteous and the humble.

25.5 From its fruit, life will be given to the chosen; towards the north it will be planted, in a Holy place, by the house of the Lord, the Eternal King.

25.6 Then they will rejoice with joy and be glad in the Holy place. They will each draw the fragrance of it into their bones, and they will live a long life on earth, as your fathers lived. And in their days sorrow and pain, and toil and punishment, will not touch them."

25.7 Then I blessed the Lord of Glory, the Eternal King, because he has prepared such things for righteous men, and has created such things, and said that they are to be given to them.

26.1 And from there, I went to the middle of the earth, and saw a blessed, well watered place, which had branches which remained alive, and sprouted from a tree which had been cut down.

26.2 And there I saw a holy mountain, and under the mountain, to the east of it, there was water, and it flowed towards the south.

26.3 And I saw towards the east, another mountain, which was of the same height, and between them, there was a deep and narrow valley; and in it, a stream ran by the mountain.

26.4 And to the west of this one, was another mountain, which was lower than it was and not high; and under it, there was a valley between them. And there were other deep and dry valleys at the end of the three mountains.

26.5 And all the valleys were deep and narrow, of hard rock, and trees were planted on them.

26.6 And I was amazed at the rock, and I was amazed at the valley; I was very much amazed.

7.1 Then I said: "What is the purpose of this blessed land, which is completely full of trees, and of this accursed valley in the middle of them?"

27.2 Then Raphael, one of the Holy Angels who was with me, answered me, and said to me: "This accursed valley, is for those who are cursed for ever. Here will be gathered together all who speak with their mouths against the Lord - words that are not fitting, and say hard things about His Glory. Here they will gather them together, and here will be their place of Judgment.

27.3 And in the last days there will be the spectacle of the righteous judgment upon them, in front of the righteous, forever. For here, the merciful will bless the Lord of Glory the Eternal King.

27.4 And in the days of the judgment on them they will bless Him, on account of his mercy, according as He has assigned to them their lot."

27.5 Then I myself blessed the Lord of Glory, I addressed Him, and I remembered His majesty, as was fitting.

28.1 And from there, I went towards the east, to the middle of the mountain of the wilderness, and I saw only desert.

28.2 But it was full of trees from this seed and water gushed out over it from above.

28.3 The torrent, which flowed towards the northwest, seemed copious, and from all sides, there went up spray and mist.

29.1 And I went to another place, away from the wilderness; I came near to the east of this mountain.

29.2 And there I saw Trees of Judgment, especially vessels of the fragrance of incense and myrrh, and the trees were not alike.

30.1 And above it, above these, above the mountains of the east, and not far away, I saw another place, valleys of water, like that which does not fail.

30.2 And I saw a beautiful tree, and its fragrance was like that of the mastic.

30.3 And by the banks of these valleys I saw fragrant cinnamon. And beyond those valleys I came towards the east.

31.1 And I saw another mountain on which there were trees, and there flowed out water, and there flowed out from it, as it were, a nectar whose name is styrax and galbanum.

31.2 And beyond this mountain I saw another mountain, and on it there were aloe trees, and those trees were full of a fruit, which is like an almond, and is hard.

31.3 And when they take this fruit it is better than any fragrance.

32.1 And after these fragrances, to the north, as I looked over the mountains, I saw seven mountains full of fine nard, and fragrant trees of cinnamon and pepper.

32.2 And from there, I went over the summits of those mountains, far away to the east, and I went over the Red Sea, and I was far from it, and I went over the Angel Zotiel.

32.3 And I came to the Garden of Righteousness, and I saw beyond those trees many large trees growing there, sweet smelling, large, very beautiful and glorious, the Trees of Wisdom, from which they eat and know great wisdom.

32.4 And it is like the carob tree, and its fruit is like bunches of grapes on a vine, very beautiful, and the smell of this tree spreads and penetrates afar.

32.5 And I said: "This tree is beautiful! How beautiful and pleasing is its appearance!"

32.6 And the Holy Angel Raphael, who was with me, answered me and said to me: "This is the Tree of Wisdom, from which your ancient father and ancient mother, who were before you, ate and learnt wisdom; and their eyes were opened, and they knew that they were naked. And they were driven from the garden."

33.1 And from there I went to the ends of the earth, and I saw there large animals, each different from the other, and also birds, which differed in form, beauty, and call - each different from the other.

33.2 And to the east of these animals, I saw the ends of the Earth, on which Heaven rests, and the open Gates of Heaven.

33.3 And I saw how the stars of Heaven come out, and counted the Gates out of which they come, and wrote down all their outlets, for each one, individually, according to their number. And their names, according to their constellations, their positions, their times, and their months, as the Angel Uriel, who was with me, showed me.

33.4 And he showed me everything, and wrote it down, and also their names he wrote down for me, and their laws and their functions.

34.1 And from there I went towards the north, to the ends of the Earth, and there I saw a great and glorious wonder at the ends of the whole Earth.

34.2 And there I saw three Gates of Heaven; through each of them north winds go out; when they blow there is cold, hail, hoarfrost, snow, fog, and rain.

34.3 And from one Gate, it blows for good; but when they blow through the other two Gates, it is with force, and it brings torment over the earth, and they blow with force.

35.1 And from there I went towards the west, to the ends of the Earth, and I saw there, as I saw in the east, three open Gates - as many Gates and as many outlets.

36.1 And from there I went towards the south, to the ends of the Earth, and there I saw three Gates of Heaven open; and the south wind, the mist, and the rain, and wind, come out from there.

36.2 And from there I went towards the east of the ends of Heaven, and there I saw the three eastern Gates of Heaven open, and above them, there were smaller Gates.
36.3 Through each of these smaller Gates, the stars of Heaven pass, and go.

THE BOOK OF METHUSELAH

106.1 And after those days my son Methuselah chose a wife for his son Lamech and she became pregnant by him and bore a son.
106.2 And his body was white like snow, and red like the flower of a rose, and the hair of his head was white like wool. And his eyes were beautiful and when he opened his eyes he made the whole house bright, like the Sun, so that the whole house was exceptionally bright.
106.3 And when he was taken from the hand of the midwife he opened his mouth and spoke to the Lord of Righteousness.

106.4 And his father Lamech was afraid of him, and fled, and went to his father Methuselah.

106.5 And he said to him: "I have begotten a strange son; he is not like a man but is like the children of the Angels of Heaven, of a different type and not like us. And his eyes are like the rays of the Sun and his face glorious.

106.6 And it seems to me that he is not sprung from me but from the Angels and I am afraid that something extraordinary may be done on the earth in his days.

106.7 And now, my father, I am entreating you and petitioning you, to go to our father Enoch, and learn from him the truth, for his dwelling is with the Angels."

106.8 And when Methuselah heard the words of his son he came to me, at the ends of the Earth, for he had heard that I was there. And he cried out, and I heard his voice and went to him. And I said to him: "Behold I am here my son, for you have come to me."

106.9 And he answered me, and said: "Because of a great matter I have come to you, and because of a disturbing vision, have I come near.

106.10 And now hear me, my father, for a child has been born to my son Lamech, whose form and type are not like the type of a man. His colour is whiter than snow, and redder than the flower of the rose, and the hair of his head is whiter than white wool. And his eyes are like the rays of the Sun; and he opened his eyes and made the whole house bright.

106.11 And he was taken from the hand of the midwife, and he opened his mouth, and blessed the Lord of Heaven.

106.12 And his father Lamech was afraid and fled to me. And he does not believe he is sprung from him but thinks him to be from the Angels of Heaven. And behold, I have come to you, so that you may make known to me the truth."

106.13 And I, Enoch, answered and said to him: "The Lord will do new things on Earth, and this I have already seen in a vision, and made known to you. For in the generation of my father, Jared, some from the height of Heaven transgressed the word of the Lord.

106.14 And behold, they commit sin and transgress the law, and have been promiscuous with women, and commit sin with them, and have married some of them, and have begotten children by them.

106.15 And there will be great destruction over the whole Earth, and there will be a deluge, and there will be great destruction for one year.

106.16 But this child, who has been born to you, will be left on the Earth, and his three sons will be saved with him. When all the men who are on the Earth die he and his sons will be saved.

106.17 They will beget on the Earth giants, not of spirit, but of flesh, and there will be great wrath on Earth, and the Earth will be cleansed of all corruption.

106.18 And now make known to your son Lamech that the one who has been born is truly his son. And call his name Noah, for he will be a remnant for you and he and his sons will be saved from the destruction which is coming on the earth because of all the sin and all the iniquity, which will be committed on the Earth in his days.

106.19 But after this, there will be yet greater iniquity than that which was committed on the earth before. For I know the mysteries of the Holy Ones, for the Lord showed them to me and made them known to me, and I read them in the Tablets of Heaven.

107.1 And I saw written on them, that generation upon generation will do wrong, until a generation of righteousness shall arise, and wrongdoing shall be destroyed, and sin shall depart from the earth, and everything good shall come upon it.

107.2 And now, my son, go, make known to your son Lamech, that this child that has been born, is truly his son, and this is no lie.

107.3 And when Methuselah had heard the words of his father Enoch - for he showed him everything which is secret - he returned, having seen him, and called the name of that child Noah; for he will comfort the Earth after all the destruction.

65.1 And in those days, Noah saw the Earth had tilted and that its destruction was near.

65.2 And he set off from there and went to the ends of the Earth and cried out to his great-grandfather Enoch; and Noah said three times in a bitter voice: "Hear me, hear me, hear me!"

65.3 And he said to him: "Tell me, what is it that is being done on the Earth, that the Earth is so afflicted and shaken, lest I be destroyed with it!"

65.4 And immediately there was a great disturbance on the Earth and a
voice was heard from Heaven and I fell upon my face.

65.5 And my great-grandfather Enoch came, stood by me, and said to me: "Why did you cry out to me, with such bitter crying and weeping?

65.6 And a command has gone out from the Lord against those who dwell upon the dry ground that this must be their end. For they have learnt all the secrets of the Angels, and all the wrongdoings of the satans, and all their secret power, and all the power of those who practice magic arts, and the power of enchantments, and the power of those who cast molten images for all the Earth.

65.7 And further, how silver is produced from the dust of the earth and how soft metal occurs on the earth.

65.8 For lead and tin are not produced from the earth, like the former; there is a spring which produces them, and an Angel who stands in it, and that Angel distributes them."

65.9 And after this, my great-grandfather Enoch took hold of me with his hand, and raised me, and said to me:"Go, for I have asked the Lord of Spirits about this disturbance on the earth."

65.10 And he said to me:"Because of their iniquity, their judgment has been completed, and they will no longer be counted before me; because of the sorceries they have searched out and learnt, the Earth and those who dwell upon it will be destroyed.

65.11 And for these, there will be no place of refuge, for ever, for they showed to them what is secret, and they have been condemned; but not so for you, my son; the Lord of Spirits knows that you are pure and innocent of this reproach concerning the secrets.

65.12 And he has established your name among the Holy, and will keep you from amongst those who dwell upon the dry ground; and he has destined your offspring in righteousness, to be kings, and for great honours. And from your offspring will flow out a spring of the Righteous and Holy, without number forever."

66.1 And after this, he showed me the Angels of Punishment, who were ready to come and release all the forces of the water, which is under the earth, in order to bring judgment and destruction on all those who reside and dwell upon the dry ground.

66.2 And the Lord of Spirits commanded the Angels who were coming out, not to raise their hands, but to keep watch; for those Angels were in charge of the forces of the waters.

66.3 And I came out from before Enoch.

67.1 And in those days, the word of the Lord came to me, and he said to me: "Noah, behold; your lot has come up before me, a lot without reproach, a lot of love and uprightness.

67.2 And now the Angels are making a wooden structure, and when the Angels come out from that task, I will put my hand on it, and keep it safe. And a change shall take place so that the dry ground may not remain Empty.

67.3 And I will establish your offspring before me, forever and ever, and I will scatter those who dwell with you, over the face of the dry ground. I blessed and increase on the dry ground in the name of the Lord."

67.4 And they will shut up those Angels, who showed iniquity, in that burning valley, which my great-grandfather Enoch had shown to me previously, in the west, near the mountains of gold and silver and iron and soft metal and tin.

67.5 And I saw that valley, in which there was a great disturbance, and a heaving of the waters.

67.6 And when all this happened, from the fiery molten metal, and the disturbance, which disturbed the waters in that place, a smell of sulphur was produced, and it was associated with those waters. And that valley of the Angels, who led men astray, burns under the ground.

67.7 And through the valleys of that same area, flow out rivers of fire where those Angels will be punished, who led astray those on the dry ground.

67.8 And in those days, those waters will serve the kings, and the mighty, and the exalted, and those who dwell upon dry ground, for the healing of soul and body, but also for the punishment of the spirit. And their spirits are so full of lust that they will be punished in their bodies, for they denied the Lord of Spirits. And they see their punishment every day yet they do not believe in His Name.

67.9 And the more their bodies are burnt, the more a change will come over their spirits, for ever and ever; for no one can speak an idle word in front of the Lord of Spirits.

67.10 For judgment will come upon them, for they believe in the lust of their bodies, but deny the spirit of the Lord.

67.11 And those same waters will undergo a change in those days; for when those Angels are punished in those days, the temperature of those springs of water will change, and when the Angels come up, that water of the springs will change, and become cold.

67.12 And I heard the Holy Michael answering and saying: "This judgment, with which the Angels are judged, is a testimony for the kings and the mighty who possess the dry ground.

67.13 For these waters of judgment serve for the healing of the bodies of the kings, and for the lust of their bodies; but they do not see, and do not believe, that these waters will change, and will become a fire which burns forever."

68.1 And after this, my great-grandfather Enoch gave me the explanation of all the secrets, in a book, and the parables that had been given to him; and will not again put them to the test, on the face of the Earth, but they will be

38.1 The First Parable. When the community of the righteous appears and the sinners are judged for their sins and are driven from the face of the dry ground.

38.2 And when the Righteous One appears, in front of the chosen righteous, whose works are weighed by the Lord of Spirits. And when light appears to the righteous and chosen who dwell on the dry ground. Where will be the dwelling of the sinners? And where will be the resting place of those who denied the Lord of Spirits? It would have been better for them, if they had not been born.

38.3 And when the secrets of the righteous are revealed, the sinners will be judged, and the impious driven from the presence of the righteous and the chosen.

38.4 And from then on, those who possess the earth will not be mighty and exalted. Nor will they be able to look at the face of the Holy ones, for the light of the Lord of the Spirits will have appeared on the face of the Holy, the righteous, and the chosen.

38.5 And the mighty kings will at that time be destroyed and given into the hand of the righteous and the Holy.

38.6 And from then on no one will be able to seek the Lord of Spirits for their life will be at an end.

39.1 And it will come to pass in these days that the chosen and holy children will come down from the high Heavens and their offspring will become one with the sons of men.

39.2 In those days Enoch received books of indignation and anger and books of tumult and confusion. And there will be no mercy for them, says the Lord of Spirits.

39.3 And at that time clouds and a storm wind carried me off from the face of the earth and set me down at the end of Heaven.

39.4 And there I saw another vision; the Dwelling of the Righteous and the .1 The second vision that he saw, the vision of wisdom, which Enoch, the son of Jared, the son of Malalel, the son of Cainan, the son of Enosh, the son of Seth, the son of Adam, saw.

37.2 And this is the beginning of the words of wisdom, which I raised my voice to speak, and say. "To those who dwell on dry ground: - Hear, you men of old, and see, those who come after; the words of the Holy One, which I will speak, in front of the Lord of Spirits."

37.3 "It would have been better to have said these things before, but from those who come after, we will not withhold the beginning of wisdom."

37.4 Until now, there has not been given, by the Lord of Spirits, such wisdom as I have received. In accordance with my insight, in accordance with the wish of the Lord of Spirits: by whom the lot of eternal life has been given to me.

37.5 And the three parables were imparted to me and I raised my voice, and said to those who dwell on the dry ground: he put them together for me, in the words of the

Book of Parables.

Resting-Places of the Holy.

39.5 There my eyes saw their dwelling with the Angels, and their resting places with the Holy Ones, and they were petitioning and supplicating and praying, on behalf of the sons of men; and righteousness, like water, flowed in front of them, and mercy like dew on the ground. Thus it is among them forever and ever.

39.6 And in those days my eyes saw the Place of the Chosen Ones of Righteousness and Faith; and there will be righteousness in their days, and the righteous and chosen will be without number, in front of him, forever and ever.

39.7 And I saw their dwelling, under the Wings of the Lord of Spirits, and all the righteous and chosen shone in front of him, like the light of fire. And their mouths were full of blessing, and their lips praised the name of the Lord of Spirits. And righteousness will not fail in front of him, and truth will not fail in front of him.

39.8 There I wished to dwell, and my soul longed for that dwelling; there had my lot been assigned before, for thus it was decided about me, in front of the Lord of Spirits.

39.9 And in those days I praised and exalted the name of the Lord of Spirits, with blessing and praise, for he has destined me for blessing and praise, in accordance with the Lord of Spirits.

39.10 And for a long time my eyes looked at that place, and I blessed him and praised him, saying: "Blessed is He, and may He be blessed from the beginning and for ever!"

39.11 And in his presence there is no end. He knew before the world was created what the world would be, even for all the generations that are to come.

39.12 Those who do not sleep bless you, and they stand before Your Glory, and bless and praise and exalt, saying: "Holy, Holy, Holy, Lord of Spirits; he fills the earth with spirits."

39.13 And there, my eyes saw all those who do not sleep; standing in front of Him, and blessing, and saying: "Blessed are you, and blessed is the name of the Lord, for ever and ever!"

39.14 And my face was transformed until I was unable to see. 40.1 And after this I saw a thousand thousands and ten thousand times ten thousand! A multitude beyond number, or reckoning, who stood in front of the Glory of the Lord of Spirits.

40.2 I looked, and on the four sides of the Lord of Spirits, I saw four figures, different from those who were standing; and I learnt their names, because the Angel who went with me made known their names, and showed me all the secret things.

40.3 And I heard the voices of those four figures as they sang praises in front of the Lord of Glory.

40.4 The first voice blesses the Lord of Spirits forever and ever.

40.5 And the second voice I heard blessing the Chosen One and the chosen who depend on the Lord of Spirits.

40.6 And the third voice I heard, petitioned, and prayed, on behalf of those who dwell on dry ground and supplicate in the name of the Lord of Spirits.

40.7 And the fourth voice I heard driving away the Satans and not allowing them to come in front of the Lord of Spirits to accuse those who dwell on the high ground.

40.8 And after this I asked the Angel of Peace, who went with me, and showed me everything which is secret: "Who are those four figures, whom I have seen, and whose words I have heard and written down?"

40.9 And he said to me: "This first one, is the Holy Michael, the merciful and long-suffering. And the second, who is in charge of all the diseases, and in charge of all the wounds of the sons of men, is Raphael. And the third, who is in charge of all the powers, is the Holy Gabriel. And the fourth, who is in charge of repentance and hope of those who will inherit eternal life, is Phanuel."

40.10 And these are the four Angels of the Lord Most High; and the four voices that I heard in those days.

41.1 And after this, I saw all the secrets of Heaven, and how the Kingdom is divided, and how the deeds of men are weighed in the Balance.

41.2 There I saw the Dwelling of the Chosen, and the Resting Places of the Holy; and my eyes saw there all the sinners who deny the name of the Lord of Spirits being driven from there. And they dragged them off, and they were not able to remain, because of the punishment that went out from the Lord of Spirits.

41.3 And there my eyes saw the secrets of the flashes of lightning and of the thunder. And the secrets of the winds, how they are distributed in order to blow over the earth, and the secrets of the clouds, and of the dew; and there I saw from where they go out, in that place. And how, from there, the dust of the earth is saturated.

41.4 And there I saw closed storehouses from which the winds are distributed, and the storehouse of the hail, and the storehouse of the mist, and the storehouse of the clouds; and its cloud remained over the earth, from the beginning of the world.

41.5 And I saw the Chambers of the Sun and the Moon, where they go out, and where they return. And their glorious return; and how one is more honoured than the other is. And their magnificent course, and how they do not leave their course, neither adding nor subtracting from their course. And how they keep faith in one another, observing their oath.

41.6 And the Sun goes out first, and completes its journey at the command of the Lord of Spirits - and his Name endures forever and ever.

41.7 And after this is the hidden, and visible, path of the Moon, and it travels the course of its journey, in that place, by day and by night. One stands opposite the other, in front of the Lord of Spirits, and they give thanks, and sing praise, and do not rest, because their thanksgiving is like rest to them.

41.8 For the shining Sun makes many revolutions; for a blessing and for a curse. And the path of the journey of the Moon is for the righteous light but for the sinners; darkness. In the Name of the Lord, who has created a division between light and darkness, and has divided the spirits of men, and has established the spirits of the righteous, in the name of His Righteousness.

41.9 For no Angel hinders, and no power is able to hinder, because the judge sees them all, and judges them all Himself.

42.1 Wisdom found no place where she could dwell, and her dwelling was in Heaven.

42.2 Wisdom went out, in order to dwell among the sons of men, but did not find a dwelling; wisdom returned to her place, and took her seat in the midst of the Angels.

42.3 And iniquity came out from her chambers; those whom she did not seek she found, and dwelt among them, like rain in the desert, and like dew on the parched ground.

43.1 And again I saw flashes of lightning and the stars of Heaven, and I saw how He called them all by their names, and they obeyed Him.

43.2 And I saw the Balance of Righteousness, how they are weighed according to their light, according to the width of their areas, and the day of their appearing. And how their revolutions produce lightning, and I saw their revolutions, according to the number of the Angels, and how they Keep faith with one another.

43.3 And I asked the Angel, who went with me and showed me what is secret: "What are these?"

43.4 And he said to me: "Their likeness, the Lord of Spirits has shown to you; these are the names of the righteous who, dwell on the dry ground and believe in the name of the Lord of Spirits for ever and ever."

44.1 And other things I saw concerning lightning, how some of the stars rise and become lightning but cannot lose their form. 45.1 And this is The Second Parable.

About those who deny the Name of the Dwelling of the Holy Ones and of the Lord of Spirits.

45.2 They will not ascend into Heaven nor will they come upon the earth; such will be the lot of the sinners who deny the Name of the Lord of Spirits who will thus be kept for the Day of Affliction and Distress.

45.3 "On that day the Chosen One will sit on the Throne of Glory and will choose their works. And their resting places will be without number and their spirits within them will grow strong when they see My Chosen One and those who appeal to My Holy and Glorious Name.

45.4 And on that day I will cause My Chosen One to dwell among them and I will transform Heaven and make it an Eternal Blessing and Light.

45.5 And I will transform the dry ground and make it a blessing, and I will cause My Chosen Ones to dwell upon it; but those who commit sin and evil will not tread upon it.

45.6 For I have seen, and have satisfied with peace, My Righteous Ones, and have placed them in front of Me; but for the sinners My Judgement draws near so that I may destroy them from the face of the earth."

46.1 And there I saw one who had a 'Head of Days' and his head was white like wool. And with him there was another whose face had the appearance of a man and his face was full of grace like one of the Holy Angels.

46.2 And I asked one of the Holy Angels, who went with me and showed me all the secrets, about that Son of Man, who he was, and from where he was, and why he went with the Head of Days.

46.3 And he answered me, and said to me: "This is the Son of Man who has righteousness and with whom righteousness dwells. He will reveal all the treasures of that which is secret, for the Lord of Spirits has chosen him, and through uprightness his lot has surpassed all others, in front of the Lord of Spirits, forever.

46.4 And this Son of Man, who you have seen, will rouse the kings and the powerful from their resting places, and the strong from their thrones, and will loose the reins of the strong, and will break the teeth of the sinners.

46.5 And he will cast down the kings from their thrones, and from their kingdoms, for they do not exalt him, and do not praise him, and do not humbly acknowledge from where their kingdom was given to them.

46.6 And he will cast down the faces of the strong and shame will fill them, and darkness will be their dwelling, and worms will be their resting place. And they will have no hope of rising from their resting-places, for they do not exalt the name of the Lord of Spirits.

46.7 And these are they who judge the Stars of Heaven, and raise their hands against the Most High, and trample upon the dry ground, and dwell upon it. And all their deeds show iniquity, and their power rests on their riches, and their faith is in their gods that they have made with their hands, and they deny the name of the Lord of Spirits.

46.8 And they will be driven from the houses of his congregation, and of the faithful, who depend on the Name of the Lord of Spirits.

47.1 And in those days, the prayer of the righteous, and the blood of the righteous will have ascended from the Earth in front of the Lord of Spirits.

47.2 In these days the Holy Ones who live in Heaven above will unite with one voice, and supplicate, and pray, and praise, and give thanks, and bless, in the name of the Lord of Spirits. Because of the blood of the righteous that has been poured out. And because of the prayer of the righteous, so that it may not cease in front of the Lord of Spirits, so that justice might be done to them, and that their patience may not have to last forever."

47.3 And in those days, I saw the Head of Days sit down on the Throne of his Glory and the Books of the Living were opened in front of him and all His Host, which dwell in the Heavens above, and his Council were standing in front of Him.

47.4 And the hearts of the Holy Ones were full of joy that the number of righteousness had been reached, and the prayer of the righteous had been heard, and the blood of the righteous had not been required in front of the Lord of Spirits.

48.1 And in that place I saw an inexhaustible spring of righteousness and many springs of wisdom surrounded it, and all the thirsty drank from them and were filled with wisdom, and their dwelling was with the Righteous and the Holy and the Chosen.

48.2 And at that hour that Son of Man was named, in the presence of the Lord of Spirits, and his name brought to the Head of Days.

48.3 Even before the Sun and the constellations were created, before the Stars of Heaven were made, his name was named in front of the Lord of Spirits.

48.4 He will be a staff to the righteous and the Holy, so that they may lean on him and not fall, and he will be the Light of the Nations, and he will be the hope of those who grieve in their hearts.

48.5 All those who dwell upon the dry ground will fall down and worship in front of him, and they will bless, and praise, and celebrate with psalms, the name of the Lord of Spirits.

48.6 And because of this he was chosen, and hidden in front of Him, before the World was created, and forever.

48.7 But the wisdom of the Lord of Spirits has revealed him to the Holy and the righteous, for he has kept safe the lot of the righteous, for they have hated and rejected this world of iniquity. And all its works and its ways they have hated in the name of the Lord of Spirits. For in His name they are saved and he is the one who will require their lives.

48.8 And in those days the kings of the Earth, and the strong who possess the dry ground, will have downcast faces because of the works of their hands, for on the day of their distress and trouble they will not save themselves.

48.9 And I will give them into the hands of my chosen ones; like straw in the fire, and like lead in water, so they will burn in front of the righteous, and sink in front of the Holy, and no trace will be found of them.

48.10 And on the day of their trouble there will be rest on the earth and they will fall down in front of him and will not rise. And there will be no one who will take them with his hands and raise them for they denied the Lord of Spirits and his Messiah. May the name of the Lord of Spirits be blessed!

49.1 For wisdom has been poured out like water and glory will not fail in front of Him forever and ever.

49.2 For He is powerful in all the secrets of righteousness and iniquity will pass away like a shadow, and will have no existence; for the Chosen One stands in front of the Lord of Spirits and His Glory is for ever and ever, and His Power for all generations.

49.3 And in Him dwell the spirit of wisdom, and the spirit that gives understanding, and the spirit of knowledge and of power, and the spirit of those who sleep in righteousness.

49.4 And he will judge the things that are secret, and no one will be able to say an idle word in front of him, for he has been chosen in front of the Lord of Spirits, in accordance with His wish.

50.1 And in those days a change will occur for the Holy and the chosen; the Light of Days will rest upon them, and glory and honour will return to the Holy.

50.2 And on the day of trouble, calamity will be heaped up over the sinners, but the righteous will conquer in the Name of the Lord of Spirits and He will show this to others so that they might repent and abandon the works of their hands.

50.3 And they will have no honour in front of the Lord of Spirits, but in His Name they will be saved and the Lord of Spirits will have mercy on them, for his mercy is great.

50.4 And He is righteous in His judgment, and in front of His Glory iniquity will not be able to stand against His Judgment; he who does not repent will be destroyed.

50.5 "And from then on I will not have mercy on them," says the Lord of Spirits.

51.1 And in those days the Earth will return that which has been entrusted to it, and Sheol will return that which has been entrusted to it and that which it has received. And destruction will return what it owes.

51.2 And He will choose the Righteous and the Holy from among them; for the day has come near when they must be saved.

51.3 And in those days, the Chosen One will sit on his throne, and all the Secrets of Wisdom will flow out from the council of his mouth, for the Lord of Spirits has appointed him and glorified him.

51.4 And in those days the mountains will leap like rams, and the hills will skip like lambs satisfied with milk, and all will become Angels in Heaven.

51.5 Their faces will shine with joy, for in those days the Chosen One will have risen and the earth will rejoice. And the righteous will dwell upon it and the chosen will walk upon it.

52.1 And after those days, in that place where I had seen all the visions of that which is secret, for I had been carried off by a whirlwind, and they had brought me to the west.

52.2 There my eyes saw the secrets of Heaven; everything that will occur on Earth: a mountain of iron, and a mountain of copper, and a mountain of silver, and a mountain of gold, and a mountain of soft metal, and a mountain of lead.

52.3 And I asked the Angel who went with me, saying: "What are these things which I have seen in secret?"

52.4 And he said to me: "All these things which you have seen serve the authority of His Messiah, so that he may be strong and powerful on the Earth."

52.5 And that Angel of Peace answered me, saying: "Wait a little and you will see, and everything which is secret, which the Lord of Spirits has established, will be revealed to you.

52.6 And these mountains, that you have seen; the mountain of iron, and the mountain of copper, and the mountain of silver, and the mountain of gold, and the mountain of soft metal, and the mountain of lead. All these in front of the Chosen One will be like wax before fire, and like the water that comes down from above onto these mountains they will be weak under his feet.

52.7 And it will come to pass in those days, that neither by gold, nor by silver, will men save themselves; they will be unable to save themselves, or to flee.

52.8 And there will be neither iron for war nor material for a breastplate; bronze will be no use, and tin will be of no use and will count for nothing, and lead will not be wanted.

52.9 All these will be wiped out and destroyed from the face of the earth when the Chosen One appears in front of the Lord of Spirits."

53.1 And there my eyes saw a deep valley, and its mouth was open; and all those who dwell upon dry ground and the sea and the islands will bring gifts and presents and offerings to him, but that deep valley will not become full.

53.2 And their hands commit evil, and everything at which the righteous toil the sinners evilly devour; and so the sinners will be destroyed from in front of the Lord of Spirits, and will be banished from the face of His Earth, unceasingly for ever and ever.

53.3 For I saw the Angels of Punishment going and preparing all the instruments of Satan.

53.4 And I asked the Angel of Peace, who went with me, and I said to him: "These instruments - for whom are they preparing them?"

53.5 And he said to me: "They are preparing these for the kings and the powerful of this Earth, so that by means of them they may be destroyed.

53.6 And after this the Righteous and Chosen One will cause the house of his congregation to appear; from then on, in the name of the Lord of Spirits, they will not be hindered.

53.7 And in front of him these mountains will not be firm like the earth, and the hills will be like a spring of water; and the righteous will have rest from the ill-treatment of the sinners."

54.1 And I looked, and turned to another part of the Earth, and I saw there a deep valley with burning fire.

54.2 And they brought the kings and powerful and threw them into that valley.

54.3 And there my eyes saw how they made instruments for them - iron chains of immeasurable weight.

54.4 And I asked the Angel of Peace, who went with me, saying: "These chain instruments - for whom are they being prepared?"

54.5 And he said to me: "These are being prepared for the hosts of Azazel, so that they may take them, and throw them into the lowest part of hell; and they will cover their jaws with rough stones, as the Lord of Spirits commanded.

54.6 And Michael and Gabriel, Raphael and Phanuel - these will take hold of them on that great day. And throw them, on that day, into the furnace of burning fire, so that the Lord of Spirits may take vengeance on them for their iniquity, in that they became servants of Satan, and led astray those who dwell upon the dry ground.

54.7 And in those days, the punishment of the Lord of Spirits will go out, and all the storehouses of the waters which are above the sky and under the earth, will be opened.

54.8 And all the waters will be joined with the waters that are above the sky. The water that is above the sky is male and the water that is under the Earth is female.

54.9 And all those who dwell upon the dry ground, and those who dwell under the ends of Heaven, will be wiped out.

54.10 And because of this they will acknowledge their iniquity which they have committed on the Earth and through this they will be destroyed."

55.1 And after this, the Head of Days repented, and said: "I have destroyed to no purpose all those who dwell upon the dry ground."

55.2 And he swore by His Great Name: "From now on I will not act like this towards all those who dwell upon the dry ground. And I will put a sign in Heaven, and it will be a pledge of faith between me and them forever, so long as Heaven is above the Earth.

55.3 And this will be in accordance with my command. When I want to take hold of them with the hands of the Angels, on the day of distress and pain, in the face of my anger and my wrath, my wrath and anger will remain upon them" says the Lord, The Lord of Spirits.

55.4 "You powerful kings who dwell upon the dry ground will be obliged to watch my Chosen One sit down on the throne of My Glory, and judge, in the Name of the Lord of Spirits, Azazel and all his associates and all his hosts."

56.1 And I saw there the hosts of the Angels of Punishment, as they went, and they were holding chains of iron and bronze.

56.2 And I asked the Angel of Peace, who went with me, saying: "To whom are those who are holding the chains going?"

56.3 And he said to me: "Each to his own chosen ones, and to their beloved ones, so that they may be thrown into the chasm, in the depths of the valley."

56.4 And then, that valley will be filled with their chosen and beloved ones, and the days of their life will be at an end, and the days of their leading astray will no longer be counted.

56.5 And in those days, the Angels will gather together, and will throw themselves towards the east, upon the Parthians and Medes. They will stir up the kings so that a disturbing spirit will come upon them, and they will drive them from their thrones; and they will come out like lions from their lairs, and like hungry wolves in the middle of their flocks.

56.6 And they will go up and trample on the Land of My Chosen Ones, and the land of my chosen ones will become before them a tramping-ground and a beaten track.

56.7 But the City of My Righteous Ones will be a hindrance to their horses, and they will stir up slaughter amongst themselves, and their own right hand will be strong against them. And a man will not admit to knowing his neighbour, or his brother, nor a son his father, or his mother, until, through their death, there are corpses enough; and their punishment - it will not be in vain.

56.8 And in those days Sheol will open its mouth and they will sink into it and their destruction; Sheol will swallow up the sinners in front of the faces of the chosen."

57.1 And it came to pass, after this, that I saw another host of chariots with men riding on them, and they came upon the wind from the east and from the west, to the south.

57.2 And the sound of the noise of their chariots was heard. And when this occurred the Holy Ones observed it from Heaven and the Pillars of the Earth were shaken from their foundations. And the sound was heard from the ends of the Earth to the ends of Heaven throughout one day.

57.3 And all will fall down and worship the Lord of Spirits. And this is end of the second parable.

58.1 And I began to speak The Third Parable. About The Righteous and about The Chosen.

58.2 Blessed are you, the righteous and the chosen, for your lot will be glorious!

58.3 And the righteous will be in the light of the Sun and the chosen in the light of eternal life. And there will be no end to the days of their life and the days of the Holy will be without number.

58.4 And they will seek the light and will find righteousness with the Lord of Spirits. Peace be to the righteous with the Lord of the World!

58.5 And after this it will be said to the Holy that they should seek in Heaven the secrets of righteousness, the lot of faith; for it has become bright as the Sun upon the dry ground, and darkness has passed away.

58.6 And there will be ceaseless light, and to a limit of days, they will not come, for darkness will have been destroyed previously. And the light will endure in front of the Lord of Spirits, and the light of uprightness will endure in front of the Lord of Spirits, forever.

60.1 In the fiftieth year, in the seventh month, on the fourteenth day of the month of the life of Enoch. In that parable, I saw how the Heaven of Heavens was shaken violently, and the Host of the Most High and the Angels, a thousand thousands and ten thousand times ten thousand, were extremely disturbed.

60.2 And then I saw the Head of Days sitting on the throne of his glory and the Angels and righteous were sitting around him.

60.3 And a great trembling seized me, and fear took hold of me, and my loins collapsed and gave way, and my whole being melted, and I fell upon my face.

60.4 And the Holy Michael sent another Holy Angel, one of the Holy Angels, and he raised me; and when he raised me my spirit returned, for I had been unable to endure the sight of that host, and the disturbance, and the shaking of Heaven.

60.5 And the Holy Michael said to me: "What sight has disturbed you like this? Until today has the day of His mercy lasted and He has been merciful and long suffering towards those who dwell upon the dry ground.

60.6 And when the Day, and the Power, and the Punishment, and the Judgment come that the Lord of Spirits has prepared for those who worship the Righteous

Judgment, and for those who deny the Righteous Judgment, and for those who take His name in vain - and that Day has been prepared. For the chosen a covenant, but for the sinners a visitation."

60.7 And on that day two monsters will be separated from one another, a female monster whose name is Leviathan, to dwell in the depths of the sea, above the springs of the waters.

60.8 And the name of the male is Behemoth who occupies with his breast an immense desert named Dendayn on the east of the Garden where the chosen and the righteous dwell. Where my great-grandfather was received, who was seventh from Adam, the first man whom the Lord of Spirits made.

60.9 And I asked that other Angel to show me the power of those monsters, how they were separated on one day, and thrown, one into the depths of the sea and the other on to the dry ground of the desert.

60.10 And he said to me: "Son of man, you here wish to know what is secret."

60.24 And the Angel of Peace who was with me, said to me: "These two monsters, prepared in accordance with the greatness of the Lord, will feed them that Punishment of the Lord. And children will be killed with their mothers and sons with their fathers.

60.25 When the punishment of the Lord of Spirits rests upon them it will remain resting so that the punishment of the Lord of Spirits may not come in vain upon these. Afterwards, the judgment will be according to His mercy and His patience."

61.1 And in those days, I saw long cords given to those Angels and they acquired wings for themselves, and flew, and went towards the north.

61.2 And I asked the Angel, saying: "Why did these take the long cords, and go?" And he said to me: "They went so that they may measure."

61.3 And the Angel who went with me, said to me: "These will bring the measurements of the righteous, and the ropes of the righteous, to the righteous, that they may rely on the name of the Lord of Spirits for ever and ever.

61.4 The chosen will begin to dwell with the chosen, and these measurements will be given to faith, and will strengthen righteousness.

61.5 And these measurements will reveal all the secrets of the depths of the Earth, and those who were destroyed by the desert, and those who were devoured by the fish of the sea, and by animals, that they may return and rely on the Day of the Chosen One. For no one will be destroyed in front of the Lord of Spirits, and no one can be destroyed."

61.6 And all those in the Heavens above received a command, and power, and one voice, and one light like fire was given to them.

61.7 And Him, before everything, they blessed, and exalted, and praised in wisdom. And they showed themselves wise in speech and in the spirit of life.

61.8 And the Lord of Spirits set the Chosen One on the throne of his glory, and he will judge all the works of the Holy ones in Heaven above, and in the Balance he will weigh their deeds.

61.9 And when he lifts his face to judge their secret ways according to the word of the name of the Lord of Spirits, and their path according to the way of the Righteous Judgment of the Lord Most High, they will all speak with one voice and bless, and praise, and exalt, and glorify, the Name of the Lord of Spirits.

61.10 And he will call all the Host of the Heavens and all the Holy Ones above, and the Host of the Lord, the Cherubim, and the Seraphim, and the Ophannim, and all the Angels of Power, and all the Angels of the Principalities, and the Chosen One, and the other host that is upon the dry ground, and over the water, on that Day.

61.11 And they will raise one voice, and will bless, and praise, and glorify, and exalt, in the spirit of faith, and in the spirit of wisdom, and of patience, and in the spirit of mercy, and in the spirit of justice, and of peace, and in the spirit of goodness. And they will all say with one voice: "Blessed is He, and blessed be the name of the Lord of Spirits for ever and ever."

61.12 All Those Who Do Not Sleep in Heaven above will bless him. All His Holy Ones who are in Heaven, will bless Him, and all the chosen ones who dwell in the Garden of Life, and every spirit able to bless, and praise and exalt, and hallow your Holy Name. And all flesh which to the limit of its power, will praise, and bless, your Name forever and ever.

61.13 For great is the mercy of the Lord of Spirits, and he is long-suffering; and all his works and all his forces, as many as he has made, he has revealed to the righteous and the chosen, in the Name of the Lord of Spirits.

62.1 And thus the Lord commanded the kings, and the mighty and the exalted, and those who dwell upon the earth, and said: "Open your eyes and raise your horns if you are able to acknowledge the Chosen One."

62.2 And the Lord of Spirits sat on His Throne of Glory, and the spirit of righteousness was poured out on him, and the word of his mouth kills all the sinners and all the lawless, and they are destroyed in front of him.

62.3 And on that Day, all the kings and the mighty and the exalted, and those who possess the earth, will stand up and they will see and recognize how he sits on the Throne of His Glory. And the righteous are judged in righteousness, in front of him, and no idle word is spoken in front of him.

62.4 And pain will come upon them as upon a woman in labour, for whom giving birth is difficult when her child enters the mouth of the womb, and she has difficulty giving birth.

62.5 And one half of them will look at the other, and they will be terrified, and will cast down their faces, and pain will take hold of them when they see that son of a woman sitting on the throne of His Glory.

62.6 And the mighty kings, and all those who possess the earth, will praise and bless and exalt Him who rules everything that is hidden.

62.7 For from the beginning that Son of Man was hidden, and the Most High kept him in the presence of His power, and revealed him only to the chosen.

62.8 And the community of the Holy and the chosen will be sown and all the chosen will stand before him on that day.

62.9 And all the mighty kings, and the exalted, and those who rule the dry ground, will fall down before him, on their faces, and worship; and they will set their hopes on that Son of Man, and will entreat him, and will petition for mercy from him.

62.10 But the Lord of Spirits will then so press them that they will hasten to go out from before Him, and their faces will be filled with shame, and the darkness will grow deeper on their faces.

62.11 And the Angels of Punishment will take them so that they may repay them for the wrong that they did to His children and to His chosen ones.

62.12 And they will become a spectacle to the righteous and to His chosen ones; they will rejoice over them, for the anger of the Lord of Spirits will rest upon them, and the sword of the Lord of Spirits will be drunk with them.

62.13 And the righteous and the chosen will be saved on that Day and they will never see the faces of the sinners and the lawless from then on.

62.14 And the Lord of Spirits will remain over them and with that Son of Man they will dwell, and eat, and lie down, and rise up, forever and ever.

62.15 And the righteous and chosen will have risen from the earth, and will have ceased to cast down their faces, and will have put on the Garment of Life.

62.16 And this will be a Garment of Life from the Lord of Spirits; and your garments will not wear out, and your glory will not fail, in front of the Lord of Spirits.

63.1 In those days, the mighty kings who possess the dry ground will entreat the Angels of His Punishment to whom they have been handed over so that they might give them a little respite. And so that they might fall down and worship in front of the Lord of Spirits, and confess their sins in front of Him.

63.2 And they will bless and praise the Lord of Spirits, and say: "Blessed be the Lord of Spirits, and the Lord of Kings, the Lord of the Mighty, and the Lord of the Rich, and the Lord of Glory, and the Lord of Wisdom!

63.3 And everything secret is clear, in front of You, and your power is for all generations, and your glory is forever and ever. Deep and without number are all your secrets and your righteousness is beyond reckoning.

63.4 Now we realize that we ought to praise and bless the Lord of Kings and the one who is King over all Kings."

63.5 And they will say: "Would that we might be given a respite, so that we might praise and thank and bless him, and make our confession in front of His Glory.

63.6 And now we long for a respite, but do not find it; we are driven off and do not obtain it; and the light has passed away from before us, and darkness will be our dwelling forever and ever.

63.7 For we have not made our confession before him, and we have not praised the name of the Lord of Kings, and we have not praised the Lord for all his works, but our hopes have been on the sceptre of our kingdom, and of our glory.

63.8 And on the day of our affliction and distress he does not save us, and we find no respite to make our confession that our Lord is faithful in all his doings, and in all his judgments and his justice, and that his judgments show no respect for persons.

63.9 And we pass away from in front of him because of all our works and all our sins have been counted exactly."

63.10 Then they will say to them: "Our souls are sated with possessions gained through iniquity, but they do not prevent our going down into the flames of the torment of Sheol."

63.11 And after this their faces will be filled with darkness and shame, in front of that Son of Man, and they will be driven away from him. And the sword will dwell among them - in front of Him.

63.12 And thus says the Lord of Spirits: "This is the Law and the Judgment for the mighty, and the kings, and the exalted, and for those who possess the dry ground, in front of the Lord of Spirits."

64.1 And I saw other figures hidden in that place.

64.2 I heard the voice of the Angel saying: "These are the Angels who came down from Heaven onto the Earth and revealed what is secret to the sons of men, and led astray the sons of men, so that they committed sin."

68.2 And on that day the Holy Michael answered Raphael, saying: "The power of the spirit seizes me and makes me tremble because of the harshness of the judgment of the Angels. Who can endure the harshness of the judgment which has been executed and before which they melt with fear?"

68.3 And the Holy Michael answered Raphael again, and said to him: "Who would not soften his heart over it, and whose mind would not be disturbed by this word? Judgment has gone out against them, upon those whom they have led out like this.

68.4 But it came to pass, when he stood before the Lord of Spirits, that the Holy Michael spoke as follows to Raphael: "I will not take their part under the eye of the Lord, for the Lord of Spirits is angry with them, because they act as if they were the Lord.

68.5 Because of this the hidden judgment will come upon them for ever and ever; for neither any other Angel, nor any man, will receive their lot, but they alone have received their judgment for ever and ever.

69.1 And after this judgment I will terrify them, and make them tremble, for they have shown this to those who dwell upon the dry ground."

69.2 And behold, the names of those Angels: - The first of them is Semyaza, and the second Artaqifa, and the third Armen, and the fourth Kokabiel, and the fifth Turiel, and the sixth Ramiel, and the seventh Daniel, and the eighth Nuqael, and the ninth Baraqiel, and the tenth Azazel, and the eleventh Armaros, the twelfth Batriel, the thirteenth Basasael, the fourteenth Ananel, the fifteenth Turiel, the sixteenth Samsiel, the seventeenth Yetarel, the eighteenth Tumiel, the nineteenth Turiel, the twentieth Rumiel, the twenty-first Azazel.

69.3 And these are the chiefs of their Angels, and the names of the leaders of hundreds, and their leaders of fifties, and their leaders of tens.

69.4 The name of the first is Yequn; this is the one who led astray all the children of the Holy Angels, and he brought them down onto the dry ground, and led them astray through the daughters of men.

69.5 And the name of the second is Asbeel; this one suggested an evil plan to the children of the Holy Angels, and led them astray, so that they corrupted their bodies with the daughters of men.

69.6 And the name of the third is Gadreel; this is the one that showed all the deadly blows to the sons of men. And he led astray Eve. And he showed the weapons of death to the children of men, the shield and the breastplate, and the sword for slaughter, and all the weapons of death to the sons of men.

69.7 And from his hand they have gone out against those who dwell the dry ground from that time and forever and ever.

69.8 And the name of the fourth is Penemue; this one showed the sons of men the bitter and the sweet and showed them all the secrets of their wisdom.

69.9 He taught men the art of writing with ink and paper, and through this many have gone astray, from eternity to eternity, and to this day.

69.10 For men were not created for this, that they should confirm their faith like this, with pen and ink.

69.11 For men were created no differently from the Angels, so that they might remain righteous and pure, and death, which destroys everything, would not have touched them; but through this knowledge of theirs they are being destroyed and through this power death consumes them.

69.12 And the name of the fifth is Kasdeyae; this one showed the sons of men all the evil blows of the spirits and of the demons, and the blows that attack the embryo in the womb so that it miscarries. And the blows that attack the soul: the bite of the serpent. And the blows that occur at midday, and the son of the serpent - who is strong.

69.13 And this is the task of Kesbeel, the chief of the oath, who showed the oath to the Holy ones when he dwelt on high in glory. And his name is Beqa.

69.14 And this one told the Holy Michael that he should show him the secret name so that they might mention it in the oath, so that those, who showed the sons of men everything that is secret, trembled before that name and oath.

69.15 And this is the power of this oath, for it is powerful and strong, and he placed this oath, Akae, in the charge of the Holy Michael.

69.16 And these are the secrets of this oath, and they are strong through this oath, and Heaven was suspended, before the world was created, and forever.

69.17 And through it the earth was founded upon the water, and from the hidden recesses of the mountains come beautiful waters, from the creation of the world and forever.

69.18 And through that oath the sea was created, and as its foundation, for the time of anger, he placed for it the sand, and it does not go beyond it, from the creation of the world and for ever.

69.19 And through that oath the deeps were made firm, and they stand and do not move from their place, from the creation of the world and for ever.

69.20 And through that oath the Sun and the Moon complete their course and do not transgress their command, from the creation of the world and for ever.

69.21 And through that oath the stars complete their course, and he calls their names, and they answer him, from the creation of the world and for ever.

69.22 And likewise the spirits of the water, of the winds, and of all the breezes, and their paths, according to all the groups of the spirits.

69.23 And there are kept the storehouses of the sound of thunder, and of the light of the lightning; and there are kept the storehouses of the hail, and the hoarfrost, and the storehouses of the mist, and the storehouses of the rain and dew.

69.24 And all these make their confession and give thanks in front of the Lord of Spirits and sing praises with all their power. And their food consists of all their thanksgiving and they give thanks, praise, and exalt, in the name of the Lord of Spirits, forever and ever.

69.25 And this oath is strong over them and through it they are kept safe and their courses are not disturbed.

69.26 And they had great joy and they blessed, praised, and exalted, because the name of that Son of Man had been revealed to them.

69.27 And he sat on the Throne of His Glory and the whole judgment was given to the Son of Man and he will cause the sinners to pass away and be destroyed from the face of the Earth.

69.28 And those who led astray the world will be bound in chains and will be shut up in the assembly-place of their destruction, and all their works will pass away from the face of the earth.

69.29 And from then on there will be nothing corruptible. For that Son of Man has appeared, and has sat on the Throne of His Glory, and everything evil will pass away and go from in front of Him; and the word of that Son of Man will be strong in front of the Lord of Spirits. This is the Third Parable of Enoch.

REVOLUTIONS OF THE LIGHTS

72.1 The Book of the Revolutions of the Lights of Heaven. Each as it is; according to their classes, according to their period of rule and their times, according to their names and places of origin, and according to their months.

That Uriel, the Holy Angel who was with me, and is their leader, showed to me. And he showed me all their regulations, exactly as they are, for each year of the world and for ever, until the new creation shall be made which will last forever.

72.2 And this is the First Law of the Lights. The light called the Sun; its rising is in the Gates of Heaven that are towards the east, and its setting is in the western Gates of Heaven.

72.3 And I saw six Gates from which the Sun rises, and six Gates in which the Sun sets, and the Moon also rises and sets in those Gates, and the leaders of the stars together with those whom they lead. There are six in the east and six in the west, all exactly in place, one next to the other; and there are many windows to the south and the north of those Gates.

72.4 And first there rises the greater light, named the Sun, and its disc is like the disc of Heaven, and the whole of it is full of a fire which gives light and warmth.

72.5 The wind blows the chariots on which it ascends, and the Sun goes down in the sky and returns through the north in order to reach the east, and is led so that it comes to the appropriate Gate and shines in the sky.

72.6 In this way it rises in the first month, in the large Gate, namely; it rises through the fourth of those six Gates that are towards the east.

72.7 And in that fourth Gate, through which the Sun rises in the first month, there are twelve window-openings from which, whenever they are opened, flames come out.

72.8 When the Sun rises in Heaven it goes out through that fourth Gate for thirty days, and exactly in the fourth Gate, in the west of Heaven, it goes down.

72.9 And in those days the day grows daily longer, and the night grows nightly shorter, until the thirtieth morning.

72.10 And on that day the day becomes longer than the night by a double part, and the day amounts to exactly ten parts, and the night amounts to eight parts.

72.11 And the Sun rises from that fourth Gate, and sets in the fourth Gate, and returns to the fifth Gate in the east for thirty mornings; and it rises from it and sets in the fifth Gate.

72.12 And then the day becomes longer by two parts, and the day amounts to eleven parts, and the night becomes shorter and amounts to seven parts.

72.13 And the Sun returns to the east and comes to the sixth Gate, and rises and sets in the sixth Gate for thirty-one mornings, because of its sign.

72.14 And on that day the day becomes longer than the night, and the day becomes double the night; and the day amounts to twelve parts, and the night becomes shorter and amounts to six parts.

72.15 And the Sun rises up so that the day may grow shorter, and the night longer; and the Sun returns to the east, and comes to the sixth Gate, and rises from it, and sets, for thirty mornings.

72.16 And when thirty mornings have been completed the day becomes shorter, by exactly one part; and the day amounts to eleven parts, and the night to seven parts.

72.17 And the Sun goes out from the west, through that sixth Gate, and goes to the east, and rises in the fifth Gate for thirty mornings and it sets in the west again, in the fifth Gate in the west.

72.18 On that day the day becomes shorter by two parts, and the day amounts to ten parts, and the night to eight parts.

72.19 And the Sun rises from that fifth Gate, and sets in the fifth Gate in the west, and rises in the fourth Gate for thirty-one mornings because of its sign, and sets in the west.

72.20 On that day the day becomes equal with the night, and is of equal length; and the night amounts to nine parts, and the day to nine parts.

72.21 And the Sun rises from that Gate and sets in the west, and returns to the east, and rises in the third Gate for thirty mornings, and sets in the west in the third Gate.

72.22 And the Sun rises from that third Gate, and sets in the third Gate in the west, and returns to the east; and the Sun rises in the second Gate in the east for thirty mornings, and likewise, it sets in the second Gate, in the west of Heaven.

72.24 And on that day the night amounts to eleven parts and the day to seven parts.

72.25 And the Sun rises, on that day, from the second Gate, and sets in the west in the second Gate, and returns to the east to the first Gate for thirty one mornings, then sets in the west in the first Gate.

72.26 And on that day the night becomes longer, and becomes double the day; and the night amounts to exactly twelve parts, and the day to six parts.

72.27 And with this, the Sun has completed the divisions of its journey, and it turns back again, along these divisions of its journey; and it comes through that first Gate for thirty mornings, and sets in the west opposite it.

72.28 And on that day the night becomes shorter in length by one part, and amounts to eleven parts, and the day to seven parts.

72.29 And the Sun returns, and comes to the second Gate in the east, and it returns along those divisions of its journey for thirty mornings, rising and setting.

72.30 And on that day the night becomes shorter in length and the night amounts to ten parts and the day to eight parts.

72.31 And on that day, the Sun rises from the second Gate, and sets in the west, and returns to the east, and rises in the third Gate for thirty one mornings, and sets in the west of the sky.

72.32 And on that day the night becomes shorter, and amounts to nine parts, and the day amounts to nine parts, and the night becomes equal with the day. And the year amounts to exactly 364 days.

72.33 And the length of the day and the night, and the shortness of the day and the night - they are different because of the journey of the Sun.

72.34 Because of it, its journey becomes daily longer, and nightly shorter.

72.35 And this is the law and the journey of the Sun and its return, as often as it returns; sixty times it returns and rises, that is the great eternal light, which for ever and ever is named the Sun.

72.36 And this that rises is the great light, which is named after its appearance, as the Lord commanded.

72.37 And thus it rises and sets; it neither decreases, nor rests, but runs day and night in its chariot. And its light is seven times brighter than that of the Moon but in size the two are equal.

73.1 And after this law I saw another law, for the lesser light, named the Moon.

73.2 And its disc is like the disc of the Sun, and the wind blows its chariot on which it rides, and in fixed measure light is given to it.

73.3 And every month it's rising and setting change, and its days are as the days of the Sun, and when its light is uniformly full, it is a seventh part the light of the Sun.

73.4 And thus it rises, and its first phase is towards the east; it rises on the thirtieth morning. And on that day it appears, and becomes for you the first phase of the Moon, on the thirtieth morning, together with the Sun in the Gate through which the Sun rises.

73.5 And a half.(…..) .with a seventh part, and its entire disc is empty, without light, except for a seventh part, a fourteenth part of it's light.

73.6 And on the day that it receives a seventh part and a half of its light, its light amounts to a seventh, and a seventh part and a half.

73.7 It sets with the Sun, and when the Sun rises, the Moon rises with it, and receives a half of one part of light. And on that night at the beginning of its morning, at the beginning of the Moon's day, the Moon sets with the Sun, and is dark on that night in six and seven parts and a half.

73.8 And it rises on that day, with exactly a seventh part, goes out, recedes from the rising of the Sun, and becomes bright on the remainder of its days, in the other six and seven parts.

74.1 And another journey, and law, I saw for it, in that according to this law it makes its monthly journey.

74.2 And Uriel, the Holy Angel who is leader of them all, showed me everything, and I wrote down their positions as he showed them to me. And I wrote down their months, as they are, and the appearance of their light, until fifteen days have been completed.

74.3 In seventh parts it makes all its darkness full, and in seventh parts it makes all its light full, in the east and in the west.

74.4 And in certain months, it changes its setting, and in certain months, it follows its own individual course.

74.5 In two months it sets with the Sun, in those two Gates that are in the middle, in the third and in the fourth Gate.

74.6 It goes out for seven days and turns back, and returns again to the Gate from which the Sun rises. And in that Gate it makes all its light full, and it recedes from the Sun, and comes, in eight days, to the sixth Gate from which the Sun rises.

74.7 And when the Sun rises from the fourth Gate, the Moon goes out for seven days, until it rises from the fifth Gate. And again it returns in seven days to the fourth Gate, makes all its light full, recedes, and comes to the first Gate in eight days.

74.8 And again it returns in seven days to the fourth Gate from which the Sun rises.

74.9 Thus I saw their positions; how the Moon rose and the Sun set in those days.

74.10 And if five years are added together, the Sun has an excess of thirty days. For each year, of the five years, there are three hundred and sixty four days.

74.11 And the excess, of the Sun and the stars, comes to six days. In five years, with six days each, they have an excess of thirty days, and the Moon falls behind the Sun and the stars by thirty days.

74.12 And the Moon conducts the years exactly, all of them according to their eternal positions; they are neither early nor late, even by one day, but change the year in exactly 364 days.

74.13 In three years, there are 1,092 days, and in five years 1,820 days, so that in eight years there are 2,912 days.

74.14 For the Moon alone, the days in three years come to 1,062 days, and in five years it is fifty days behind.

74.15 And there are 1,770 days in five years so that for the Moon the days in eight years amount to 2,832 days.

74.16 For the difference in eight years is eighty days, and all the days that the Moon is behind, in eight years, are eighty days.

74.17 And the year is completed exactly, in accordance with their positions, and the positions of the Sun, in that they rise from the Gates from which the Sun rises and sets for thirty days.

75.1 And the leaders of the tens of thousands, who are in charge of the whole of creation, and in charge of all the stars, and also the four days which are added, and are not separated from their position, according to the whole reckoning of the year. And these serve on the four days that are not counted in the reckoning of the year.

75.2 And because of them men go wrong in them. For these lights really serve in the stations of the world, one in the first Gate, and one in the third Gate, and one in the fourth Gate, and one in the sixth Gate. And the exact harmony of the world is completed in the separate 364 stations of the world.

75.3 For the signs, and the times, and the years, and the days, were showed to me by the Angel Uriel whom the Lord of Eternal Glory has placed in charge of all the Lights of Heaven. In Heaven and in the world, so that they might rule on the Face of Heaven, and appear over the earth, and be leaders of day and night; the Sun, the Moon, the stars, and all the serving creatures who revolve in all the Chariots of Heaven.

75.4 Likewise, Uriel showed to me twelve Gate-openings in the disc of the chariot of the Sun, in the sky, from which the rays of the Sun come out. And from them heat comes out over the Earth when they are opened at the times that are appointed for them.

75.5 And there are openings for the winds, and for the spirit of the dew, when they are opened at their times, opened in Heaven, at the ends of the earth.

75.6 I saw twelve Gates in Heaven, at the ends of the earth, from which the Sun, and the Moon, and the stars, and all the works of Heaven, go out in the east and in the west.

75.7 And there are many window-openings to the north and to the south, and each window, at its appointed time, sends out heat corresponding to those Gates, from which the stars go out, in accordance with His command to them, and in which they set according to their number.

75.8 And I saw chariots in Heaven, running through the region above those Gates, in which the stars that never set rotate.

75.9 And one is bigger than all the others. And it goes round through the whole world.

76.1 And at the ends of the earth, I saw twelve Gates open to all the winds, from which the winds come out and blow over the earth.

76.2 Three of them open in the front of Heaven, and three in the back, and three on the right of Heaven, and three on the left.

76.3 And the three first are those towards the east, and then the three towards the north, and the three after these towards the south, and the three in the west.

76.4 Through four of them come winds of blessing and peace. And from the other eight come winds of punishment; when they are sent they bring devastation to the whole Earth, and to the water which is on it, and to all those who dwell upon it, and to everything that is in the water and on dry ground.

76.5 And the first wind from those Gates, called the east wind, comes out through the first Gate, which is towards the east. The one that comes from the south brings devastation, drought, heat, and destruction.

76.6 And through the second Gate, in the middle, comes what is right. And from it come rain, and fruitfulness, and prosperity, and dew. And through the third Gate, which is towards the north, comes cold and drought.

76.7 And after these, the winds towards the south come out, through three Gates. First, through the first of the Gates, which inclines towards the east, comes a hot wind.

76.8 And through the middle Gate, which is next to it, come pleasant fragrances, and dew, and rain, and prosperity, and life.

76.9 And through the third Gate, which is towards the west, come dew, and rain, and locusts, and devastation.

76.10 And after these, the winds towards the north..(...)..from the seventh Gate, which is towards the east, come dew and rain, locusts and Devastation.

76.11 And through the Gate exactly in the middle, come rain, and dew, and life, and prosperity. And through the third Gate, which is towards the west come mist and hoarfrost, and snow, and rain, and dew, and locusts.

76.12 And after these the winds towards the west. Through the first Gate, which inclines towards the north, come dew, and rain, and hoarfrost, and cold, and snow, and frost.

76.13 And from the middle Gate, come dew and rain, prosperity and blessing. And through the last Gate, which is towards the south, come drought and devastation, burning and destruction.

76.14 And thus the twelve Gates, of the four quarters of Heaven arecomplete. And all their laws, and all their punishments, and all their benefits, I have shown to you, my son Methuselah.

77.1 They called the first quarter eastern because it is the first, and they call the second the south because there the Most High descends, and there especially the one who is blessed forever descends.

77.2 And the western quarter is called waning because there all the lights of Heaven wane and go down.

77.3 And the fourth quarter, named the north, is divided into three parts. And the first of them is the dwelling place for men; and the second contains seas of water, and the deeps, and the forests, and rivers, and darkness and mist; and the third part contains the Garden of Righteousness.

77.4 I saw seven high mountains, which were higher than all other mountains on the earth; and from them snow comes. And days and times and years, pass away and go by.

77.5 I saw seven rivers on the earth, larger than all the other rivers; one of them comes from the east and pours out its waters into the Great Sea.

77.6 And two of them come from the north to the sea and pour out their water into the Erythraean Sea in the east.

77.7 And the remaining four flow out on the side of the north, to their seas, two to the Erythraean Sea, and two into the Great Sea, and they discharge themselves there, and not into the wilderness, as some say.

77.8 I saw seven large islands, in the sea and on the land, two on the land, and five in the Great Sea.

78.1 The names of the Sun are as follows: The first Oryares, and the second Tomases.

78.2 The Moon has four names: The first name is Asonya, and the second Ebla, and the third Benase, and the fourth Era'e.

78.3 These are the two great lights; their disc is like the disc of Heaven and in size the two are equal.

78.4 In the disc of the Sun, are seven parts of light, which are added to it more than to the Moon, and in fixed measure light is transferred to the Moon until a seventh part of the Sun is exhausted.

78.5 And they set, go into the Gates of the west, go round through the north, and rise through the Gates of the east, on the face of Heaven.

78.6 And when the Moon rises, it appears in the sky, and has a half of a seventh part of light, and on the fourteenth day it makes all its light full.

78.7 And fifteen parts of light are transferred to it, until on the fifteenth day its light is full, according to the sign of the year, and amounts to fifteen parts. And the Moon comes into being by halves of a seventh part.

78.8 And in its waning on the first day, it decreases to fourteen parts of its light. And on the second to thirteen parts, and on the third to twelve parts, on the fourth to eleven parts, and on the fifth to ten parts, and on the sixth to nine parts, and on the seventh to eight parts, and on the eighth to seven parts, and on the ninth to six parts, and on the tenth to five parts, and on the eleventh to four parts, and on the twelfth to three, and on the thirteenth to two, and on the fourteenth to half of a seventh part. And all the light that remains from the total disappears on the fifteenth day.

78.9 And in certain months the Moon has twenty-nine days and once twenty-eight.

78.10 And Uriel showed me another law: - when light is transferred to the Moon, and on which side it is transferred from the Sun.

78.11 All the time that the Moon is increasing in its light, it transfers as it becomes opposite the Sun, until in fourteen days it's light is full in the sky; and when it is all ablaze, it's light is full in the sky.

78.12 And on the first day it is called the New Moon, for on that, daylight rises on it.

78.13 And its light becomes full exactly on the day that as the Sun goes down in the west it rises from the east for the night. And the Moon shines for the whole night until the Sun rises opposite it, and the Moon is seen opposite the Sun.

78.14 And on the side on which the light of the Moon appears, there again it wanes, until all its light disappears, and the days of the Moon end and its disc remains empty without light.

78.15 And for three months, at its proper time, it achieves thirty days, and for three months, it achieves twenty-nine days, during which it completes its waning, in the first period, in the first Gate, 127 days.

78.16 And in the time of it's rising, for three months, it appears in each month with thirty days. And for three months it appears in each month
with twenty-nine days

78.17 By night, for twenty days each time, it looks like a man, and by day like Heaven, for there is nothing else in it except it's light.

79.1 And now, my son Methuselah, I have shown you everything, and the whole Law of the Stars of Heaven is complete.

79.2 And he showed me the whole law for these, for every day, and for every time, and for every rule, and for every year, and for the end thereof, according to its command, for every month and every week.

79.3 And the waning of the Moon, which occurs in the sixth Gate, for in that sixth Gate it's light becomes full, and after that it is the beginning of the month.

79.4 And the waning, which occurs in the first Gate, at its proper time, until 127 days are complete, or by weeks; twenty-five weeks and two days.

79.5 And how it falls behind the Sun, according to the law of the stars, by exactly five days in one period of time, when it has completed the pathway you have seen.

79.6 Such is the appearance, and likeness, of every light, which Uriel, the great Angel who is their leader, showed to me.

80.1 And in those days Uriel answered me and said to me: "Behold, I have shown you everything, Oh Enoch. And I have revealed everything to you, so that you may see this Sun, and this Moon, and those who lead the Stars of Heaven, and all those who turn them, their tasks and their times and their rising.

80.2 But in the days of the sinners the years will become shorter, and their seed will be late on their land, and on their fields. And all things on the earth will change and will not appear at their proper time. And the rain will be withheld and Heaven will retain it.

80.3 And in those times the fruits of the earth will be late, and will not grow at their proper time, and the fruits of the trees will be withheld at their proper time.

80.4 And the Moon will change its customary practice and will not appear at its proper time.

80.5 But in those days it will appear in Heaven, come on top of a large chariot in the west, and shine with more than normal brightness.

80.6 And many heads of the stars, in command, will go astray. And these will change their courses and their activities and will not appear at the times that have been prescribed for them.

80.7 And the entire law of the stars will be closed to the sinners, and the thoughts of those who dwell upon the Earth will go astray over them, and they will turn from all their ways and will go astray, and will think them gods.

80.8 And many evils will overtake them and punishment will come upon them to destroy them all."

81.1 And he said to me: "Oh Enoch, look at the book of the Tablets of Heaven and read what is written upon them, and note every individual fact."

81.2 And I looked at everything that was written and I noted everything. And I read the book and everything that was written in it, all the deeds of men, and all the children of flesh who will be upon the Earth, for all the generations of eternity.

81.3 And then I immediately blessed the Lord, the Eternal King of Glory, in that he has made all the works of the world, and I praised the Lord because of his patience, and I blessed him on account of the sons of Adam.

81.4 And at that time I said: "Blessed is the man who dies righteous and good, concerning whom no book of iniquity has been written, and against whom no guilt has been found."

ENOCH'S LETTER TO METHUSELAH

81.5 And these three Holy ones brought me and set me on the earth in front of the door of my house, and said to me: "Tell everything to your son Methuselah, and show all your children that no flesh is righteous, before the Lord, for He created them.

81.6 For one year we will leave you with your children, until you have regained your strength, so that you may teach your children and write these things down for them, and testify to all your children. And in the second year we will take you from amongst them.

81.7 Let your heart be strong, for the good will proclaim righteousness to the good, the righteous will rejoice with the righteous and they will wish each other well.

81.8 But the sinner will die with the sinner and the apostate will sink with the apostate.

81.9 And those who practice righteousness will die because of the deeds of men, and will be gathered in because of the deeds of the impious."

81.10 And in those days they finished speaking to me and I went to my family as I blessed the Lord of Ages.

82.1 And now, my son Methuselah, all these things I recount to you, and write down for you. I have revealed everything to you, and have given you books about all these things. Keep, my son Methuselah, the books from the hand of your father so that you may pass them on to the generations of eternity.

82.2 I have given wisdom to you, and to your children, and to those who will be your children, that they may give it to their children, for all the generations, forever, this wisdom that is beyond their thoughts.

82.3 And those who understand it will not sleep, but will incline their ears that they may learn this wisdom, and it will be better for those who eat from it than good food.

ENOCH'S FIRST VISION

83.1 And now, my son Methuselah, I will show you all the visions that I saw, recounting them before you.

83.2 Two visions I saw, before I took a wife, and neither one was like the other. For the first time, when I learnt the art of writing, and for the second time, before I took your mother. I saw a terrible vision and concerning this I made supplication to the Lord.

83.3 I had lain down in the house of my grandfather, Malalel, when I saw in a vision how Heaven was thrown down, and removed, and it fell upon the Earth.

83.4 And when it fell upon the Earth, I saw how the earth was swallowed up in a great abyss, and mountains were suspended on mountains, and hills sank down upon hills, and tall trees were torn up by their roots, and were thrown down, and sank into the abyss.

83.5 And then speech fell into my mouth, and I raised my voice to cry out, and said: "The earth is destroyed!"

83.6 And my grandfather, Malalel, roused me, since I lay near him, and said to me: "Why did you cry out so, my son, and why do you moan so?"

83.7 And I recounted to him the whole vision, which I had seen, and he said to me: "A terrible thing you have seen, my son! Your dream vision concerns the secrets of all the sin of the Earth; it is about to sink into the abyss and be utterly destroyed.

83.8 And now, my son, rise and make supplication to the Lord of Glory, for you are faithful, that a remnant may be left on the Earth and that he may not wipe out the whole Earth.

83.9 My son, from Heaven all this will come upon the Earth, and upon the Earth there will be great destruction."

83.10 And then I rose and prayed, and made supplication, and wrote my prayer down for the generations of eternity, and I will show everything to you my son Methuselah.

83.11 And, when I went out below and saw the sky, and the Sun rising in the east, and the Moon setting in the west, and some stars, and the whole Earth, and everything as He knew it since the beginning.

Then I blessed the Lord of Judgment and ascribed Majesty to him, for he makes the Sun come out from the windows of the east, so that it ascends and rises on the face of Heaven, and follows the path which has been shown to it.

84.1 And I raised my hands in righteousness and I blessed the Holy and Great One. And I spoke with the breath of my mouth, and with the tongue of flesh, which God has made for men born of flesh so that they might speak with it; and he has given them breath, and a tongue, and a mouth, so that they might speak with them.

84.2 "Blessed are you, Oh Lord King, and great and powerful in your majesty, Lord of the whole Creation of Heaven, King of Kings, and God of the whole world! And your kingly authority, and your Sovereignty and your Majesty will last forever, and forever and ever, and your power, for all generations. And all the Heavens are your throne, forever, and the whole Earth your footstool forever, and ever and ever.

84.3 For you made, and you rule, everything, and nothing is too hard for you, and no wisdom escapes you; it does not turn away from your throne nor from your presence. And you know, and see, and hear, everything, and nothing is hidden from you, for you see everything.

84.4 And now the Angels of your Heaven are doing wrong and your anger rests upon the flesh of men until the day of the great judgment.

84.5 And now, Oh God, Lord, and Great King, I entreat and ask that you will fulfill my prayer to leave me a posterity on Earth and not to wipe out all the flesh of men and make the earth empty so that there is destruction forever.

84.6 And now, my Lord, wipe out from the earth the flesh that has provoked your anger, but the flesh of righteousness and uprightness establish as a seed bearing plant forever. And do not hide your face from the prayer of your servant, Oh Lord."

PROPHECY OF THE TEN WEEKS

91.1 And now my son Methuselah, call to me all your brothers, and gather to me all the children of your mother. For a voice calls me, and a spirit has been poured over me, so that I may show you everything that will come upon you forever.

91.2 And after this Methuselah went and called his brothers to him and gathered his relations.

91.3 And he spoke about righteousness to all his sons, and said: "Hear, my children, all the words of your father, and listen properly to the voice of my mouth, for I will testify and speak to you - my beloved. Love uprightness and walk in it!

91.4 And do not draw near to uprightness with a double heart, and do not associate with those of a double heart, but walk in righteousness my children and it will lead you in good paths, and righteousness will be your companion.

91.5 For I know that the state of wrongdoing will continue on Earth, and a great punishment will be carried out on the Earth, and an end will be made of all iniquity. And it will be cut off at its roots and its whole edifice will pass away.

91.6 And iniquity will again be complete on the Earth, and all the deeds of iniquity, and the deeds of wrong, and of wickedness, will prevail for a second time."

92.1 Written by Enoch-the-Scribe, this complete wisdom and teaching, praised by all men and a judge of the whole Earth. For all my sons who dwell on Earth. And for the last generations who will practice justice and peace.

92.2 Let not your spirit be saddened by the times for the Holy and Great One has appointed days for all things.

92.3 And the righteous man will rise from sleep, will rise and will walk in the path of righteousness, and all his paths, and his journeys, will be in eternal goodness and mercy.

92.4 He will show mercy to the righteous man and to him give eternal uprightness, and to him give power. And he will live in goodness, and righteousness, and will walk in eternal light.

92.5 And sin will be destroyed in darkness, forever, and from that day will never again be seen.

93.1 And, after this, Enoch began to speak from the books:

93.2 And Enoch said: "Concerning the sons of righteousness, and concerning the chosen of the world, and concerning the plant of righteousness and uprightness, I will speak these things to you, and make them known to you, my children. I, Enoch, according to that which appeared to me in the Heavenly vision, and that which I know from the words of the Holy Angels, and understanding from the Tablets of Heaven."

93.3 And Enoch then began to speak from the books, and said: "I was born the seventh, in the first week, while justice and righteousness still lasted.

93.4 And, after me, in the second week, great injustice will arise, and deceit will have sprung up. And in it there will be the First End, and in it, a man will be saved. And after it has ended, iniquity will grow, and He will make a law for the sinners.

93.5 And after this in the third week, at its end, a man will be chosen as the Plant of Righteous Judgment, and after him will come the Plant of Righteousness, forever.

93.6 And after this, in the fourth week, at its end, visions of the righteous and Holy will be seen, and a Law for All Generations, and an enclosure will be made for them.

93.7 And after this, in the fifth week, at its end, a House of Glory and Sovereignty will be built forever.

93.8 And after this, in the sixth week, all those who live in it will be blinded. And the hearts of them all, lacking wisdom, will sink into impiety. And in it, a man will ascend, and at its end the House of Sovereignty will be burnt with fire. And in it the whole race of the chosen root will be scattered.

93.9 And after this, in the seventh week, an apostate generation will arise. And many will be its deeds - but all its deeds will be apostasy.

93.10 And at its end, the Chosen Righteous, from the Eternal Plant of Righteousness, will be chosen, to whom will be given sevenfold teaching, concerning his whole creation.

91.7 And when iniquity, and sin, and blasphemy, and wrong, and all kinds of evil deeds increase, and when apostasy, wickedness, and uncleanness increase, a great punishment will come from Heaven upon all these. And the Holy Lord will come in anger, and in wrath, to execute judgment on the Earth.

91.8 In those days wrongdoing will be cut off at its roots, and the roots of iniquity, together with deceit, will be destroyed from under Heaven.

91.9 And all the idols of the nations will be given up, their towers will be burnt in fire, and they will remove them from the whole Earth. And they will be thrown down into the Judgment of Fire, and will be destroyed in anger, and in the severe judgment that is forever.

91.10 And the righteous will rise from sleep, and wisdom will rise, and will be given to them.

91.11 And after this the roots of iniquity will be cut off and the sword will destroy the sinners. The blasphemers will be cut off; in every place blasphemy will be destroyed by the sword.

91.12 And after this there will be another week; the eighth, that of righteousness, and a sword will be given to it so that the Righteous Judgment may be executed on those who do wrong, and the sinners will be handed over into the hands of the righteous.

91.13 And, at its end, they will acquire Houses because of their righteousness, and a House will be built for the Great King in Glory, forever.

91.14 And after this, in the ninth week, the Righteous Judgment will be revealed to the whole world. And all the deeds of the impious will vanish from the whole Earth. And the world will be written down for destruction and all men will look to the Path of Uprightness.

91.15 And, after this, in the tenth week, in the seventh part, there will be an Eternal Judgment that will be executed on the Watchers and the Great Eternal Heaven that will spring from the midst of the Angels.

91.16 And the First Heaven will vanish and pass away and a New Heaven will appear, and all the Powers of Heaven will shine forever, with sevenfold light.

91.17 And after this, there will be many weeks without number, forever, in goodness and in righteousness. And from then on sin will never again be mentioned.

91.18 And now I tell you, my children, and show you the paths of righteousness, and the paths of wrongdoing. And I will show you again so that you may know what is to come.

91.19 And now listen, my children, walk in the paths of righteousness and do not walk in the paths of wrongdoing, for all those who walk in the path of iniquity will be destroyed forever.

93.11 For is there any man who can hear the voice of the Holy One and not be disturbed? And who is there who can think his thoughts? And who is here who can look at all the works of Heaven?

93.12 And how should there be anyone who could understand the works of Heaven, and see a soul, or a spirit, and tell about it, or ascend and see all their ends and comprehend them, or make anything like them?

93.13 And is there any man who could know the length and breadth of the Earth? And to who has all its measurements been shown?

93.14 Or is there any man who could know the length of Heaven, and what is its height, and on what is it fixed, and how large is the number of stars, and where do all the lights rest?

ENOCH'S MESSAGE OF GUIDANCE

94.1 And now I say to you, my children, love righteousness and walk in it; for the paths of righteousness are worthy of acceptance, but the paths of iniquity will quickly be destroyed and vanish.

94.2 And to certain men, from a future generation, the paths of wrongdoing and of death will be revealed; and they will keep away from them and will not follow them.

94.3 And now I say to you, the righteous: do not walk in the wicked path, or in wrongdoing, or in the paths of death, and do not draw near to them or you may be destroyed.

94.4 But seek, and choose for yourself, righteousness, and a life that is pleasing and walk in the paths of peace so that you may live and prosper.

94.5 And hold my words firmly in the thoughts of your heart, and do not let them be erased from your heart, for I know that sinners will tempt men to debase wisdom, and no place will be found for it, and temptation will in no way decrease.

94.6 Woe to those who build iniquity and found deceit for they will quickly be thrown down and will not have peace.

94.7 Woe to those who build their houses with sin, for from their whole foundation they will be thrown down, and by the sword they shall fall, and those who acquire gold and silver will quickly be destroyed in the judgment.

94.8 Woe to you, you rich, for you have trusted in your riches, but from your riches you will depart for you did not remember the Most High in the days of your riches.

94.9 You have committed blasphemy, and iniquity, and are ready for the days of the outpouring of blood, and for the day of darkness, and for the day of the Great Judgment.

94.10 Thus I say, and make known to you, that He who created you will throw you down, and over your fall there will be no mercy, but your creator will rejoice at your destruction.

94.11 And your righteousness in those days will be a reproach to the sinners and to the impious.

95.1 Would that my eyes were a rain-cloud, so that I might weep over you, and pour out my tears like rain, so that I might have rest from the sorrow of my heart!

95.2 Who permitted you to practice hatred and wickedness? May judgment come upon you, the sinners!

95.3 Do not be afraid of the sinners, you righteous, for the Lord will again deliver them into your hands, so that you may execute judgment on them as you desire.

95.4 Woe to you who pronounce anathema that you cannot remove. Healing will be far from you because of your sin.

95.5 Woe to you who repay your neighbours with evil for you will be repaid according to your deeds.

95.6 Woe to you, you lying witnesses, and to those who weigh out iniquity, for you will quickly be destroyed.

95.7 Woe to you, you sinners, because you persecute the righteous, for you yourselves will be handed over and persecuted, you men of iniquity, and their yoke will be heavy on you.

96.1 Be hopeful, you righteous, for the sinners will quickly be destroyed before you, and you will have power over them, as you desire.

96.2 And in the day of the distress of the sinners, your young will rise up, like eagles, and your nest will be higher than that of vultures. And you will go up, and like badgers, enter the crevices of the earth, and the clefts of the rock, forever, before the lawless, but they will groan and weep because of you, like satyrs.

96.3 And do not be afraid you who have suffered, for you will receive healing, and a bright light will shine upon you, and the Voice of Rest you will hear from Heaven.

96.4 Woes to you, you sinners, for your riches make you appear righteous, but your hearts prove you to be sinners. And this word will be a testimony against you as a reminder of your evil deeds.

96.5 Woe to you who devour the finest of the wheat, and drink the best of the water, and trample upon the humble through your power.

96.6 Woe to you who drink water all the time, for you will quickly be repaid, and will become exhausted and dry for you have left the spring of life.

96.7 Woe to you who commit iniquity, and deceit, and blasphemy, it will be a reminder of evil against you.

96.8 Woe to you, you powerful, who through power oppress the righteous; for the day of your destruction will come. In those days many good days will come for the righteous in the day of your judgment.

97.1 Believe, you righteous, that the sinners will become an object of shame and will be destroyed on the Day of Judgment.

97.2 Be it known to you, sinners, that the Most High remembers your destruction and that the Angels rejoice over your destruction.

97.3 What will you do, you sinners, and where will you flee on that day of judgment when you hear the sound of prayer of the righteous?

97.4 But you will not be like them against whom this word will be a testimony: "You have been associated with the sinners."

97.5 And in those days, the prayer of the Holy will be in front of the Lord, and for you will come the days of your judgment.

97.6 And the words of your iniquity will be read out before the Great and Holy One, and your faces will blush with shame, and every deed which is founded upon iniquity will be rejected.

97.7 Woe to you, you sinners, who are in the middle of the sea, or on dry ground, their memory will be harmful to you.

97.8 Woe to you who acquire silver and gold, but not in righteousness, and say: "We have become very rich and have possessions, and have acquired everything that we desired.

97.9 And now let us do what we planned, for we have gathered silver and filled our storehouses, and as many as water are the servants of our houses."

97.10 And like the water your life will flow away, for your riches will not stay with you, but will quickly go up from you, for you acquired everything in iniquity and you will be given over to a great curse.

98.1 Now I swear to you, the wise, and the foolish, that you will see many things on the earth.

98.2 For you men will put on yourselves more adornments than a woman, and more coloured garments than a girl, clothed in sovereignty, and in majesty, and in power, and silver, and gold, and purple, and honours, and food will be poured out like water.

98.3 Because of this they will have neither knowledge nor wisdom. And through this, they will be destroyed, together with their possessions, and with all their glory and their honour. And in shame, and in slaughter, and in great destitution, their spirits will be thrown into the fiery furnace.

98.4 I swear to you, you sinners, that as a mountain has not, and will not, become a slave, nor a hill a woman's maid, so sin was not sent on the Earth but man, of himself, created it. And those who commit it will be subject to a great curse.

98.5 And barrenness has not been given to a woman but because of the deeds of her hand she dies without children.

98.6 I swear to you, you sinners, by the Holy and Great One, that all your evil deeds are revealed in Heaven and that your wrongdoing is not covered or hidden.

98.7 And do not think in your spirit nor say in your heart, that you do not know, or do not see, every sin is written down every day in Heaven in front of the Most High.

98.8 From now on, you know that all your wrongdoing that you do will be written down every day, until the day of your judgment.

98.9 Woe to you, you fools, for you will be destroyed through your folly. And you do not listen to the wise and good will not come upon you.

98.10 And now know that you are ready for the day of destruction. And do not hope that you will live, you sinners; rather you will go and die, for you know no ransom. You are ready for the Day of the Great Judgment and for the day of distress and great shame for your spirits.

98.11 Woe to you, you stubborn of heart who do evil and eat blood, from where do you have good things to eat and drink and to be satisfied? From all the good things which our Lord the Most High has placed in abundance on the earth. Therefore you will not have peace.

98.12 Woe to you who love deeds of iniquity. Why do you hope for good for yourselves? Know that you will be given into the hands of the righteous, and they will cut your throats and kill you, and will not have mercy on you.

98.13 Woe to you who rejoice in the distress of the righteous for graves will not be dug for you.

98.14 Woe to you who declare the words of the righteous empty for you will have no hope of life.

98.15 Woe to you who write lying words, and the words of the impious, for they write their lies so that men may hear and continue their folly. And they will not have peace but will die a sudden death.

99.1 Woe to you who do impious deeds and praise and honour lying words; you will be destroyed and will not have a good life.

99.2 Woe to you who alter the words of truth, and they distort the eternal law and count themselves as being without sin; they will be trampled underfoot on the ground.

99.3 In those days make ready, you righteous, to raise your prayers as a reminder and lay them as a testimony before the Angels, that they may lay the sin of the sinners before the Most High as a reminder.

99.4 In those days the nations will be thrown into confusion and the races of the nations will rise on the Day of Destruction.

99.5 And in those days, those who are in need will go out, seize their children, and cast out their children. And their offspring will slip from them, and they will cast out their children while they are still sucklings, and will not return to them, and will not have mercy on their beloved ones.

99.6 And again I swear to you, the sinners, that sin is ready for the Day of Unceasing Bloodshed.

99.7 And they worship stone, and some carve images of gold and of silver, and of wood and of clay. And some, with no knowledge, worship unclean spirits and demons, and every kind of error. But no help will be obtained from them.

99.8 And they will sink into impiety because of the folly of their hearts, and their eyes will be blinded through the fear of their hearts, and through the vision of their ambitions.

99.9 Through these they will become impious and fearful, for they do all their deeds with lies, and worship stones, and they will be destroyed at the same moment.

99.10 And in those days, blessed are those who accept the words of wisdom, and understand them, and follow the paths of the Most High, and walk in the path of righteousness, and do not act impiously with the impious, for they will be saved.

99.11 Woe to you who extend evil to your neighbours; for you will be killed in Sheol.

99.12 Woe to you who lay foundations of sin and deceit, and who cause bitterness on the Earth, for because of this an end will be made of them.

99.13 Woe to you who build your houses with the toil of others, and all their building materials are the sticks and stones of sin; I say to you: "You will not have peace."

99.14 Woe to those who reject the measure, and the eternal inheritance of their fathers, and cause their souls to follow error, for they will not have rest.

99.15 Woe to those who commit iniquity, and help wrong, and kill their neighbours, until the Day of the Great Judgment; for he will throw down your glory.

99.16 And you put evil into your hearts, and rouse the spirit of his anger, so that he may destroy you all with the sword. And all the righteous and the Holy will remember your sin.

100.1 And in those days, and in one place, fathers and sons will strike one another, and brothers will together fall in death, until their blood flows as if it were a stream.

100.2 For a man will not, in mercy, withhold his hand from his sons, nor from his son's sons, in order to kill them. And the sinner will not withhold his hand from his honoured brother from dawn until the Sun sets they will kill one another.

100.3 And the horse will walk up to its chest in the blood of sinners and the chariot will sink up to its height.

100.4 And in those days the Angels will come down into the hidden places, and gather together in one place all those who have helped sin, and the Most High will rise on that day to execute the Great Judgment on all the sinners.

100.5 And he will set guards, from the Holy Angels, over all the righteous and Holy, and they will guard them like the apple of an eye, until an end is made of all evil and all sin. And even if the righteous sleep a long sleep they have nothing to fear.

100.6 And the wise men will see the truth, and the sons of the Earth will understand all the words of this book, and they will know that their riches will not be able to save them or overthrow their sin.

100.7 Woe to you, you sinners, when you afflict the righteous on the day of severe trouble, and burn them with fire, you will be repaid according to your deeds.

100.8 Woe to you, you perverse of heart who watch to devise evil; fear will come upon you and there is no one who will help you.

100.9 Woe to you, you sinners, for an account of the words of your mouth, and for an account of the deeds of your hands that you have impiously done; you will burn in blazing flames of fire.

100.10 And now know that the Angels will inquire in Heaven into your deeds, from the Sun and the Moon and the Stars, into your sins, for on earth you execute judgment on the righteous.

100.11 And all the clouds and mist and dew and rain will testify against you, for they will be withheld from you so that they do not fall on you, and they will think about your sins.

100.12 And now give gifts to the rain, so that it may not be withheld from falling on you, and so that the dew, if it has accepted gold and silver from you, may fall.

100.13 When the hoarfrost and snow, with their cold, and all the snow winds with their torments fall on you. In those days, you will not be able to stand before them.

101.1 Contemplate Heaven, all you sons of Heaven, and all the works of the Most High, and fear him, and do not do evil in front of Him.

101.2 If He closes the Windows of Heaven, and withholds the rain and the dew, so that it does not fall on the earth because of you, what will you do?

101.3 And if he sends his anger upon you, and upon all your deeds, will you not entreat him? For you speak proud and hard against his righteousness. And you will not have peace.

101.4 And do you not see the captains of the ships; how their ships are tossed by the waves and rocked by the winds and are in distress?

101.5 And because of this they are afraid, for all their good possessions that go out on the sea with them, and they think nothing good in their hearts, only that the sea will swallow them up, and that they will be destroyed in it.

101.6 Is not all the sea, and all its waters, and all its movement, the work of the Most High, and did he not seal all it's doings and bind it all with sand?

101.7 And at his rebuke it dries up and becomes afraid, and all its fish die, and everything in it; but you sinners who are on Earth do not fear him.

101.8 Did he not make Heaven, Earth, and everything that is in them? And who gave knowledge, and wisdom, to all things that move on the ground and in the sea?

101.9 And do not those captains of the ships fear the sea? Yet, sinners do not fear the Most High.

102.1 And in those days, if he brings a fierce fire upon you, where will you flee, and where will you be safe? And when he utters his voice against you will you not be terrified and afraid?

102.2 And all the Lights will shake with great fear, and the whole Earth will be terrified, and will tremble and quail.

102.3 And all the Angels will carry out their commands, and will seek to hide from the One who is Great in Glory, and the children of the Earth will tremble and shake; and you sinners will be cursed forever and will not have peace.

102.4 Do not be afraid you souls of the righteous, and be hopeful, you who have died in righteousness.

102.5 And do not be sad that your souls have gone down into Sheol in sadness and that your bodies did not obtain during your life a reward in accordance with your goodness.

102.6 But when you die the sinners will say about you: "As we die, the righteous have also died, and of what use to them were their deeds?"

102.7 "Behold, like us they have died in sadness and in darkness, and what advantage do they have over us? From now on we are equal."

102.8 "And what will they receive and what will they see forever? For behold, they too have died, and from now on they will never again see the light."

102.9 And I say to you, you sinners: "You are content to eat and drink, and strip men naked, and steal, and sin, and acquire possessions, and see good days.

102.10 But you saw the righteous, how their end was peace, for no wrong was found in them until the day of their death."

102.11 "But they were destroyed and became as though they had not been and their souls went down to Sheol in distress."

103.1 And now I swear to you, the righteous, by His Great Glory and His Honour, and by His Magnificent Sovereignty, and by His Majesty: - I swear to you that I understand this mystery.

103.2 And I have read the Tablets of Heaven and seen the writing of the Holy Ones. And I found written and engraved in it, concerning them, that all good, and joy, and honour, have been made ready, and written down, for the spirits of those who died in righteousness.

103.3 And much good will be given to you in recompense for your toil and that your lot will be more excellent than the lot of the living.

103.4 And the spirits of you who have died in righteousness will live, and your spirits will rejoice and be glad, and the memory of them will remain in front of the Great One for all the generations of eternity. Therefore do not fear their abuse.

103.5 Woe to you, you sinners, when you die in your sin, and those who are like you say about you: "Blessed were the sinners they saw their days.

103.6 And now they have died in prosperity and wealth, distress and slaughter they did not see during their life, but they have died in glory, and judgment was not executed on them in their life."

103.7 Know that their souls will be made to go down into Sheol, they will be wretched, and their distress will be great.

103.8 And in darkness, and in chains, and in burning flames, your spirits will come to the Great Judgment. And the Great Judgment will last for all generations, forever. Woe to you for you will not have peace.

103.9 Do not say, the righteous and the good who were alive;"In the days of our affliction we toiled laboriously, and saw every affliction, and met many evils. We were spent and became few and our spirit small.

103.10 We were destroyed and there was no one who helped us with words or with deeds. We were powerless and found nothing. We were tortured and destroyed and did not expect to see life from one day to the next.

103 11 We hoped to become the head but became the tail. We toiled and laboured, but were not masters of the fruits of our toil; we became food for the sinners, and the lawless made their yoke heavy upon us.

103.12 Those who hated us, those who goaded us, were masters of us. And to those who hated us we bowed our necks but they did not have mercy on us.

103.13 We sought to escape from them so that we might flee and be at rest. But we found no place where we might flee and be safe from them.

103.14 We complained about them to the rulers, in our distress, and cried out against those who devoured us, but they took no notice of our cries, and did not wish to listen to our voice.

103.15 And they helped those who plundered us and devoured us, and those who made us few, and they concealed their wrongdoing, and did not remove from us the yoke of those who devoured us, and scattered us, and killed us. And they concealed our slaughter and did not remember that they had raised their hands against us."

104.1 I swear to you, you righteous, that in Heaven the Angels remember you for good in front of the Glory of the Great One, and that your names are written down in front of the Glory of the Great One.

104.2 Be hopeful! For you were formerly put to shame through evils and afflictions, but now you will shine like the Lights of Heaven, and will be seen, and the Gate of Heaven will be opened to you.

104.3 And persevere in your cry for judgment and it will appear to you, for justice will be exacted from the rulers for all your distress, and from all those who helped those who plundered you.

104.4 Be hopeful, and do not abandon your hope, for you will have great joy like the Angels of Heaven.

104.5 What will you have to do? You will not have to hide on the day of the Great Judgment, nor will you be found to be sinners. The Eternal Judgment will be upon you for all the generations of eternity.

104.6 And now do not be afraid, you righteous, when you see the sinners growing strong and prospering in their desires, and do not be associated with them but keep far away from their wrongdoing, for you will be associates of the Host of Heaven.

104.7 For you sinners say: "None of our sins will be inquired into and written down!" But they will write down your sins every day.

104.8 And now I show you that light and darkness, day and night, see all your sins.

104.9 Do not be impious in your hearts, and do not lie, and do not alter the words f truth, nor say that the words of the Holy and Great One are lies, and do not praise your idols. For all your lies, and all your impiety, lead not to righteousness but to great sin.

104.10 And now I know this mystery; that many sinners will alter and distort the words of truth, and speak evil words, and lie, and concoct great fabrications, and write books in their own words.

104.11 But when they write my words exactly in their languages, and do not alter or omit anything from my words, but write everything exactly, everything that I testified about before; then I know another mystery:

104.12 That books will be given to the righteous and wise and will be a source of joy and truth and much wisdom.

104.13 And books will be given to them, and they will believe in them and rejoice over them; and all the righteous who have learnt from them all the ways of truth will be glad.

105.1 And in those days, says the Lord, they shall call and testify to the sons of the Earth about the wisdom in them. Show it to them for you are their leaders and the rewards will be over all the Earth.

105.2 For my son and I will join ourselves with them, forever, in the paths of uprightness during their lives. And you will have peace. Rejoice you sons of uprightness! Amen

ENOCH'S CONCLUDING WORDS

108.1 Another book which Enoch wrote for his son Methuselah and for those who should come after him and keep the law in the last days.

108.2 You who have observed, and are waiting in these days, until an end shall be made of those who do evil, and an end shall be made of the power of the wrongdoers.

108.3 Do indeed wait until sin shall pass away, for their names shall be erased from the Books of the Holy Ones, and their offspring will be destroyed forever. And their spirits will be killed, and they will cry out and moan in a chaotic desert place, and will burn in fire, for there is no Earth there.

108.4 And there I saw something like a cloud, which could not be discerned, for because of its depth I was not able to look into it. And the flames of a fire I saw, burning brightly, and things like bright mountains revolved and shook from side to side.

108.5 And I asked one of the Holy Angels, who were with me, and I said to him: "What is this bright place? For there is no sky, but only the flames of a burning fire, and the sounds of crying, and weeping, and moaning, and severe pain."

108.6 And he said to me: "This place which you see; here will be thrown the spirits of the sinners, and of the blasphemers, and of those who do evil. And of those who alter everything that the Lord has spoken through the mouths of the prophets about the things that shall be done.

108.7 For there are books, and records, about them in Heaven above so that the Angels may read them and know what is about to come upon the sinners. And upon the spirits of the humble, and of those who afflicted their bodies and were recompensed by God, and of those who were abused by evil men.

THE KOLBRIN BIBLE

INTRODUCTION
The Kolbrin, in its present production, incorporates a body of enlightened teachings which are the treasure of the centuries, a light on the path of Truth, and as applicable to the world today as they were in the past. There has, however, been a considerable amount of reconstruction, as the original writings survived only precariously. Most of what is presented here was actually salvaged from a pile of discarded manuscripts and was partially burned and damaged by the weather before being reconstructed into a manuscript from which this is rewritten. Undoubtedly, additional material has been incorporated with good intent, to fill gaps and elaborate on the original. Something may have been lost in the modernization of various parts.

The important point, however, is that this is not intended to be a historical record, an intellectual work or literary effort, it falls short of these and is rather a coherent and consistent body of spiritual teachings. It is on this aspect alone that it stands or falls. The spiritual truths presented here are all that matters, the rest can be regarded as an embellishment, a vehicle for presentation and conveyance. The message conveyed, whatever its form of presentation, is always the essential core, and ethically, morally and spiritually the Kolbrin concedes nothing to other works of a like nature. It should be seen as an inspirational work, the substance of which can be accepted with confidence and trust.

While great care was exercised in the past, to ensure that these transcriptions would be transmitted through the centuries in a form as unadulterated and

unaltered as possible, little is known about the actual persons or body of people concerned. From what is known, the name 'Kolbrin' was originally applied to a collection of manuscripts which were salvaged from Glastonbury Abbey at the time of its burning. The fire, which was arson, was intended to destroy those manuscripts, but they were secretly housed otherwise than in the scriptorium and library at the time of the fire.
In any event, it was believed that these 'heretical works' were destroyed, and as it happened the fire proved to be a good cover for their preservation Some of the manuscripts were transcribed, at some time, on to thin metal plates and, collectively, these were known as 'The Bronzebook of Britain'. This designation was carried forward when they were written out in book STITCH from in the seventeenth century.

The subject matter was then divided into chapters and the paragraphs were numbered. The whole was modernized in the latter part of the nineteenth or early part of the twentieth century. Incorporated in the modern Kolbrin are manuscripts which were traditionally clamed to have been copied from salvaged manuscripts which were not transcribed on to metal plates and formed a work known as 'The Coelbook'. During the second and third decades of this century these books were in possession of a religious group in England which was never very powerful, because requirements for membership were too restrictive. It would seem that throughout history the Kolbrin has always been on the brink of extinction, yet it has survived, safeguarded by a few who barely knew what it was all about, who were neither intellectual nor wealthy and for whom the practicalities of life took precedence.

Originally, there were twenty-one books, which were said to be twelve books of Britain, eight books of Egypt and one of the Trojans, but of their names there is little certainty. Only a portion of these books remains and it seems that much of historical nature has been trimmed away. It is known that at the beginning of the fourteenth century there was a settled community in Scotland under the leadership of one John Culdy. The old Culdians, who were guardians of what they called 'The Treasures of Britain', were never numerous and loosely organized, membership being maintained by itinerant smiths and other craftsmen. They seem to have previously been loosely known as 'Koferils'. The Kolbrin makes mention of 'Wise Strangers' and there is a tradition to the effect that these were the original Culdians (Kailedy).

There are other explanations, but the writer is in no position to express any positive or worthwhile opinion. Does it really matter anyway? We are told that the Ferilmaster (a word of uncertain meaning) was Nathaniel Smith, martyred in the beginning of the seventeenth century.

This appears to mark the end of the Old Culdians as a coherent body, but steps were taken to preserve the Kolbrin. For a long time it was buried or otherwise hidden, but some time during the early part of the last century, copies were written out in 'biblical English' and two of the books were in existence just before the first World War. Since then the various books of the Kolbrin have suffered many vicissitudes and what remains is only part of the original. During the last world war the old books were thrown out as 'worthless junk', saved and again discarded as 'heathen works of the Devil', but luckily, again salvaged before irreparable damage was done. It has not been easy to reconstitute them, even with the assistance of a more knowledgeable co-worker who filled in a few gaps with compatible references to modern works. No doubt, in its present form the Kolbrin leaves much to be desired.

The contents could perhaps have been condensed and much irrelevant matter deleted, but the compiler considered it his prime duty to preserve and retain every possible fragment and leave it to others better qualified to sift, revise and condense. Obviously, some of the proper names are spelled wrongly, and some of the original correct ones may have been replaced by others, for it seems that in the past there was a biased selection of material to be included. No claim is made regarding historical accuracy, for the compiler is totally unqualified to voice any opinion in this respect; but, as stated before this is not an historical work but the corpus of a doctrine and way of life. Whose hands originally wrote its many parts is unimportant and it is even less important to know who transcribed it later, though some details appear in the modern section. The phraseology may be cumbersome and even ungrammatical, because of the manner in which the biblical form of English has been modernized by one who has no scholarly pretensions whatsoever. It may be argued that this work should have been presented in its archaic form, to preserve its authenticity, but the compiler disagrees, and we concur.

The criterion by which any literary work should be judged is its message and intent, not its format. The words, of themselves, are sterile, it is the spirit of the whole that give the Kolbrin meaning and life. What is presented here is an attempt to pass on, as near as possible in its original form, with all its defects and shortcomings in style and presentation, something which will be of benefit to all. The original writers attempted to make words convey something beyond inherent meaning, they endeavoured to build an edifice of glory out of common clay. The importance of what is given here lies in what is projected out of the past into the present lamentable spiritual vacuum; in the help it can offer to the ordinary man and woman, not in what it offers to the literary world. On this basis alone these writings must stand to be judged. The worth of any knowledge is in its value here and now, in present day circumstances. We know, from the later books of the Kolbrin, that for centuries its contents had to be kept secret because they may have been misunderstood or found unacceptable. Perhaps they will fare better now. This book is resurrected with the sole intent of ranging it alongside the Forces of Good. Its publication will undoubtedly be difficult, for such a work can scarcely be deemed to have popular appeal. It deals with goodness and virtue, courage and mortality, with spiritual ideals and human aspirations, all unpopular and despised fare in these the Days of Decision.

It seeks to enshrine love in a place beyond clamour and craving of the mortal flesh, and this alone may be sufficient to call down derision upon it. The same effort as was put in the piecing together and reconstruction of the Kolbrin, put into a book pandering to the moral weaknesses of society and exploiting the jaded, degenerate appetites of modern life, would undoubtedly prove more popular. But can it be said, even in these morally unwholesome times, that the value of a publication depends solely on its popular appeal? In the Kolbrin, the Masters can record only the outcome of their own searching. They found assurance but cannot convey it directly to others. If others want it they too must tread the path the Masters trod, a long weary road not for the fainthearted. The first step along that road is the study of the moral code and standard of conduct required. The next step is to put these into practice, making them the rule of life.

They are the disciplines which enabled the truly enlightened ones of the past to awaken inner perception and make direct contact with The Universal Source of Truth. Only by following in their steps can anyone be assured of a path certain of reaching the desired goal. Originally, the Kolbrin was in two parts, 'The Open Book' and 'The Closed Book', the latter being more properly called 'The Great Book of Eternity', the former being "The Great Book of life". What is presented here is "The Open Book". Actually, this book contains nothing not already known, for mankind has never been without guidance.

Truth and wisdom can be no one's monopoly, therefore many things expressed therein are to be found elsewhere. Superficially the Kolbrin may appear to be just a jumbled collection of maxims and old stories, some incomplete, but to judge it from this standpoint is like analyzing the pigments of the paint in a painting and counting and classifying the brushmarks to discover what an artist wants to convey. To understand it fully one must stand off and view it as a whole, even then comprehension must flow from the heart and mind, not from the eyes. A society progresses through social evolution, not revolution, but the woes displayed by present day society indicate that the evolutionary trend has taken a wrong direction. The standards of the past, formulated to stabilize society, have been spurned, without any adequate substitutes being put in their place. That is the tragedy of the times. To get a more comprehensive view of where our society is heading, perhaps a better understanding of where we have been is needed. It is in this context that the Kolbrin is launched, to take its place in the greater scheme of things.

THE AFFLICTION OF GOD

This comes from the scroll of Kerobal Pakthermin who wrote, "The forbears of all the nations of man were once one people, and they were the elect of God who delivered all the Earth over to them, all the people, the beasts of the field, the creatures of the wasteland and the things that grow. They dwelt through long ages in lands of peace and plenty."

"There were some who struggled harder, were more disciplined; because their forefathers had crossed the great dark void, their desires were turned Godward and they were called The Children of God". "Their country was undulating and forested. It was fertile, having many rivers and marshes. There were great mountains to the East and to the West, and in the North was a vast stony plain." "Then came the day when all things became still and apprehensive, for God caused a sign to appear in the Heavens, so that men should know the Earth would be afflicted, and the sign was a strange star".

"The star grew and waxed to a great brightness and was awesome to behold. It put forth horns and sang, being unlike any other ever seen. So men, seeing it, said among themselves, 'Surely, this is God appearing in the Heavens above us'. The star was not God, though it was directed by His design, but the people had not the wisdom to understand'. "Then God manifested Himself in the Heavens. His voice was as the roll of thunders and He was clothed with smoke and fire. He carried lightings in His hand and His breath, falling upon the Earth, brought forth brimstone and embers. His eye was a black void and His mouth an abyss containing the winds of Destruction. He encircled the whole of the Heavens, bearing upon His back a black robe adorned with stars".

"Such was the likeness and manifestation of God in those days. Awesome was His countenance, terrible His voice of wrath, the sun and moon hid themselves in fear and there was a heavy darkness over the face of the Earth".

"God passed through the spaces of the Heavens above with a mighty roar and a loud trumpeting. Then came the grim dead silence and black red lit twilight of doom. Great fires and smoke rose up from the ground and men gasped for air. The land was rent asunder and swept clean by a mighty deluge of waters. A hole opened up in the middle of the land, the waters entered and it sank beneath the seas".

"The mountains of the East and West were split apart and stood up in the midst of the waters which raged about. The Northland tilted and turned over on its side".

"Then again the tumult and clamour ceased and all was silent. In the quiet stillness madness broke out among men, frenzy and shouting filled the air. They fell upon one another in senseless wanton bloodshed; neither did they spare woman or child, for they knew not what they did. They ran unseeing, dashing themselves to destruction. They fled to caves and were buried and, taking refuge in trees, they were hung. There was rape, murder and violence of every kind".

"The deluge of waters swept back and the land was purged clean. Rain beat down unceasingly and there were great winds. The surging waters overwhelmed the land and man, his flocks and his gardens and all his works ceased to exist.".

"Some of the people were saved upon the mountainsides and upon the flotsam, but they were scattered far apart over the face of the Earth. They fought for survival in the lands of uncouth people. Amid coldness they survived in caves and sheltered places".

"The Land of the Little People and the Land of Giants, the Land of the Neckless Ones and the Land of Marshes and Mists, the Lands of the East and West were all inundated. The Mountain Land and the Lands of the South, where there is gold and great beasts, were not covered by the waters".

"Men were distracted and in despair. They rejected the Unseen God behind all things for something which they had seen and known by its manifestation. They were less than children in those days and could not know that God had afflicted the Earth in understanding and not willfully, for the sake of man and the correction of his ways".

"The Earth is not for the pleasure of man, but is a place of instruction for his Soul. A man more readily feels the stirrings of his Spirit in the face of disaster than in the lap of luxury. The tuition of the Soul is a long and arduous course of instruction and training".

"God is good and from good evil cannot come. He is perfect and perfection cannot produce imperfection. Only the limited understanding of man sees imperfection in that which is perfect for its purpose".

"This grievous affliction of man was another of his great tests. He failed and in so doing followed the paths of unnatural gods of his making. Man makes gods by naming them, but where in this is the benefit to him?"

"Evil comes in to the midst of mankind spawned by the fears and ignorance of men. An evil man becomes an evil spirit, and whatever evil there is on Earth comes either from the evil of spirits or the evil of men".

IN THE BEGINNING

Now, the Children of God were moulded by the Hand of God which is called Awen, and it manifested according to their desires. For all things which have life are moulded by Awen. The fox, shivering in the coldlands, longs for warmth and so its cubs have warmer coats. The owl, clumsy in the dark, longs to see its prey more clearly, and in generations of longing the desire is granted. Awen makes everything what it is, for all things change under its law.

Men, too, are moulded by their desires, but unlike the beasts and birds their yearnings are circumscribed by the laws of fate and destiny and the law of sowing and reaping. These, the desires, modified by the laws, are called Enidvadew. Unlike the beasts and birds, this, in man, is something relating to him rather than to his offspring, though they are not untouched by it. Destiny may be likened to a man who must travel to a distant city whether or not he wishes to make the journey, the destination being his destiny. He may choose whether to go by way of a river or by way of a plain; whether across mountains or through forests, on foot or horseback, slow or fast, and whatever befalls because of this decision is fate. If a tree falls on him because he chose the forest path, it was fated, for luck is an element of fate. Destiny leaves no choice, fate gives limited choice which may be good or bad, but it cannot be averted. What is fated must be, for at no point can there be any turning back.

The circumstances, Enidvadew, of the traveler conform to the law of sowing and reaping; he may travel in comfort or pain, happily or sorrowfully, with strength or weakness, heavily burdened or lightly burdened, well prepared or ill prepared. When the destination is set according to the degrees of a former life, then the circumstances of the journey should conform with the desire. For what use is it desiring a great destination when the law of sowing and reaping decrees that an intolerable burden must be carried on the way? Far better to have lesser aspirations. The decrees of fate are many, the decrees of destiny are few. When the Earth was young and the race of man still as children,

there were fertile green pastures in the lands where all is now sand and barren wasteland.
In the midst of it was a gardenland which lay against the edge of the Earth, eastward and towards the sunrising, and it was called Meruah, meaning The Place of The Garden on the Plain. It lay at the foot of a mountain which was cleft at its rising, and out of it flowed the river of Tardana which watered the plain. From the mountain, on the other side, ran the river Kal which watered the plain through the land of Kaledan. The river Nara flowed westward and then turned back to flow around the gardenland. It was a fertile place, for out of the ground grew every kind of tree that was good for food and every tree that was pleasant to the sight. Every herb that could be eaten and every herb that flowered was there.

The Tree of Life, which was called Glasir, having leaves of gold and copper, was within the Sacred Enclosure. There, too, was the Great Tree of Wisdom bearing the fruits of knowledge granting the choice and ability to know the true from the false. It is the same tree which can be read as men read a book. There also was the Tree of Trespass beneath which grew the Lotus of Rapture, and in the centre was The Place of Power where God made His presence known. Time passed and The Children of God were grown strong and upright under the tempering hammer of God, and Earth, The Anvil of God, became more kindly. All was pleasant and food plentiful, but life palls in such places, for it is against the nature of man to flourish in these circumstances.

Earth is not for pleasurable dallying, it is a place of teaching, trial and testing. The Children of God were not yet the heirs of God nor inheritors of godhood, but there was one among them who had almost completed the Pilgrimage of Enidvadew. He had unraveled the tangled skeins of fate and traversed the tumultuous seas of life to the many ports of destiny, and having paid the debts of sowing and reaping was one triumphant over Enidvadew. He was Fanvar, son of Auma and Atem. He was wise and knew all things, he beheld mysteries and the secret things hidden from the eyes of other men. He saw sunrise and the sunsetting in their splendour, but longed for things not realisable in the place where he lived. So because he walked with God he was culled out from his kind and brought to Meruah, The Gardenplace.

He came to it across the mountains and wastelands, arriving after many days journeying. Weary and close to death because of the privations he suffered, he could just reach the refreshing waters from which he drank deeply, and filled with exhaustion he slept. In his sleep he dreamed and this was the manner of his dreaming: he saw before him a being of indescribably glory and majesty, who said,

"I am the God above all, even above the God of your people, I am that which fulfils the aspirations of men and I am that in which they are fulfilled. You, having traversed all the Circles of Enidvadew and established your worthiness, are now made my governor on Earth and you shall rule all things here, guiding them in my ways, leading them ever upwards into glory. This will be your labour and, behold, here is your reward.".

A cloud mist seemed to gather about The Glorious Being, enfolding Him so He was no longer visible. Then the mist gradually cleared and the man saw another form emerging. It was that of a woman, but one such as Fanvar had never seen before, beautiful beyond his conception of beauty, with such perfection of form and grace that he was dumbfounded. Yet the vision was not substantial, she was a wraith, an ethereal being. The man awoke and sought food from the fruits about him and having refreshed himself wandered about the garden. Wherever he went he saw the wraith, but was unafraid because she smiled encouragingly, bringing comfort to his heart.

He built himself a shelter and grew strong again, but always, wherever he went, the wraith was not far distant. One day, near the edge of the garden, he fell asleep in the heat of the day and awoke to find himself surrounded by the Sons of Bothas, not true men but Yoslings, kinsfolk to the beasts of the forest. Before they could take his strength and wisdom he loosed himself among them, slaying some in his rage and might before the rest ran away. When it was done he sat himself down beneath a great tree, for he was wounded and blood gushed out from his side and gathered thickly beside him. He became faint, falling into a deep sleep and while he slept a wondrous thing happened. The wraith came and lay beside him, taking blood from his wound upon herself so it congealed about her. Thus the Spiritbeing became clothed with flesh, born of congealing blood, and being sundered from his side she rose a mortal woman. In his heart Fanvar was not at rest, because of her likeness, but she was gentle, ministering to him with solicitude and, being skillful in the ways of healing, she made him whole. Therefore, when he had grown strong again he made her Queen of The Gardenland, and she was so called even by our fathers who named her Gulah, but Fanvar called her Aruah, meaning helpmate. In our tongue she is called The Lady of Lanevid.

Now, God enlightened Fanvar concerning the woman, saying, "This woman was drawn from her compatible abode in a realm of beauty through the yearning aspirations of men. Her coming accomplishes something which would otherwise have taken countless generations, for Earth is more fitting for men to learn manly things than for women to learn womanly ones. This woman is not as other women, being in no way like yourself; every hair of her head is unlike that of a man, every drop of blood and every particle of flesh is that of a woman and quite unlike that of a man. Her thoughts and desires are different; she is neither coarse nor uncouth, being altogether of another, more refined realm. Her daughters will walk proudly, endowed with every womanly perfection and grace. Delicacy, modesty and charm will be the lovely jewels enhancing their womanliness. enceforth, man will be truly man and woman will be truly woman, men being girded with manliness and women clothed with womanliness. Yet they shall walk together, hand in hand, towards the ascending glory before them, each the helpmate and inspiration of the other".

So Fanvar and Aruah lived in contentment amid bounty and fruitfulness, with freedom from afflictions and sickness. They delighted in each other and because of their differences were drawn closer together. Aruah brought but one thing with her when she crossed the misty frontier, the treasure of Lanevid, the jewel contained in the moonchalice, the stone of inspiration fashioned by the desires of men.

Never owned by any but the daughters of Aruah, this, the Lengil, Aruah gave to Fanvar as her dowry and her pledge of purity and exclusiveness. She followed the ways of the cradleland, not the ways of Earth. Within the Gardenland was the Sacred Enclosure, the domain of Fanvar and Aruah, forbidden to those of The Children of God who had now come to this place. It contained the Chalice of Fulfilment granting any who drank from it the realization of all things to which they aspired.

None might drink from this save Fanvar and Aruah. Also there was the Cauldron of Immortality containing an essence distilled from the fruits growing in the garden, and this guarded against mortal ills. Aruah brought forth a son by Fanvar and he was called Rautoki, and a daughter who was called Armena. Each knew the mysteries of magic and the ways of the stars. In the fullness of time Rautoki married among the daughters of the Sons of God and had two sons, Enanari and Nenduka. It was Enanari who first taught the weaving of cloth from plants, and Nenduka was a mighty hunter.

Armena also married among the Sons of God and brought forth a son who was called Belenki and daughters called Ananua and Mameta. Ananua knew the making of pots and things of clay and Mameta the taming of beasts and birds. Nenduka had two sons, Namtara and Kainan. Namtara had two sons also, Nenduka and Dadam, before dying in the fullness of manhood. Belenki married Enidva and had a son called Enkidua and a daughter called Estartha, meaning Maid of the Morning, and she became a great teacher among The Children of God. This was the Estartha who became the first Moonmaiden, being later called Lady of The Morning Star. Enkidua had a daughter and her name was Maeva. Outside the Sacred Enclosure, known as Gisar, but forming a gateway into it was a circular structure of stones called Gilgal, and within this was a shrine wherein was kept a sacred vessel called Gwinduiva. This was like a goblet and was made of rainbow-hued crystal set in gold with pearls. Above the cup appeared a shimmering moon-coloured mist like a thin cold flame.

At certain times, when the Heavens were in a proper position, the Gwinduiva was filled with moondew and potions from the cauldron within the Sacred Enclosure, making a pale honey-coloured liquor, and this the people drank from the goblet. However, there were different proportions in the vessel for those of the blood of Fanvar and Aruah and those who were Children of God but not of their blood. It was the potion from the Gwinduiva which kept sickness and disease away from those who drank it.

Dadam, the Firstfather, married Leitha and they had a son called Herthew. Dadam then married Maeva who had a daughter, not by him, and this was Gwineva, the cuckoochild fathered by Abrimenid of Gwarthon, son of Namtenigal, whom we call Lewid the Darkfather. About the land of The Children of God was the wasteland where Yoslings, called The Children of Zumat, which means They Who Inherit Death, dwelt. Amongst these, Namtenigal, the wily hunter, was the most wise and cunning; he alone was unafraid of The Children of God and he alone dared enter the Gardenland.

In the days when Estartha was teaching, Namtenigal often came to hear her words and The Children of God were not displeased, for teaching the wild men about them was a duty with which they had been charged. Namtenigal, therefore, participated in their rites but could not partake of the elixir from the Gwinduiva, because this was forbidden. While it gave health and strength to The Children of God, safeguarding them from the sicknesses of the Yoslings, if given to others it caused a wasting away. It was also altogether forbidden for any of The Children of God to mate with the Yoslings, for this was deemed to be the most unforgivable of sins. Now, the wily one learned much from Estartha and in the fullness of time brought his own son to her and he became as her son, living in her house and forsaking the ways of his people. Estartha called him Lewid the Lightbringer, for it was her intention that he should be taught the ways of those who walked in light, that he might in time enlighten his own people. Lewid grew up tall and handsome, he was quick to learn and became wise. He was also a man of the chase, strong and enduring, a hunter of renown.
But there were times when the call of his people was strong, then he would go out furtively into the night to indulge in their dark rituals. Thus he became

knowledgeable in the ways of the flesh and in the carnal indulgences of the body. Dadam became a servant of the Sacred Enclosure where the misty veil between the realms could be penetrated, for all those having the blood of Aruah had twinsight, an ability to see wraiths and sithfolk, ansis and spiritbeings, all the things of the Otherworld, not clearly but as through a veil.

Beside the place called Gisar was a pleasant parkland with trees of every kind and a stream, also thickets of flowering bushes and all manner of plants growing lushly. It was the custom of Maeva to wander there in the sunshine and Lewid also went there; so it came about that they met among the trees. Maeva knew the man but had shunned him in the past, now she saw he was handsome, possessed of many attractions, so her foot was stayed and she did not run away. As the days passed they dallied longer together and Lewid talked of things Maeva had not heard before. She felt a stirring in her blood but did not respond or heed his temptations, because of the things which were forbidden. So Lewid went to the Moonmother, wise woman of the Yoslings, and telling of his desires beseeched her to help him.

The Moonmother gave him two apples containing a vile substance which they had drawn through their stalks; this Lewid gave to Maeva who then became helpless in his hands. They met again after this, for Maeva became enamoured towards Lewid, but it happened that she became ill with a strange sickness and was afraid. Then Dadam became ill and Lewid also, and Lewid said to the woman, "You must obtain the pure essences from within the Sacred Enclosure, and Setina, the Moonmother, will prepare an elixir which will cure us". This he said because none of his kind had ever been able to obtain the Sacred Substances, though they had always coveted what had been denied them. Now, because of her frailty, the woman was pliable in his hands and Lewid seized the opportunity. To achieve his ends Lewid gave Maeva a potion which had been prepared by the Moonmother and she administered this to Dadam and those with him, by guile and deceit, so that they fell asleep.

While they slept Maeva stole from the Sacred Substances and took them to Lewid who gave them to the Moonmother, and she made a brew. Part of this was given to Maeva and the rest was drunk by the Yoslings, from their awful ankital during their night rites. When the morning came they were all smitten with grievous pains, and before the sun set that day all the Yoslings were stricken with a sickness such as they had not known before. Maeva took what had been given to her and finding Dadam laid low in his bed gave him a draught from her vessel, though she had to use womanly wiles to get him to drink it. She drank the remainder and they both slept. But when they awoke in the morning both were suffering pains and this was something they had not known before.

Dadam said to the woman, "What have you done, for what has happened to us cannot be unless the things which are forbidden have been done". The woman replied, "Lord, I was tempted and I fell, I have done that which is forbidden and unforgivable". Dadam said, "I am bound by duty to do certain things, but first let us go into the Gisar to the place called Bethkelcris, where I will seek enlightenment".

So they went there together and stood before the shrine beneath the Tree of Wisdom. There they were filled with an inflowing vision, seeing themselves as they were and as they should have been, and they were ashamed. He because he had not followed the proper path of a man and she because of her falsity. There, in the reflecting mist, the contamination of the woman was revealed, and the man's heart shriveled within him like a flower licked by flame. Then they saw a great Spiritbeing materializing in the reflecting mist and he said to them, "Woe to you and your house, for the greatest of evils has befallen the race of The Children of God and it is defiled. The heritage of Kadamhapa is lost. The fetid flow defiling the woman results from the incompatible intermingling, but it is not all, for sicknesses and diseases are also generating from the ferments of the impure implantation".

Dadam said, "The fault is with the woman, wherefore should I suffer?" The Spiritbeing replied, "Because you two are now as one the conkerworms of disease and sickness strike both equally, but you shall not again defile this place. Henceforth, the misty veil becomes an impenetrable barrier severing our two realms from each other, so they can no longer be easily spanned. Between us there will now be no means of communication. Henceforth, man and woman, fated to unite in love divine, shall be divided and set apart, though ever yearning reunion. They may cleave one to the other, seeking the unity which will rekindle the flame, but unless their efforts transcend the limitations of earthly things they will be in vain.

The spirit of man is now severed from the whole and cast again into unconsciousness, and it too shall long for reunion with the whole. The spark shall seek to return to the fire, for otherwise it becomes nothing. The web of fate is rewoven and the paths of destiny remade, the design of life is redrawn; again the progression begins in ignorance, birth and death, pain and pleasure, joy and sorrow, success and failure, love and hate, peace and war, all the light and shade, the many hues making the splendidly intricate pattern of life on Earth. This is a new beginning but a beginning not in purity and unencumbered, but one already weighted with debts and burdens".

The Spiritbeing continued, "Enough wickedness has been wrought by your willfulness and disobedience, for the decrees forbidding certain things were for your own benefit. Immortality was nearly within your reach, but had you achieved this you would have brought an even more grievous evil upon yourselves and your inheritors, for freed from servitude to change, you and they would have been unable to progress".

The Children of God were driven out of the gardenland by Spiritbeings, and then guardians were set at its gates so none could re-enter. Then it was withdrawn beyond the misty veil, the waters ceased to flow and the fertility departed, only a wilderness remained. The Children of God went to dwell in the land of Amanigel, which is beyond the mountains of Mashur by the sea of Dalemuna.

From this time onward man fashioned his own spiritlikeness. Some, who were loathsome in aspect even unto themselves, went apart and were mercifully veiled in dark depths, and they said among themselves,

"Let us dwell here in the darkness and prepare a place for others like ourselves, so that when they follow they abide here and join us". Thus were the Dark Regions formed and inhabited by demons who are nought but the hideously fashioned spirits of evil men. These things have been written into the record. In Siboit they used to say this was the manner of man's making, "God sent His creating Craftsman Spirit down to Earth and the reflection of The One was drawn into a spiritless body, and this became the heart of man".

These are the words written by Thonis of Myra in Ludicia in his day:- "You ask me what is man and I answer: He is life becoming aware of itself. He is the intangible knowing the tangible, Spirit in matter, fire in water. When this first happened, none remembers and only the old folktales remain. There was the beginning and then the garden, and it was in this garden man found himself; before this he was not free, being one with everything about him. As he could not disobey, good and evil could not be, they were non-existent".

"Man became free through awareness of himself, and with this knowledge denied any kinship with the beast. As he was no longer in harmonious relationship with things of the Earth, he became discontented, dissatisfied and restless, he wanted to belong but felt his place of belonging was not there. He had been reborn as a mangod, and therefore it is truly said that man was born of Earth and Spirit, under a tree, the symbol of life, and in a garden".

"There the eyes of the man and woman were opened and, being above the beasts, they knew they were different and set apart from all else that breathed. They separated themselves, being now ashamed of their state and strangers to each other. The carnal satisfaction of lesser creatures now no longer sufficed, they had lost contact with the Source of Love; but, though knowing something was lacking, knew not what.
They had fallen into carnal knowledge which only man can know, for only he feels the reproach of divinity. They were removed from The Garden of Content by an inhalation of the Divine Substance and could not return because of the barrier between man an non-man".

Kamelik has written: "The entwined were cut apart and since that day have never known content. They wander restlessly ever seeking to unite again and together find the jewel which is lost to Earth forever".

Lupisis has written: "This first woman, who came from the void, is the eternally glorified goddess, the inspirer of hearts, the ideal of womanhood honoured by all men, the priestess at the shrines of delicacy and tenderness. She was the ideal woman who, because of man's nature, is always tempted by his twinshade, the beast in his form. If the beast triumphs and she falls, the ideal becomes enshrouded in winding cloths of disillusionment, and something is lost to the heart of a man".

These words are also there: "They did not partake of wisdom, and fruit from the tree of knowledge is bitter. Men are denied their true birthright. The fall of man was a fall from loving contact with God into material carnality. The Soul that had shared the consciousness of God fell into unconsciousness by becoming ensnared in matter. The fall severed man from the source of his spiritual sustenance; thereafter his efforts were to struggle back. In his blind groping for God, after the fall he discovered demons and found it easier to worship them than to continue the search". "God is always waiting, man has only to look up, but it is easier to go down the hill than to climb it. It is easier for man's spiritual beliefs to degenerate than to evolve.

Who among men knows the truth and can write with certain knowledge? Would not this certainty be against the Law? No man was there at the beginning to see and write, but of one thing alone we can be sure, The Creating God knows how and why, and could the acts of One so great be without purpose?

HERTHEW - SON OF THE FIRSTFATHER

The Book of Beginnings tells us all things began with Varkelfa, therein called Awenkelifa, from whom flows gwinin, the energizer which stabilizes all things so they maintain their proper form, and awen which responds to the moulding desires. This is well enough, but men concern themselves more with the beginnings of their race, and ours is rooted in Herthew the Sunfaced, son of the Firstfather.

While Herthew was still young he was expelled from the lushlands where he was born, and he journeyed across the hasrshlands in the company and keeping of wise Habaris. After many days they came to Krowkasis, cradleland of our race, land of mountains and rivers, which is beside Ardis, and they encamped there in a valley. With them were retainers and flocks. Herthew grew to manhood there and always Habaris was at his side, instructing him in all the things he should know. He taught Herthew the Nine essential disciplines of Imain, and the secrets of the three sacred vessels. Herthew learned that there was a place of gloom, where the air was foul and malodorous breezes carried pestilence and poisonous particles. This was the source of all maladies and ailments and of the things which cause putrefaction and decay. This place had been closed off from Earth, for it existed in another realm beyond the ken of mortals; but it had been brought into attunement with Earth when a forbidden act was accomplished. Thus the bodies of mortals became susceptible to influences from the baleful place. To this and similar parts of the Otherworld the wicked would be drawn when they passed through the grim gates of death.

But Habaris taught a different conception of wickedness, one where lack of effort, indolence and indifference to duty and obligations, the taking of the easy path, were just as wrong as actual deeds of wickedness. He taught that men reach the true goal of life by transmuting lustlove into truelove. That true victory is gained only over the defeated bodies of their vanquished passions and baser selves. These and many other things were taught by Habaris, but many of his teachings displeased the people of Krowkasis who were then as they were before Herthew's forefather was led away.
So Habaris concealed many things from them and taught, by simple tales, things within their understanding. He taught them the mysteries concerning the wheel of the years and divided the year into a Summer half and a Winter half, with a great year circle of fifty-two years, a hundred and four of which

was the circle of the Destroyer. He gave them the Laws of Weal and Woe and established the folkfeasts of harvest-tide and seeding-tide.

He taught them the ritual of Ulisidui. But Habaris instructed Herthew in the ways of the Otherworld. He taught him concerning the three rays from the central invisible sun, which manifest all things, upholding them in stability of form. Also concerning the Oversoul which filled everything in creation, as the Soulself filled the mortal body. This Soulself, he declared, would develop from mortal sensitivity and feeling transmuted into divine sensitivity and feeling, through suppression of the baser instincts within mortals. It was strengthened by development of feelings of love between man and woman and between these and their kindred; by the appreciation of beauty and devotion to duty; by the development of all qualities that pertain to humans and not to animals. Herthew learned that the Soulself is quickened by soul substances outflowing from the Godhead. That the strong soul is transformed and moulded to the soul's desire, but the weak soul is not its own master, it is flabby, unstable and is pulled into a state of distortion by its own vices.

In the afterlife there is unbounded joy for the entry of a noble soul, it will glow with splendour and stand out proudly. The mean soul of the wicked is dull-hued, twisted and drab, and, being drawn towards its own compatible state, it shrinks into the dark places. When Herthew had barely crossed the threshold of manhood, black-bearded spearmen began to ravish the borders of Krowkasis, and Idalvar, king of that country, called his fighting men together and when word came to Herthew he prepared to depart. But Habaris bid him stay awhile, for he was unprepared for battle. Then Habaris prepared a strange fire with stones, unlike any fire seen before, and when it burnt low he plucked out that which is called 'child of the green flame' and he beat it out so it became a blade. This he fitted to a horned handgrip and when it was edged and blooded gave it to Herthew, saying, "Behold, Dislana the Bitterbiter, faithful servant of he who strikes hard and true".
Then he made a shield of wicker covered with ox-hide and a cap of hide which came down over the face and neck. So equipped Herthew went to the encampment of Idalvar, taking eight fighting men with him. In those days men fought with hand-thrown spears and clubs, with flung stones and sticks

sharpened by fire and weighted, but they did not close in the battle clash. So when Idalvar saw the battleblade of Herthew, he wondered and it passed his understanding; but when he saw Herthew close on the battleline and the foeman fall before him, he was amazed. No man about the king could understand the making of such weapons, offspring of fire and stone, but Habaris made others and Herthew became the king's right hand man and the first hero of the Noble Race. The king offered Herthew his daughter's hand in marriage, but Herthew declined saying, "The days of my manhood are not yet fulfilled".

When the war-filled days had passed, Herthew withdrew to the place where Habaris made the bright battleblade, and already he had taught the mysteries of their making to others, sealing their mouths with magic. But Herthew was less concerned with the weaponry of war than with the mysteries of life and the battles of the Spirit beset by mortality. So while his workmen drew bright blades from the thunderstones, Habaris taught Herthew and his battlebrothers, and these were the things they learned from his mouth. "Beyond God there is an Absolute which no man should try to understand, for it exists and has always existed in a state beyond man's finite comprehension. It is from this Absolute that God, The Ultimate in all Perfections, was engendered".

"To create, God first visualized in thought, then He produced an outflowing wave of power which, in a manner of speaking, solidified what might be called building stones. The outflowing power also produced the Celestial Hymn which brought the building stones together in harmonious forms. So it is truly said that all creation is the harp of God and it responds to His song and manipulations. It is an everlasting unfoldment. The voice of God can also be heard in the voice of His beautiful daughter who endows all growing things with life and beauty".

"There is a divine purpose in creation which may be known only to the few, this knowledge is the key to all unanswered questions. Acquiring it is like the drawing back of heavy curtains which have kept a room in gloomy half light, so all things suddenly became clear and distinct. He who gains this knowledge knows the Grand Secret, the answer to the riddle of the ages, and knows beyond a shadow of a doubt. This divine purpose, and the divine secret concerning it, is called Gwenkelva".

"Apart from Gwenkelva God gains nothing from His creation, except that as a Being possessing infinite love and goodness He must have something to receive the gift of love and respond to it. Even among mortal beings, who is there that could find satisfactory fulfillment in self-love? Also, He needed something wherewith He could contract Himself, some medium wherein He could perform, and this is creation".

"Creation is also, for mortals, the school of life. The training ground for godhood. There are Three Circles of Reality, three realms, three stages of existence. They are: Heaven, where perfection visualized on Earth may be realized and desires and ideals materialized; where hard-striven-for aspirations are attained; it is the place where all the properly developed spiritual potential latent in man reaches maturity and fulfillment. Earth, the place of training, development and preparation, the testing ground, the battlefield where men discover their true natures when confronted by life's challenges, contests and contentions; where competition and controversy are the rule. It is here that aims and objectives are conceived and thought-out for realization later in the proper place. It is a starting point, the beginning of the journey; it is here that the proper road must be wisely chosen. Then there is the Realm of the Misty Horizon, the intermediate place, the place of spirits, where those above can commune with those below and where free spirits wander within their limitations".

These things which Habaris taught in those far off days have been rewritten in transmission to accord with our understanding, but it is unwise to voice them in these troublesome days, when words become snares to entrap the unwary.

Now, Idalvar desired to learn the secret of the bright blade engendering thunderstones, but no man who came with Habaris or laboured for him would disclose any part of it, and the king was afraid to put them to the test. So, having thought the matter out the king sent for his daughters and told them what he expected them to do, for he had devised a plan to learn the secret. Then he sent an invitation to Herthew and Habaris. When they arrived at the king's encampment they found a great gathering in their honour and the king's daughters favourably inclined towards them, one smiling upon Herthew and the other upon Habaris who was at the age of hoaryheadedness.

Though at first Habaris was indifferent and wearied her, the king's daughter pandered to him, encouraging even his follies, setting out to charm him with her wit and beauty. It was no great length of time before her womanly wiles ensnared the heart of Habaris and though he was almost ripe for the surrender of secrets, the damsel's efforts had taxed her and the game became tiresome, so there came an evening when she could not endure his company. In the midst of the merrymaking, when the alebowls had made many rounds and the sound of song and story was at its height, she slipped away with a young battleman who attended upon her father.

Many who sat among the benches saw this and whispered to one another, nodding knowingly in the directions of Habaris who was not unaware, though he appeared to have drunk to his capacity. Habaris had learned to love the young woman, so he was sorely heartsmitten, but within himself he knew the tree of Winter love bears only Winter's fruits. Yet he made excuses to himself for her, thinking perhaps it was just some girlishness with no more weight than a floating feather, nothing of serious import, for it was true the merrymaking was better suited to the natures of men than the natures of women. Maybe, he thought, it is just an innocent indiscretion. So when the day came to its fullness and those who had made merry went heavily about their tasks, Habaris approached the king and asked for his daughter's hand in marriage. He said, "Your daughter Klara has delighted me with her winsome ways, she has charmed me with her gaiety and beauty; she has displayed much pleasure in my company, surely I have not misread the signs".
The king was not overpleased, for though he greatly desired to know the secret of the bright blade he had not intended giving his daughter's hand to Habaris, but neither did he wish to offend him. Therefore, he was wary in his reply, saying, "It is the custom for any suitor for a high born woman's hand to

be himself highborn and worthily battleblooded. Yet such is my affection for you that I would not let even the custom become a bar to this marriage, and you may be a battleblooded man among your own people. But let us not enter lightly into this thing, for the girl is still young and it would be well if you established yourself favourably with her. She will be a worthy wife indeed, for she is one who is ever ready to learn, one with an enquiring mind. Nothing gives her greater pleasure than the acquisition of knowledge". So the matter was left.

Now, some days later Idalvar and his retinue, accompanied by Herthew and Habaris, went to the gathering place for folkfeasts, some five days journey away. People were accustomed to meeting here every thirteen moons to celebrate the season of fruitfulness, many coming a great distance. Beside the gathering place was the compound of a far-framed seer and warlock called Gwidon, who, in the fullness of the moon on the third night, would prophesy events for the forthcoming year. Idalvar and those with him presented their gifts and took their places before the compound. Presently, Gwidon came out cloaked in the skins of wild dogs, with a horned crown and skull-headed staff. He seated himself before a small fire into which he threw prescriptions, making a cloud of smoke which completely enveloped him. When this had drifted away he seemed to be asleep, but after a while he lifted his head, then raising himself up he started to prophesy. He talked awhile of small matters, then told of dangers to the people through enemies who would bear down from the Northlands.

He prophesied a great bloodletting, telling people they could be saved by a great war leader, a king knowing the secret of the bright blade, himself a war-wielder of one. He exhorted the people to bestir themselves and prepare, wasting no time in finding their leader. No man among the people knew the mysteries of the bright blade except Habaris, but he was not a man of battle and Herthew was not high born among them.
So, though they talked long they talked in tangles, failing to resolve the issue. It was then decided each should go his own way, but they should meet at the same place again at the next full moon, when Gwidon would be able to help with their decision.

When Idalvar returned to his encampment he was no longer hesitant about the marriage of his daughter, ordering that it should take place forthwith. But he stipulated that Habaris must initiate him and his sons into the mysteries of the bright blade immediately. This being agreed, arrangements for the marriage were put in hand. Habaris and Klara were married and Idalvar and his sons partially initiated into the mysteries of the bright blade, for the king was told it would take some time for the initiation to be completed. So when they next went to the meeting place, Idalvar was proclaimed the war leader, with his sons to follow according to their ages, should he fall in battle. But Habaris had spoken to Gwidon in secret and matters were so arranged that should the sons of Idalvar fall, then Herthew would become the battle chief.

The king and those with him returned to their homecompound where they were to prepare battlemen, but Herthew was to go back to the gathering place and there train fighting men in the battle tactics which brought them clashing into the fore. Now, on their wedding night, when they had retired to their bower, Klara burst into tears and fell weeping with her head on the knees of Habaris, confessing she was not a virgin and had deceived him, begging his forgiveness. Habaris raised her up and said, "Even the wisest of men becomes a fool when his heart blinds him to reason. The older the fool the bigger the fool". He did not question her regarding love, for he knew she could not love and deceive him, she had given her heart and with it her virginity to another. Yet he made an excuse for her to himself, thinking that she had not willfully deceived him but had acted out of duty to her father. Also, truly loving someone and wishing to demonstrate that love, she necessarily had to sacrifice the happiness and content, the self-respect of her husband-to-be, the choice had been hers to make.

It is ever so. Habaris asked if her father had known how things were and she said, "He suspected, for am I not his daughter?" Thus Habaris found himself tied to an unloving wife, for he chose to disregard the custom of the people. He wondered, was she also to be an undutiful and unfaithful one? A woman reserves herself for her husband or she does not, according to her marriage criterion. A woman reserved for marriage is one unlikely to be unfaithful; a woman easily come by before marriage is no less attainable afterwards, for if she says love is the criterion, then she measures by something unstandardised, which may figuratively vary from one inch to a mile. A man declaring his love may have seduction in mind or a lifetime of protective devotion, the marriage proposal determines the difference and establishes the intent.

After the marriage the king showed little concern for Habaris, for he kept Klara's young battleman in his retinue when he should have dispatched him elsewhere. Nor did Klara maintain the restraint and decorum, which dignifies wifehood, except in their outward manifestations, which is no more than a deceptive crust disguising the polluted love beneath. Thus Habaris bore the shame of belittlement in the eyes of men, for Klara was furtively unfaithful. Habaris visited Herthew and on his return told the king that he and his sons would now receive their final initiation. So, having made preparation, they set off, accompanied by Klara, to the place of the thunderstones, this being a deeply cleft mountain wherein there was a large cavern from which flowed a river.

Entering the cave Habaris told those with him to bide where they were, for only Idalvar, his sons and Klara were to accompany him into the place of initiation, a small cave entered through a long narrow passage closed off by a heavy door and lit by fire already prepared, a fire which burnt tardily with a blue flame. When a length of time had passed those who waited without grew uneasy, but it was long before they approached the door and when they did their throats were seized, so they were affrighted and fled, and one among them died. Then those who knew the mysteries of the thunderstones came and cleared the way, and all within the cave were found dead.
Habaris did what had to be done, for though it is well for men to conform to the laws of men, there is a superlaw by which men who are men should live and which sometimes decrees that they must die. Herthew married the daughter of Idalvar and they had a son who died in his seventh year. Idalvar's daughter died in childbirth. The invaders came and were defeated with a great slaughtering, and Herthew became the first king over all the people of Krowkasis.

THE BOOK OF GLEANINGS
Being writings from Various Old Culdee books which were partially destroyed in Ancient Times.

CHAPTER ONE. MAYA AND LILA

This was formerly called The Book of Conception and said to be The First Book of the Bronzebook. It concerns man's conception of The True God in olden days, during the struggle back towards the light. Once all men were dark and hairy and in those days woman was tempted by the strength and wildness of the beast which dwelt in the forest, and the race of man was defiled again.

Therefore, the Spirit of God was wrathful against woman, for hers was the responsibility to reject the beast within and without, that she might bring forth children of the light to walk in the light; for in man there is beast and god, and the god walks in light and the beast walks in darkness. Now, because of the wickedness that was done, there are among men those who are the Children of the Beast, and they are a different people. The race of man alone was punished, for the beast acted according to its nature. In man the beast and god strive to decide whether he shall take his place among the gods that live or the beasts that die, and woman, in her weakness, betrayed him to the beast.

Men struggle daily with the beast and wrest their living from the soil, their day being encompassed with strife and toil. So women bring forth children with suffering, and because they are frail their husbands rule over them. Man is conceived in the womb of woman and she brings him forth to life. Therefore, when God raised man up from among the beasts, choosing him as His heir and endowing him with an immortal spirit, He placed a veil over the portals of life. This, that woman should not forget she is unlike all other living creatures and the trustee of a divine mission. For a woman not only gives life to a mortal being, she also bears a spark of divinity to Earth, and there can be no greater responsibility.

The eye that sees earthly things is deceitful, but the eye that sees spiritual things is true. Then, because of the things that happened, the Great Eye that saw Truth was closed and henceforth man walked in falsity. Unable to perceive Truth he saw only that which deceived him, and so it shall be until his awakening. Not knowing God, man worshipped Earth who mothered him and supplied his needs. God was not displeased, for such is the nature of children; but when no longer children they must put aside childish things. Nor, having blinded them, was He wrathful that they could not see, for God is, above all else understanding. The face of a good father is stern and his ways are hard, for fatherly duty is no light burden, but his heart is ruled by compassion. His children walk in Truth and uprightness, their feet do not wander, nor are they willful and wayward.

Man is born of mud, sun and Spirit. In the days of conception the Spirit of God impregnated the receptive Earth, and she brought forth her children. Then came man who walked like a little child, but God took him in hand and taught him to walk in the uprightness of God.

A race of men came out of the cold northlands. They were under a wise father and above them was The Grand Company which later withdrew in disgust. This race was The Children of God; they knew Truth and lived in the midst of peace and plenty. The Children of Men about them were wild and savage; clothed in the skins of beasts they lived like beasts. Even more wild were the Men of Zumat who lived beyond them. Among the Children of God woman had equality with man, for her counsels were known to be wise. She heard with understanding and her speech was considered; in those days her words were weighed, for then her tongue did not rattle in her head like seed in a dried pod. Woman knew that though man could subdue her with his strength, he was weak in his desire for her. In his weakness lay her power and in those days it was used wisely, it was the foundation of people.

The race was good, but because of its goodness it was destined to be smitten, for only the good vessel is worthy of the fire. It is burnt, that its shape may be set and its design endure. This path of peace is not the path of progress.

The people were not governed by princes or by statutes, but wise men sat in council. They had only a code of conduct and moral tradition binding each one to the others in symmetrical web of life. Those who transgressed the code and tradition were deemed to be unworthy of life among the people and were banished into exile. Among The Children of Men woman was a chattel. She was subject to man, an object for the satisfaction of his lust and the servant to supply his needs. He subdued her and kept her in servitude, for her betrayal of man was known even among them, and it was never forgotten, nor could it be forgiven.

The Children of God valued woman highly and protected her from crudeness and cruelty, and her standing was such that she was awarded only to the most worthy of men. They held her in respect, for to them she was the fountain of life within their race, the designer of its future. Yet even so they had to restrict her, for she was inclined to be wilful and unheeding of her responsibility. The people flourished and, from generation to generation, grew in stature and comeliness. They were the rising tidewaters of mankind surging towards its destiny. The right of a man to mate was decided according to his standard of thought, his uprightness, the manner in which he upheld the code and tradition and his dealings with man and woman.

The fittest men could choose a mate among all woman, but lesser men could seek only among the less desirable, according to a known standard. To some, having only the outward appearance of men, no mate was given, while the noblest men could take additional ones from among the ranks of lesser women. Thus, the race ever tended to improve, to accord with its design.

The council of the people knew well the strength of man's desire for woman. The force of the urge was not wasted, for their forbears had harnessed it to the vehicle which carried their race to greatness above others. The race which could properly channel the forces contained within itself was ready to control the forces beyond itself.

The greatest forces man can harness to his benefit are those lying within himself, but the underlying strength of the people lay in the morality of its women, for this was the strength that governed, because it was the safe guard for something of value. Men strive for gold, and value it because it is something not easily attained. If gold would be gathered by the handful, men would scorn it, its power is in its scarcity. Then it happened that one man became arrogant in the strength of his manhood and pride of place, his thoughts inclined towards himself rather than towards the welfare of the people. He scorned the old ways, declaring the code and tradition an unnecessary burden laid on the backs of men. He said, "Why should we carry the burden of things which have come down to us from our fathers? How do we know they walked with wisdom?

How can we say that what was good for them is good for us?" Because of his unruly speech and wayward ways, the council banished him for a time and had he remained apart, his heart would have been humbled in wisdom. But among The Children of God there was a woman, one of the most desirable and fair, who interceded for him so he might return to dwell among them, it being in their code that the wayward could always regain their place. The woman sought him out in the wilderness and, coming upon him,. said, "Though, because of my heart, you appear to me as the finest of men, in the eyes of the elders you are unworthy to claim me. Therefore, I have spoken for you; now come, go before them yourself and say the wilderness has changed your ways. By so doing you will find favour with the council and, perchance, I may become your mate. The strength and courage I admire place you high in the regard of men and in favour with the elders, but your wayward and inconsiderate spirit is unworthy of your body. Though you find favour in the eyes of the young and foolish women who see only the outwardness of your body and thereby become more foolish, the eyes of the wise women see your naked spirit and are not deceived. Therefore, disregard the glances of foolish maidens and carry yourself well. Act in such manner that you find favour in the sight of the wise women". And, said she, "Am I not Maya, the most desirable of women, one whom all men seek? Yet will I remain reserved only for you, therefore be not unworthy of me".

The man came out of the wilderness and wastelands. He went before the council of wise women and said, "What must I do that I may have this woman for a mate? For I desire her above all things, even above my own life. For her I will become the most worthy of men among the people, her standard being high I may not possess her otherwise". The wise women answered him, saying, "For so long shall you conduct yourself in this manner", and they set him a time and a task. That it should be well, the task was to be done with heart as well as deed, but the man accepted it gladly, his heart not in that day but in the days to come. The council and the elders said, "what the wise women have done is good, it will be well and to the people's benefit".

The man rose manfully to the task and was magnificent in his manhood, his new ways gladdening the hearts of all the maidens, many of whom were disturbed by strange stirrings within their breasts. Among these was one less comely and desirable whose heart burned hotly for him, her thoughts resting upon him continually; but she knew that in his sights she was of little account. Here name was Lila. It happened that, arising early one day, she saw the man depart into the forest by the swampland, going about his task, and she took counsel with herself and followed him. She came upon the man while he rested in a place of solitude and approaching spoke softly, saying "It is your servant Lila. O my Lord, are you not weary with the task burdening your days, also that you lack companionable gladness to lighten it? Where is she who set the load upon your strong back? Where is my kinswoman who, without doubt, is more comely and very much more desirable than I and therefore a very fitting reward for your heavy labours? Does she rest in the shade or is she gathering fruit back in the gardens? Without doubt her thoughts are with you, but is she not unduly hardhearted in that she fails to comfort you, for is it not in the nature of woman to come to man and lighten his burden with her softness? Is it not in the nature of woman to be yielding and submissive, that man may rejoice in his strength? Is it, perhaps, that despite her loveliness the heart of this woman of your desire is not the heart of a woman? Is it like the mock orange, sweet to look at but bitter to bite? "Or is her heart in the keeping of the elders, that she prefers the ways of the old to the ways of the young?

What has she done to you, has she not humiliated your manliness by harnessing it like an ox to the customs of the people? Can it be right that the decrees of old men long dead should come between living man and woman? Is it not more fitting that the customs of men submit to the law of Her who gave us our natures? This desirable woman is yours, providing you toil and wait. She is yours, but not without conditions. She does not come without reservations as a woman should, but like a man who comes to an ass bridle in hand. Alas, that I lack the loveliness which places the yoke upon you, but beneath I lack nothing and am as much a woman as any. My heart burns for you with a flame that comes nigh to consuming my body. Take me, accept my humble offering. I give all freely, I will be yours without any conditions.

O my Lord, which of us women truly offers the most? She who concedes nothing, or I who will even be accursed by God and men for your sake? I who am nothing in your sight require no sacrifice from you on my behalf. I ask nothing and I offer all a woman can". Then Lila knelt at the feet of the man and placed her head on his knee.

The man was sorely troubled in his body and he wrestled with it, but his spirit brought before his eyes the vision of the more desirable maiden, and he was strengthened. He arose and said, "Begone and tempt me no more!" Then Lila departed and went her way, but within herself she brooded and in the course of days her thoughts hatched a dark scheme. She mixed a forbidden potion from herbs and, putting it into a pitcher of water with honey, took it to the man as he toiled in the heat of the declining day. Seeing her, the man said, "Wherefore have you come again?' And she answered him, saying "My Lord, your servant brings a much lesser offering, one you need not fear as you did the greater one, a humble gift of refreshment". The day being hot and the toil arduous, the gift was not unwelcome.

The man drank heavily from the pitcher and because of the potion his spirit slept while the beast entered his body in strength. When the fire of his passion was quenched by the waters of lust, his spirit returned and he reviled the woman, saying, "What have you wrought? Would you destroy me in this manner?" The woman replied, "The deed is yours, my Lord, for you are a man and I am a woman".

Then the man became afraid, for he knew the code and custom. He became angry after the manner of frightened men and shouted, "Begone from my sight, you viper, lest I crush you!" Lila answered quietly, "My Lord, why be wrathful or afraid without cause? For this thing shall be a secret between us, none will ever know of it. Behold, my Lord, are you not free again and the yoke removed from your neck? Now you may know the joys a woman can give, without submitting to the task; therefore, take your ease, for life is good to you". The words of the woman were not sweet to the ears of the man, for he was filled with remorse for what had been done. He said, "You are not the maiden of my tender desires, in whom my heart delighted and for whom I gladly undertook the task. What now of her whose beauty compares with the glory of the sun, whose gentleness caresses as the sunbeam, beside whose brightness you are no more than a gloomy shadow?

Lila replied, "She is indeed as the sun, you may worship from afar but never touch lest you be burnt and destroyed". "I am the woman of your body whom your flesh has chosen. What has this other woman done for you? Did she not sharpen the sword on which you cut yourself? If one lights a fire among reeds, knowing a man sleeps there, who is to blame for his burning? The fire, he who lit it or the reeds? It is beneath your manliness to turn on me thus, am I not shamed for your sake? And who among women would invite the wrath of gods and men as I have done? Be content with the wrong your lust has already wrought. This is an evil deed you have committed, but because we are now united in the flesh no harm shall befall you through me". Thenceforth, among the people they went their separate ways, but flesh called to flesh, bringing them furtively together in secret places. Each dwelt with the reproachful whispers of their spirit, and each walked in the shadow of fear because of the code and tradition. Now, the elders were not without shrewdness and they saw that the man was no longer diligent in the task and had returned to his former ways. Also he avoided the eyes of Maya and was no longer reserved with women, having sampled forbidden fruit he now sought other varieties. He was not a man with an end in view towards which he strove, his bearing was not that of a free man. The glances between the man and the woman, and their uneasiness, were not difficult to interpret.

The elders and wise women said among themselves, "Such is the manner of those carrying a burden in their hearts, whose shadowy love is a feeble furtive thing blooming shamefully in dark and hidden places". Therefore, they set a watch on the pair. The watch came upon them as they lay together in nakedness upon their skins and mocked them with ribaldry, for their passion was profane and a thing for jest. It was a fungus upon the tree of love.

They were brought before the high council, which was the council of elders, and the council of wise women, which questioned them, saying, "Wherefore have you done evil unto us?" The man answered, "The woman put my spirit to sleep with an evil brew, and my body became weak because of my manhood". They replied, "Truly you have little manhood now and are a lesser man because of this woman". The woman stood up before the high council and answered them boldly, "Am I then the stronger of the two? Can I lift the biggest stone or run the fastest race? Do not the strong always prevail against the weak, and is not this man the strongest among men? Is this even a matter for your concern? For in what way have we caused harm to any but ourselves? Shall we be punished for that which concerns us two alone and wrongs no other?"

The high council replied, "The deeds of any person affecting the lives of others are the concern of others. Though it were done in secret between yourselves, were not the effects displayed in your eyes for all to see? Does the man serve the people better because of this thing, or does he serve them less well? Has something been added to the people, or has something been taken away? Have not the people lost?"

"Therefore, is not that which you did the concern of the people and not of yourselves alone? The deed of itself was not wrong, except in the manner of its accomplishment. A woman who places no value on herself steals something from all women, for they are then less valued in the eyes of men. Would men value gold were it gathered by the wayside? Above all this, what of God-given love? Have you elevated or degraded its means of expression among men and women? Among people who value gold above all else, he who debases or adulterates it commits a wrong against them.

Here, where love is valued above all else and woman honoured as its custodian, those who debase it are regarded likewise". "We dwell in a pleasant place, amid peace and plenty, an inheritance from our fathers. The Children of Men have inherited the wastelands. Are our fathers less wise than theirs, that the customs of our fathers should be spurned? What you have done relates to your two selves and by your two selves shall your punishment be carried out. This is not a punishment for any wrong done to us, for we are old and it affects us little. We punish because we have a duty to the young, to the unborn of our race. We have an even greater duty to the hallowed things which inspire mankind and enthrone man above the beasts".

"Your wrongdoing affects no one man or woman, yet it affects all men and women, and if left unheeded would not be without effect on children yet unborn. The code and tradition is the pillar of our people, and the pillar may not be struck with impunity. Though it be strong and one blow will not damage it, many blows will bring down even the stoutest pillar. A blow left unheeded encourages another. A deed disregarded is a deed encouraged".

"A people can be judged by the things it punishes and the things it permits. The swine revels in filth and therefore attacks anyone who enters his pen. Were we wholly of the Earth, we need only protect earthly things".

"Thus we banish you forever from among us, unless in your old age you are permitted, in mercy, to return". In this manner were the man and woman banished from the tilled land to wander the wilderness beyond. They dwelt in a cavern in the wasteland, against the outer border of the tilled land, and they ate weeds and wild creatures. There they were in a place defended from hostile men and made safe from ambushes. In the first days of their banishment the man was wrathful against the woman and spoke to her spitefully, saying, "Like a lamp that gives no light you are a woman without womanly virtue, no longer deserving of the honoured treatment accorded women of our race. You spoke truly when you said that I am strong and you are weak.
So be it, henceforth your weakness shall be my strength; no longer will the weakness of man be the strength of woman and the backbone of a people clinging to things without substance. Henceforth, I am obligated to no one and owe a duty to none but myself. Man is weak only in his desire for woman, but the weakness of woman shall henceforth assure satisfaction of the desire". So the man subdued the woman after the fashion of The Children of Men; she was the wife who ministered unto him, saying "My Lord, I am but a woman and your handmaiden".

The beast of the wastelands were the keepers of the woman and she was in bondage to the barrenland, for the wilderness was beyond reach of the waters, a place of desolation yielding only weeds and thorns. The man hunted afield for wild creatures while the woman delved for roots, seeking sustenance among the weeds. Thus it happened that one day, being overcome with hunger, the woman went among the reeds growing on the edge of the tilled land, for flowering plants grew there, the roots of which could be eaten. While engaged in gathering she was seen by a husbandman tilling the fields, who, coming upon her stealthily, said, "Woman I see you, are you not the one who was banished? If so the custom decrees you will have to die, for it is forbidden to re-enter the fertile land, having been cast out". Then the woman, being still in the water, loosened her girdle and, letting down her hair, said, "honoured I may no longer be, perhaps die I must, but am I not still a woman while I live? If you see me otherwise than as a woman who can please a man by the ways of women, then I say you cannot be a man. Yes, I am the woman your brother seduced, the frail victim of his lust. Perhaps it is better that I die quickly by your hand than starve slowly in the wasteland. Death can hurt me no more than life which has revealed me to the evil of men. Let me die now for the wrongdoing of your brother". So saying she came out of the water. The husbandman did not slay, but instead he dallied with her until the evening. The woman said, ere he departed, "This shall be a secret between us, for there is none other nearby to see us here. Give me food, that my flesh may be firm and my heart gladdened, that I may come often to this place". Thus, in the days that followed the woman went many times to the waters and in other places where there were other men. Therefore, she no longer had to delve for roots, nor did she toil in the wilderness.

Then The Children of God banished other men into the wastelands because of the woman, and the man, seeing how this came about, said, "Is my affliction because of you never to end?" The woman answered, "My Lord, this thing I did for your sake; see these others, are they not outcasts in the wilderness, men without a chief to rule over them or a hand to guide? Gather them together, that they may hunt for you and serve you, rule over them and become powerful. What I have done I have done for you alone. To your strength will be added their strength, and the loss of the people in fertile lands will thus become your gain. What is there that strength cannon obtain? If your desire is for other women, will not strength obtain them? Therefore, revile me not, because I have now placed in your hands the means to that which you desire".

"Now I say to you, and speak truly of things only a woman can know, that you are a better man than those who live bound to the tilled lands, whose women secretly despise them for their servility to the code and tradition". The man was stirred up by these words and went out and about to the others, approaching them, saying, "Behold, we have been cast out because we have followed the ways of men according to the nature of men. Our manhood is good within us, let it therefore assert itself so our strength may be greater". So it came about that the men who were outcasts entered the fertile tilled land stealthily at night time, burning the houses and overthrowing the water towers, saying, "Let this land rejoin the wilderness". They slew menfolk and carried the women and children away. They stole sheep, goats and cattle. Then they withdrew to the fastnesses of the wastelands. There they built an encampment and fortified it about with walls and ditches, and they made war upon The Children of Men and prevailed against them. They ruled their women sternly and made them chattels, buying and selling them like cattle. When man said "Come", the woman came, and when he said "Go", she went. On her yielding back and on her submissive head he dissipated his wrath, on her servile body he satisfied his lust. Lila was a true daughter of the woman who betrayed the first race of men. It is written of her that when her sons grew to manhood, she caused then to kill and eat their father, so they might gain lifelong strength and wisdom.

Man kept woman in bondage, for he knew from his own knowledge of her ways that she was not to be trusted. Henceforth, she could not walk freely among men, for they knew that though woman was weak and man strong, by womanly guile she could exploit his weakness. Among the outcast people and The Children of Men woman was subject to man, and he imposed his will upon her and dominated her. In this manner woman wrought her own downfall and the destruction of those who held her in high regard. Her charms she cast at the feet of those who trampled them underfoot. Woman was not yet fitted to be the free guardian of the portals of life. She was never wise enough to choose the fathers of the race, for she was ruled by womanly waywardness, not by wisdom.

It came about that the sons of The Children of God mated with the daughters of The Children Men, who knew well the ways of men and were not reserved. The covenant had been broken and strange women were taken into the households, some even as wives, but though the daughters were lesser women, the sons were wonderfully big and mighty fighting men. These new people came out of the wastelands and crossed to Kithermis, which they divided in three parts between them, and there were rivers on the boundaries. This was when the years of man's life were lessened because he became fully Earthsustained, but he remained full of vigour though filled with hostility, particularly towards those who loved. To the East was the land of Ubal which was mountainous and the Ubalites were herdsmen. Westward was the land of Chaisen and it joined Ubak on the North. Southward were the land of Utoh and the land of Kayman, whose peoples dwelt on the plains and tilled the soil. Some from the households of The Children of God went into the land of Chaisen and gave the people laws and taught them to build with brick. Netar and Baletsheramam, the sons of Enanari, taught them writing and set their letters on a pillar in Herak. Enkilgal, son of Nenduka, built Keridor which stands between two rivers. Then came the lengthening of the years, when the time of sowing was confused and seed died in the ground. In those days, Enos came up out of Chaisen and spoke for the god of The Children of Men. In those days, there were many having the blood of The Children of God who inclined their ears towards his words, for they thought the Great God of their fathers had abandoned them.
Therefore, the enlightening word of God came to Eloma. Eloma, daughter of Kahema, heard the voice of God and was carried into the wilderness unto a place where there was a cave and clear running waters, and she dwelt there for seven years.

Eloma had three sons and they all heard the voice of God and walked with Him. Her firstborn son was Haryanah and he carried the word of God to the Children of God who dwelt in the Northlands, for they had forgotten His Ways. He married Didi, daughter of a great king and became an even greater king; he had many sons who all became kings among men of renown. Yahama, her secondborn son, carried the word of God to those who dwelt towards the sunrising, and Manum, her thirdborn son, carried it to those towards sunsetting. When the ear of the Spirit was opened in Eloma, she returned to her people and became The Interpreter of God. In the days when some men left to dwell among The Children of Men, others came to Eloma and said, "Behold, men leave and we become weak, while The Children of Men become strong. Can this be the will of our Father?" Then Eloma called upon God and He heard her cry and said unto her, "Let your spirit be at peace, for things happen as they will; it is the grain being winnowed from the chaff. It is always easier for men to follow the ways of the flesh than the ways of the spirit, yet the deeper man descends into the vale of earthly things, the harder the climb out to the heights of glory.

A generation to go down, ten generations to rise again. Man must struggle or degenerate, but the path of pleasure is pleasant, while the path of progress is beset with pain and strife". God said to Eloma, His servant, "Behold, I have been good to My children, they have been given everything that is pleasant, everything has come easily to their hand. The lot of The Children of Men is more harsh and yet they prosper. Childish things are expected from a child, but when it grows up more is anticipated, yet still My children come to me as children". God then said, "Go, return to the place from whence you came and remain there for seven years" and she did so. The seven years passed and Eloma returned to the people and, behold, the fertile fields were unsown, the water channels were dry and there was desolation in the midst of the waters.
Eloma sought among the fields and when she came upon the habitations her heart was rent apart. For she saw the daughters of The Children of God consorted with the sons of The Children of Men and were become unlike true women. Then Eloma said to them, "Wherefore has this thing come about?" And they answered, "Behold, men came from out of the wilderness and our men were like sheep before wolves; see, even now they labour within a pen of servitude". Eloma then went unto the men and said, "Wherefore has this thing come about?" and they answered her, "Behold, the god of The Children of Men is, unlike ours, a god of battles and we were delivered into their hands". Then Eloma was heavy of heart and called upon God, saying, "Behold the plight of Your children" and God heard her and answered, "I am not indifferent, for their sufferings are My sufferings. They are not under the whips of men but under the flail of God, the grain is being separated from the

chaff. They toil not under the blows of men but under the hammer of God, they are not imprisoned but are upon an anvil. I am not the God of battles, not the God of nations, not even the God of men. I am the God of Souls, The Keeper of the Treasures of Eternity. I have not turned away from My children, My children have turned away from Me, disobeying my laws. This cry will echo down through the generations of man: "My God, why have You deserted me?" And it will come from those who have deserted their God".

"Arise, go seek among the people and you will find a maiden who is pure at heart, but she is mocked and degraded by being made a swine attendant. Take her with you and go to Shinara, guard her well, for she is the daughter of a new dawning". Eloma sought among the people and found Nanua, Maid of the Morning, and they went into Shinara. The Voice of God came to Eloma in Shinara, saying, "This is the way things shall be with those who aspire to godhood. They must follow only the paths which I have shown through the words of My interpreters. The unfolding spirit residing in those who have the blood of The Children of God and the greatness that dwells in men shall be magnified in the blood of their children. Their wisdom shall be greatly multiplied, if the tie of blood be strong. As good wine become bad if diluted overmuch, so is greatness in the blood of man. There is a virtue in the blood of those whose forbears were The Children of God, and if two people having this blood marry, then this virtue is increased in their children, so it is greater than either parent.
There is a law of inheritance from which no man is exempt, for man is governed by the laws of earthly creatures as well as by greater laws. Is not the best ram chosen to sire the new flock?

So let women choose the best among men that they can and let men choose the best among women, and they who heed My words will know which is the best. Let the truly great ones rule". God said, "The creative words remain on this side of the veil, but their echoes resound on your side. The real remains here, but its reflection is there; creation is My mirror, though it is not without distortions. I have created in spirit and in matter, My thoughts have ranged from the unseeable smallest to the incomprehensible largest. My greatest thoughts formed substance for the spirits of the sons and daughters of Earth".

"Truth and justice, perfection of beauty and goodness remain with Me, and these you can know on Earth only by their reflection. In the universe of Truth all things are free from illusion and are seen in reality, but on Earth even the reflection is distorted. I have crated light and called it substance; it is illuminated within by the light of an ever present love potential".

"Men call on many gods, though above all there is but One; yet whatever they call Me I will hear them, for I am The God Above Names, The God Embracing All Names. Whatever men believe, if it serves Good it serves God. But gold necklaces are not for sheep and outward forms of worship must suffice for the spiritually undeveloped. The rituals of men may often be empty ceremonials, but they may also guard the Great Mysteries behind them".

"If a man seeks to enter My presence by prayer and says, "God grant me this or give me that", the thing will be neither granted no given, unless it be for his spiritual good or benefit another. I am no huxter bargaining blessings in exchange for worship, nothing man can give can add to what I have. Also me do Me little honour when they fail to recognize that I am above concern for mere bodies which decay and fall apart when the enlivening spirit leaves them. Yet man is but man, know that I am a God of understanding and compassion.
If man cries out to Me, in genuine stress and suffering, he will not go unrelieved and uncomforted. Yet understand that suffering and sorrow are the lot of man, that he may become Mangod. There is also the Great Law to which man must conform; there are intricacies of enidvadew to be unwoven and the challenging paths of destiny and fate to be followed. Too often the price to paid for things done or not done is pain and suffering, sorrow and distress, but where would be the benefit to the debtor were I to wipe out such debts? Yet will I see that never, be even a single grain, will they exceed that which is absolutely necessary and just. On earth, joy and gladness will always outweigh pain and sorrow". "Earth is Earth, take it as you find it, do not expect to find heavenly things there. It is a place of tuition and the purpose of life is learning. All things of Earth are limited and mortal, immortality will not be found there. When the things of Earth have fulfilled their hidden

purposes, each passes away, returning to the dust from whence it came". "Behold, in the days to come Truth shall be unfolded to all peoples, revealed in a degree and manner which will accord with their needs and capabilities. It will be passed on from generation to generation and from man to man.

The purity of its flame will accord with the quality of the oil of spirituality with which it is fed and replenished; hence there will be many differing degrees of purity and revelation. The food which one man enjoys may sit heavily on the stomach of another, yet it would be foolish to say that the food enjoyed by one should become the food of all. So it is with the spiritual things which men believe".

"I will not send prophets, nor will I appoint spokesmen, but such will arise through their own efforts and enter into conscious union with Me. They will point the way, which will be followed by the spiritually sturdy, but others less strong in spirit must take a slower path, and many will advance only by faith and service, by justice and kindliness towards others".

"The spark of divinity in man generates inspiring dreams which will ever lure him onward and upward, yet the road is long, the journey wearing and often unpleasant. Man has unnecessarily encumbered himself, he has enshrouded his spirit under a winding sheet of earthly passions.
With his Great Eye blinded by indulgence in vice and his spirit corroded by corruption, his fallible senses only are left to him, and these deceive him into believing the mortal vehicle is his total being. Affliction and decay are now the lot of man and he has passed into a long, dark night of ignorance. Now only by journeying the long and painful road of earthly experience can his soul be cleansed and awakened to the realization of the glory within him".

"Man may conceive Me as he will and it will be well. I am not a God of pettishness. As I brought forth the creation, so shall he bring forth the revelation of his God. Unto you, Eloma My child, I grant the keys of Communion and Union". Then Eloma went out among the people and taught them about their Creator in this manner, "I bring you the soul-whispered words of God, The Eternal Tower of Strength, The Fathomless Ocean of

Compassion. He has hung the Earth in the void, surrounding it with nothingness, yet by His power it remains in its appointed place. He veils His glory behind the shield of illusion, lest it overpower the spirits of men. He is obscured by the dark cloud of mortal ignorance.

He is the inspirational spirit ever entering the hearts of man, striving to arouse them to reach out towards greatness and achievement". "He has moulded the sky above us and bedecked it with splendour and awesome beauty. He taught the stars their song of joy and the winds their wondrous music. All the widespread Earth proclaim His creativity, while the high vaults reveal His skill and handiwork. His messages go out to men, not in the speech of men but in wordless whispers to their hearts. His finger prescribes a course for the fertilizing waters which nourish the desolate sands, making tender buds burst forth from the dead soil. The soft waters caress the ground and pastures arise to become the habitations of great flocks and herds".

"The rose unfolds its beauty to honour Him and the woodbine delights Him with perfume delivered upon the wind. The cornfields bow in humility, then the wheatstalks raise upwards in praise. The trees spread wide their worshipping branches and the barleyheads whisper together of His sungiven bounty. He is the Fountainhead of All Life, the Overseer of the Fertilising Waters and the Captain of the Stars".
"Men stand beneath the great dome of the nightskies and are overawed by the work of their architect and by the bright mysteries displayed in such a pattern of beauty. They become dismayed at their own smallness, but are reassured by His words which have come down to them from ancient times".

"God has crowned man with life and set the scepter of intellect in his hand. He has given him the flail of mastery over all other living creatures and set him on the throne of creation. He disciplines us when young and stretches out a welcoming hand when we near the end of life's journey. He accompanies men on their pilgrimage along the road of life, mitigating their misfortunes and rejoicing with them in its pleasant surprises. He balances the lives of all men, so they continually encounter conditions and situations meet for them".

"The widespread, mysterious Heavens are His throne and bountiful Earth His footstool; no structure man could build would contain Him. Did He need a residence, no place built by the hands of man could compare with that which His hands could erect. There is nothing on Earth that man can give God which could add to God's glory or increase what He has. The only acceptable sacrifice man can offer is service to the will of God, and God's will is that man should spiritualise himself and improve the Earth. To offer goods or money as a sacrifice is an insult to God, it is shirking the needful effort, evading the necessary duty and obligation; it is the easy way and not acceptable".

"God is the refuge of the poor and the comforter of the needy. His compassion encompasses men when troubles weigh heavily upon them. Yet tribulation and adversity, sorrow and suffering are not to be thought of as needless burdens imposed upon the difficulties inseparable from earthly life. They are things of value which open the eyes to Truth, tempering the spirit, as iron is tempered in the flame".

Eloma taught many things and she forbade any man to fornicate with unwedded matrons whose silver tongue beguiled and whose winsome ways led men astray. She also decreed that men should not fornicate with any maid or another's wife, for none so doing could call himself an honourable man, and such deeds canker the spirit. It was Eloma who taught men the wisdom of the stars which journeyed according to their destinies. She taught them to interpret the pattern of each man's life, which is woven from the threads of fate and destiny and interwoven with the many coloured strands of enidvadew. These things were learned and written down by Ishkiga.

THE FLOOD OF ATUMA

Behold, was this not written in the days of our fathers' fathers and of their fathers before them, and given unto us that we should pass it in to you, the children of days yet unborn? That if the ability of the scribe remains with you it could be read in your generation. Read, O children of the unborn years, and absorb the wisdom of the past which is your heritage. The enlightening words from a past which is to you, in days so far away and yet in Truth so near. We are taught that we live forever, and this is true, but it is equally true that no moment of life must be wasted; for each hour and day on Earth is a shaping for the future. We are the inheritors of a portion of time, we can dissipate it on futile things or utilize it to our everlasting benefit. In the days of our fathers, before barren teachings clogged the thoughts of men, and vain, formal ritual built a wall which obscured understanding, men walked in the light of Truth.

Then they knew there was One God alone, but because they allowed their higher abilities to fall to disuse, they saw less clearly. Because He appeared in different aspects, they thought He was many. Now, in our days, God has many varied forms in the eyes of men and each declares he alone knows the true name and likeness of God. Here all men fall into error, though all have spoken truly according to their understanding. But Truth can never bow to the limited understanding of man, the comprehension of man must expand to grasp it. In olden times there were spawned great monsters and beasts in fearful form, with frightful gnashing teeth and long ripping claws; an elephant was but a cat in comparison with them. Then, because of heavenly rebellion and turmoil, and the terror overwhelming the hearts of men, The Great One hardened the face of the land, which had become unstable, and the beasts were changed to stone. This was beforetimes, when the Destroyer still slumbered in the upper vaults of Heaven. Thus, it is written in the record of Beltshera; In those days the people were wicked and though the wise men among them gave many warnings of the wrath to come, they would not listen, such is the way of the wicked. So it came about that the Chastening Spirit became stirred up against them because of the odour of wickedness arising from the Earth, for her nostrils abhor the smell of evil.

This is a smell no man can know, for as the hounds know the smell of fear, which no man can detect, so can other beings know the smell of wickedness. The great floodgates which are above Earth were all opened. Thus, the floodwaters rose up to cover the land and great rainstorms lashed down. The winds could no longer discover their destinations. The people left the plain of Shinara and fled up into a great mountain rising above the flatlands below, and here, near the summit, they camped. Feeling themselves secured, the wicked mocked, saying, "No water can ever reach up here, for there is not enough of it in Heaven or Earth". Still the waters rose ever higher and the mouths of the wicked were silenced.

The priests of the people danced and chanted in vain, and many rituals were performed to appease the wrath above. There came a period of quietness, then the people built a gateway to Heaven wherein the Chief of Interpreters might commune with the Other Realm. He entered into the silence and cast his spirit, and when he had done so it contacted the Chastening Spirit which men call by other names. Her voice was heard within his heart and it said, "I am that which has been called forth by the odour of wickedness arising from the bodies of men, which no incense can disguise. For as the smell of putrefaction assails the nostrils of men, so does wickedness give forth something which assails us in this realm. Wickedness is, therefore, an offence against us. If a man threw filth over the wall into your courtyard, would you not consider this an act of hostility? Could any among you live in harmony with those who were insensitive to your own sensitivity? Thus, I am awakened to happenings in the world of men and am now clothed in a performing substance". The Spirit being said, "I have no desire to unduly punish men. Go out to the people and tell them that if they will but mend their ways and walk no more in the path of wickedness, I shall depart".

But when the Chief of Interpreters returned to the people he found them fearful and distraught, clay in the hands of false priests, devotees of the baleful gods. The false priests were crying out for a sacrifice to their gods and had seized Anis, a young man more handsome than any other, a messenger and runner between cities.

Then, though they whispered fearfully among themselves concerning the deed, the people had seized Nanua, handmaiden of Eloma, the Enlightened One, whose life was dedicated to Illana, for she had cried out curses upon their heads when the young man was taken. Nanua and Anis were held by the false priests and about them surged the great mass of the people, and though the Chief of Interpreters raised his voice it went unheeded.

Then the mass of the people moved down to the water's edge and there they stopped while the priests shouted prayers to the gods raging above. All the Heavens were darkened with great rolling clouds and there were high winds and lightning about the mountain top. The people rent their garments, the women wailed and men struck their forearms. Anis was beaten with a club and delivered to the waters. Then, as he who wielded the club turned towards Nanua, she said to those about her, "Let be, I will deliver myself to the waters, for if I must be sacrificed I would be a better sacrifice so given". Then she went down to the waters, but as her feet entered she drew back from the cold dark watery depths before her. But as the one who wielded the club moved forward, a young man, Sheluat the Scribe, a man of quiet ways, neither handsome nor strong in body, pushed forward and, taking her by the hand, went down into the waters with her. The waters had risen high and men shared the place where they stood with wild beasts and with sheep and cattle, but now the tumult quietened and the waters drew back. Seeing this, the people shouted praises to the baleful gods and cried out, "Great are the mighty gods, and great their holy priests!"

The Chief of Interpreters went sorrowfully apart, hiding himself, for now he was fearful for his life. When the waters had subsided, he cast his spirit and entered into communion with the Chastening Spirit, and he said, "Shall I also enter the falling waters as a sacrifice? For life is now futile, as I am without God or honour". The Great One answered, "Men see in events the things they wish to see, they can interpret only according to their understanding. The waters rose to their limitations and did not fall because of the needless sacrifices. The Powers above may ordain events to chasten men, but more often such events are challenges and tests. However, divine intervention is rare indeed".

"These priests follow another, a longer path, but they too condemn wickedness and they too point the way to Truth, though that way may be indirect and beset with hazards. So whether they or you reached the ears of the people the odour of wickedness will be diminished. Divine ends are achieved by diverse means, and the eyes of few men are opened to see either the means or the end".

"Life is never futile, but your sacrifice would be. No man can lose his God, for He is always there; but the prestige of a man because of that God such prestige is a worldly thing of little real value. How do you know whether you have lost or gained? Events of the moment cannot be weighed in the moment, but can be assessed only by the judgement of the years. Only eternity knows whether this or that was good or bad, a gain or loss".

Then the Great One opened the eyes of the Chief of Interpreters, so he saw beyond the earthly border into the realm beyond. Behold, he saw Anis who had been strong and handsome on Earth, and now he was something not pleasant to gaze upon. He saw also the true beauty of Nanua who was now a being of dazzling loveliness, and beside her was Sheluat who had always loved her secretly, and he was now glowing with youth and handsome as Helith. The Chief of the Interpreters then understood that evil could be transmuted into good, and that men had little knowledge of the true nature of things. Upon the mountain there is now a grove of trees and a temple built in the form of a circle of white stones, where the people remember the day of their deliverance. But what they recall and what happened are not the same, nor is the cause in their minds the true cause. They say, "We are the children of Atuma who saved us". Many who have gone often to the Temple of Deliverance say they have seen two shades, one radiantly beautiful and one gloriously handsome, wandering hand in hand through the trees or sitting in the sunlit glades. All about is now a place of peace. Men walk under the shadow of dread and fear of unknown powers fills their hearts. They have fashioned images in the likeness of the things which frighten them in the gloom of their ignorance, and they spurn the real for the unreal. Did they see more clearly they would know that the things they fear are but gentle and sturdy hands which can lead them to fields of contentment.

THE DELUGE

It is written, in The Great Book of the Firehawks, that Earth was destroyed twice, once altogether by fire and once partially by water. The destruction by water was the lesser destruction and came about in this manner. The people of those times spurned all spiritual things and men lived only for pleasure, caring little for the good of mankind or the future of the people. Lewdness and lies were upon the tongues of all men and brother could not deal justly with brother. The princes and governors were corrupt and proper tribute was not paid, the statues were held up to scorn.

The lives of men were ruled by their desires and they spent their days in gluttony, drunkedness, fornication, dancing and singing to instruments of music. The land was unattended, for men dissipated their strength in unproductive lusts and pleasures. Women lacked shame, for many would cast their glances after one man. Men fought among themselves and even slew one another because of their lusts for worthless women, while the chaste women were not sought. They were even rejected, for men declined the effort of being worthy of them in the eyes of their fathers. Wives were unhonoured and only the women of pleasure commanded the attentions of men. Women were unclean and immodest and men lay with them shamelessly in the presence of one another.

Old women were more lustful than the young ones, while virgins were seduced and corrupted in their childhood. Fathers fornicated before their sons and were admired for their prowess. They made no distinction between their sons and other men, or between their wives and other women. Deceit and violence were seen on every hand. To the East and North were high mountains upon which dwelt a tribe called The Sons of Nezirah, The Men of the Mountains, who were hardy men and mighty hunters, skillful in the chase and valiant in battle. The men were upright, their wives were faithful and their sons noble. In their hearts were no unworthy thoughts, no envy or hate, no malice or deceitfulness. They did not smile before a man's face, uttering smooth words, then when he turned his back reach out to stab him.
In their wives and daughters there was no impure longing, and neither cursing nor lying was heard among them. The womenfolk respected their men and maintained decency and decorum. Yet they were men with men's ways, abhorring all forms of unmanliness and degeneracy. Therefore, the treasures in the cities of the plains and the weakness of the people to whom these belonged did not go unnoticed by The Sons of Nezirah. So they said among themselves, "Let us go down and do a good deed among these people, let us show them the ways of men who are strong, making them slaves and possessing ourselves of their goods". This talk continued among the men in the marketplaces and gatherings, until they were stirred up to deeds, and they gathered together a warband of fighting men. The Mountain Men chose leaders from among themselves, after their custom, and prepared to fall upon the soft-living people of the plains and become their masters.

When the chiefs of The Mountain Men saw what was happening, they became wroth and ordered their men to return to their flocks and pastures. The chief of chiefs stood up before the gathered warband and said, "It is our decree that this thing shall not be done, you must not go down from these mountains bringing the sword to these people. Leave them alone, as rotted fruit is left on the tree to whither and die. Leave them to follow their own ways a little longer and in the fullness of time they will destroy themselves. Make no widows among your own people. If you go down there carrying fire and sword, you may find a trap laid for you among the fleshpots. The attraction of their pleasure and the temptations of their luxury is, to strong men such as you, like the lure the flame has for the moth. Do not lay yourselves open to destruction, even though the manner of its accomplishment be pleasant. If you must destroy this people, then destroy utterly so nothing remains.

They are many while we are few, and though by the keen hardhitting sword we may prevail in battle, yet might we not be lost under a deluge of soft feathers? Will you be wise enough to sup on milk and honey without being drowned in it?" For a time the fighting men heeded the words of their chiefs, for they were neither willful nor reckless, but there were some among them who went down to the plains in peace.

They returned with tales of treasures and pleasures awaiting below, reporting that the time was ripe for an attack, the warmen hired by the lowlanders having departed. For in those days the gods of Sharapik strove against the gods of Elishdur and Ladek. Then the fighting men disregarded the commands of their chiefs and, choosing war captains from among themselves, went down and fell upon the people of the plain. The people of the plain bowed before the strength of the men of the mountains. They did not fight, for among all their possessions they regarded their lives as the most valuable thing, precious above all else. They said, "Take whatever we have, our riches and harvests, the treasured things from our dwellings, even our daughters for your amusement, but leave us enough that we may live under your shadow".

The sturdy men of the mountains were sickened by these half men who had lived for three generations without fighting, and they despised them. The battlehardened men who had come down from the highlands took whatsoever they desired. The plainsmen demurred, but because their stomachs turned to water before the virility of their conquerors, their protestations were words of wind. The victors clothed themselves in plundered finery and indulged themselves in the wines and delicacies of the food tables. They slept in beds of luxury and dissipation, every want being attended to by the vanquished. They learned the ways of sensuality which goes with soft-living, and when sated with natural pleasures some lightened their boredom with unnatural ones.

The Mountain Men saw that the women of the cities were beautiful but they were not modest, casting their charms before the masters, unashamed; so it followed they were taken when required and treated as chattels. The women did not complain, though hitherto they had stood equal with their menfolk, but woman's equality with half men is not something of value. With women like this the men placed no restraint on their lust and went from excess to excess. The women, rejoicing in the strength and vigour of the men, said among themselves, "Here are men indeed such as we have not known before".

Then, in the manner of women, they turned away from their own men and from the households of their husbands and fathers, for now they despised them. They threw off all womanly restraint and grappled with the victors like ravening beasts, and the strong were vanquished by weakness. Always do women behave thus when their menfolk are defeated in battle, it is for this men fight. None came to do battle with the victors, for they who had fought for the gods had destroyed themselves and in the fullness of time the victors, too, were destroyed by the fleshpots, by fornication and drunkenness, by ease and luxury. Their fighting strength and valour departed with the passing years, they grew fat and slothful. They who had come down in manly array to fight and win, who could not be challenged in battle by the lesser men of the plains, were eaten up in the mansions of pleasure, in the drinking booths, with music, wine and fine linen.

Upon the mountain and in the mountain homes there was weeping and sadness among the women. Fields were untilled and cattle strayed away, sheep went unplucked. The best craftsmen were gone and few remained willing to learn their skill, the teachers of learning taught no more. The gnarled hand that had wielded the sword and terrorized the foe now plucked the strings of psaltery and lyre. The rough jerkins and corselets were cast off and now garments were of fine linen dyed purple and crimson. Men arrayed their softening bodies in gaudy attire and bathed in scented waters. They rejected their own women for those of the cities whose hands and feet were stained with bright colours and whose faces were marked with blue. One day, from afar off came three men of Ardis, their country having been stricken by a mountain burst. They were worshippers of The One God whose light shines within men, and when they had lived in the two cities for a number of days they were stirred up in their hearts because of the things they saw. So they called upon their God to see these evil things. Their God sent down a curse upon the men of the cities, and there came a strange light and a smoky mist which caught at the throats of men. All things became still and apprehensive, there were strange clouds in the skies and the nights were hung with heaviness. Many days passed before a northwind came and the skies cleared; but then, when women conceived they bore devils. Monstrosities came forth from their wombs, whose faces were terrible and whose limbs were unproportioned.

In those days men knew the art of working clay and making linen in bright colours, and also the use of eye paint. They had knowledge of herbs and magic, of enchantment, and the wisdom of The Book of Heaven; the knowledge of signs and omens, the secrets of the seasons, of the moon and the coming of the waters. The remnants of the Sons of Nezirah remained upon the mountains which are against Ardis, by the land about the encampment of Lamak. In Ardis there were wise men filled with the inner wisdom, who read The Book of Heaven with understanding and knew the signs. They saw that the deeds of men in all the lands about the mountains had brought them to their hour. Then the day came when The Lady of the Night changed her garment for one of a different hue, and her form swept more swiftly across the skies. Her tresses streamed out behind in gold and copper, and she rode in a chariot of fire. The people in those days were a great multitude and a loud cry ascended into Heaven.

Then the wise men went to Sharepik, now called Sarapesh, and said to Sisuda, the King, "Behold, the years are shortened and the hour of trial draws nigh. The shadow of doom approaches this land because of its wickedness; Yet, because you have not mingled with the wicked, you are set apart and shall not perish, this so your seeds may be preserved". Then the king sent for Hanok, son of Hogaretur, and he came out of Ardis, for there he had heard a voice among the reeds saying, "Abandon your abode and possessions, for the hour of doom is at hand; neither gold nor treasure can buy a reprieve". Then Hanok came into the cities and said to the governors, "Behold, I would go down to the sea and would therefore build a great ship, that I may take my people upon it. With me will go those who trouble you and they will take the things which cause you concern; therefore, you will be left in peace to your own enjoyment".

The governors said, "Go down to the sea and build your ship there, and it will be well, for you go with our blessing". But Hanok answered, "It has been told to me in a dream that the ship should be built against the mountains, and the sea will come up to me". When he had gone away they declared him mad. The people mocked him, calling him Commander of the Sea, but they did not hinder him, seeing gain in his undertaking.

Therefore a great ship was laid down under the leadership of Hanok, son of Hogaretur, for Sisuda, king of Sarapesh, from whose treasury came payment for the building of the vessel. It was built on the Lake of Namos, close by the river of gold, where it divides. All the household of Hanok was there and the household of his brother who directed the men at the task. Dwyvan, captain of ships, from the land beyond Ardis, was overseer of the craftsmen. The women and children carried and the men built. The length of the great ship was three hundred cubits, and its breadth was fifty cubits, and it was finished off above by one cubit. It had three storeys which were built without a break. The lowermost was for the beasts and cattle and their provender, and it was laid over with sand from the river. The middle one was for birds and fowls, for plants of every kind that are good for man and beast, and the uppermost one was for the people. Each storey was divided in twain, so that there were six floors below and one above, and they were divided across with seven partitions.

In it were cisterns for water and storehouses for food, and it was built with askara wood, which water cannot rot or worms enter. It was pitched within and without and the cisterns were lined. The planks were edged and the joints made fast with hair and oil. Great stones were hung from ropes of plaited leather, and the ship was without mast or oars. There were no poles and no openings, except for a hatch beneath the eaves above whereby all things entered. The hatch was secured by great beams. Into the great ship they carried the seed of all living things; grain was laid up in baskets and many cattle and sheep were slain for meat which was smoked by fire. They also took all kinds of beasts of the field and wild beasts, birds and fowls, all things that crawl. Also gold and silver, metals and stones. The people of the plains came up and camped about to see this wonder, even the Sons of Nezirah were among them, and they daily mocked the builders of the great ship; but these were not dismayed and toiled harder at the task. They said to the mockers, "Have your hour, for ours will surely come".

On the appointed day, they who were to go with the great ship departed from their homes and the encampment. They kissed the stones and embraced the trees, and they gathered up handfuls of the Earth, for all this they would see no more. They loaded the great ship with their possessions and all their provender went with them. They set a ram's head over the hatch, pouring out blood, milk, honey and beer. Beating upon their breasts, weeping and lamenting, the people entered the great shop and closed the hatch, making it secure within.

The king had entered and with him those of his blood, in all fourteen, for it was forbidden that his household go into the ship. Of all the people who entered with him, two understood the ways of the sun and moon and the ways of the year and the seasons. One the quarrying of stones, one the making of bricks and one the making of axes and weapons. One the playing of musical instruments, one bread, one the making of pottery, one the care of gardens and one the carving of wood and stone. One the making of roofs, one the working of timbers, one the making of cheese and butter. One the growing of trees and plants, one the making of ploughs, one the weaving of cloth and making of dyes, and one the brewing of beer. One the felling and cutting of trees, one the making of chariots, one dancing, one the mysteries of the scribe, one the building of houses and the working of leather. There was one skilled in the working of cedar and willow wood, and he was a hunter; one who knew the cunning of games and circus, and he was a watchman.

There was an inspector of of water and walls, a magistrate and a captain of men. There were three servants of God. There was Hanok and his brother and their households, and Dwyvan and six men who were strangers. Then, with the dawning, men saw an awesome sight. There, riding on a great black rolling cloud came the Destroyer, newly released from the confines of the sky vaults, and she raged about the Heavens, for it was her day of judgment. The beast with her opened its mouth and belched forth fire and hot stones and a vile smoke. It covered the whole sky above and the meeting place of Earth and Heaven could no longer be seen. In the evening the places of the stars were changed, they rolled across the sky to new stations, then the floodwaters came. The floodgates of Heaven were opened and the foundations of Earth were broken apart.
The surrounding waters poured over the land and broke upon the mountains. The storehouses of the winds burst their bolts asunder, so storms and whirlwinds were loosed, to hurl themselves upon the Earth. In the seething waters and howling gales all buildings were destroyed, trees were uprooted and mountains cast down. There was a time of great heat, then came a time of bitter cold. The waves over the waters did not rise and fall but seethed and swirled, there was an awful sound above. The pillars of Heaven were broken and fell down to Earth.

The skyvault was rent and broken, the whole of creation was in chaos. The stars in the Heavens were loosened from their places, so they dashed about in confusion. There was a revolt on high, a new ruler appeared there and swept across the sky in majesty. Those who had not laboured at the building of the great ship and those who had mocked the builders came quickly to the place where it was lying. They climbed upon the ship and beat upon it with their hands; they raged and pleaded, but could not enter inside, nor could they break the wood. As the great ship was borne up by the waters it rolled and they were swept off, for there was no foothold for them. The ship was lifted by the mighty surge of waters and hurled among the debris, but it was not dashed upon the mountainside because of the place where it was built. All the people not saved within the ship were swallowed up in the midst of raging confusion, and their wickedness and corruption was purged away from the face of the Earth.

The swelling waters swept up to the mountain top and filled the valleys. They did not rise like water poured into a bowl, but came in great surging torrents; but when the tumult quietened and the waters became still, they stood no more than three cubits above the Earth. The Destroyer passed away into the fastness of Heaven and the great flood remained seven days, diminishing day by day as the waters drained away to their places. Then the waters spread out calmly and the great ship drifted amid a brown scum and debris of all kinds. After many days the great ship came to rest upon Kardo, in the mountains of Ashtar, against Nishim in The Land of God.

THE TEACHINGS OF YOSIRA

These are the words for the Sons of the True Doctrine, written in the temple of Sacred Mysteries at Yankeb in the Days of Darkness, by the Unnamed Lord of the Secret Belief, who then lived. The true knowledge of the teachings and mysteries of Yosira concerning the spirit within the body, taken from his books and rewritten truly after the custom of writing.

Yosira spoke to his sons in this manner, "I am the Viceregent of the God of Gods. I am the custodian of the Books of Power. I am the Voice of Heaven. I am one sent into Tamerua as a lightbearer, that a call may go thence throughout all lands. Let every man be watchful of his deeds and ways. Whosoever be watchful of himself is a man of wisdom, for he shall be saved from the terror of everlasting darkness". "I am the torchbearer running before the chairlitter of Truth. I come to reveal the greatness of men, to tell them of their immortal selves, of their spirits which have to be ransomed from the doom of devouring darkness".

'The God of Gods spoke unto me, saying, "Long have you dwelt under my shadow and listened to my words. Now arise and go hence to a land where these things of which we have spoken can be established. To a place whither I shall lead you, for it is not proper that those who dwell there should remain uninstructed. Behold, I have given you the secret of immortality, but know that though all men are born into a heritage of immortality, not all enjoy it. The God of Gods, in His infinite mercy, plunges many into the waters of forgetfulness. Yet even from there they may return to be renewed, not of themselves but through the supplications of others".

When Yosira came into Tamerua he gathered his sons together on the stones beneath the place called Homtree and spoke to them in this manner, "I am the Dawnlighter and a torchbearer for the God of Gods. These are my words which you will do well to absorb, as the dry sands soaks up water. Though they are words of wisdom, they are useless unless accepted by men who have control over themselves. They have no value to men who are unable to feel compassion for others or who close their ears to Truth".
"You are the few chosen ones, my sons, light of my light, who shall hand the light on down through the generations. To you I give the true conception of God. To you I give this standard, that it may be a rallying point for those who will accompany us; for we stand on the borders of a land which has found favour in the eyes of our God".

"With us are fighting men, but they are few while those who stand ready to repel us are many. Therefore, we will not set ourselves against them in battle array, but go among them with guile, to gather many who will fight with us. You shall be the light of the fighting men, even as I am your hght and the God of Gods my light".

"The light that is with me was kindled at The Supreme Source, which is the God of Gods. Therefore, my hght shines with such brilliance that it must be veiled in part, lest it blind you. It is even as the sun be seen through a veil of cloud, it may be gazed upon for as long as desired. Seen thus it is a thing of beauty and mystery, not something which bums and consumes the eyes of the beholder".

"Therefore, even as I veil my light from you, so shall you veil your lights from the eyes of the uninstructed. Yet in all matters not pertaining to the light you shall instruct them in the fullness of Truth. In all matters concerning their bodies you shall instruct them in Truth. But in all matters concerning the Lord of the Body you shall instruct them with a light that is veiled".

"Behold the nature of man. Within him is a spark from the Divine Source and this is the Lord of the Body. This alone is everlasting, this alone of man is his true self. This spark is enwrapped within a heavy mantle of matter, it is enclosed in a covering of earthly clay. This spark alone is the seat of life, it alone has understanding and thought. Such things are not with the clay of the flesh, neither are they kin to the stones from which the bones come. The life within man radiates out from the enclosed spark, and through the blood endows the body with life and heat. life gives forth heat and the greater the life the greater the heat".

"As the sun gives light and fire spreads heat, as the flower radiates perfume, so does the Central Light give forth a vaporous unseeable glow, and this our fathers called the Breath of God. This Breath comes forth in two manifestations: there is a heavy form and a hght form, and from these all things are compounded. From The One comes the Sacred Glow in its two aspects, which men call the Breath of God, and from this are made all things which are in Heaven and Earth".

"Above is the God of Gods and below Him are Heaven and Earth. Heaven is divided in twain, there is a Place of Light and a Place of Darkness. Within the Place of Light dwell the spirits of Good and within the Place of Darkness dwell the spirits of evil. Between them the boundary is not fixed but flows back and forth according to their fluctuating strengths. But they who abide in the hght shall always prevail, for light will ever dispel darkness. Therefore, those who dwell in darkness withdraw before the brilliance of those who dwell in the light. This light and darkness are not such as men can understand, for it is not the light and darkness known on Earth".

"Before the Gates of Heaven is the Land of the Horizon, whence go all who depart from their earthly body. From here there are two great gates, one leads to the Place of Light and the other to the Place of Darkness, and the Lord of the Body is admitted into its appointed place according to its likeness. He who is filled with the light and is a Brilliant One cannot go to the Place of Darkness, for it would draw back before him. Neither can he who is a Dark One go into the Place of Light, for there he would shrivel before the light, as the white worm coming forth from the damp darkness of its hole shrivels in the light of the sun".

"Between Heaven and Earth there is a great gulf across which the dwellers in Heaven may not return, but Earth is not wholly beyond their reach. Man receives, from the Place of Light, that which influences him for good, and from the Place of Darkness that which affects him for evil. These things may be written, but the secret things concerning them may not be recorded in such manner that they come to the knowledge of the unenlightened men".

"That which comes from Heaven, whether influencing for good or evil, comes forth as shades in the likeness of men, which is rare; or much more often as lukim, which are like unto motes. It may also come as waves of air, but not air such as we breathe and feel. It is something altogether different in nature. Things come forth which are not stable, and these are the formless Ones. All things are held in form by the Breath of God, which changes formlessness, but the formless Ones can alter form into instability".

"There are three great spheres and that containing the Earth is held together by the Great Glow outflowing from the God of Gods. That part of the Great Glow which is light and contains life is called Manah, while that which is heavy and contains the flesh of things of the Earth is called Manyu". "The One Who is the God of Gods is so great that He cannot be defined in the speech of men. Neither can they conceive Him in their thoughts, for He is beyond thenunderstanding. Mortal man has limitations, therefore let men conceive Him as they will. It is of no importance, providing their conception serves both His purpose and the glorification of man".

"Man is not yet great and until he becomes so it is well that he worship the many Godforms conceived within his thoughts, providing they be such as tend to raise him above himself. Nor do ritual and worship do harm of themselves, unless they, too, thickly overlay the truth so it is buried from sight. Ritual and outward forms of worship can be aids to purification of thought and provide a kind of sustenance for the Lord of the Body. What are the Lesser Gods beloved by unawakened men but thought-conceived friends and guides? Yet this is a dangerous path men tread, balanced between light and darkness. Therefore, when man wanders towards the abyss of darkness, reveal a little more light, that he may see and so return to the path. Beware, too, lest he follow gods that are false guides and would lure him into the quicksand of carnality, or into the wilderness of ignorance".

Before crossing into Tamuera Yosira chose captains to be over the fighting men, and they sent forth men to spy out the land. He also sent some from among his sons into the land of Tewar, that they might talk with the people there, and these came back bringing hostages from the governors of the land of Tewar.
Then Yosira spoke with the sons of the governors and they gave ear to his words, they were receptive to his speech. Yosira spoke to the people, "These are the words of the God of the Gods. Henceforth, no child shall be sold into bondage by its father or by any man who has ward over it. Such may not yet be the custom of all the people in this land, but if they become mighty, this they may do, for such is the nature of men".

"If a man have a woman in bondage he shall not cause her to become a harlot unto men, for this is a great wickedness and he shall not go unpunished. If she become with child unto her master, then neither she nor the child shall be given in bondage
to another. But if she be given to a freeman who takes her in marriage, then it will be well".

'The greatest wickedness m the eyes of the God of Gods is all incest of the first degree, which is that between mother and son or father and daughter; or between the mother's mother and the son of the mother, or between the mother's father and the daughter of the mother; or between the father's father and the father's daughter, or between the father's mother and the father's son. This is a wickedness unto the God of Gods, for it calls forth the strongest of the Formless Ones, causing it to enter into an earthly body to become an abomination before the eyes of God and man. Therefore, they who commit such an act shall perish by fire. If it be committed with a child, then the child shall not perish, but it shall be branded with the mark of incest".

"Adultery is a foul and evil thing which you shall abhor, for it permits the lukim to pollute the fountain of life. In a far off land there lived a queen more beautiful than the Dawnflower, who, because she was powerful, disregarded her heritage of womanhood. As powerful kings had many wives she thought she could do likewise with men. The God of Gods and Creator of Life created men and women intending that each should play a different role. They are in no wise alike, for as men have their function so do women have theirs. What is meet for one is not meet for the other, and because the Creator made them as they are, each should follow their own path, never seeking to journey along the other's.
Now, while the seed of one man was yet with her this queen took the seed of another, and the seed of one man strove with that of the other so that both perished and became a corrupt pasture. Thus, the way was cleared for lukim to enter into the antechamber of life and the sacred shrine of life was polluted, becoming the breeding place of foulness. So it was that when other men came unto her, the flesh of their bodies was seized upon by the lukim and corrupted, for foul lukim had made their abode within the woman. So the wellspring of life became a fountain of polluting evil. Adultery is an abomination to the Bestower of life, therefore let it not go unpunished".

"None shall sleep in the bed of another, unless the spell of his presence be first removed. For he who goes into any place or takes up any thing while it is under the spell of another's presence, shall surely suffer. They who are of the same kin living under the one roof, will not suffer unless sickness already be there".

"None shall eat from the platter of another or drink from his drinking vessel until the spell of his presence has been removed. None among those who know the God of Gods shall walk in anything poured out for a libation unto strange gods, neither shall he touch any part of the Libation. If it come upon him he shall go forthwith to the Master of Mysteries and be cleansed".

Yosira said unto the people, "These are the words of the God of Gods. None among you shall wash himself in water used by another and contained within anything made by the hand of man. None among those who know God shall touch a woman while the days of her heritage are upon her. No man shall go unto a woman with unwashed hands, and when man and woman have lain together both shall purify themselves before going about their tasks".
"Among the lukim none is more subtle than the nableh which seek sustenance among the food of men. Therefore, if you have bread within your dwelling, then it shall not be hung up; but if there be meat or fish, then it shall be suspended within the dwelling. If you have bran or meal which has been pounded, then it shall be kept in a capped container with nowrata flowers, thus the lukim will not come upon it.
Neither crushed corn nor the crumbs of any repast shall be left within the sight of man or within the boundaries of the dwelling, lest the nableh seize upon them for sustenance. All things that have held life but have not been used for food shall be buried within the ground. All vessels which have held food but hold it no longer shall be made clean with sun and sand".

"When the flesh of any beast or of fish or fowl becomes dark in your keeping or has the smell of rottenness upon it, then it is a sign that the nableh have come upon it and it shall be taken out and buried where no beast can come upon it. Thus, the nableh are left without sustenance and will be forced back into their dark abode. But if you permit them to sustain themselves, then they will come in their hosts and, being fattened and strengthened, will afflict you with many terrors during night watches".

"If the pouring place or the spout of any pitcher or pot have a blackness upon it, then that pitcher or pot shall be broken, for it has been entered by the fiery lukim. If any who know God eat with strangers, they shall purify themselves at the rising of the sun on the following day. If any among you eat with a hand uncleansed by water or sand, then be prepared for attack by the lukim of the night. He who draws the blood of any beast must cleanse himself of all blood, lest he be attacked by the dark lukim. Neither food nor drink of any kind shall be kept under a bed or against a sleeping place, lest the lukim of the night come and take up their abode therein". These are words of the God of Gods spoken through the mouth of Yosira.

Yosira said this also, "All things which may sustain the lukim are to be buried or burnt. Anything coming forth from the nostrils or mouth of any man or woman is rejected from within and becomes sustenance for the lukim. Still waters that lie upon the ground are their drinking places and forbidden to men. Water shall not be used as drink unless it be drawn from within the ground, or be in a place where it is shaded by trees". "Eat only food known to be wholesome and which gives contentment to the stomach. In taste it should be soothing and refreshing, never bringing pain and discomfort. Eat not of anything that is too dry or oversalted, or which brings sickness upon you.
Any food of which men eat and has become rotten or mouldy has been seized by the lukim for sustenance; this you can see, for the rottenness and mould upon it is the excreta of lukim".

"Anything that has blood in it and is dead, having died of itself, shall not be eaten, for the lukim have made their abode in it. No man shall eat uncooked meat, even that which the sandfarers carry shall not be eaten".

"The slaying of any man or any woman is forbidden, but it is not unlawful to slay in war or in self-defence, or to uphold the purity of the household and home. To kill deceitfully or to strike from behind is murder and shall not go unpunished. If blood
be shed it shall not cry out from the ground in vain, and unto the kinsmen of each one slain shall be the order of revenge"

"If you swear an oath one with another, saying, "Great God bear witness" or before any strange god, to deceive another man, then consider, for only the most foolhardy turn their back on such an oath. For it is sworn on the life of the Lord of the Body, and if it be broken the Lord of your Body will be everlastingly disfigured with an unremovable scar. Man has many trials to overcome in his life and not the least of these, tests is oathkeeping. Though an oath may diminish and become nothing with the passing years according to the memories of men, it is everlastingly impressed on the Lord of the Body. Wiser far is he who never makes an oath".

"If any man say, 'The whirlwind and the sandstorm, the floodwaters and the burning fire, these do I fear because these I see, but the lukim which I see not neither do I fear, that man is a fool, for he knows not the deficiencies of his own eyes. The lukim, he will learn to know by their manifestations, for they will seize upon his body and torment it, sometimes even unto death. It is likewise with the God of Gods, none may see Him, but by His manifestations is He made known unto men".

Yosira spoke to the captains of the fighting men and to those who were with them and said, "When we come into this new land all things that the people who dwell therein hold sacred you will neither defile nor mock. Neither shall you stir up strife with any man, for we come to them as friends not foes".

Therefore, when Yosira and all those with him came up into the land of Tewar and dwelt there, peace was in the land. Then Yosira taught the people of Tewar the weaving of cloth and the working of metals, and showed them how to make tools and weapons of metal cast in a mysterious manner. But the secret of the sharp-edged weapons he revealed only to his own. The people of Tewar built a habitation for Yosira and a temple of brick bound with reeds. There were skins upon the walls and on the floor, and the door were of wood. Then Yosira spoke to his sons in this manner, 'These are the things in which the people of this place shall be instructed: The dove is the most sacred of birds and shall not be eaten, but if people say, "Forbid it not to us for sacrifice to our gods", then it shall not be forbidden them".

"The milk of all beasts which do not have horns and part the hoof is not for the sustenance of man, but if the people say, "Forbid it not, for it is our custom", then it shall not be forbidden them". 'The sacrifice of breast children at the burial of the dead shall be forbidden, for the blood of the young cannot provide life for the old, each man being the fashioner of his own destiny. He that has life shall bear it with him, and none can possess the body and life of a breast child except the God who gave it life. He who buries a living breast child with the dead shall himself die". "All things buried with the departed one, whether they be weapons or dishes, instruments or ornaments, shall have the form released from them before they are placed within the ground". 'This shall be the law unto all those who work with metal, whether it be gold, silver or copper: One day in seven shall be a day of rest for the fires herewith the metals are wrought. On this day no fire will be lit and no metal touched or moved from its place. On the even of this day all things of metal that have been made since the last day of rest shall be placed in a trough of sanctified oil, remaining there until their appointed time. Nothing shall go out from the workplace of a craftsman in metal until it has passed through the oil".

THE RULE OF YOSIRA

Yosira gathered his sons about him and spoke to them thus, "These are the days of the dawnlight and I am the Dawnlighter from beyond Bashiru. I am the Torchbearer for the God of Gods. These are the laws which I made for my people in the land of Tewar, the laws of one speaking with the mouth of the God above all gods".

"He who places a spear or arrow within a dead body shall be accursed and his hand and arm will become things of evil. They will swell up and become consumed by fire. Likewise shall be accursed who looses these weapons against another, but if it be a man of Tamuera who looses the weapons, then he shall die by them himself, for he is beyond the reach of the curse".

"A tree that reaches up above twice the height of a man shall not be stricken for burning or to take away its land. But if it be dedicated to the adze and is then used by a craftsman in wood, then it may be stricken and cut. Trees are not things to be lightly dealt with, for they move the winds which cross the face of the Earth and generate these in great forests of the North and South. The slaughter of a tree is no less wrong than the slaughter of an ox or a sheep, for the same breath of life is in each. Therefore, never bring them low wantonly. Are not trees held sacred by the people of this land? Is it not more reasonable to dedicate a mighty tree or a grove of trees to a god than a mute stone or object cut from wood?" Therefore, when Yosira moved among the people he did not forbid them their grave groves, nor did he silence the words of the women who tended them. But Yosira said, "These things are for women and not for men, let the women bide, but men should follow the callings of men and their place is not among the grave groves".

Now, when Yosira came among the people they dwelt away from the river, fearing the god of moving waters who molested them at night. But Yosira bound the god of moving waters, so he no longer troubled the people. Then Yosira bade them build their dwelling places beside the moving waters, decreeing that none should dwell beside still waters unless the still waters be filled with the life of fishes.

In those days men sought to appease the Formless Ones and the Spirits of the Night with offerings and worship. But Yosira forbade them this and he surrounded the whole land with a protective wall which no Dark Spirit could penetrate, while all those within were dissolved. Every Dark Spirit being neither male nor female and every Dark Spirit which clothed itself in the shape of a beast or bird was bound and cast back into the Place of Darkness.

All men who were blood kindred with the beasts of the forest or with fowl or with serpent, dwelt together according to their kinship, and were divided thereby. Yosira forbade them not their kinship but did forbid the rule of blood. He spoke to the people in this manner: "Great are the ties of that thing which binds men together and joins them with their forefathers, but greater still is each man in himself, his destiny lying within himself alone and not within his kindred. Man is not a drop of water in the stream of life, but a fish that swims within the stream. Yet insofar as these things have ever been, the twenty-four great kinships shall remain secured in their establishment".

Before the coming of Yosira a man could not take to wife a woman of his own blood, but Yosira redeemed the land with blood, safeguarding it against barrenness. So henceforth men could take wives from among their own blood kindred, and the land remained fruitful. This, the Spirit of Life, became strong among men, for it was not spread out to become diluted and weakened. Until Yosira came none in this land knew of hokew, and it filled men with fear and awe, but Yosira revealed all its secrets to his sons, and the secrets are known even in these days. Hokew is that which sustains the Dawndwellers. It is but thinly spread throughout the Earth and before the days of Yosira men could gather it, storing it in stones and in sacred objects. It may be drawn upon by the spirits of men, as women draw water from a well. It is hokew which bestows fertility, causing flocks to multiply and crops to increase. Its secrets are known by the Twice Born. Though in the days of his distress Yosira called upon his Father in Kanogmahu, he forbade his sons to call upon Him likewise, for Yosira was their father on Earth and their advocate in the Hall of Admission.

Therefore, none can call upon Him with impunity, for if He dealt with them He would neglect His task among the Dawndwellers. Nor is any man justified in calling upon the spirit of a Departed One, for they are beyond concern for the everyday affairs of men. When the sons of Yosira had established their rule over the people, the leaders of the people came to Yosira desiring to make him their king, so he would rule over them. But when they came before him, Yosira replied to their wish in this manner,

"I am the mouth of the God of Gods and the light of my people. I will be the father of your king and the director of his footsteps, but your king I cannot be, for I am dedicated in service to the God of Gods". Saying this Yosira then took his son, who was grown to manhood, and led him forth by the hand, giving him to the people to be their king. Later, while the leaders and governors of the people still remained gathered after the anointing of their king, Yosira spoke to them as the mouth of God. He said, 'To judge justly between man and man is one of the greatest obligations of a king and those who stand in his place. So from this day hence judgement shall not be given by those who sit under the trees, listening to the words whispered among the leaves. However, if three men sit far apart and each gives a like judgement, the words from their mouths being the same, then the judgement shall be good. However, if it is a matter where a life can be forfeit or property taken away, a family divided or a man or woman enslaved, then judgement shall be given only by the king or by one who wears his mantle and bears his burden". "Sacred waters are living waters filled with the power of hokew and shall no longer be used for any purpose other than sanctification and purification. No longer shall they be used to decide whether a wife be guilty of adultery; henceforth she shall be tested by the bitter draught alone".

"He who eats the flesh of swine shall be accursed, for to eat the flesh of swine is to eat something dedicated to the fathers of men and an abomination. Flesh of the ass shall not be eaten, for it diminishes the vigour of men". "Henceforth, the bodies of the dead shall not be broken or burnt, for the hokew within them departs with the Lord of the Body. Therefore, nothing can be added unto a Victorious One by rendering up the essence of his earthly mantle through the flames of the fire".
"The people shall not be denied their feasts, nor shall they be forbidden the rituals of fruitfulness. Their offerings to any god shall not be taken away. As the gods of the people are today, so shall they remain, for they serve their end. They may depict their gods after their own fashion, for the likeness of such gods is of small consequence. But the likeness of the God of Gods shall not be fashioned by any man, for He is beyond the understanding of men. No man shall seek to find His likeness in water".

"The festival to the god who draws up the land is not to be denied the people, but no longer shall they eat the flesh of asses, for now this is forbidden. The days for the feast of the forefathers shall not be diminished, lest the gift of long life be thereby curtailed. With them alone is the distribution of the life forces and in their keeping are the powers granting fertility and good fortune. Unto those who control the sprouting of com, the increase of herds and the harvests of fishes, the potency of men and the fertility of women, success in hunting and victory in war shall be given all due honour and worship".

"He who causes injury or death, sickness or suffering by drawing the likeness of another in sand and piercing it with a fire-hardened stick, or who makes the likeness of another in wax to burn in the fire, or in clay to be pierced by stake or thorn, is henceforth accursed. He will be delivered to the lukim of disease or death". "He shall be accursed who mixes living grain with fat to enslave the earthshade of another man or woman. He shall be accursed who calls up the nightshade of another or the nightfrightener. All who are so accursed will be delivered to the lukim of sickness or shall become the prey of Formless Ones".

"It is not wrong to make an image of a breast child, that a woman may conceive, but to make the hkeness of a man's private organ so that a woman may conceive, is wrong and any woman making or lying with such a likeness shall be accursed. She who is so accursed will be delivered to the lukim of sickness and pain".

When Yosira came up into Harfanti he found there people with strange customs which displeased him, but he forbade them none except those which were evil in the sight of the God of Gods. While there he laid a great curse upon any who transgressed his laws. These were words spoken through the mouth of Yosira, which he caused to be recorded: "Henceforth, no maiden shall be enclosed in bark and kept in darkness for seven days before marriage, but she may be kept in seclusion among women. If she has to be purified, it must be done with water and not with fire. A woman shall never be mutilated to purge her wickedness".

"Henceforth, the private parts of young women shall not be sewn up to preserve their maidenhood. This shall remain in their own keeping and in the keeping of the young women's kindred in good faith and trust. To sew or cut the private parts of any woman is a great wickedness, for this is the portal of life and woman is not an unworthy guardian. It is best that women remain maidens, until their marriage day, of their own free will and choice; but if, because of the maiden's weakness, this seems doubtful, then the obligation shall be on her kindred".

"The custom of the Habshasti whereby the legs of young women are bound together, after which young men may enter their chamber to lie with them, is a thing of wickedness and no longer permitted. Now, if any man discover the nakedness of a maiden, he shall not go unpunished". "Man shall not see the nakedness of woman in childbirth, even though the woman be bis wife. The hut of childbirth and all within its circle is a place forbidden unto men. Henceforth, no woman shall be suspended at childbirth". "If the wife of a hunter he with another man while her husband is absent so that he be slain or wounded during the hunt, then no wrong is done if her husband or the kindred of her husband slay her. Neither shall it be cause for bloodslaying if the kindred or husband slay he who lay with her".

"The foreskin of a man is cut to defy the lukim of impotency. This is not forbidden to the people, but they shall not preserve the foreskin in fat and use it to endow stones with hokew. The binding of foreskins is forbidden". Yosira laid the greatest of all curses upon those who captured and enslaved the Lord of the Body belonging to another.
Since that day none has done so and lived. He also laid a curse upon women who baked their new born children and ate them because of the barrenness of the land. He also cursed the chief of the women's kindred. Beforetimes, that which grew to fullness within the wombs of cattle and sheep was sustenance for men alone, but when the beast cast it forth before its day it became sustenance appointed for women.

Yosira forbade this and cursed all that came forth from the womb of beast before its time. Yosira had these things recorded in Yapu: "No child shall be slain wilfully, saying, "Our god has denied it proper sustenance". Above all gods is the God of Gods who is the God of Life and they who proclaim these things proclaim a falsehood against Him. Yet they shall not be accursed until after the day when they have heard the laws of the God of Gods spoken unto them. Before then they have been led astray by those who should guide them, and on the leaders shall be the curse".

"Henceforth, the empty body shall not be bound tight against itself, but stretched out, for the earthly body cannot be reborn when once its Lord has departed. The people shall not be forbidden the carrying of it, nor shall they be stopped from elevating it, but it shall not be hung over the living waters, lest it call forth a Formless One in the darkness of the night".

"If the kindred of a man come up to molest him at night, the nightshade shall be bound by the power of hokew transmitted into a hollow log filled with fire-retaining substances. The log will then be burnt in purifying fire and the ashes buried after the fashion of your fathers, but the hokew shall not be given back. That hokew which comes from a man whose crops and trees yield abundantly is best".

"The spirit of the life of men does not dwell in the moving waters and therefore it cannot enter into a woman from the waters, neither does her own water bear it up from the ground. Even as a tree springs out from a single seed and the barley from a single grain, so is it with the seed of men.
That which forms within the womb of woman is not built up from many outpourings of man, once will suffice. If the blood of a woman be not stopped, then she carry no child, for the life within is blood of her blood".

"No man shall fashion the likeness of any beast to lay with it so that his flocks and herds be increased, for henceforth he who does so, and all his beasts, shall be accursed so they sicken and perish. Nor shall any man spill his seed into an object of wood or stone and bury it. If he does so, then be he accursed, so that he is forever molested by the nightshades of terror".

"It is foolishness to resort to the charmers who make likenesses of beast so their kind may be brought to the arrow and spear. Unless he who seeks the wild beasts be empowered with the hokew gathered by the kindred of his habitation, nought can guide his steps or strengthen his arm, neither will his eye see keenly. The success of the hunter is not to be found with the charmers, but lies in the goodness and uprightness of the kindred within his habitation".

"If a woman take seed from a young man and deliver it to the charmers so that barrenness be removed from her, then she and the youth, and if she bear any children they also, shall be accursed. The young man will be seized by the lukim which feasts on the hearts of men, and the woman by those which tear open the bowels".

"It is an abomination in the sight of the God of Gods for men to deball themselves, and all who do shall be accursed. Those who would deball themselves for the sake of their god may instead make an offering of their foreskin, and this will be acceptable by any god. The prayer of thankfulness that they are not born women shall be made at the time of sacrifice upon the altar".

"The excreta of man and woman shall never be left exposed to the eyes of anyone, nor in a place where its smell can come to the nostrils. Nor shall anyone pass water where another can smell it, for they whose nostrils the smell enters thereby gain power over the other. The smell from human waste draws up the formless lambata which afflict men and women at night and turn their bowels to water".

"No offering of meat shall be eaten raw. It shall be roasted before a fire and the bones pounded into flour and eaten with meal. If the offering be consumed within a dwelling place, then the blood which has been spared must be smeared upon the door posts, so that the dark shades of the night haunters and the death bringers be repulsed by the power of life".

"It is the duty of a son to provide sustenance for a Departed One who was his mother or his father, and he shall not neglect his brother or his sister or any of his kinsfolk who lack children. If he be neglectful of his duty he shall not escape molestation by the earthshades of the Departed Ones, which will wander relentlessly until satisfied. If Formless Ones be called forth by neglect so that they reach stability on Earth, they ll haunt the dark watches of the night and suck life-filled blood to sustain their awful forms. No man may keep them from his dwelling, for they will slide in stealthily even as snakes".

"It is wrong for charmers to call forth Dark Spirits. Any charmer so doing within the borders of the enlightened land shall be accursed, so he be seized by the nightfiend. If such be done, and the Dark Spirits wander out of control, then one of the Twice Born shall be called upon to return them to their dark abode". "It is not sufficient for men to shun the ways of wickedness, for unless the Lord of the Body be clothed in brightness they who watch for him in the Land of the Dawning will wait in vain. Those who lack that which would bring them into the Place of Light will fall prey to the Lords of the Dark Places and be forever lost to those who love them".

"All those who are Awakeners of the Dead shall be accursed and delivered to the lukim of madness. If any of my people deal with them, then they too shall be accursed so that they become prey to the terrors of the night. It is futile to consult the Departed Ones, for what can they do but advise on matters of little import? If they have anything of importance to impart they will come unbidden to men of understanding and made it known".

When Yosira came with his sons and those with them into the true land of Tamuera, he strove with the people of Kantiyamtu who followed the ways of wickedness and ignorance. He remained among the people of Tamerua during the days of Gabu, dwelling at the place where now stands the Temple of the Skyseer, in an abode of reeds, by the moving waters. In those days the people of Earth united themselves with those who were in the land of Morning Light by the powers within the body of a womanchild, seeking in this manner to preserve the hokew of their kindred.

When Yosira saw the wickedness of the custom he placed a great curse upon all the land and upon those who split the body of a womanchild, so that her flesh cried out from within them. Therefore, the land became stricken with a great plague. Since then never has anyone in the enlightened lands eaten the flesh of man or woman, and no womanchild is violated in the great wickedness of ignorance. The people of Tamuera greatly feared the curse of Yosira.

Yosira taught the people that the power of hokew resided not in the flesh of the body but in the bones, and that each bone contained the essence of all the being, man and woman. Then the people began to seek union with the Departed Ones in the land of the Morning Light, by the power of the bones, and Yosira forbade this not, though he knew it was futile. But where there was healing in the bones and they were able to draw it forth, Yosira was not displeased, for all things pertaining to the good of the people were well in his sight. Nevertheless, he forbade to women the burden of the bones of their husbands, and since then no shades has risen to molest them. This was because of the protecting power which he drew forth to fill all the land, it relieved the women of their burden, raising it from their backs.

All the charmers who brought forth shades from the Land of Dawning and all the Questioners of the Dead and the Awakeners of the Dead were cursed, and this curse hovers over the land even to this day. Yet there are still some who seek to call forth a shade from the swathed body made eternal, but all they raise up is an ill-omened messenger from the Place of Darkness.

Yosira did not forbid to the people the rites of homage due to their departed kinsfolk, for in the Place of Morning Light these were the powers most interested in the welfare of any mortal man. Yosira never forbade anything that was to the benefit of men, taking away nought but the things which were futile or harmful. In those days there were no rites of written record, but Yosira caused them to be given to the people. Not so that these should renew life in the Departed Ones upon Earth, but so that the Lord of the Body should be sustained and strengthened in the Place of the Morning Light by the link of hokew, sacrificed by those remaining on Earth.

Yosira spoke to the people, giving them laws which were recorded in this manner: 'These are words of the God of Gods Who created man and beast upon the sacred island. No beast shall be mated with another not of its kind, and if this happen, then both shall be slain and their bodies burnt. If this be done with the permission of a man, that man will be accursed. Neither shall any beast be yoked together with another not of its own kind. During the first year of its life no beast shall be made to take up the burden of man".

When Yosira came to Kambusis he found there a man of the Hestabwis bound and prepared for sacrifice, and he cried out against the deed but none gave ear to his word. So, standing off, Yosira placed a staff of power upright into the ground and danced around it, singing the song for drawing forth the spirit. When they saw this, the people were wroth against him and called upon their charmers to curse him so he departed from the Earth. Their curses were ineffective and when one charmer approached the dance ring of Yosira, Yosira called forth a tongue of flame which consumed the charmer. Then the people became afraid and fled. So Yosira released the man who was bound upon the place of sacrifice, but he was not yet whole.

Yosira also cursed all those who offered the Hestabwis as a sacrifice to their gods; since that day no man of the Hestabwis was ever slain upon the altars. Yosira did not curse the charmers of that place, instead he called them to him and gave them dominion over the Dark Spirits which left their abode to wander Earth, molesting men in their habitation.

Thus the charmers became greater in the eyes of the people, and from that day onward they have cleansed the land of all Dark Spirits. However, Yosira forbade them the calling forth of the Lord of the Body from any man so that he became the servant of another, and he placed a great curse upon any charmer who disobeyed this law. Yet this is done even now, but those who transgress the laws of Yosira do not escape the awful fate due to them, for his power is yet potent in the lands of his people. When the transgressors stand before him in awful judgement, their deeds will witness against them.

Yosira forbade those who sat in judgement the right to judge men by the fat of crocodiles or by the horn or skin. Instead he revealed to them the manner of making judgement through corn and by the burning sword. He also taught them how to brew drink which loosened the bonds from the tongues of men, so that Truth was no longer restrained. The people dwelling among the trees, along the banks of the moving waters, lived in fear of tree apes. They held these sacred and would never harm them. They believed that these tree apes snatched the departing Lord of the Body and ate it, that they lurked in wait to catch it in a mighty unseen net. So Yosira went about cursing the food reserve for the tree apes so that it became fire in their bellies, causing the life within them to come up as foam out of their mouths. Thus the land was freed from fear of the tree apes, and henceforth the Departed Ones have gone in peace, no longer being molested by the tree apes.

THE WAY OF YOSIRA

Yosira taught that within each man resides a little man who is the Lord of the Body, and this is the life of men. While man sleeps the little man wanders abroad to journey as it will, at death departing from him forever. The Lord of the Body cannot be seen by mortal eyes, but it is not hidden from all seeing eyes of the Twice Born. When departing at death it comes out from the mortal mouth, waiting awhile until it grows celestial wings. Then it flies away to the Western Kingdom where the wings are shed. In the place whither it journeys the Lord of the Body needs no earth-made abode, therefore burning the earthly habitations of a Departed One is futile. However, if the habitation remains and it is not purified, it becomes the gathering place for shades arising from the Place of Darkness, for the habitation need not be destroyed, it must be purified by incense and water and refilled with protective hokew.

If a man come upon another asleep, the sleeper must be awakened quietly and with gentleness, so the Lord of the Body may re-enter peacefully. For if the sleeper be awakened before it has re-entered, or if it jump back in fright, then the man will become sick. Therefore, when awakening a sleeper it is well to call gently to the being without. When the mortal body becomes sickened without the heat of the lukim being present, or if the man or woman be seized and tormented by the Dark Spirits of madness, this may be caused by the daysleeping of the Lord of the Body.

Thus, if the Lord of the Body be awakened from its daysleeping, or restored from its restlessness, then the man or woman may be cured. These things Yosira permitted to be done after the fashion of charmers. Yosira taught the curing of many kinds of ills within the mortal body and the use of draughts containing the life of herbs and growing things. He used fire to stop life leaving the mortal body. The manner of effecting these things is written in the Book of Medications.

When Yosira came with his sons into the land of Tamuera, the people there dwelt in darkness and they were ignorant of all knowledge. They were divided among themselves into many kindreds, and strife was frequent. They had no kings and only the old men ruled. There were many charmers who ruled the people by delusions and also those called the Keepers of Customs and the Teller of Tales.

One people dwelt among great trees and thick forests in the midst of swamplands. Their habitations were made of reeds and stood upon high platforms. These people were called the Children of Panheta, for he was their god in the days following those during which men were first created in the midst of the waters. Another people dwelt beyond reach of the waters and away from the trees, and they were nameless. They dug holes for their habitations or sought abodes in caves within
the hillsides.

This people had no gods but worshipped the Dark Spirits and the Kamawam of the forest which seized men at night. When the men who had been seized returned to their kindred, they were without words, being dumb. They died in the midst of madness, tearing at their bodies. But there was no Kamawam in the forest, this madness being the work of charmers wishing to instil fear into the hearts of men. This is the manner in which it was brought about: When the charmers seized men at night they took them to a secret place where their tongues were pierced well back with thin thorns. Thus the tongue swelled up, so they whose tongues were so pierced lost the power of speech. The charmers also pierced the victims about the waist with slivers of wood, so none could discover where they were inserted. They drove other splinters into them at the bridge between the private parts and the rear channel, and none could discover them there and know the victim was pierced with thorns and splinters.

Yosira cursed all the charmers who practised this evil with a great curse, so they were driven to madness by a demon which ate away their bellies. Since then the Kamawam has been known no more in the land. Yosira taught men to beat metal out of stones and to burn stones, so that they gave up their heart. He taught men to work with clay and he taught them the weaving of cloth and the making of beer. When Yosira came into the land, the people knew nought about the cutting of water channels and the sowing of corn, but Yosira taught them these things. It was he who brought fertility to the land; it was he who died in the midst of the waters to give them life, and his life is in them still. Therefore, it was through the Spirit of the Great One who died in the days of old that the soil became fruitful. Beyond the reach of the living waters which rise and fall like the chest of a breathing man, the land is dead. It remains barren like a woman who has not known a man.

It was known even to the men of old that if the land was not refreshed with the living waters but with other waters, then its increase would diminish from year to year until it became waste. The increase within the soil comes not from water alone but from the life within the water. Life comes forth from life, and that which has not life cannot beget life. Therefore, the good land is that which is married to the threefold god, and land not so married remains barren. The married land is covered with the rising waters, but the land not married is ignored by them. These things were written concerning The Children of Panheta: Yosira spoke with Panheta as man speaks to man, therefore the laws of the Inta were not changed, remaining to bind alike those of them who dwelt on the soil or dwelt on the sand. If any man went among the Inta their laws became his laws and if any woman left the people to dwell among the Inta she became even as they and might not return. Even as the Sunspirit journeys on a road set between the stars, so does the spirit of man journey with the movement of the waters. Therefore, when a man dies his body shall be buried lengthwise with the great river. Even as the land upon which things grow belongs to the kindred whose blood is within it, so shall no man own to himself alone anything growing up from it, whether it be grass or herb or tree.

But each man and woman may take of every herb and fruit as much as can be gathered in the hands and eaten before sunsetting. Of all things which are a seed and can be eaten, each one may gather for themselves as much as can be stored within a jar or suspended from the foodpole. All things which are a seed and can be eaten but which are not stored in a jar or suspended from a foodpole, shall be stored in the pit of the kindred. Nothing shall be placed within the pit unless it has been heated by fire and cooled.
Even as the Spirit of Life resides in the things which men eat, so does it reside in the living things from whence they came. Therefore, any tree or bush bearing the food of men shall not be cut or broken. The blood of beasts cries from the soil even as does the blood of men; therefore, if shed it must be appeased. Slay no beast unless it be needed for food, and bury the head and whatever comes out of its belly. Every other part which is taken shall be eaten or burned, except for the bones and the skin which are to be used.

Fire serves man, but it can also become his master. Consider its nature. Does it spring out of the wood unbidden or of its own volition, or does it require the agency of man? Does it reside in the wood or is there a firespirit? Only the fools among men start something which they cannot control. Never let a fire grow into a thing of much smoke, keep it bright, using no more wood than is needful for the purpose. Let it not stray from its proper place, which is the place where it serves without menace.

When they become of an age to do so every man and woman should take themselves a mate. Those who fail to do so are not held in the highest esteem. By the things whereby a man commits a wrong, so shall he be punished. Likewise, he shall be dealt with according to the nature of the wrong. The customs from times past are not unhelpful guides. When Yosira came to the place where the Inta dwelt they made him welcome in this manner, "When we saw you our hearts were gladdened. The life was renewed in us and though content as we were you brought refreshment and joy". Yosira called these people his unweaned children.

THE TRIBULATIONS OF YOSIRA

These things were written in the Book of the Two Roads: Yosira, whois therein called Yoshira, came from beyond the Realm of Athor and was the first king of Tehamut. He established the festivals of the new moon, the festival of wool drawing and the days of devotion. When first he brightened this land by his presence, the welfare of its people was in the hands of false priests who taught that man was a double-spirited being in whom the Spirit of Good struggled with the Spirit of Evil for possession of his soul. Each deed and thought was said to strengthen one or other of the opponents. The people were not completely deceived in accepting this, it is perhaps an earthly distortion of reflected Truth, but neither is it wholly true. In the days of old, men saw Truth but dimly, for it could be only partially revealed in accordance with their ability to understand it. Truth is a light growing even brighter in the darkness of man's ignorance, and as the generations pass and go down into dust, men see more clearly. Each lightbearer dispels a little more darkness, and Yosira was a lightbearer, the greatest of them all.

Before Yosira came, bearing the lamp of brilliant light, Truth was but dimly perceived in this land. The false priests of those days taught that when the Great God created man He held back immortality as a special gift for those whom he favoured. This is not the attitude of One Who is Great, and therefore such doctrine cannot be accepted. That these priests were misled themselves was not so great an evil as their misleading of others who trusted them. A true priest should approach as close as possible to the shrine of Truth and interpret whatever he sees there as clearly as his ability and the understanding of his followers permit. In those olden days no man had yet been reborn to wisdom and enlightenment. Therefore, nothing was known about the Gardens of light, and men believed in the Dark Abode alone. This Dark Abode was a place where sand and dust were the sustenance of the dead whose bodies were clothed in long hair and feathers. Men, in those olden days, knew little more than that. They also believed that souls risen to glory really consumed the food and wore the garments and ornaments provided for their use.

They did not know, as we do, that as the soul is subtle itself so can it use nought but the subtle elements of earthly things. Even now incense is burned before the statues of those risen to glory, so that they may receive their portion. There are those who believe that the sustenance of the soul, and its continued life, depends upon the monthly communion sacrifice of its kinsmen on Earth. As a man who walks with a lamp at night is attacked by those who lurk in the darkness, so are enlighteners who seek to bring light into the gloom of ignorance attacked by those whom it would reveal in their true likeness. Thus, when Yosira cried out against those who, while not permitting the slaying of men and women in their daily lives, nevertheless allowed a child to be slain as sacrifice, or buried beneath the pillars they raised up, he was condemned as an enemy of the gods.

When Yosira was in the land far up the River of life, one named Azulah who stood close to the right hand of Yosira slew a man who was kindred to the

Leopard. This enraged the god of these people, for the slain man's blood cried out to him. Therefore, men of the Leopard came into the land of the East seeking to slay Azulah for his offence against their god, but he had withdrawn to a place of hiding. So when they found their search to be in vain the men of the Leopard returned to their place, informing their priests of their failure. The priests then held the rituals for calling down the war power, drawing it down in strength. Then, because Yosira was the overlord of Azulah, the men of the Leopard went forth against him, claiming the right of war. But in the night, when the hostile host waited before the camp of Yosira, the war priest defiled himself and so the war power failed to make faint the hearts of those with Yosira, the war priest having lost control over it.

Thus, the war power came into the hands of Yosira and he cast it back so it fell upon the Men of the Leopard, and their knees were loosened and their bowels went to water, and they fled from that place. The Men of the Leopard dwelt within the forests, towards the sunsetting side of the moving waters, and Yosira pursued them there. He did not enter the thick forest, but, coming to an island in the midst of the waters, he made camp there. He had a prisoner whom he released, sending him to the priests with this message, "Come in peace, that I may hear your complaint and judge whether it be just".
But the priests of the Men of the Leopard came down only to the edge of the waters and would go no further, and they called out across the waters, "What was just heretofore is just no longer, for this is now a matter to be settled between our kindred and those who are with you, for blood still cries out for blood".

Hearing this Yosira answered, "Let us be wise, there are judges above us, so let the God of the Moving Waters decide the matter". To diis the priests said, "It is well". Then Yosira took Azulah into a boat, rowing him through the waters against the South wind. Stopping the boat Yosira commanded Azulah to leap into the waters so he might be tested by swimming, and this Azulah did. He swam powerfully and the God of the Moving Waters did not take him, for Yosira had covered the waters with his power, so the waters bore up the swimmer, carrying him in safety to the shore. Then Yosira sat down with the chiefs of the Men of the Leopard and made a covenant with them and with other peoples likewise. This was that when a man slays another among his own kindred, none among them shall protect him, and he shall be either slain or cut off from those of his own blood. However, if the slain man be of a kindred different to that of the slayer, then the slayer may be slain by men of either kindred. If the kindred of the slayer would avoid the toll of blood, then they must send a token to the kindred of the slain man, together with an account of the deed. They must also agree that the blood be upon their own heads and revenge in their hands, and account of such revenge shall be sent to the kindred of the slain man together with their forfeiture.

Then all the kindred bound themselves with a great oath, declaring that if blood cried out from the ground in vain, then the night terrors and blood shades would be called upon to fall upon the kindred of the slayer and not upon the kindred of the slain. It was at the time when this covenant was made that Yosira spoke in this manner to his sons, "These are the meats which are accursed and shall not be eaten. All the meat of any beast which dies of itself. All the meat of any beast which has been slain as a sacrifice to the small gods. All the meat of any beast which has been slain by wild beasts and all meat which has been offered up on the door stones. These are unclean meats".
When Yosira had gone throughout the land and purified it, and bound up its wickedness with curses, he taught those who dwelt there the making of waterways. He also instructed them in the meanings of the heavenly signs. He built Piseti in the midst of the reedlands and drained the swamps. Then he raised up the first temple of brick and stone. At this time he established those who were recorders of the days and seasons.

While Yosira was at Piseti, the priests stirred up the people against him, and so he fled to the Land of God with his sons and blood kindred. But his wife and youngest son did not go with him, for they were with her father in the land from whence the great river flowed. This was the land of Kantoyamtu, where priests taught that death is not the normal lot of man. These priests said that though their forefathers of old were just as mortal as men, their forefather's fathers were heirs to immortality on Earth. This is an erroneous teaching, one belonging to the childhood of man, but later men were taught that death is just the departure of life which takes flight with the soul.

While Yosira was at Piseti, his true son, Manindu, commanded the Mesiti who were a host of men and workers in brass. They subdued the whole land, returning it to Yosira. Later it was delivered into the hands of Manindu whose seal is on it even yet. After the time of Manindu the people forgot the God of Gods, for He appeared distant from them, and they worshipped other gods whom the priests devised. The light was dimmed and only poorly reflected in small hidden shrines.

THE VOICE OF GOD

(This is a modernised, revised version of a difficult to understand original and it probably contains some interpolated material). The Voice of God came out of the Heavens unto His servants even before the days of Wunis, but in these days it has come to certain of His Devoted Ones who heard it within the cavern of visions. Afterwards, each wrote it down according to his own hearing, and lo, when they came together it was seen that each had recorded the same words. Thus, the things which were heard by the three and set down by them in writing, all being agreed alike are things recorded forever.

"I am the Voice of God Who is the God of All Men and Ruler of their Hearts. I have many aspects and come differently to all men, I am the God of Many Faces. To you, My servants, I give these words, that they may be carried to all men. Obey My commands and I will be Your God. I will enlighten and instruct you, guiding you along the way. I desire your love and loyalty, and your adherence to My plans, but I do not desire your servility. I am not only your God but your Commander as well, and so I expect obedience and discipline, as befits those who prepare for harsh and grim battles such as those which lie ahead".

"My desire is for love rather than futile sacrifices of burnt offerings, but it should not be a passive love but one expressing service in My Cause. A certain knowledge of right and wrong, with free choice of the former, is of greater value in My sight than pointless ritualistic worship. I derive no pleasure from the wasteful shedding of blood from bulls and lambs. I gain nothing from the fat of sheep and the flesh of goats. I am the Creator of All, so what can men give that would increase My greatness? Men are misled if they believe that their sins can be purged by vain rituals. Only active goodness can obliterate the stain of sin".

"Men approach Me in fear, they come to me with servility. They beg forgiveness for their sins and request My help in worldly matters. To sing My praises is their excuse for coming into places made sacred unto Me, but they come wanting something, be it only reassurance. With this attitude towards Me, do you wonder that I remain mute before their pleas? Bring Me no more vain offerings of flesh and blood, for such wastefulness of life is an offence to the God of Life. What benefit do I derive from all your feasts or festivals? Give me dedication and effort, that is all I ask. Above all be true to yourselves, for I abhor the face of hypocrisy, the face now all too familiar when men approach Me".

"Men bring Me meat and wine, fine flour and wheaten cakes, thinking I can consume these, or that I have need of such sustenance. I would be far better served were these to be given to the widow and orphan, to the multitudinous poor whom you suffer to exist in your midst. Poverty is man-made and it is not sufficient for the wealthy to give alms to the poor; those with power and position, with wealth and plenty must strike at the roots of poverty. If they fail to do this, then the alms they give have no merit in My sight".

"Your solemn assemblies, your tedious processions, your long faces and melancholy expressions bring no gladness to My heart. Your burdensome ceremonials and futile offerings of life and food benefit Me in no way at all. Men themselves may derive benefit from these, but their hypocrisy when they proclaim they do this in My name is not hidden from Me".

"The reek of your incense smoke rises and disappears into the air, but it comes not unto Me, nor do I have need of it. Yet I will not deny you the pleasure of its fragrance which can bring inner harmony and peace by soothing the spirits of men. Nor will I deny you your feasts, if the fetters of wickedness be thereby loosened from your souls, but do not say they are undertaken for My benefit or glorification. Fasting and the denial of bodily appetites may serve useful ends for men, but though you may deceive yourselves regarding their intent, do not try to deceive Me by mis-stating their purpose.
I have no desire to repress the joy and exuberance welling up in the hearts of men, far rather would I prefer that such humanising emotions be cultivated. Therefore, pray if prayer serves its true purpose, which is to harmonise your spirit with Mine so communication becomes possible. Keep your festivals and feasts if they serve their purpose, which is to inspire and refine your spirit. Do all that elevates your spirit and develops your souls, that is the true purpose of life. Do all that is good for you, nothing wholly beneficial is denied you, but do not declare that in so doing you confer benefit upon Me. I am the God Above and Beyond All".

"I do not deny you your rituals and ceremonials, worship Me if you will as you will, but bear in mind that this cannot substitute for your obligations. Ritual and worship cannot be an adjustment or payment for the things you have failed to do, or be an apology for your own shortcomings. Neither do they compensate for iniquities against your fellowmen. If you attach importance to ritual and ceremonial let it be in a proper proportion, and never let them dull your conscience against deeds of wickedness, of usury and injustice. Never let your duty and obligations be neglected because you worship Me diligently, following a formalised ritual and ceremonial. Let this not become an excuse for failing to share your bread with the hungry or for neglecting the needs of the destitute or weak. I am not deceived.

A life dedicated to Me is not one preoccupied with worship, that is more the life of a coward trembling before the unknown. He who dedicates bis life to Me gives shelter to the homeless and succours those in distress, but even these are not the ultimate in goodness, for they are passively accepted. The ultimate in goodness is to actively combat all the root causes of evil. Those who are my true followers live a life of service and goodness. They live in harmony with their neighbours, harm none and do not shirk the burdens and obligations of earthly existence". "I am better served by obedience to My laws and conformity with My plans than by ritual and offerings. To listen to the words of the Sacred Writings while striving to understand them is better in My sight than offerings of flesh and treasure which benefit the priests more than they do Me.
Among the things which I abhor few are more detestable than the hypocritical offerings of the evildoer. The offerings and worship of a hypocrite are an abomination to Me. Evil enters the realm beyond Earth as a foul smell, and the worse one of all is the smell of hypocrisy. Those who pander to hypocrites or do not actively oppose them are also creatures of evil".

"I know too well the deceit to which men are prone. The adulterer and fornicator preach chastity for others, while the liar declares the virtues of Truth. The thief preaches honesty and the lewd-minded professes modesty. Men say one thing and mean another, while all too often the half or slanted truth replaces the real thing. Men may deceive themselves and other men, but I am not deceived. Now I say, let men first cleanse their own souls and eradicate hypocrisy before presuming to approach Me. Men may well cry out, "Why does God remain mute, why has He deserted Me? " Do they think their deeds are hidden or that I cannot read the secrets of their hearts?"

"Worship by men of iniquity is mere mockery. How rare the sincere and genuine heart! Were men indeed deserted by their God, they would have none to blame but themselves. Do men think their lack of kindness and consideration for others, their insincerity and inconsistency are truly hidden from Me? I am the All Knowing One. I see too little love of goodness in the hearts of men and too much fear for the consequences of their deeds".

"Real and sincere worship is to obey My laws and to shoulder the responsibilities of men, to steadfastly conform to My plan and to live in neighbourly harmony. He who devotes his life to Me also devotes it t his own welfare. He who serves Me well likewise serves himself. This is the Law of Laws. For the whole purpose of life is not the service of God but the development of the soul of man. He who worships Me with empty ritual and vain ceremonial but neglects the wellbeing of his own soul, does not serve Me well, for he thwarts My purpose. I have endowed the creature made in My likeness with a religious instinct, for this springs from its everlasting spirit, as fire generates heat; therefore, to worship is not unnatural.
But blind worship lacks the vitalising element, it defeats its own end, for in true worship man should reach out beyond himself to discover his own soul. Then, having done so, he should develop it until the soul aspires to godhood itself". "Therefore, dedicate all your labours and the skill of your hands unto Me, and let your heart ever dwell on the borders of the spiritual. Let the life which you cherish be the spiritlife. Free yourself from all vain hopes and selfish thoughts; from all worthless encumbrances; from ungainful avarice and unbeneficial lusts; from the domination of the flesh. life is not easy, nor is it wholly pleasant; it is not meant to be, but bear your burdens with cheerfulness and fortitude. Entrench yourself within an inner fortress of peace".

"Whatever you do or give, do or give in My name, and whatsoever sufferings descend upon you, suffer them for Me. Thus, you will avoid the stigma of false pride and all given and suffered will be without any taint of selfinterest".

"The path of godliness is not an easy one to follow, for it is beset with the pitfalls of perplexity and doubt. Then, too, there is not one path but several, and few among men know which is the best. There are many false paths leading nowhere, there are paths that lead to a wilderness of disillusion and some which lead to destruction. Yet among the many beliefs springing up from time to rime in various lands, there are always those which lead to the same Truth, to the one Fountainhead of Light, though some may be devious and some wander through dangerous territory. They are like many roads leading pilgrims to the one shrine. Though all true paths are lit by the guiding light of Truth, not all see it alike; but the fault lies not so much in the light as in the beholder. It is this which leads to misunderstandings concerning each other's teachings and to disputes between those who prefer one road and those preferring another. Each considers his own way, his own interpretation of the light to be the best, if not the only, way".

'There are few, even among truly enlightened men, who are able to conceive My true nature, and these know that I am even above unchangeability in manifestation. I can think of Myself as some other and forthwith that other comes into being.

There are those among men who declare all life, all My creation to be an illusion of the senses, a dream without sustenance. They are in error, for all that is real and all that exists was ever latent, awaiting the awakening kiss. Because men cannot know reality as it actually is but only as they can conceive it to be with their deceptive sense, does not make it any less real. If all men were blind, the stars would still exist".

"Neither reality nor Truth, nor the God Who is beyond and above both will be inconceivable to the minds of the ultimate man. Only man in his present undeveloped state and in his ignorance cannot conceive such things and therefore, because in his blindness they are beyond his sight, he says they do not exist". "In the beginning I established the Law, without which the souls of men could not develop and progress. As each soul is itself a divine fragment, with all the powers of divinity latent within itself, it can modify all but the Great Law. Man thinks but his thoughts alone do not create, for, as yet, he lacks knowledge of the power which creates in substance. First I created the firmament, which is the matrix of all; then when I took thought the creative power flowed outward and, operating upon the medium, brought into being things of substance".

"My creation arose before Me as light does before a flame or heat before a fire. It came and still comes into being because I exist, it is because I Am. Creation in no way affects Me any more than a man is affected by his shadow, or light by its reflection. As raindrops, waves, rivers, dew and mist are all forms of water, so is everything existing and knowable by man but various forms of the one substance. This substance has its origin in Me, but it is not Me".

"I am the source of all things, supporting but not being supported by them. Even as the mighty winds which sweep across the Earth find their rest in the tranquil vastness above, so all beings and all things have their rest in Me. It is a power outflowing from Me which holds all things in stability and form".
'They who devote their lives to My service must do more than love and worship Me, for such service entails the elevation of mankind, the spreading of good and the combating of evil.
They must not only fight against the ungodly, but also overcome the wickedness welling up in their own thoughts. They who love Me desire the wellbeing of all men, and their souls are filled with harmony and peace. Dearer to Me than their love for Me is the labour and tribulations of those who serve Me. I am their end. I am never the God of Inertia but the God of Effort; if you offer no more than deeds done in My service or in conformity with My design, then you serve Me adequately".

"However, too rarely do the ways of men conform to My plan and the ranks of those who serve are too thin. Therefore, I shall call forth leaders from among men and send out the clarion cry to service. I shall seek out men who will serve Me diligently and loyally. They will be men of goodwill who are of a friendly nature. They will be kind and compassionate, men who can love deeply and truly, whose steadfastness is the same in pleasure and affliction; whose resolve remains equally unbroken in the sweet embrace of good fortune as under the harsh blows of misfortune. I will send men who are fair and just, proud and resolute, but these qualities mean nothing unless they also have courage and resolution, fortitude and tenacity".

"I shall seek the man who is himself ever seeking, who seeks to unravel the riddle of life. One whose determination is strong, who detests wickedness and delights in the good; whose heart and inner vision reach out for enlightenment. His tranquillity will remain unshaken under stress and within his heart will be a haven of peace beyond the reach of excitement and anger. He will be a lover of wisdom and seeker of truth. He who is wise, he who knows what to do, who remains calm when others lose their self-control; he who is clearheaded under stress, who enjoys the challenge of the task, that man is Mine, He who labours uncomplainingly, who disdains to satisfy deforming lusts, whose spirit remains the same under the temptations of honours or the pressure of disgrace; he who is free from the shackles of unworthy earthly attachments, who retains his balance under praise or blame, who can shoulder his own burdens, whose spirit is calm, silent and strong under all circumstances; he who can bear the responsibilities of life and the obligations of love, that man is Mine. I am the God of Inspiration, I am the God of Love".

"I am the Knower and you are the known. I am the Source of Life. In the vastness of My nature I place the seed of things to be, from which come forth all things that are now or ever will exist".

"Men must nourish their spirit and sustain it with spiritual fare. They must also learn that the spirit is not something seperate from man, or something within him. Man is spirit, man is soul. There is no need to engage in long-winded empty discussions about far away things lying beyond the reach and understanding of men. To know the reality of the spirit and to establish the existence of the soul, man has only to delve within his nature, to seek within himself. The spiritual part of man is not a mysterious something outside his being, or a thing difficult to understand. To discover it requires no more than the effort of seeking".

"Men with sincere hearts, seeking a path ask for a starting point. However, for most the key is self-discipline, and this is the reason for many laws and restrictions. But these must never be unnecessarily restrictive, each must have a definite purpose and beneficial end, obscure though these may be. The means for overcoming unwholesome desires and for harmonising with the divine chord he within the reach of all, but effort must be expended in their cultivation. If the end is great beyond man's conception, it is no less true that the task before man is arduous and difficult in the extreme. To master himself and gain complete self-control is no more than the first step along the path".

"Though men may despair because I am veiled from them, though they may seek without finding, I am not indifferent to their needs and desires. Doubt and uncertainty are essential earthly conditions serving a definite end. I have not surrounded men with perplexities and obscurities unnecessarily. The climate of unbelief and materialism, strange though it may seem to men, is best for their spiritual health. I know better than men themselves what is best for them, for I alone can see the broad design spread over the ages, I alone see the end and objective. Though unenlightened men expect it, it is not meet for Me to interfere unduly in the affairs of Earth".

"All things are Mine and under My dominion, but man may deal with them as he will. I do not interfere, but finally man is accountable. Though I have all and nothing can add to My grandeur, with all this I still labour. Therefore, man should never disdain to labour, for this is an attribute of the Highest. I do not require of any man that he do something I would not do, or be something I would not be, I am the God of Righteousness. If ever I ceased to labour, the universe would be without order, chaos would prevail and precede its destruction".

"I am the God of Many Aspects, for men may conceive Me in any form they wish, or even as something without form. I am the God of Men's Hearts. In whichever way and by whatever name men serve Me, abiding by My laws and conforming with the Great Design, is right in My eyes. Any path which will bring man to his goal is the right road. Truly the paths chosen by men are many and varied, some are even devious, but if they be true paths of enlightenment and development, they are acceptable in My sight. However, those who lust for earthly power, offering sacrifice and worship to earthly gods conceived to accord with their desires, are not acceptable to Me. It is true that earthly success and power may come to those who strive for them, but do they achieve anything more than fleeting satisfaction? What manner of being would now dominate Earth, had all men been without divine enlightenment from the beginning, if earthly ends alone had dominated men's minds? Consider what earthly life would have been like, had it been left to develop predominated by materialism, if it had not been mitigated by injections of the divine".

"There are four main types of men who are good and serve Me well. They are those who suffer courageously the afflictions and sorrows which develop the soul. Those who labour, that Earth and man may benefit. Those who seek after Truth and those with vision and creativity. Yet how rare are those among these who do not besmirch their record with deeds of evil and thoughts of wickedness. All too many may have, by their carnal desires and acts of wickedness, countered their goodness to the detriment of their immortal souls".

"If a man follow a false god with goodwill and honesty, serving men well and living in accordance with My laws, I will not repudiate him and he will not be denied enlightenment on the way. There are many roads along which the soul may travel to bring about its development and awakening to self-consciousness, but is it not advantageous to choose the best one? Only the foolish travel blindly, without seeking guidance and directions. Those who have little wisdom or who are easily misled follow roads which go nowhere. They who follow a barren faith reach a barren destination, they find only an empty place devoid of hope, incapable of fulfilling their dreams and aspirations".

"Those who worship gods of their imagination, gods in strange likenesses, which have been brought into being by man's creative conceptions, will go to these gods who have an existence in a dim shadow realm. Those who worship lower spirits will go to them and those who worship the demons of darkness will join them, for what a man desires he deserves. There is a link between that which men desire and what becomes established in existence. Provision is made for man to receive the fruits of his own creations".

"Whatsoever you do, whatsoever you plan or create, whatsoever you suffer, let it be an offering unto Me, not for My sake but for yours. I am the God of

Compassion, the God of Understanding. From those who in their devotion offer Me but a single leaf, a flower or fruit, or even a little water, this I will gladly accept, thus lightening their loving spirit, for it is offered in sincerity of heart. He who comes before any god, whatsoever its image, with pureness of heart and good motives, comes unto Me, for I gaze upon him with compassion and understanding. I am not concerned with the deeds alone of men, but with their motives. Empty gestures are ignored, but that which is done with good intent and a loving heart never goes unheeded".

"I am the Hidden God, hidden to serve an end. Veiled in mystery, I am further obscured by the mists of mortal delusion. Unable to see me, men declare I do not exist, yet I declare to you that man, with his mortal limitations, sees only a minute part of the whole. Man is the slave of illusion and deception.
Though man is born to delusion, for it is a needful state, he is further inflicted by deceptions wrought by men. Though man cannot perceive the greatness above him, because of its greatness, neither can he see the smallness beneath him, because of its smallness. From the greatest came the smallest and from the smallest came creation, and within the smallest is greatness and power. For the smallest is far less than the mote, yet it is the upholder of the universe and it shines like the sun beyond the darkness. It lies out towards the edge of the reach of man's thought. In the beginning all things arose from the invisible and into the invisible all things will disappear in the end, but the end is not the end of the spirit. Out beyond this material creation born of the invisible, there is a higher eternal invisible of greater substance.

When all material things have passed away, this will remain. Above all is timelessness, which is eternity, and there is My abode, the supreme goal of man, and those who attain it dwell in eternity. I am the Eternal God". "Few are they who can conceive of Me as I really am, the Unborn and Uncreated, Beginningless and Without End, Lord of All the Spheres. Those few who can conceive Me as I am are awakened spirits freed from mortal delusions. As thick clouds of smoke rise up and spread out from a fire burning in damp wood, so did the material universe come forth from Me. As a lump of salt dropped into a pool of water dissolves and cannot be removed afterwards, yet from whatever part of the water you draw there is salt, so it is with My pervading Spirit.

I am the Great Luminary, the everlasting source of light sparks, which, imprisoned in matter, become the slumbering souls of men. These, unconsciously guided, spread out the five senses under the control of unconscious thought. That which the senses harvest departs with the spirit. It is borne away by the spirit, even as perfume is carried by the wind. I am the Boundless One, The One Beyond Limitations. I remain free and unencumbered by the effort of creation. I Am and I watch life unfold. I set the course which nature follows to bring forth all that lives". "The fools on Earth, who shut their eyes and complain because they stumble, the ignorant who choose to walk in darkness and the apathetic who choose paths of ease and comfort, have no knowledge of Me. Their hopes are sterile.

Theirs the choice of darkness, theirs the choice of ignorance, theirs the choice of apathetic inertia. Their learning is futile, their thoughts fruitless and their deeds without purpose. Though man is born in ignorance and darkness, he is also heir to the guiding light which dispels them. The light is his for the taking. Then there are the awakened souls among men, their sustenance is My own nature. They know My Spirit is among men as an everlasting source of strength and refreshment to the weary and disheartened. They are in harmony with My Spirit and therefore know Me". "Men call Me the God of Battles, which I am not, for good men fight each other when kings declare war.

Men call Me many things, but this does not make Me become what they think I am. I am the hidden power which ultimately rights all wrongs, which will eventually redress all injustices. I come to all who are worthy, but it is the lonely, the unwanted, the undesirable whom I seek. To Me, the dispirited, the perplexed, the sorrowful and humiliated soul is an irresistible magnet. I am the welcoming light at the end of the road, the companion who watches in compassionate silence, the understanding friend, the ever ready arm. I am He Who presides over the haven of peace within your heart".

"To those who unite their spirit with Mine and to those who are in harmony but not united, I increase that which they have and provide what they lack. I turn a like countenance to all men. My love for them remains constant, but those who join Me in devotion to My cause are truly in Me and I am in them. This is My everlasting and unchanging promise unto me: He who walks with Me, serving My cause, shall not perish. So join your spirit with Mine, giving me your confidence and trust, and thus united in a harmonious relationship you will come to know the supreme goal. Men say they cannot know Me through their senses, and this is true, for I am above and beyond the reach of their finite senses. The senses of man are not meant to be the means for experiencing Me, they are for experiencing the material spheres. They are also limiting, shutting out far more man they reveal. Yet men have within mem a greater sense which can know Me, but it lies dormant in the mass of men. I am the Light Widiin the Heart, the Consciousness of All Living Things. I am the God of Consciousness, the Listener in the Silences".

"I do not manifest to man through his mortal senses, for these are bounded by earthly limitations. I manifest through the great sense which is of the spirit, the sense of the soul. As pure light hides many colours, so am I hidden in the hearts of men. As sparks fly from a bellows-blown fire, so from the Eternal Fire the life sparks fly out to glow for an instant in matter and then fall back. As the sun radiates heat, a flower perfume and a lamp light, so does the heart of man create his own spiritual state. The eye of man sees a pebble, a star, a sheep or a tree and these do not appear to him in anyway alike. Yet all are differing forms manifesting in the one outflowing force originating with Me. This outflowing force generated mat which gave birth to substance and endowed it with the matrix for form. The fragments of Divine Spirit interpret that which the Divine Spirit created, but they cannot know it in its reality, for, enshrouded in matter, they sleep. Because the material sphere is a separate part of the greater whole, the mortal part of man can never hope to know in full its boundless beauty, or experience its limitless bliss. Out beyond the limits of man's thought and conception, beyond reach of even the most vivid imagination, the wonder and glory of it all stretch out into absolute perfection. Even at the outer reaches where eternity begins the wonder of the inner glory remains veiled. No words of man can ever hope to describe the true nature of divine things, to the divine alone can the divine be known. The radiant living heart pulsating with love can never be known to man as man, but when man becomes more than man he may take his first glimpse behind the veil. I am the Inspiration and Goal of Man".

"Before creation I was the One Alone. I thought and the thought became a command of power, and into the void of the invisible came that which was the potential of substance, though itself then part of the invisible. light was born of the power and My Spirit was in the midst of the light, but it was not that light which lightens the day. A firmament became the foundation of all things, matter gradually forming there, becoming ever denser as it thrust outward from the invisible. It moved from a subtle state to something more solid, from intangibility to substance, from incoherent substance into a state of density and form.

I commanded the subtle substance, with light but without form, to mate with the subtle substance of darkness and become dense. It did so and became water. Then I spread water over the darkness below the light, placing a fountain of light about the waters. This brought forth the light of mortal vision, which is not the light of the spirit, nor the light of power. At that time the universe was made and then Earth received her form. It slept warmly in the midst of the waters, which were not the waters of Earth, and this was before the beginning of life in earthly substance. I am the God of Creation".

"At the foundations of My creations are Truth and Reality, these are with Me and of Me, but they are not My substance, neither are they things comprehensible on Earth. These are truly great things indescribable in the inadequate words of men, which can do no more than form an imperfect, incomplete and distorted picture of them; simple things can be described clearly in a few words to the understanding of man, but greater things become increasingly difficult to deal with through mere words. What words of man can be used to describe the indescribable? How can tilings beyond the comprehension of mortal men be brought within the limits of their understanding? Before the shadow there was the reflecting light, a light so bright that were it not veiled in the darkness it would consume the shadow. Seeking to explain and describe transcendental things in the limited language of man only leads to obscurity and confusion, the words form incomprehensible sentences and unthinking men will declare them to be incoherence. Therefore, look behind the sentences strung together with mere words. I am the Unknown God veiled from man by man's mortal limitations".

"The universe came into being and exist because I AM. It is My reflection in matter. As a man remains unaffected by the manifestations of his shadow, so do I remain unaffected by the material creation. As heat comes forth from fire and contains its essence and nature, though it is not fire, neither has it the substance of fire, so does My creation relate to Me. I am as an object reflected in water. The water may not know the reflection or find it within itself, but this inability has no effect on the reality of the object, nor on the fact of its reflection.

It is as a man looking into clear water on a calm day sees his reflection therein, but if the wind blows the image becomes distorted, and if the sun hides its face the image disappears. Yet none of these effects touches upon the image itself, nor upon that which casts the image. When the wind drops, the cloud vanishes and the sun reappears, both distortion and deception end, and the reality is again reflected. Within My creation is My Spirit, which supports it, and this Spirit is the bond between My creation and Myself. No man acknowledges the air because it is still, but when this same air becomes a whirlwind men give it their whole attention. With Me all is real, while with man all is illusion; but man may abandon his illusions in seeking Me, and he will thereby discover reality. I am the Realty Behind the Reflection, I am the Uncaused Cause".

"Those who turn away from the glorious jewel within to seek an outside god, a separate, unresponsive being, are looking for a mere trinket, while disregarding the priceless treasure already in their keeping. Men of light worship the vision of light, men of darkness and ignorance worship ghosts and dark spirits, demons of the night. There are men who, moved by dark beliefs or their carnal lusts and perverted passions, perform awful austerities and self-mutilations never ordained by Me. They delight in tormenting the life and spirit within their bodies. They are truly deluded victims of the darkest form of ignorance. Yet some derive pleasure from their pains and torments, and so continue them, but these may be truly described as mutilated souls. Some men follow gods who punish wickedness and reward good, and therefore tend towards goodness, but is it not folly to follow nonexistent gods? All men choose their own spiritual destiny, whether it be done knowingly or not, for under the Law their future state must rest in their own hands.

I am the God Who ordained the Law, and nothing man can do will change it. My love alone mitigates the consequences of man's unredeemed wickedness. I am the Changeless One. Could a God of Love become a God of Vengeance? Revenge is something alien to Me. Therefore, is it reasonable that men should believe I could be one thing today and then because they fall into error become something else tomorrow? My nature is not as that of man. I AM as I AM. "I am not influenced by the mere formal actions of men, or by empty sacrifice.

Lighted lamps and candles, days of fasting and self-mortification by man cannot sway Me in his favour. I am not to be bribed, for I am God. He who handles fire carelessly and gets burnt cannot blame the fire, neither can he who goes into swift waters and drowns blame the waters. There are laws, the violation of which brings retribution in its train. They who by their own deeds bring pain and suffering upon themselves cannot blame Me for what ensues. These are the effects of the lesser laws which are easily understood, but above these is the Great Law which is not so incomprehensible. Under this the link between the deed and its effect is not so apparent; men bring down calamity and suffering upon their own heads and blame Me, when the fault lies with them and the cause is their own misconduct or misconception. Men reap as they sow and I am the Fertile Field which takes no part in the sowing or the reaping. Man is his own master and the lord of his own destiny. He cannot expect help from any great power, unless he himself expend effort to contact such power or be deserving of help. Everything a man is or becomes is the result of his own striving and efforts, or his lack of them. I made man to be a man, not a mere puppet or nurseling.

I am the God of the Law. I am the God of the Stalwart". "Man is the heir to divinity, and the road to divinity is spirituality. Man cannot become spiritual except through his own efforts and striving. He cannot achieve it by being led by the hand or through fear of punishment, nor by greed through anticipation of a reward. He who enters into his heritage of divinity will be no weakling, he will have trodden a hard and stony path".

"Man has two ways of knowing Me. He can know Me through his own spiritual awakening or through the continued revelation of moral law and divine purpose by My inspired servants. To know Me through a spiritually awakened self is the way of certainty, but few can suffer its austerities and disciplines". "When the spirit of man is unawakened he cannot know the great self within him, of which he is a part. Not knowing his true nature and unable to see clearly, he is blinded by material delusions.

Would not the creatures of the night, which never see the sun, deem the moon to be the most brilliant light in the sky above? So it is with the man walking in the darkness of spiritual unconsciousness, He says, "I am the body and the body is my whole being", and in the delusion of that belief he becomes ensnared in an existence bound to matter. Like the creatures bound to an existence in the night, which cannot know the glories of things flourishing in the brilliance of daylight, so it is with men bound to the darkness of spiritual ignorance".

"As a shadow in the night is mistaken for an intruder, or a mirage is mistaken for a pool of clear water, so does the spiritually immature man mistake the material body for the whole living being. As the shimmering heat haze appears like solid water, so does the outer body appear as the whole being to the spiritually unawakened. As, to a man in a moving boat, another boat lying still on the water will often appear to be moving while he himself seems to remain still, so the unawakened spirit is deluded by appearances, seeing the mortal body as a whole being. When in fact the clouds are flying overhead, it appears as though the moon itself is speeding across the Heavens, it is only the knowledge and experience we have of the skies above, which tell us this cannot be the truth. Thus it is with the spiritually unawakened man who, in his ignorance, thinks the mortal body is the whole being, and, having no knowledge or experience of the spiritual region, is deceived. In fact all the beliefs of man which hold that the mortal body is the whole being are generated in the darkness of ignorance. A man may be wise in the ways of men, but completely ignorant and unaware of the higher, more glorious things which are revealed in the light of the spirit".

"The man held in bondage to delusion says, "If mere be another body, a part of me of which I am unaware, it cannot be real, neither can I know it. My eyes are infallible guides, seeing things just as they are, and any feelings I may experience have their origin within my mortal being. I am the child of my body". This man is deluded, like the creatures of the night, or as the man who sees a mirage. Are the eyes which see mirages totally reliable?

Motes swimming in the sunbeam are unsubstantial things, yet things such as these are the bricks of man's body, the eyes making them appear solid and substantial, the unreal for the real, his mortal body for his whole self. The deluded man ignores the spiritual part of his being and its needs. He cherishes the mortal body, gratifying its desires with earthly pleasures. Like the silkworm, he becomes captive in a cocoon of his own making. The man who lavishes undue care on the mortal body displays his own spiritual ignorance and inadequacy. To be free from existence in the darkness of ignorance, to know the glory of life in the light of spiritual consciousness, a man must first awaken his spirit, in this way alone can he become aware of his true nature".

"Ask yourselves, "What am I? What is real within myself? What comprises the whole man? Can it be that I am truly no more than this fleshy thing, the petty, immature, unstable being balanced between futile unearthly ideals and carnal cruelty and lust? Or am I something greater which is undiscoverable by mortal senses? Am I really akin to something divine and glorious from which source alone could have come the ideals and virtues which transcend the mundane needs of earthly existence? " Ask yourselves, in the solitudes, and perchance you will not go unanswered. I am the God of Silences".

"The words of men are inadequate to express just what man really is, the knowledge of his true nature is beyond the understanding of the unawakened spirit. The inheritance within the grasp of man is without limitation, for it is the totality of all things. Man has not been misled in the hope and belief that the seemingly mortal is in fact immortal. The spirit does not mislead men. They are deceived by their own eyes, they are misled, so they are unable to see things as they are in reality. All that men see and experience throughout earthly existence is veiled in illusion. Man may think his eyes reveal things as they are, but no mortal eye has ever beheld a thing as it actually is. It appears to man through the coloured distorting glass of his own mortality. Spiritually, men as a whole are little different from the madman who builds himself a kingdom from the fabric of his imagination.

The flowing life existence about him is seen as a distorted image, a distortion which his own defects have imparted to it. Yet it was meant to be thus, for man is surrounded by the conditions meet for him. It is for man to discover why this is so, and in discovering he will find himself. I am the Truth, I am the Reality".

"This earthly life, which I have given you, should not be viewed in its minute aspect but in the light of infinitude. All the suffering and disillusionment, the futility, the forlorn hopes and wasted efforts, the oppressions and injustices are not without a purpose. That purpose is beyond anything man can understand and infinitely greater than his conception can grasp. The truly awakened man, alone among men, can have any insight into life's end and goal".

"These are divine things, yet they can be set down only in the mere words of men and will thus be reduced to things of mortal frailty. Mere words will be read and the pattern formed by them will be far short of Truth and Reality. The taste of a fruit or the fragrance of a flower cannot be known by reading about them. The fruit must be eaten and the flower smelt. Only in union with Me, spirit communicating with Spirit, can proof of My reality be found. Yet, because things are as they are, Truth must ever be veiled from man as man. But who would labour, if labourers were paid whether they worked or not?

Were they revealed to him, the ignorant man would not comprehend great things, therefore the light is not for him.

The insincere and shallow seeker after diversion and pleasure will find little entertainment in these words. The really illuminated man will already know something of the Truth and will therefore seek it more diligently along a higher path. So these words are given just for those sincere seekers who are aware of their own shortcomings and ignorance. These will be people whose thoughts are not smothered by prejudice, who are not set in their opinions. For who among men is the most confirmed in his opinions? Who states things in the most assertive manner and talks with the loudest voice? Is it not the most ignorant? I will not let the sincere seeker go unguided. I am the Light on the Path".

"Well do I know the hearts of men, they ever seek to deceive themselves. They clearly see the errors and follies of others but are blind to their own. There are those whose idea of righteousness is mumbled words and repetitious prayers. Their souls are warped with selfish desires and their Heaven is the fulfilment of these. Their prayers are pleas for pleasure or power, for freedom from the things which develop the spirit. The lovers of pleasure and power delight in following the path of their own inclinations, they build a creed of their own desires. They have neither courage nor the will to follow a sterner and true path. Avoid the companionship of such as these, setting your heart upon the task in hand rather than the reward. I am the Knower, I am the Rewarder".

"If a man fixes his attention wholly upon one goal or one thing for his own selfish purpose, as if it were an independent, all unrelated to others, thing, then he moves in darkness of ignorance. If he undertakes a task with a confused mind, not considering the outcome or where it will lead him, or the harm it may do to others or himself, then it is an undertaking of evil. There is a wisdom which knows when to go and when to stay, when to speak and when to remain silent, what is to be done and what is to be left undone. It knows, too, the limitations set by fear and by courage, what constitutes bondage and what freedom. This is the wisdom I have placed at the disposal of man, if he would but seek it, the true wisdom of the spirit.

Opposed to this clear-sighted wisdom is the false, man-made wisdom obscured by the darkness arising from delusion. Here wrong is thought to be right and error passes as Truth, things are thought to be what they are not. The unenlightened men dwelling in comfortable darkness, unperturbed by the challenge of reality as revealed by the light of Truth, lack any understanding of true values. That which appears to them to be no more than a cup of sorrow is in fact a chalice filled with the wine of immortality. The vain pleasures that come from pandering to the carnal cravings of the senses appear at first to be a cup of sweetness, but in the end it is found to hold the brew of bitterness. He who does right does it not for Me but for himself; he is the one who benefits, not his God. He who does wrong inflicts himself for it, and he is the sufferer. He who does right does it to bis own good and he who works wickedness does it to his own hurt.
It could not be possible, in a just creation, that those whose ways are evil should be dealt with as are those who live godly lives and perform good deeds. The fate of the selfish and that of the unselfish could not be alike. I am the God of Justice, the Maker of the Law".

'The spirit of man has the. potential for doing all things, it can even rise above earthly limitations. The awakened soul can do whatsoever it wills. Man makes the
environment for his own development; as it is now, so countless wills from the past have fashioned it. When the body awakens in the morning, it is like a man entering his habitation, it becomes a place of awareness. The soul becomes active in matter, that with which you hear, taste, smell and feel is the soul. Physically, the ear of a dead man is still in perfect condition for hearing, but the hearer, the interpreter, has gone. The eyes of a corpse are not blinded, but that which operated them is no longer there".

"So long as the soul looks outward only, into the deceptive environment of matter and is satisfied with the material pleasures it finds there, and which its baser body finds compatible, it remains cut off from the greater realm of the spirit. It binds itself to matter, failing to find the greater pleasures always there in the silent depths of its being. Confirmed in his attitude by experiences in a deceptive environment, mortal man becomes convinced that all desirable things lie outside himself. He concludes that satisfaction comes from gaining the things which promote material welfare. This is the folly of the unbalanced man. However, balance is the keyword, for it is equally foolish to turn away from material things altogether. Man is made of earthly things, because it is intended that he should live and express himself on Earth. It is also intended that he should discover his nature through earthly conditions and experiences".

"However, the Divine Spark must kindle the spirit. It must not be smothered. Balance is the ideal, the whole becoming neither wholly inwardly nor outwardly oriented. Man needs his body and must not repudiate it, and if it requires man's labour to sustain it, then is not man entitled to enjoy its pleasures? Here also it is simply a matter of proper balance.

Man lives in a sea of material manifestation where I am only indirectly reflected, as the soul of man is indirectly reflected in his body. If a man sees with nothing but the eyes of the body, then he cannot perceive Me, for I am beyond his vision. I am the God veiled Behind Matter, I am the God of the Spirit".

"Yet there is a vision possible to man, which pierces the universal veil, a vision free from all obscurity, a vision uncontaminated by the dark shadows of base desires or fear, by unstable emotions or unworthy motives. It is the vision seen when man develops a new faculty, a new sense. It is an inward vision of splendour. A wave of spiritual light will engulf him, a mysterious power indescribable in mere words sweeps like a shooting star over the expanse of his spirit, giving a sudden illuminating flash which floods his whole inner being, his soul, with a glorious light. In its brilliance he is granted, for a brief moment in time, a glimpse of the vision splendid. He is then united with the living heart of the universe by a bond reaching out to infinity. Nothing known to man, no symbols of his conception can express the joyousness which floods his whole being. It can be experienced in quiet tranquillity of spirit. It can burst all the bounds of restraint, expressing itself in an all embracing, overwhelming feeling of love. Lost in an unfathomable sea of silent contemplation, the body will shine with radiance from the inner light, and all about will be bathed in a luminous spiritual glow.

Having once been in divine communication, these awakened spirits know a joy supreme, and never again do they walk through the veil of mortal sorrows. The truly awakened soul is beyond carnal lust and mortal grief, his love is alike for all My creation and thus he shows supreme love for Me. By this love alone he knows Me in Truth, Who and What I am, and knowing Me in Truth he participates in My Whole Being. Those who seek union with Me must first prepare a dwelling place for Me in their hearts; but those who are not pure, those who do not fight for Me, those who have not suffered under the discipline of love and those without wisdom cannot attain union, no matter how much they strive. I am the God of Illumination, I am the God of Enlightenment".

"Would you know the ultimate state of man when he has finally reached his goal, when he has entered into his inheritance of divinity? It is a state of glory transcending anything conceivable by him during an earthbound existence. His consciousness expands to embrace everything, all that ever was or will be. He sees all. He knows all. He is in all and he contains all. These things come to him through infinite powers of perception, yet he is above all such powers. He is beyond all yet within all. He is beyond the realm of matter, freed from all restrictions, yet he is not denied its joys and may, if he so desires, manifest again in matter. His thoughts have the power of creation. He is one with the Light of Lights, the Light transcending vision. He is the partaker of My Substance, My son in eternity, the inheritor of everlasting life. I am your God, the Father of Man".

THE SPIRIT OF GOD

"I am the immortality latent in all things mortal. The light filling all things with radiance, the power holding all things to their form. I am the pure, invulnerable stream untouchable by evil, the supreme fountain-head of thoughts, the unfailing well of consciousness, the light of eternity. I am that to which the soul of man is related. I am its power, its life, its strength. I am that to which it responds".

"I am the sweet coolness in refreshing waters and the comforting warmth in the sun. I am the calmness of peace in the radiance of the moon and the delicacy in the moonbeam. I am the sound heard in the stillness, the companionship felt in the solitude and the stirring in the hearts of men. I am the cheerfulness in the laugh of a youth and the gentleness in the sigh of a maiden. I am the joy in the life of all living things and the content in the hearts of awakened souls. I am the beauty in the beautiful and the fragrance in the fragrant. I am the sweetness in honey and the scent in perfume. I am the power in the strong arm and the wistfulness in a smile. I am the urge in good and moderate desires. I am the gaiety in gladness, the restlessness in life, the refreshment in sleep. Yet though I am in all these, I am not contained in them and they are in me rather than I am in them. How pitiful are the words of men to depict sublime things! With the souls of men asleep, enwrapped in clouds of delusion, how can I be known to them?"

"I am of the Supreme, the Eternal, of God and from God, yet not God. As heat to fire, as fragrance to flowers, as light to a lamp, so am I to God. I am the power of God operating in matter. I am the first created of creation, I am the eternal thread upon which all creation is strung. I am the effective thought of God. I am that brought forth by His creating command, wherein all things share life. I am the Lord of forms holding all things together". "I am the power giving form, I am the comforting companion of the way. I am that which gives substance to the hopes and desires of men. Think of me therefore in any way you will. I am the companionable one, the comforter. I am the waters of inspiration springing from the Eternal Fount. I am the glory of love shining forth from the Central Sun. I am in all things".

"I am the root of the tree of life, the words written in the Book of God. I am the guardian of knowledge, the wisdom of the soul. I am the harmoniser of sound, the controller of power, the keeper of matter and the sustainer of shapes. I unroll the scroll of time and record its changes. I am the reader of past and present, the scribe of change, the chooser of chance". "I am victory and the struggle for victory, but I am more, I am that which defeats defeat, for I am the victory in defeat. I am the goodness of those who are good, but I am more, for I am the success that arises out of failure. I am the achievement remaining when all else has gone".

"I am the sublime veiling secret mysteries. I am the guardian who jealously discloses hidden things. I am the knowledge of the knower. I am the seed within the seed from which all things spring. I am the bricks of which all things are built. I am more, I am the clay and water within the bricks. I am the motion in all things that move, without me there is no movement. I am the stability in all things stable, without me nothing holds to its shape".

"I am the craftsman with innumerable shapes, the artist with countless colours. My labours are outside the knowledge of men, my works beyond their sight. My masterpieces will never be seen by mortal eyes". "That which abides in breath and yet is other than breath, which breath itself cannot know or influence, which controls it from within itself, that am I. That which is behind the voice, which voice itself cannot know or influence, which controls it from behind itself, that am I. That which is in the eye yet is other than the eye, which the eye itself cannot know or influence, which controls it from within, that am I. That which is behind the touch and yet is other than touch, which touch itself cannot know or influence, which manipulates it from behind itself, that am I. Yet this you must know: I am not you, nor are you me, though I abide in you as you abide in me. Let wisdom disentangle these feeble words set down through the hands of mortal men". "The glory that shines from the Lord of the Day, the gentle gleam radiating from the Mistress of the Night, the comforting glow from the hearth fire, all these are of my substance. I penetrate Earth with love. I raise up the seed. I am the breath within the breath of all living things. 1 am the sweet scent of flowers and the bitter tang of vinegar. I am the differentiating essence in all things".

THE SONG OF THE SOUL

"I am the sleeper awakened from slumber. I am the seed of life eternal. I am the everlasting hope of man. I am a shoot of the Spirit Divine. I am the soul". "I have been since the beginning of time and shall be forever. I am the design interwoven in the warp and weft of creation. I am the indestructible essence of life. I am the treasure chest of man's hopes and aspirations, the storehouse of lost loves and fulfilled dreams".

"Before time I was an unconscious spirit potential united with the Supreme All. Ever since time began I was in the slumbering sea of spirit, waiting to be drawn forth into separate mortal incarnation. Now, though the mortal body enwrapping me fall apart and decay, I remain everlasting and immortal. Through all the ebb and flow of life, whatever destiny decrees, I remain the everlasting jewel of ages, invisible to mortal eyes and untouchable by mortal hands"

"I am the eternal bride of mortal men, ever awaiting the awakening kiss, the whisper of recognition. O being of flesh, deny me not; let me not dwell in forgotten solitude, left alone, unwanted and unheeded. Hold me to you as a lover holds the beloved, reach out beyond earthly things and kiss the lips that are yours eternally. Look out beyond the sphere of earthly opposites, out beyond the pettiness of gains and possessions. Grasp and possess me, your own everlasting and responsive soul".

"You will not find me where emotional tempests rage, or while sensual storms bring turmoil and disquiet. First subdue these, for I await beyond, in the quietness of calm waters. I must be sought as a lover seeks the loved one, in solitude, amid quietness and tranquillity, only there will I respond to the awakening kiss of recognition". "Do not neglect me, O my beloved, or tarnish me; for I come to you as an inestimable treasure. I bring beauty and innocence, gaiety and wholesomeness, decency and consideration, a jewel of potential perfection. Do not drag me down with you into the demon-haunted regions of darkness and terror. I am yours, closer to you than any loved one of Earth.
If you spurn me, I go down to a terrible doom in darkness, there to be purged and purified from the corruption of your touch. The best I can then hope for is to be bestowed upon another". "I am the sublime vehicle awaiting the command to bear your trueself to its destiny of glory. Could anyone be so foolhardy as not to cherish me? Without moving I am swifter than thought, on celestial wings I far outstrip the range of mortal senses. I drink at the fountain of life and feed on the fruits of eternal energy".

"What are you, my beloved, but a passing thing fashioned of clay? A handful of dust given life by a spark from the everlasting flame. I, myself, am no more than potential. Yet together we are so great that Earth of itself alone cannot contain us, we transcend it to reach out into the spheres of divinity. Take me, awaken me, acknowledge me, cherish me, and I will carry you to realms of glory unimaginable on Earth".

"I am the imprisoned captive longing for return to the freedom of the infinite. Yet, because of my mortal love I feel heartpangs of sorrow for things that pass away. But I know that beyond the pains inseparable from a sojourn in the vale of tears, there shines a glorious rainbow of hope and joy. There is a place of abiding love centred on the infinite; there, if you will but cherish me, we shall not be denied expression".

"I am drawn, by the law of spiritual gravitation, towards union with the Universal Soul and can no more escape return there than the mortal elements of man can escape their return to dust. Man sees glory by the reflected light of glory within him, he knows love by the love within himself. The sun is seen by the light of the sun and not by any light within man. Man sees the spirit by the light of the spirit, and not by any light within his mortal self. Only by the light of the spirit can the spirit of man be lit". "I am at peace when awakened to communion with my God. I am joyful when enthroned in consciousness and when endowed with wisdom and vision transcending that of Earth.

I delight in communion with the great sphere with which I am akin. I rejoice in union with the Divine Spirit from whence I came. I am your own trueself which should be forever cherished. By listening to my whispers, by letting your thoughts dwell on me and by knowing me, the whole glory of the greater spheres is opened unto you".

"I am that which reads what the eye sees, understands what the ear hears, knows what the hand feels, tastes whatever enters the mouth and smells whatever is borne on the nose. I am the indwelling consciousness which knows and enjoys all the good things of Earth. Those who dwell in the darkness of delusion cannot know me, and to them is lost the greatest glory of life. All conceptions of beauty, love and kindness are due to the consciousness residing in me. When I depart from my earthly abode I will carry with me the knowledge of the senses, as the wind carries perfume from the flower".

"I am not born, nor will I ever die. Once awakened to an existence in consciousness I can never become nothingness. I am the everlasting one who dies not when life departs from the body. O call me forth, awaken me from sleep with the kiss bestowing conscious life. Let me not lie unnoticed, wrapped in the heavy mantle of perpetual slumber, dreamless, unknowing".

"I am the indestructible one. Fire cannot burn me, swords cannot maim me or water smother me. When a drum is beaten, the sound it gives forth cannot be grasped or held. As that sound, so am I. When a shell is blown, the note it gives forth cannot be grasped or held. As that note, so am I. When a pipe is played, the music it gives forth cannot be grasped or held. As that music, so am I.

I am the immaterial in the material awaiting recognition, but in my own sphere I am the substantial one. There, man-known matter is no more substantial than the dawn mists are here". "I am the fire of life in all things that breathe, and in union with the breath I consume the nourishing substance within the food which feeds the body. I am the kernel within the seed in the heart of all. 1 am the guardian of memory and the arbiter of wisdom".
'These things are mine and ever with me. They are to me what the bones and muscles are to the mortal body. The waking and sleeping consciousness. The awareness of self. The five powers of feeling and the five of activity. The controlling spirit, which is the sensitive being".

"I am the living consciousness within you, I am the knower. The things seen by the eye and the things smelt by the nose are received by me. The things heard and the things felt are registered by me. I am the inner being causing all decisions to be made, though the tongue report back outside the things that I, the soul and the spirit, hold recorded. Everything done and undertaken, such as the working of the hands and movement of the legs, all are done in accordance with my command".

"When I depart, the body without me is as useless as a worn-out garment which is discarded and cast aside. Do we go together, my beloved, hand in hand as lovers? Do I return home radiant in the pride of blooming consciousness, or, spurned and humiliated, return without sensitivity, memory or knowledge? Do I return to be welcomed with joy in the light of glory, or must I shamefully seek refuge in the darkness? I am yours, my beloved, do with me as you will. I am yours everlastingly".

AFRIKAN BIBLE

THE BOOK OF SCROLLS

formerly called **THE BOOK OF BOOKS** or **THE LESSER BOOK OF THE SONS OF FIRE** this being **THE THIRD BOOK OF THE BRONZEBOOK** Compiled from remaining portions of a much damaged part of The Bronzebook and rewritten in our tongue and retold to our understanding according to present usage.

CHAPTER ONE. THE SACRED REGISTERS - PART 1

Herein are recorded sacred things which should never be written, but the memory of man is like a storehouse made of straw, or like a storepit dug in sand. Even less enduring is his body, for it. is a frail thing of fleeting substance which passes away like the dew in the morning. And what of the mortal chain which links the generations in knowledge? Behold, it is a thing prone to distortion, a transmuter of tradition and Truth. Therefore, when the command went forth from the Great One Illuminated With Wisdom, and came to your servant, he saw fit to quell the doubts engendered by fear and undertook to do the thing which had not been done before, placing his trust fully in the protecting wings which are spread by the words issuing from the Royal Residence.

These are the words spoken by the Great Interpreter, who, through the powers inherited by him from above and by the powers now in his keeping, all freely bestowed upon him by the grateful hearts of his people below, will lead us into the Fields Of Everlasting Glory. O Exalted One, intermediate between gods and men, what we now do for you do you for us. Let your deeds and your words become our words. Thus it ever was and thus it will ever be, while mortal beings make pilgrimage through this valley of tears. Speak thus in your hour. The High Born One has not blasphemed the Divine Powers, nor has he paid undue homage to earthly desires. He has not been loudmouthed in the Sacred Places, nor laughed when he should have been grave. His tongue is pure, for when fed with the words of men he absorbs Truth and excretes falsehood. His mouth has never spewed forth words of malice or envy, words of oppression or injustice never passed his lips.

Look now at the great dark water mirror and see what is reflected there from the mists swirling along the corridor of time. Seeing your place, make ready, so that when the summons comes from the Dark One you are not caught unprepared. These are the words to be spoken to those who peer from beyond the Dark Portal: His arm was ever ready to help those who did good for others, and he lent his power to those who ordered what was good. He stood for those who could no longer stand and commanded for those who could no longer command. He carried the weary and succoured the helpless. He never oppressed the weak, nor did he permit injustices to go unpunished and unrectified. He stood by the side of the Great Potter, and because of his plea the clay was shaped to a more pleasing form. He erased disfiguring faults and smoothed the roughness. He added stiffness to the mixture. He has done no evil, his words have always been true.

He stands unashamed and fearless before the twin shrines. Even as it was in the Land of the Great River, so let it be here. Let him not be cut off by distance. Let not his power be cut off, for he stands between the worlds. Let it flow out like living waters unto the living and be as shining rays to the Radiant Ones. For here we see the power darkly, while beyond the horizon it shines brightly. He is everlastingly faithful in heart, for he has admitted no other who would defile him.

He has remained loyal to the sacred words and has diligently perused the great writings. He has navigated the shallows of the winding waters. Now he draws near. He has left his kingdom of trial, he has overcome the challenges of life, he has done all things written on the tablets of Truth, and he has sojourned in the Chamber of Profound Silence. He has done all things which are proper and been reassured that he has followed the right path. He does not fear judgement. Let him reunite with The Supreme One who sent him forth, so that he will not be separated from the waters of life. Let the Holy Heat enwrap him when he passes through the Place of Coldness. Let his nostrils inhale the breath of nourishment, that he may live and that we may partake of his existence. Do not repudiate him, but make him welcome. Do you not recognise the one you endowed with power? Has he become too radiant? Is his form too glorious? Read what is written in the books of his heart.

You set him in darkness and he saw. You set him in silence and he heard. You set him in emptiness and he felt. You established him in nothingness and he gathered substance. Therefore, he returns with manifold powers. He is well fitted to be presented to those who stand before The Supreme One. When the bright sun shines with splendour in the dayskies above, the gentle morning star hides her face in modesty and becomes unseen. All the great Company of the radiant nightlights withdraw before the majesty of the greater light. Yet when darkness eats the shining disk we know again the comforting presence of the eternal stars, so let it be with your servant.

The Dark Ones who dwell in their compatible gloom cannot claim him as one of their own, he cannot be numbered among their dreadful company. His heart is pure, his deeds were good, no creature spawned in murkiness has gained control of his thoughts. His desires have not been generated by denizens of the darkness. He who was afflicted here is not afflicted forever, he is made whole, he is freed from pain, his sickness has departed. He rejoices in the light, therefore let him be drawn towards the greater light where you are.

Let him not see the place of darkness, let him not behold the Hideous Ones fashioned by wickedness, the Dwellers in the Dark Recesses, who shrink before the light, or the Twisted Ones moulded by lewd desires. He brings with him a lamp lit from the flame of Truth, he bears the rod of righteousness which rewards those who have overcome tribulations. O let him pass to the right side of the dividing flame! He has left us, he is coming to you, he approaches, he throws off the earthly wrappings, he stands free, he stands glorious. Does he not glow with splendour? Behold him, your worthy companion in brightness. Is he not wholly compatible with those of your company? See, he is a Shining One, a Hero of the Horizon. Is he not one destined to abide everlastingly? Take him, lead him to the Realm of Glory, show him his place in the Spheres of Splendour. The eyes that were deceived on Earth now see clearly, O what splendours are revealed! The music unheard by earthly ears now sounds sweet melodious music. O what joyous rapture it brings!

The nostrils inhale perfumes too delicate for the earthly nose, O how the heart sings! All drabness, all dullness and all sordidness, which are of the Earth, are left behind. Turn him from the place where these can regather about him. The unmoving, empty body remains here before our eyes; it is nothing, it sees not, it hears not, it speaks not, it smells not, its breath is stilled, it begins to fall apart. There is no life and the overseer has departed. Nothing remains here with us but this unresponsive thing.

The greatness, the feeling, the sensitivity have departed from the body and are now beyond our ken. These are with the real surviving being. O receive him into the life of splendour! We, who are here, stand blinded behind the veil of flesh, we cannot see beyond ourselves, we hope, we believe and we trust. Thus it has ever been with men, for they pass their lives behind a wall of limitations, there is a barrier shutting them in. They are imprisoned within a mortal body. O grant us fulfilment, grant us that which is that which is the ultimate desire and aspiration of men! We speak for this man. He is one who came with us from afar. He is one who has travelled a long weary road. No taint of meanness stained the purity of his spirit, no corruption of deceit discoloured the garments of his soulself. He has gone over shining in radiant splendour, so even the doomed in their darkness can hope when they sight his distant glow. May it shed some small warmth into their grim coldness!

O Great Welcomer, who greets the newcomers, help our departed one. He served well in this place of trial and tribulation, let him not go unrewarded. He is the son of hope. Like us, like those who went before, he hoped as men have always hoped, for this is not a place of certainties. If it were, our heritage of glory would be badly earned.

He lives because it is ordained that he live; he lives, for all men live everlastingly. They die not, they perish not, they endure through ages. His Kohar awaits him and needs hide no awful aspect in shame. Let his face shine in greeting, welcome home the wanderer. This tombed structure is not a place of finality. The grave is not the goal of earthly life, anymore than the soil is the goal of the seed. Does seed die within the ground? Is it planted intending that it be mingled with the soil and lost?

O Great Welcomer, let your face shine with gladness when you greet the homecoming wanderer. Lead him to the Kohar which is his inheritance, that he may enter into it and enjoy its embrace. Let him find completion and fulfilment by absorption into his Kohar. Our departed one was the whole part which came forth from the whole, and he returns to the whole. Nothing is lost, nothing is gone. He lives over there, lives more fully than he ever lived. He lives in splendour, he lives in beauty, he lives in knowledge and in the waters of life. He is everlasting.

O departed one risen to glory, you are now a released spirit united with your spirit whole, the companionable Kohar, the everlasting one. Arise alive in the Land Beyond the Horizon and journey to the Land of Dawning; the stars accompanying you will sing for joy, while the heavenly signs voice hymns of praise and gladness. You are not far removed from us, it is as if we were in one room divided by a curtain, therefore we are not sorrowful. If we weep it is because we cannot share your joys and because we no longer know your touch.

O everlasting Kohar, take this man of goodness into your eternal embrace, let your life become his life and your breath his breath. He is your own, he is the drop returning to the filled pitcher, the leaf returning to the tree, you are the repository of his incarnations. As you grew there, so he grew here; you are everlastingly whole and he lives in you. If he is not even as you in face, let him enter, hide his faults, for they are not many. For this you were fashioned, for this you came into being, you are the overbody awaiting the returning spirit, and the spirit now comes. You are that which will clothe the newly arrived spirit in heavenly flesh. You are that in which our departed one will express himself.

O Kohar, hear us. Here is your vitalising essence; before you were incomplete, now you are whole. Draw your own, your compatible one, to you and observe the many likenesses. We send fragrances, that they may spread around you. Now take the eye which will perfect your face, it is the perfecting eye, the eye which sees things as they are. See the fluctuating wraith, is it not beautiful? Does it not come with an aura of fragrance, sweetness filling the air?
It has been purged of all impurities, all about it is fragrant. Therefore, grant it your substance, that it may become solid and firm.

O Kohar, long have you awaited the day of fulfilment, the day of your destiny. That day is here, it is now; therefore, take the spirit which is your own and enfold it with your wings. Each to his own and to his own each goes. You and he are bound together with unseverable bonds, each without the other is nothing. Now bear him up, for in that place you are greater than he, for you are the generator. While he rested in the womb you were active, as he grew you grew before him. If he has done wrong, and who among men is guiltless, then in you let the wrong be adjusted. You are his hope, you are his shield and you are his refuge. This we say to the Brilliant One, the Guardian of Goodness: The departed one has not walked with ignorance, he has not been slothful in carrying the burden of his duty. He has not been swayed by passions of the body, he has not despoiled the house of another, he has not caused undue sorrow, nor has he maltreated a child for pleasure. He has succoured the poor and weak, he has done all that is good; therefore, let none of Those Who Lurk in Darkness seize him. His radiant light is strong, those who would seize him are repulsed by the light and slink away. He lives, he lives forever. He has lived worthily, he has been purified by the fires of earthly life, he has been refined in the furnace of tribulation, he has overcome all earthly temptations. He has lived the life which enhances goodness, he has prepared himself for life in the light. Receive him,

O Brilliant One! O Kohar, absorb into yourself the lifeforce, it was meant for you, it is yours. It is the enlivening spirit which spans the two worlds. He, the departed one, was you and even more so were you he. Come to him as the Beauteous One came to Belusis, a great king, and gathered him in compassion and love. Come, that he may awaken to new life in your arms. This man, the departed one, who in unity with you becomes the Glorious One, was born of a god and is the child of two gods, after the nature of greater men. Now you are impregnated with the living spirit of he who was prepared by trial on Earth for you. Behold, in unity your twain are now throbbing with life and your brightness bedazzles the eyes. You are now a Star of Life, a Living Star, and to a star you shall ascend to rule its life.
The departed one is now freed, he is loosed from the bonds of illusion, he is saved from the dark waters of unreality and is one with the Eternal Light. These things we declare, so let them be.

Our thoughts mould a new reality beyond the present real, and this becomes the reality of tomorrow. O great substantial Kohar, protect this departed one, your own, from the accusations of false-fronted beings, remembering the faithful heart ever prevailing before the balances of our forefathers from far away. Put into his mouth those words which open doors. Let the goodness in him prevail, but you, yourself, stand up and bear witness for him. He suffered from the frailties of men. He was wrathful when provoked and surly when enduring great burdens. His temper flashed quickly when his words were not accepted or his ways followed, and at times he lacked consideration. However, these are small things inseparable from the frailties of mortal men, and in all greater things he was good. Let not the false-fronted one disguised in his brother's form possess him, guard him from the beings lurking in the shadows this side of the darkness.

I see this, my brothers. Behold, the departed one goes to meet his own image. It is his own self reflected in his image. It is his own self that comes to greet him. It is his Kohar which embraces him. It welcomes him as though he were one ransomed from captivity. I see them blend and he becomes a new seed in the heart of his Kohar. I hear the Kohar speak, it names itself Nevakohar, it says, "O man of pure thoughts, of kindly words, of quiet speech, of good deeds, come to me. I am your being, yet I am not you; as you have loved and cherished me, so I now love and cherish you. I am your reward, as I would have been your affliction". They are now united and this is the place of the first threshold, from whence the Completed Beings depart. The departed one now stands in his own form and likeness. He becomes the Great Ship-Borne Voyager and passes over the waters to the Place of Reeds, but his weaknesses do not bear him down and he goes through. Great Ones, lift him up, let him not fall into the fetid waters of decay. He is a worthy son of Lewth. Then the lesser is carried by the greater, while Dark Ones gaze up from their misery and wait silently to see if he is borne up.

The Glorious One goes past in peace, for he is not compatible with their dark company. He remains unmolested, for flame confounds the hands of slime. An unloosed Dark One comes up saying it will take this man, but is repulsed by brightness. It is a thing of maimed rottenness, for on Earth it was clothed in lustsaturated flesh, though contained in a form of beauty. The heart of this man is not faint; see him now, is he not sure of his welcome among Beings of Glory? He is as the wild bull, the prince of herds, he is a Great One among the Everlasting Spirits. He reaches the firm ground where a Bright Being welcomes him, and he is named 'The Newcomer'. He has landed on the shore and climbed the Steps of Splendour. He is in the company of Shining Spirits and his earthlife companions greet him, they welcome him, saying, "All this beauty and splendour is yours to enjoy". They bring garments of beauty, bright clothes of radiance. He has passed through the Hall of Judgement. The Twin Truths have heard his plea, and those who bore witness have departed. He has crossed the waters and ascended the steps, now he has attained the threshold of immortality and stands in rapture. He has passed by the regions of darkness and gloom and is with glory. He comes to everlasting hfe in a true form of splendour, to dwell evermore as a living spirit within his Kohar. How wonderful it is to be united and one with the Kohar!

The Newcomer looks back across the waters to the Place of Decision, then he turns and ascends the steps to the threshold of immortality. He is in his true form, yet he is a spirit within his Kohar. He speaks, but it is not the speech of men and all understand him. His hearing is all-embracing. He sees both the powers of Light and the powers of Darkness, but the powers of Darkness no longer affect him. The Newcomer has reached his compatible abode. He has fought the battle which is mortal life and risen supreme to victory. He has not been vanquished by the Raging Ones which are the bodily passions. At each step forward he has left a lifeless form, at each step he has fought a shadow, at each step he has won the clash of arms. The Newcomer has sought out and discovered the One Hidden Behind the Two, and the Three which stand before them. He knows the secrets of the Nine which veil the others from the eyes of men. He has unravelled the skein of life's mysteries, even as those enlightened ones yet living on Earth must do.

There is no suffering or pain in the Newcomer, he cannot feel hurt, neither can he be sorrowful. If a companion of his Earth journey be numbered among the Dark Ones, then his heart is soothed with forgetfulness; but later he will remember, and because of his efforts the Dark One will be returned to the crucible.

CHAPTER TWO. THE SACRED REGISTERS - PART 2

The writings of Garmi were brought by the hands of Nadayeth The Enlightener, of the twin cities whence come the Sons of Fire, when he fled the wrath of kings. He spread out before the Learned Ones beauteous things of many colours and spoke to them after this fashion, and I, Lavos, recorded it in the tongue of the Sons of Fire: Behold this, it is the Land of the Dawning. It stands between the Land of Light ever splendid and the Land of Darkness ever gloomy. They are the lands beyond the veil, before the veil is the Land of the Living. The Aspiring One has embarked on the waters of illusion, his craft is afloat but it has not yet reached the shores where the promise of new life is fulfilled. Now he is guided by two beings, one a lovely maiden and the other an ill-visaged man. These two strive one with the other, each grasping one side of the craft, now it overturns. The maiden seeks to drag the Aspiring One down, while the ill-favoured man seeks to keep him afloat. But the Aspiring One struggles against him. They come to the sands of the shining shore where the Light of Truth turns the maiden into a vile-faced hag and the man into a handsome youth.

The Aspiring One lies on the sands of Shadow as one dead, for he had fought against the man who sought to save him. The Beauteous One comes attended by handmaidens, and with them are the companions of the Aspiring One's earthly life. There, too, is his soulself, awaiting his embrace. The Aspiring One lies as dead, for he did not know his saviour. They who stand about, who are

The Welcomers, wait in uncertainty. The Beauteous One bends over the prostrate man and says, "Revive, this is not a place where death rules". He moves and she says, "Raise yourself and cast away the residue of your mortality".

The Aspiring One opens his eyes, he sits up, he shields his eyes before the vision of beauty, he is blinded by it and she gives him his heart. The handmaidens weep and their tears are the blood of the Aspiring One's life.

The Beauteous One says, "I have come that you who were dead might live, that you who were blinded might see, that you who were deceived might know Truth". The soulself says, "I have come to embrace you, I have come to protect you, I have come to shield you, I am your refuge". That which is the Kohar says, "I have come to brighten up your face, I am you as you are me. I have waited for you, I have wept for you and rejoiced when you rejoiced. I have never forgotten you while we have been apart. I have heard every word spoken and these are recorded for you. I have recorded every sight. I have recorded every sound. I have recorded every smell and every taste. Every memory is secure for you. Here I give you form and substantiality". This is The Herald, he stands between this man and his Kohar, and they, together with The Adjuster and The Welcomers, go to the Hall of Judgement and stand before The Lord of Life, The Master of Destinies. Now come The Lords of Eternity who are The Lesser Gods, and they enter the Gates of Splendour. The Balancer comes from his secret place.

The Greeter to Darkness stands at his door and The Greeter to Splendour stands at his door, they face each other. The Welcomers, compatible companions of this man's earthly life, stand about, they are there, in the Hall of Judgement. The Balancer causes two fluid-like, fluctuating columns which stand on either side of the Kohar and one takes the form of the Aspiring One, but it is horribly malformed because it mirrors all his wickednesses and weaknesses. The other shines brightly, for it mirrors all his goodness and spiritual qualities. Then the two columns merge back into the Kohar and The

Adjuster adjusts with justice and mercy. Then the Aspiring One stands forth in his Kohar and in his true likeness, which is a blending together of all his incarnational likenesses.

The Aspiring One is drawn towards the right hand door, he passes through and sets foot on the rainbow road. He is accompanied by The Welcomers, the companions of his earthly life who are now revealed to him in their true likeness. They sing, they dance, they rejoice, and there is much gladness in the reunion. The word of Truth is established, it is fulfilled. The ancient promises are fulfilled. He who departs shall return, he who sleeps shall awaken, he who dies shall live. The Aspiring One has passed into the Regions of Glory.

Now, behold the body vacated by the vehicle of life. It slumbers in its death wrappings, for the enlivening spirit has flown. The earthly body alone stays and cannot hold itself together. It prepares to fall apart and decay. The Companions of the Dead take it into their company, it will be made incorruptible and become a communicating door. It is given the things which rightly belong to the dead. Those who remain on Earth fear the Life Shadow of the One who has gone on before them. The body is bandaged in its death wrappings. It is purified, it is made clean, it is provided with the necessities. Thus, the Life Shadow shall dwell at peace within the empty body, it believes it to be its abode. It shall not wander.

O Shadow, do not wander, remain within the tomb, seize any who come to steal, seize any who would break the body, seize any who would open that which is closed. Seize and haunt, seize and haunt! The Companions of the Dead speak thus, "The Life Shadow of this man who was is never restless, it never wanders, it is ever protecting, it is ever watchful. It remains, for it is bound to the empty corpse by the restraining throngs". They say, "The spirit of this man has awakened in the Land of Immortality, it rejoices in the Land Beyond the Horizon. He is a Hero of the Horizon. Offend him not by thinking that he is dead, he cannot die, for he is with the Ever Living. He has not gone away to die, he has departed to live elsewhere. Let the moisture of his body return to the waters of the Earth from whence it came. Let the things of hardness in his body return to the dust from whence they came. Let his bones rejoin the stones which once they were".

"Weep not, for your tears and lamentations restrain his eager spirit. Sing the death dirge, that its echoes may sound the toscin in the Region of Light and The Splendid Ones and The Welcomers come to the place of appointment. It is unfitting to force gladness on a sorrowful heart, but be sad only for a temporary parting". "Let not the earthly body of this man who was, become destitute, surround it with care and affection, so that it may transmit the substance of life. Sustain it, so the Life Shadow remain within". "What see you now? Gaze upon it, the frail mortal remains enwrapped and silent, unresponsive. Ponder, this you see with the eyes of the body, which cannot perceive things of the spirit.

Were the eyes of your spirit opened but a brief moment, you would perceive something entirely different and then you would know that his shining, immortal spirit walks in the company of those risen to glory." " It is the time for parting, the time for farewell, for the closing of the door." "O departed one risen to glory,who has left us to sorrow. As we have helped you and surrounded you with the protection of our love and our offerings, so now help us in the days of life left to us on Earth."

CHAPTER THREE. THE SACRED REGISTERS - PART 3

Behold, one comes wearing white sandals and clad in fine linen. Arise, stand up to greet him. He bears the staff of righteousness. He brings a pearl of priceless value, take it and become perfect. Others come, fair women and young children. His father's heir has come and the four great ones who bear sweet waters, who spread the feast and rejoice under the strong arm of their protector. He who has gone is not forgotten, but this is the day of the living. He who has inherited ceases from weeping and begins to smile, the protecting one comes in peace. The heart in the sky is no longer small, it expands, it grows large. Thus it is also with the heart of he who lives, his days of lamentations are over and his heart swells and grows large. The good son never ceases from faithful service on behalf of the absent one who has escaped from the confinement of the body. The dutiful son now calls upon the absent one for protection from wandering shadows and from the molestations of life Shadows.

O Bountiful, Ever Considerate One, hear the words of your faithful and dutiful son, as they ascend with the blue, penetrating smoke of fragrant incense. Let no shadow wander from your safe abode to haunt our habitations, for they who dwell therein have done you no dishonour. Safeguard the Dark Doorway, that things in vile forms come not near us to pollute our bodies with sickness and disease. You left, and before the waters rose again the man of Shodu, he who dealt harshly with the widow dwelling beside the channel of black stones, departed for his judgement. Is not he whom you judged, and did you not deal rightly with him when the scales went down against him? Therefore, might he not return from the Region of Darkness with others of his kind and cause misfortune to fall upon us? You he cannot harm, you are now in the Place of Glory, in the land beyond the Westera waters. Therefore, send us guardians from among the Glorious Company, that they may spread protecting wings over our habitations. Many come, bearing cakes of fine meal and barley cakes, large, fat-bodied fish and meats of many kinds, honey wine in jars and fruits in plenty. He who is absent from the feast is joyful.his arm is strong and he issues his commands to the guardians. Cast off all gloom and be joyful, for this is not the time of sorrow, and tears have no place in your eyes.

If there be benevolent Life Shadows beyond the protective pale, they may enter. Join with us in our rejoicing. Let us all enjoy what we have and what we share, for life is irrepressible. These are things from a foreign place said for our brother Gwelm, according to the rites of the Sons of Fire, and thus it shall be for those who enter the chambers of stone.

CHAPTER FOUR. THE SACRED REGISTERS - PART 4

No longer can the man who was speak with men on Earth, for he now lives in splendour among The Eternal Ones. He was weighed before the Assessors, and though his faults were not few he was not outweighed in goodness. He has become a Shining One and journeys on into the spaces of Heavenland, accompanied only by his compatible companions. He has ascended into the Place of Glory, the Place of Fulfilment. The years have fallen off his shoulders, like a cast off cloak, and he is young again. He is vigorous, he lives. Time cannot touch him with change, nor sorrow enter his heart. He rests, awaiting a new call to duty. He has passed through the Wide Hall and through the Narrow Portal. He has entered the Land of a New Dawning and he is welcomed, his Earth companions greet him, he lives. He is beyond harm, he sees the sublime visions which fulfil his yearnings. He who has served is now served. As he has sown and husbanded, so now he reaps.

He continues past the Place of Waiting Souls and sees the awaiting Kohars who will unite with the ascending spirits of men. He bears in his hand the Book of Life and glides over the pure pastures, past the bright dividing flame. He turns the face of compassion towards the darkness, but sees nought but fleeting shadows against the red glare. The Lost Ones shrink back in shame and the man who was passes the entrance to their foul abode. Those who are left to mourn for the Glorious One have dried their tears, for all is well with him. He delights in the good life in a place of glory. He is safe in the embrace of his Kohar, he is the Adoring One whose eyes are opened to splendour, he sees the sublime visions. The man who was seeks the Illuminator who will direct him in his duties, he cleanses himself in the Lake of Beauty and refreshes himself at the Fountain of Life. He sees spirits of the twilight who are purged of all their wickedness and lusts yet remain captive to The Lords of Destinies, for they are still unproven. The Lord of Life will direct their passage back for trial and testing. For these there is always hope. The man who was has navigated the winding waters of life and crossed the dark waters of death, and is now strengthened in wisdom. He takes a seat on high, that he may become an instructor and guide on the path. He becomes a brazier in the distance, a homing light to guide those who seek Truth.

He is purified and comes forth wearing the White Mantle of Greatness. Behold the splendour of his raiment and the purity of his adornments, as he sits awaiting calls from those in the Heavy Kingdom, who seek his counsel. The seers in dark waters will amaze the people with the clarity of their visions and revelations, for the power goes forth from the man who was, with manifold strength. A great being has joined the Splendid Company in the Land of Dawnlight. Over there they will say, "Earth is worthily fulfilling its purpose when it produces men such as this".

You may wonder what are the occupations of the man who was. Does he illuminate the dark waters alone? May he not be among those who seek to enter the hearts of those who close the doors of their spirit to the instructors of wisdom? Alas, they who are heavily enshrouded in earthly wrappings are ever set of face before the instructors of wisdom, they say, "What have we to do with this babble?", yet they, most of all, require enlightenment, for they are men of small minds. May he not have become a pathfinder in the night, a guide through the darkness, the star illuminating the night at its darkest hour as the herald of The Great Illuminator? May he not have become a Director of Rays that dance on the waters, or a Controller of the Winds which caress the cheek? Suffice that he rejoices in a life of splendour, so let it remain with him and his Kohar until the day when all is known, the day of full knowing.

CHAPTER FIVE. THE SACRED REGISTERS - PART 5

These are the instructions for those who journey the outer track of the twinway, for those who have been laid in the chambered tombs, who followed the ways of Kemwelith. The words are those from the distant past, first spoken in a far land beyond the rolling billows: The Risen One has become the Newcomer, and having passed through the clearing house his departure is not delayed. No toll is required on the ferry, for the Newcomer has with him the words of entrance which have become known to him according to his deeds. He has not deviated from the path and all is well. The ferryman comes to the Place of Waiting, he of the winding river which is the tortuous channel of purification.

The Newcomer stands at the mooring place and proclaims, "O ferryman, away to the Region of the Blessed Ones. I am purified, purged of polluting evils; make haste, do not delay. I am a wanderer anxious to reach my destination". The ferryman says, "From whence come you?" The Newcomer says, "I am from Restaw and am weary. Take me to my compatible place of abode, let us not delay, I wish to join those united with their soulselves. Let us not dally. Do not tarry, for I am anxious to depart from this sombre shore. Have no fear, cautious one, for no evil dogs my footsteps. Come, let us away, bear me over the waters to the appointed place. Carry me swiftly to where spirits are regenerated and made young again. Carry me to the foot of the Great Stairway that ascends to the Place of the Immortals, to the Courtyard of The Great God". The ferryman hesitates, he says, "Show me your token, that I may know you have truly passed the tests, that I may know your true destination. For it is the way with men that they think one thing but Truth lies elsewhere". The Newcomer says, "My token is the brightness, which, if you be no imposter, you may see shining above my head, and my introduction is the writing concerning me, written in the Book of Sacred Mysteries. Come, bear me over the waters, so that I may tread the Field of Peace. See, have I not four attendants, two on either side? Let them speak for me, for they are witnesses walking in the light of Truth".

The ferryman says, "Who stands to the pole?" and the Risen One answers, "I will stand to the pole with my attendants, two on either side. You stand by to bear at the steering oar, so that our course remains straight". The ferryman says, "It is well, for the current is sullen and changeful". The Newcomer says, "O ferryman of the boatless ones, I am truly a man justified before all on both sides of the horizon, before Heaven and Earth. I have passed the tests of the examiners and am free to proceed. I am one who can claim passage by virtue of my deeds. Have not men spoken well of me after I departed from their midst, is this not enough? It is the way with Earth, that if men speak of the goodness of an absent one, then he is good indeed. Truly I am a Bright One".

The ferryman says, "Draw aside your mantle, that I may see your likeness, for this is a good boat which may not be polluted. The path henceforth is hard for those who cannot be faced without revulsion. O Great One, draw your mantle over again, for you are indeed among the brightest of those who pass this way, great will be the rejoicing when you appear among your own kind, the pure of heart". "Delay no longer, ferryman. Quickly over the waters to the other side. If you delay further I will name the names of gods to men, that their unreality be exposed. I am not one to be trifled with, I am one who can dispel the clouds of illusion. I am a man of no mean qualities, therefore tarry no more, let us depart".

CHAPTER SIX. THE SACRED REGISTERS - PART 6

The man who was becomes the Pilgrim. He has crossed the waters, he has passed the Grim Guardian, he waits without the Place of Union and stands firmly. He is not afraid and stands resolute. The Cool Gracious One approaches with three jars of water and refreshes him. The Pilgrim says, "Behold, O Watcher at the Gate, I have laid up treasure enough in the storehouse of love, therefore allow me to pass. The love of those who have gone before, see is it not a large quantity and sufficient to draw me upward? See the love of those who remain behind, is it not a large quantity and sufficient to draw me upward?" The Watcher hears his words. The Grim Guardian counts and weighs and says, "Pass". Then this man passes and goes beyond the Lake of Wisdom, past the Winding Channel of Experiences, over the flooded Field of Reeds, to the Eastern side of the Region of Light where he will be renewed in birth into the Higher Spheres. The Pilgrim now stands before the Womb of Heaven where those who enter as pure seed are brought forth into union with God.

This man passes by to where the attendants help him to assume the Robe of Glory. They welcome him. "Behold", they say, "His Kohar has brought this man powers to make him complete. The powers he gave into the keeping of his Kohar during the prayer times on Earth have returned greatly magnified. This man has joined the Joyful Company, he has left his old, discarded body in the Region of Heaviness, to assume another more glorified one in the Region of Light. The Kohar greets the Pilgrim and says, "I welcome you, my own". The Kohar says to those about, "This is my own, he has washed in the Lake of Wisdom and passed by the Caverns of Distrust and Doubt. Let us, therefore, enter in peace when the Great Door is opened for the United Being in the East, the door leading to the Place of The One True God above all gods, whose manifestations are secret mysteries".

Before going further they pass by a side entrance to the Region of Darkness where vile and sorrowful things lurk, the Lost Ones, those who served in the ranks of evil on Earth.

O Great Kohar, stop the ears of your own; that he may not hear the mournful waitings of the doomed ones left behind! They who are the companions of the Pilgrim cry out, "O Kohar, guide your own right, guide him up the Ladder of Life which he must traverse again; strengthen its rungs, support him, so he bears lightly upon them, let not the rungs break beneath his weight. This is the test of deeds long since done, where evil bears down heavily".

"O Kohar, your ownis weak and falters, yet your arms are strong, therefore lift them to support him, that he may surmount to the heights above. Do this, that he may sit with those who have understanding and perception, that his feet may be welcomed in the Fields of Peace and that he may take his place among the Glorious Ones". Blessed is the Kohar who safeguards all memories, storing them as men store corn; who retains these for the use of the Reborn Ones; who can recall all that men forget and can draw forth a memory as men draw water from a well. The Kohar is the eternal recorder, Pilgrims become Risen Ones and enter their Kohars as a soul enters a body, and in unity they become Glorious Ones.

CHAPTER SEVEN. THE SACRED REGISTERS - PART 7

This is the manner whereby the Aspiring Ones of Earth may cross the dread horizon through residence within the Cavern of Stone. It is thus that men come to know the Truth concerning the Realms of Glory beyond the Western Horizon, but it is a path beset by great dangers and manifold terrors, and many return witless. The Aspiring One is of Earth, he is earthbound. He sits within the cavern before the Cauldron of Rebirth and Regeneration, and inhales the smoke from the brew of release. He rises above himself, flying on wings of five feathers, the names of which are recorded in the Book of Secret Mysteries, wherein are the awful recipes. There it is written that he may ascend like a falcon and cannot go otherwise than as a falcon. He may not go in the manner of any other bird. He escapes the call of Earth, its fetters fall from him. The Aspiring One leaves his attendants behind, he is not with them, he is not of Earth, neither is he of Heaven. He is at the place where the two meet and intermingle. His body moves without the spirit and partakes of the sour yellow bread of wide vision.

The Aspiring One drinks the brew of grey barley and sips long at the wine of harish, eating the cakes of green brown horris. He eats the fruit of the releasing tree and drinks the brew of black fungus, which is in the smoke goblet. Thus, he sleeps and the attendants lay him down in the receptacle called the Womb of Rebirth. He is in the Place of Visions but remains like the masthead bird. He shall be covered and made so that in his struggles he rise not. His voice is heard speaking in a strange tongue, as he calls on his fathers who have gone before and now preside over affairs beyond the Wide Lake. His body becomes still, as he enters the dazzling chamber which is the doorway to twin vision. Now he must penetrate the Walls of Dry Air which bar his passage, and rise into the rainbow-coloured Clouds of Radiance which

are above. High up he looks below him and sees the waters of the Winding Canal of Experience and understands the meaning of all that had befallen him. Now he has four eyes, these being the inner and outer eyes, and rising higher he attains the heights of wide consciousness. Here he meets the Pathfinder and follows him swiftly. He speaks rightly to the Guardian.
He shields bis eyes when passing the Lurker on the Threshold, and goes on until he comes to the abode of the Opener of the Ways. Now the body of the Aspiring One becomes restless and those who attend him place the power of Hori over his face. He hears the voice of The Sungod, which says, "I know the necessary names, I am The Knower of Names. I know the name of The Limitless One, above The Lords of the East and West, I am One Most Powerful".

The Aspiring One becomes covered with moisture, he writhes, he shouts, he struggles. The Companionable Watchers know he has left the protection of The Sungod, that he has been seized by the Fiends of Darkness, but he struggles and prevails over them, and all is well. Then the Aspiring One returns. A hundred shining suns whirl above, a whisper rolls around like thunder, lights of manifold hues sway above, like the river reeds in the wind. All things appear to dance in a shimmering haze, then turn over and fold back into themselves, and such beauty is produced that the human tongue cannot describe it.

All things take upon themselves shimmering forms through which other forms can be seen. Great melodic music throbs all around, while everything pulsates a soft rhythm. The air is filled with voices of unearthly sweetness, glory and splendour are everywhere. Then the Aspiring One awakes. He is raised, behold he comes forth and walks as one bemused by a vision of glory. He staggers, he cannot walk unsupported. His throat burns and his mouth is overgrown with dryness. His head resounds with drumbeats. He is given the sweet waters in the cup of forgetfulness and drinks deeply, all is well. He is a Reborn One, he is an Enlightened One. He is one resurrected from the Cavern of Stone.

CHAPTER EIGHT. THE SACRED REGISTERS - PART 8

These are the supplications of Dkeb, the Stranger, who came from the Land of Rising Waters and was known to us as the Opener of the Ways, he came under the wings of the Firehawk. He was the first of the Scarlet Robed Ones, the right hand of Glanvanis. That was in the time of our fathers' fathers, and the tongue of the seafarers is no longer in the mouth of men. O Great Being of Beauty, Brilliant One who greets the Newcomers arriving in the Place Beyond the Western Horizon, this woman is your daughter, your daughter is she. See, she is pure in spirit and clean in heart. She is modest and womanlike, so let her pass to live in the Pastures of Life, in the Land of New Dawning where all is wholesome. Let her be purified by the maidens of Orshafa, let them purify her, let her be washed and dried by the attendants at the clean, sweet waters of life. Let the nine Delicate Ones minister to her, let her be clothed in garments of decency, for she is a womanly woman.

O Great and Glorious One, give this woman your hand, clasp her hand with womanly tenderness. Spread out your falcon wings over her, spread protecting wings around her. She has followed the tedious ways of womankind and has glorified life with her presence. She has endured affliction with patience and made her home hearth a place of peace and content. Let her roam the pastures of the Blessed Ones and penetrate into the farthest regions of light. I raise my hands in supplication. The flame is lit, it burns brightly, fragrant incense is placed in the bowl and it becomes aglow. Its sweet perfume rises into the recesses above.

O Happy Risen One, O Beautiful Being glowing with womanly goodness, treasurer of all the virtues, purify yourself for admittance into the Higher Regions. The incense we offer here is your indrawn breath of renewed life. It fills your lungs, you breathe and because you breathe you live. This is the best incense from the Land of Gwemi, differing not from that which our fathers knew when they travelled the water road. O Beautified One, my heart lingers at the place where you rest, my heart is with you, entwined with yours. How sweet your breath, how pleasant your perfume, how gentle your whispers, how delicate the rustle of your attire.

O newly become Beauteous One, you are not alone. Rise blue perfumed smoke, rise cleaning fragrance, rise sweet wholesome offerings, rise like fluttering birds on wings of purified air to the glorious regions of light which he away beyond our poor perception. Accept our sweet fragrance, O Beautified One, inhale our sweet smoke, O Ever Delicate One, may you enjoy the due reward of your labours and privations, of your selfless sacrifices. Be ever contented and peaceful, O dutiful wife and loving mother, hear our words, as they rise to you in the softly smouldering incense which comes shipborne to these shores. Hear the voices of the waiting Welcomers greeting the Beauteous One who now joins them.

They say, "Cast off the old worn garment and array yourself in garments of radiant light, in the clothes of splendour which have awaited you. Bedeck yourself in the well earned jewels of spiritual reward. "Henceforth you shall dwell here, walking about freely, to be honoured and loved. Here you will be renewed, be alert, vigorous and far reaching. The power of your spirit shall stretch out to every place. You take thought and fly on hawks wings. Your desire becomes a chariot with wings of light".

"Beyond the place of your first destination is the kingdom of the Lord of the Distant Sky. There he will permit manifestations in glory. There, henceforth, you shall walk in strength and beauty, being ever filled with life and power, garmented in loveliness for all eternity". "There floodwaters of a glorious fluid light unknown here rise and fall in moderation, and therein you may bathe daily and taste the revitalising rests. Here your thirst may be slaked at the well of Divine Essence and your appetite appeased by the strange bread of everlasting life". "This is your destiny, in the Land Beyond the Veil, therefore lift up your face in joy. Rise, lovely liveliness. You are one destined to be numbered among the Shining Ones and are warmly welcomed into the company of the Fragrant Ones. O happy one who enhanced earthly life with your presence, this is your reward. Many have done mighty things, but you have served with constancy and diligence, adding the small grains of goodness to the pile of merits until it exceeded in weight the great things done by others. We hail you, O victorious one!"

The Welcomers say among themselves, "How fair and bright the face of this Newcomer. How fine must have been her life in the Region of Heaviness. Behold, here she is, renewed and made young again but with a loveliness unknown in the life left behind". When she goes forward from here she is within her Kohar, they are one. Her vision is through the Kohar, her smell is through the Kohar. All she senses is through the Kohar. All she does and knows is through the Kohar. Behold, she is among the Chosen. Henceforth, she becomes an Opener of the Way for those of her blood. Glorious is she and blessed are they! Those are the supplications made for Milven, daughter of Mailon, son of Market the Stranger, according to the rites of the Sons of Fire. Ardwith kept it and it was done into this form at the place called Korinamba.

CHAPTER NINE. THE SACRED REGISTERS - PART 9

This concerns the mystery of the Twice Born. It relates to those born again, to those who have endured the awfulness of the false death which many do not survive; who have drunk deeply from Koriladwen, the smooth bitter brew which releases the spirit; who have entered Ogofnaum through the thundering doors. This is their path. The door of Heaven stands ajar, the doors of vision have been opened and now the Cavern of Vision is revealed. The spirit-bearing waves from the abyss have been freed, the rays of the Great light have been set free and the Guides and Watchers have been placed in their positions by the Constant One.

The Welcomers stand back, for this is not their stage. The Brilliant One is there and another who is the Reciter, and he explains the visions: "O Brave stouthearted one, Syoltash to be, the things you behold are the things seen by the Great Ones of Earth when they came this way in their hour and were returned back to life. They were truly men of wisdom, well versed in the mystic procedures, men who knew their position and parts." "Behold the twin stars. These embody the midwifery powers drawing the Twice Born back to their places of origin. They who are with them are the champions of light and darkness. One you must choose as your companion, but the choice must be made according to the law of affinity, otherwise you are lost."

"The pool wherein you gaze is earthlife. The brilliant light above, far greater than the sun, is the manifestation of The One God, but it is not He. The rays dancing about are the gods, distorted reflections of what is, distorted reflections of Truth, shadows of reality. The sparkling motes are souls, they descend from the light to manifest in darkness." "The clouds obscuring the lesser lights are the clouds of misconception, which darken the face of wisdom. The dark twins standing by the pillar are Delusion and Illusion, the constant beguilers of men. The stream of clear water is Truth and the waters of Truth constantly sheer away the clay pedestal of falsehood." "The brightness you see

before you and to the right is the naked spirit displaying itself in isolation. It is neither in a mortal body nor within the Kohar.
Beyond it is a much greater brightness reflected from afar, which is the Kohar of Kohars, which men cannot yet understand."
"The repulsive shapes which are behind the flame on your left are doomed spirits which once were the enlivening forces within men. Now they grovel in slime and filth, denizens of the mire, but their fate is just, for they themselves were the judges. The darkness beyond the murk will not become greater. Darkness cannot change to light, for when light comes into darkness there is no darkness, it ceases to exist." "The gloominess and shadow scene you see, forward on your left hand side, is the Region of Heaviness where mortals sojourn. The flickering lights which appear here and there are the joys of Earth, while the darker spots are where there are sorrows and suffering. The redness is anger and strife. The blue whiteness is love and compassion."

"The brightness above and ahead is the Region of Lightness where the Risen Ones rejoice, for there they welcome their Earth companions and are happy in reunion. Behold, here is a Rising One newly arrived, see, she flies upward on the wide wings of spirit and loving arms reach out to welcome her. The star-girt roadway you see rising before you is that trodden by the countless Risen Ones who have gone before. Now, advance towards the left."

"The abyss now before you is the mouth of Earth, and see, it opens and speaks to you, bidding you farewell. Listen carefully, for it will retell your deeds, your accomplishments and your omissions. If they weigh against you, then cast yourself into the abyss, for you are unworthy to survive this trial; go no further, nor can you turn back, lest you become prey to the Foul Lurker in Darkness." "If you have not been found wanting in the weighing, then step forward boldly and without fear, for the mouth will close to let you pass. If you are not numbered among the triumphant ones, then better by far that you be swallowed forthwith than that you survive to meet the Dread Lurker, the Devouring Horror, and be returned to Earth a witless, empty shell." "Beyond the abyss lies a stretch of blue water which contains the Pool of Wisdom and the Pool of Purification. Therein you must bathe and refresh yourself. The trees growing to your right bear the fruits of spiritual nourishment, eat and become strong.

Know, as doing so, that the things done, thought and visualised on Earth become qualities which are here transmuted into the things and experiences of this nature." "Pass between the waters and the trees and you will see a cliff against which is a ladder, the rungs of which are bound in leathern throngs made from the hide of the Bull of the Nightsky. This ladder, which rises before you, is the Ladder of Experience. Its two supports are experience in the body and experience in the spirit. The rungs are your daily deeds and thoughts and fantasies of your earthly life.

Now is the test. Will your daily deeds and secret thoughts support your ascent, or are they incapable of bearing you upward? See, above is your Kohar, call upon it for help, for therein you may have stored a reserve of spiritual strength. Or, perchance, it may be barren and empty, only you know. Those who uphold the ladder are the Lords of the Ladder, and they greet you as the Ascending One." "The ladder leads onto a plateau, and beside you appears the strangely garbed Reciter who sweeps his arms about and says, "All wherein things manifest is the firmament, which was before the beginning and still is. In the beginning its darkness was pierced by just a single ray from The Sun of God, but later, when the first spirits entered, the firmament was brightened and it was divided by heaviness and lightness. Then, when it was set apart, it was divided by the entry of dark spirits whose need was for a place with which they had a sombre affinity. Therefore, the firmament of lightness is divided, there is a Place of Light for the Victorious Ones and a Place of Darkness for those who could not rise to victory.

There are regions of gloom and shadow, regions of twilight and shade. There are regions of light in many hues, regions ranging from dazzling lights to dim light. There is a veil across the firmament, dividing Heaven from Earth, and each spirit departing from Earth penetrates through this veil, going to its appointed place, carried by the winds of affinity. Arriving there, the spirit, good or bad, strengthens and extends its compatible territory." "The Kohar is the Knower and the spirit is the known. All knowledge is with the Knower,

but the known can tap it so it flows out into the known. The Kohar receives the spirit seed in Heaven, for there it is as the body is on Earth.
Even as the earthly body is made of things from the Region of Heaviness, so is the Kohar made of things from the Region of Lightness." "These things are said by the Reciter before he leads you to the place where sleeps a serpent, and pointing to it he says, "Behold the serpent it sleeps at the bole of a tree from which hangs the body of man, the tree of his backbone. It is on guard, safeguarding the precious gem of spiritual powers, which lies enwrapped in the threefold covering. To obtain the gem the serpent must be aroused and then overcome. To rouse this serpent is a thing not to be lightly undertaken, for it causes a fire to mount into the heart, which may destroy the brain with delusions and madness. Only the Twice Born can really obtain the gem."

"You pass on with the Reciter who will say: "These are the things you must establish in your heart, the knowledge of the eight roads along which you must travel to reach the Land of the Westerners. These will bring you to the twelve first portals leading to the Land of Shadows. Here I will recite for you the twenty-two deeds of wickedness you have not done. You will then pass through the Land of Shadows as if it were your hour, and, beyond it, come to the Great Portal where it must be established, before the Great Guardian, that you have ever done all within your power to live according to the twelve virtues. Then you pass through the portal to the Hall of Judgement. Here, for the first time, your light is revealed and it is made known whether your tongue has spoken in accordance with the things within your heart."

"Many are they who know the words of the tongue but sever these from what is written in the heart. If the words of the tongue are copied from the writings of the heart and are a true copy, then cross to the Place of Assessment where your true form and likeness will be displayed for all to see." A curtain of darkness descends, there is a heavy dark mist, then the muffled crash of Thundering Doors. The aching body reclines within the tomb of stone. The questing pilgrim has returned to his homehaven. He has learned truths he could never learn on Earth and now knows the Grand Secret. Faith is replaced with certainty and he is now an Initiated One.

CHAPTER TEN. THE SACRED REGISTERS - PART 10

My God and Father, my Creator and Governor, Supreme and Immortal Spirit, I come to you as a wayward son comes to his father. I come as the world-weary wanderer comes home. I come as the victorious battle-bludgeoned warrior comes to the place of his rest. I am one who has passed the trials. I am one who has survived the challenges. I have returned full of wisdom and knowledge, the fruits of long years in Your earthly place of instruction. There I was diligent, I was not a waster of time, I was not a man of idleness. I am proved worthy. I, Your son, have come home. The virtues I developed on Earth are the messengers that sped before me, my qualities hastened to announce my coming. They sped on invisible wings, so that only those sensitive to that which emanated from me knew of their coming. They came as perfume carried on the wind. They announced me, they heralded me. They gave salutations to the Spirits in the Bright Abodes.

Yet I have not forgotten the Dwellers in Terror, and a small dark spirit of the Twilight has gone forth to make known to them my departure from Earth. This, that should any there know of me they may be made aware that I am not of their dismal company. Will there be weeping there in the dank, dreary darkness? I surmounted the trials of existence in heaviness. Now my spirit can speed like the lightning flash. I am one who has accomplished what had to be done. I have governed my affairs, not wholly by earthly standards but by the greater ordinances of Heaven. I have carefully read the books of instruction and listened to the interpreting words of the wise. He who tests hearts and reads thoughts has weighed me and I was not found wanting in the balances. I am a Cool One, for my thoughts rest in peace. I am not numbered among the Hot Ones whose thoughts consume them as fire consumes wood. I have passed the Nameless Ones, to come into the presence of The Great One whom no man names, whose name is not knowable to men. I have reached the destination of ages, I have achieved the ultimate goal. I have put on the mantle of immortality and the robe of light which the Heavenly Weavers prepared for Me. I am a Little One, one who comes in littleness and not greatness. I am a

Humble One and come not in pomp and grandeur, for these are things of the four quartered Earth having no place here.

I have done things which have been wrong, but these were done in ignorance and not wilfully or with malice. O Watchers, announce to the Lords of Light and to the Lords of Darkness that I am one who has penetrated the Mystic Veil but is destined to return to the Realm of Heaviness. O Watchers, announce that I am now a selfknowing everlasting spirit. O Father of the Gods, who is above all, issue the decrees of fate which ensure that henceforth I live a life of service, that I may live purposefully when I return to fulfil my destiny.

CHAPTER ELEVEN. THE SACRED REGISTERS - PART 11

My Heart, my Spirit, my Kohar, guardian of my memories, cast not your words in the balances against me. My faults and failings are not few, for no mortal man is perfect, yet they weigh tightly against my qualities and good deeds. Say not that I have wrought evil to any man wilfully or with malice, say not that I am a man of wickedness. Let me not suffer sorrowful remorse in the gloom and darkness, but let me live forever within the Region of Light. I have done deeds of goodness and led a goodly life. I have overcome the wiles of wickedness and avoided the snares of temptation. I have lived in peace with my neighbours. I have dealt justly and fairly with them and have not uttered words of malice to stir up strife. I have not gossiped about my neighbours, nor engaged in idle chatter concerning their affairs.

These things are not easy, and as no man is perfect I have at times been bad tempered under provocation. Therefore, speak words that will weigh in the balances against my failings. I have not slandered any man, nor have I wilfully caused pain and suffering. I have not caused the widow to weep, nor the child to cry without cause. I have dealt justly with my servants and with the servants of others, and I have been loyal to my masters. I have not slain unlawfully, nor wounded any man wilfully. Yet no man is perfect and when my burdens have weighed heavily upon me I have spoken harshly. Therefore, speak words that will weigh in the balances against my failings. I have never oppressed a poor man or taken from him what is his by virtue of my position. I have never oppressed the weak or cheated in the substance of metals. I have never said to a hungry woman, "Lay with me and you shall eat", for this is a vile thing. I have not lain with the wife of another man or seduced a child, for these are abominations. Yet no man is perfect and few are commanders of their thoughts, Therefore, speak words that will lighten these things in the balances.

I have not turned the water of another so that he is deprived of his full measure. I have not stopped flowing waters in their course. I have not kept fodder from cattle, nor allowed the pastures to be neglected. I have not caused any child to know fear without reason, nor have I beaten one in bad temper.

I have not transgressed the statutes of the king. Yet no man is perfect and sometimes that which is right in its day becomes wrong in another. Therefore, speak words that will weigh in the balances against my wrongdoings. I have not stolen, neither have I taken the possessions of any man by deceit. I have not divided the household of any man, nor separated him from his wife or children. I have not quarrelled with any man because of ignorance. I have not turned from my duties or failed in my obligations. I have not hidden my errors or buried my failings. Yet no man is perfect, therefore speak words that will weigh in the balances for me.

I have never behaved boisterously in a sacred place, nor have I ever defiled one. My hand has not been demanding because of my office, nor have I dealt haughtily with those who came to me with a plea. I have not increased my position by false words or writings. Yet my burden has been increased because of the perversity and wilfulness of men, and no man is perfect. Therefore, speak words that will weigh in the balances against my weaknesses. I have not permitted envy to eat my heart, nor malice to corrupt it. I have not been loud of mouth, nor spoken words of boastfulness. I have never slandered another or uttered words of falsehood. My tongue has never escaped from the control of my heart. I have never derided the words of another because they passed my understanding, nor have I stopped my ears to words of enlightenment.

I have never hidden myself to observe others, nor have I ever disclosed the secret designs or doings of others, unless they be of evil intent. Yet no man is perfect, therefore speak words that will weigh in the balances for me. When I have done wrong I have adjusted the scales that weighed down heavily against me. I have not hidden my weaknesses and failings in dark places, but washed them clean in the sunlight of honest compensation. I have not succumbed to the lures of lewdness, nor has my tongue spoken slyly of things which should be kept private. I have not peeped at nakedness or pryed into another's privacy. I have respected the modesty of womankind and the innocent delicacy of childhood. Yet men are as they are and imperfect, while thoughts stray wilfully and are not easily restrained. Therefore, speak words that will weigh in the balances for me.

O Great One, protect me. O Kohar, save me. Hear the words of my heart. I was one who was ever mindful of what was right and what was wrong. I did what I thought was right and shunned that which I thought was wrong. I listened to those who were wiser than I and helped those who were less privileged. Can man do more?

CHAPTER TWELVE. THE SACRED REGISTERS - PART 12

Know me and understand my ways. I am one who sees the past and the future, I look into hidden places, I am one who wanders freely. I am one who can be reborn, I am one who knows the speech of the released. I am an Uplifter. The Climbers come to me and I support them, I lift them up, I strengthen. Therefore, bring me the sustenance of smoke.

I hear and I hear not, for what I hear is heard by others. I speak and I speak not, for what I speak is in the mouths of others. I weep and I weep not, for my weeping is the weeping of others. I am an Uplifter. The Climbers come to me and I console them. I enlighten them with words of hidden wisdom. Thus they find the way. I am one who comes forth when the circle is formed, when the twin lamps have been lit and the incantations made. I come forth from the consecrated place and bear the staff of power. I know the secrets of the dark waters and the secrets of blood. I am a wanderer in strange places.

I am one who does not fear to tread the forbidden paths. I am an Uplifter. The Climbers come to me and I reveal the way. I am the Opener of Tombs. I am the Dweller in the Stone Caverns. I am the one who precedes the Herald of the Companions. I am the Swimmer in the Waters of Wisdom. I am the Discoverer of Hidden Places. I am the one who hovers above the Still Waters. I am the Wanderer with the Winds.

I am an Uplifter. The Climbers come to me and are comforted. They thirst and I refresh them, they hunger and I fill them with food. I am the Sitter Beneath the Sycamore. I am the Eater of the Rowan. I am the heart within the heat of the fire and the eye within the candle flame. I am the uprising hawk and the contented dove. I am one who has tamed the serpent and drawn forth its secrets. I am one who has many eyes and sees what is written in the nightskies; whose ears hear the whispers at the edge of the Great Waters. I am one whose right foot rests on the Earth and whose left foot rests oh the firmament.

I am one who faces all spirits alike and knows their true nature. I am an Uplifter. The Climbers come to me and I give them peace. I am one who gazes into the deep dark pool, reading the things hidden therein. I am the Caller Forth of the Deformed Ones and the Tongue of the Bright Ones. I am he of the Everlasting Form. I am he who provides stability to falterings forms and the interpreter who spans the veil.

I am an Uplifter. The Climbers come to me and I provide their Guide and their Guardian. Know me and understand my ways. Invoke me through the rite of smoke and wine. Call me forth into the circle of stone, but beware, for lest you hold the seven keys and understand the nature of the three rays, you are lost.

CHAPTER THIRTEEN. THE SCROLL OF RAMKAT

Awful is the great day of judgement at its dawning in the Netherworld. The soul stands naked in the Hall of Judgement, nothing can now be hidden. Hypocrisy is no avail; to maintain goodness when the soul reveals its own repulsiveness is futile. To mumble empty ritual is foolishness. To call upon gods who have no existence is a waste of time. In the Hall of Judgement the wrongdoer is judged. On that day and henceforth his qualities shall form his food. His soul, soft as clay upon Earth, is hardened and set into shape according to its moulding. The balances are adjusted. One arrives. The Forty-Two Virtues are his assessors. Shall he dwell among beauty as a godling, or be given captive to the Keeper of Horrors, to dwell among vile things under a merciful mantle of darkness?

One arrives. The twisted body, tormented on Earth, and the ugly face have gone, discarded at the portal. He strides through the Hall in radiance, to pass into the Place of Everlasting Beauty. One arrives. Now no earthly body sheilds the horror which is the true likeness of the evildoer upon Earth. He runs from the light which he cannot tolerate, and hides himself in the shadows near the Place of Terror. Soon he will be drawn to his compatible place among the Dismal Company.

One arrives. He has been upright and a just one. His failings and weaknesses were of little account. This upright man fears nothing, for he is welcomed among the Bright Ones and shall go unhampered among the Everlasting Lords.

One arrives. He trembles before the Unseen Judges, he is lost, he knows nothing, earthly knowledge and confidence are left behind. The balance drops, he sees his soul and recognises his true self, he rushes into the merciful darkness. It enfolds him and dark arms embrace him, drawing him into the terrible gloom, into the Place of Dark Secret Horrors. One arrives. She graced the court with beauty, men sang of her loveliness and grace. Now, as when a mantle is removed, all is discarded, it is the time of unveiling. Who can

describe the lustful thoughts and secret unclean deeds which fashioned the horror coming through the portal?
There is a hush among the compassionate. One arrives. On Earth she was pitied by the compassionate and scorned by the hardhearted. There her lot was degradation and servitude, privation and sacrifice, few and meagre were the gifts from life. Yet she triumphed. Now she comes forward surrounded by brilliance, even the Shining Ones are dazzled by her beauty. One arrives. The twisted face and pain-wracked body of the cripple have been left behind. A kind and loving soul dwelt imprisoned within its confines. Now the relieved spirit steps forward into the great Hall, unencumbered and free, glorious to behold.

One arrives. The splendid body which graced Earth remains there, an empty, decaying thing. The naked soul enters the Everlasting Halls. It is a deformed, misshapen thing fit only to dwell in the merciful gloom of the place with which it has compatible affinity.

One arrives. Neither goodness nor wickedness bears down upon the scales. The balances remain straight. The soul departs to the twilight borderland between the Region of Light and the Region of Darkness. O Great Lords of Eternity, who once were in the flesh, even as I, hear not the outpourings of an overburdened and sorrowful heart. For who am I to presume to call upon The Great God of All? Who am not without wickedness and weak in spirit. I have filled my heart with knowledge of the Secret Writings but still I fear the judgement. Therefore, Great Lords of Eternity, I call upon you who once walked the Earth, even as I, and who, therefore, understand the failings and weaknesses of men. I am not weak in my standing with earthly things, but I am weak beside the Greater Beings. Will I, too, ever be worthy of the grandeur of the Eternal Mansions ?

O Great Beings whose nature is beyond understanding, grant me just a spark of the Eternal Wisdom, that it might light my soul and kindle the flame of immortal life. What is the destined fate of a man who knows the existence of things beyond his understanding? I see but I do not know, therefore I am afraid. Man can swim against the current towards the bank, but he needs a helping hand to pull him ashore when he is exhausted from the struggle. This is the fate of man. He must strive for that which he cannot attain.

He must believe in that which he cannot prove. He must seek that which he cannot find. He must travel a road without knowing his destination. Only thus can the purpose of life be fulfilled. Man may believe he knows his destiny, but he cannot be assured with certainty; in no other way can he fulfil it. In this way alone can his soul be properly awakened to flower with its full potential. This alone he may know: The purpose of all human life is a goal so glorious it surpasses all earthly understanding. We may visualise our individual goals as we will, it is ordained that we have this freedom. How close or how far we are from reality is of little consequence, what is, is. He who seeks a non-existent destination will, nevertheless, get somewhere. He who seeks not at all will get nowhere. Earthly life fulfils itself without attainment.

CHAPTER FOURTEEN. THE SCROLL OF YONUA

Away from my eyes, O Hideous One. Slink back into the dark shadows about the black sunless abode where dwell the self-distorted souls of the Fearsomely Formed Ones. Back to your murky haven of sombre compatibility. Away, out of sight, for your repulsiveness brings back into my heart the thoughts of evils and temptations I have encountered and overcome, thoughts which I now so gladly forget. You poor, doomed fiend, mis-shapen, horny-headed, slit-snouted, stunted in arms and legs, horrible to behold. What dreadful thoughts and unclean deeds must have been yours, to fashion you in this manner! Away, back to your own kind, back from the twilit border where you lurk furtively, afraid, pitifully seeking a glimpse of the bright joys denied to your own folly. Back to the place with which you have pitiful affinity, back to your own dark, compatible companions.

The Guardians of the Hidden Gates repel you, lest you befoul the pathways of the Glorious Ones who once struggled to find beauty and cleanliness. The light of this place is ever spreading, and soon a Glorious One may walk where you now slink in the gloom. Back, back from the dividing flame, back into the sad comfort of enveloping darkness. Back to your foul companions in misery, back into the mercifully enshrouding gloom. Your fate saddens my heart. Can you find consolation there, hidden in the comforting darkness? Does a kind word ever lighten the burden of your days? Is there a place of rest among the slime and excreta?

O Fallen One, who once walked Earth so proudly in self-esteem, selfishness and arrogance, go back, torment yourself no more with the sights of beauty and joy which lie beyond your reach. O Wriggler in the Slime, back from the purifying flame, what can it avail you now? O Repellent One, who by wrongdoing and non-good doing thus cursed yourself and were delivered into the comfortless arms of decay and filth; who on Earth appeared arrayed in such deceptive softness and complacency; who dwelt amid pleasure and luxury, away, back into the shadows, hide yourself from the pure gaze of the Glorious Ones.

O Squirming One, turned back are you, the shameful flesh is unworthy even of the flame. The unshapely mass, unchiselled by the forming blows of self-discipline and selfless service, unmoulded by the touch of compassion and love, unpolished by conformity to the burnishing blows of sincere goodness, has no place near the region of revealing light. See, are you not seared with pain when the pure light falls upon you?

Miserable indeed is your lot in that dread, dreary abode! See, your slimy hide shrinks from the pure glare, it splits, it cracks, back, back into your dark cavern with its floor of slime. Back out of sight, out of hearing, back from the pure gaze of righteousness. How miserable the lot of one who finds unconsoling comfort in the depths of dread darkness lit only by shadowy gloom! How awful to dwell in companionship with distorted shades! What became of the loveliness which once clothed you on Earth?

Whose fault that you brought it not with you? Did you ever pause, even for one moment, to gaze into the self-revealing mirror within you and see the awful creature you were forming? Amid your pleasures and luxury, did you not think of the wellbeing of your inner self? Did you not care? O if I could but help you now, but the hideousness was set firm in the furnace fire of death. Then the enveloping flesh was stripped away and the hidden horror within the mould revealed. As the butterfly emerges from the chrysalis, so should the soul emerge from its earthly body. An unnatural thing like this was never intended, yet you freely made the choice. Not a single disfiguring line was made by another. What words are those which rasp forth from the unlipped, fish-shaped mouth?

O ears, say you deceive me! O heart, cease this pounding clamour! O hand of horror, release your awful grip! Would that I could swoon, that I could find relief in unconsciousness, but facts have to be faced here as on Earth. I must look in trembling terror. Yes, I loved on Earth, nothing there was more precious to me than my sister in love. I forgave her wilfulness and was not stirred up when her words were unkind. I ever remained a man of cool temper.

I clothed her well and good food she never lacked. My heart sang in her presence, I rejoiced in her loveliness, she was my life, my wife. Yet she was unfaithful, she was cruel, she found pleasure in deceit and perversion. As the years passed they became heavy, clouded and bitter because of her wayward ways.

O horror, O terror, O cringing fear, keep away from me! O my eyes, O my heart, it is true. It is the one I loved. O let me die once more, that consciousness may pass from me! It is her whom I loved, she for whom I waited in joyful anticipation, hoping to find the light of my youth, hoping the overlay of later evils would be sloughed away by death, hoping to find the warm, throbbing liveliness I once held. I would gladly have forgiven the pain she caused in her maturity. O what has become of the smooth flesh, the warm touch? Where is the beauty of face, the grace of form?

O raise not the crocodile-skinned arms to shield the awful snout, the green-rimmed, red-veined eyes! O racing heart! I hear the misformed words amidst the hiss and gurgle issuing forth from the oozing aperture. O say not that I was so blind, so greatly deceived, that you cared for nought but the earthly things we shared; that your affection was the false front of hypocrisy, your love a lie. Did I not always forgive? Was I not always patient? With whom did you share the terrible thoughts and desires that fashioned you thus ? Surely this cannot be the work of your own nature alone. Fickle you were and pleasure loving, selfish, cruel and deceitful, but all this I forgave because of the plea of my heart. Was this not enough?

O where is the companion I awaited? Lost, and worse than lost. O compassion, O mercy, come to my aid! My heart fails me, I cannot face what I thought to greet so joyously. O powers of solicitude, strengthen me. What can I do to mitigate the Law? Is there hope? Is there a way? A whisper of comfort, O gratefully I hear it, "There is hope and there is a way, but between this self-shaped horror and the Glorious Ones there is an uncrossable chasm. In sorrow and anguish it must seek a road, it must go its own dark way as you must go yours in the light. Turn back, turn again towards the light, the compassion in your own heart does nought to bridge the gulf between, unless it strikes a responsive spark within the other heart".

"Let the memory be erased, this is not the companion of your path. The trials and sorrows borne so well, the uncomplaining unselfishness fashioned you in glory. Nor would you have reached the present degree of perfection had she not been as she was, and is now revealed to be. This fearful fate was wrought by the lost one alone, for each is the sole keeper of his spirit. Each soul is fashioned by every thought, desire and deed, every emotion that touched it during its sojourn in an earthly body". "Each is the maker of his own future, the fashioner of his own being".

CHAPTER FIFTEEN. A SCROLL FRAGMENT - ONE

Salvaged from the Great Book of The Sons of Fire this is all that remains of some sixteen damaged pages relating to an initiation ceremony.

Who will reward or punish me? I will.

Who besets my path with sorrow? I do.

Who can grant me a life of everlasting glory? I can.

Who must save me from the horror of malformation? I must.

Who will guide my footsteps through life? I will.

Who brings joy into my life and gladdens my heart? I do.

Who brings peace and contentment to my spirit? I do.

Who lightens the burdens of my labour? None but myself.

Whose courage will protect me from the workers of evil? My courage.

Whose wisdom will guide me and enlighten my heart? My wisdom.

Whose will rules my destiny? My will.

Whose duty is it to attend to my wants? My duty.

Who is responsible for my future state of being? I alone am responsible.

Who shields me from temptation? No one.

Who shields me from sorrow and suffering? No one.

Who shields me from pain and affliction? No one.

Who benefits from my toil and tribulation, my sorrow and suffering? Myself, if wise.

Who benefits from my temptations and afflictions, my sacrifices and austerities? Myself, if wise.

CHAPTER SIXTEEN. THE THIRD OF THE EGYPTIAN SCROLLS

(A Fragment) If a man would know Heaven, he must first know Earth. Man cannot understand Heaven until he understands Earth. He cannot understand God until he understands himself, and he cannot know love unless he has been loveless.

God is unknown but not unknowable. He is unseen but not unseeable. God is unheard but not unhearable. He is not understood but He is understandable. The goal of life is upstream, not downstream. Man must struggle against the current, not drift with the flow. A child is born knowing all God intended it to know, the rest it must discover for itself.

Man does not live to increase the glory of God, this cannot be done, but to increase the glory of man. He who worships with empty rituals wastes his time and displays the shallowness of his thought. That which man does to benefit man is good, but if he seeks to gratify God it is a labour of ignorance showing disrespect for God whose nature is above that of earthly princes.

A lifting hand is worth ten wagging tongues. Be a man of fortitude and courage. Prepare to fight, for Earth gives man but two choices: to struggle or perish. There is work to be done in the Garden of God, therefore cease useless performances and word-wasting discussions, go, pick up the hoe and tackle the task to hand.

This is the secret of life: Man lives in God and God lives in man. This answers all questions.

CHAPTER SEVENTEEN. THE SIXTH OF THE EGYPTIAN SCROLLS

God is in all and He encompasses all. There is no God but The True God, and His existence is our assurance of life everlasting. He was before the beginning and will be after the end. He is mighty and all powerful. In His magnificence and majesty no man can conceive Him. His divine nature is beyond the understanding of man. His creation is awesome. His ways unfathomable. His creative thought brought all things forth and the power which flows from Him is life.

He holds life within His mind and the universe within His body. If a man, in ignorance and foolishness, conceives a more understandable god in his own image or builds gods of wood and stone, that will not take anything away from the stature of God. The Supreme One is ever God, The Creator of man, and if man makes earthly gods to worship, then it is man who loses thereby and not God.

Among earthly things man shall find nothing greater than himself. Man worships, not to make God greater, for this he cannot do, but to make himself greater. Nothing man can do can add to what God already has. Men conceive God as a Being having greatly magnified human qualities, as a kinglike Being greater than any king. Thus man falls into error.

As the sun surrounds man with light, though it be hidden behind the stormclouds, so is man in the thoughts of God, though God Himself be hidden from him. Such is our God who, though Himself eternal, lives with each man and with him passes through the Dark Portal of Death into the light of the Glorious Region beyond. God rules over all earths and all spheres. He is in them and they are in Him. All things are in God and He is in all things. What is was to be, all things begin and end in God. This alone is wisdom, understand and live forever.

CHAPTER EIGHTEEN. A SCROLL FRAGMENT - TWO

The Book of Initiation and Rites says of God, "All our hopes rest in God who created all things, sustaining them with His breath, whatever their state, wherever they may be, in this place on Earth, or in any other place visible or invisible".

"He alone causes herbs to blossom in beauty and causes all things to come forth in their proper order and time, all flow from His directing thoughts. The peaceful beauty enfolding the face of the land at eventide, the melody of song and speech, the fragrance of flowers, the soft delicacy of petal and wing. All beauty and charm that delight the hearts of men flow from God".

"His wisdom is unbounded and in His goodness He has provided all things in which He has created a need in man. The daylight and wind, food and water, heat and coolness, the materials of his dwelling and the substance of his garments, all things for his daily use and enjoyment. Man lacks nothing which would increase his skill and knowledge, to all useful things guideposts have been planted along the way. What need can man know for which God has not already made provision, even before man was born?"

"He has established the nature of all things, so they remain stable and come forth in their proper order without change. When a man sows barley he knows what will come up out of the ground, the rewards of his toil are not confusion".

"A man lights a fire knowing it will cook his food, it is not sometimes hot and at other times cold. He knows that day will follow night and that the hours of darkness are prescribed, it is not a matter of chance. The hours of darkness are not one day long and the next day short. Oil is ordained for lamps and water to drink, man knows that never can he light a wick in water. Man looks about him and sees order, not confusion, and he knows that where there is organisation there must be an organiser".

"The ordinances of God are established for the benefit of man, were they not set in stability man would be nothing but the plaything of chance and the victim of chaos. Therefore, on the days of feast and fasting, each following in their due season, I will ever remember the obligations due to my God".

"I will rejoice and sing songs of praise with a full heart, I will shun the hypocrisy of moving lips. I will be joyful in the fullness of spirit at the beginning and at the end of the appointed seasons". 'The decrees of God are fulfilled at the appointed times and the days of labour pass one into the other. The season of first gathering to the full time of harvest, the season of sowing to the season of fruitfulness, all pass away as the kiss of the wind on the waters".

"I will raise my voice, and my hands will move with the music. I will pluck strings and send sweet musical sounds rising to my God, and my breath will fill pipes with
tunes to His Glory. When the sky blushes in the dawning I will lift up my voice in gladness, and when it reddens in the evening I will not remain silent". "O how I rejoice that God has made me as I am! Truly He is in all and encompasses all. In His magnificence and majesty no man can conceive Him, for His divine nature is beyond the understanding of man. His creation is awesome, His ways unfathomable".

"The love of God for His wayward children has been limitless and abounding. It has remained changeless throughout the ages, filled with His noble purpose. He created so that He might express and share that love, which is the very essence of His nature, with beings created in His likeness, beings which could absorb and reflect that love. Yet, that his love might be wholly free man was endowed with freewill, the freewill he has used perversely".

CHAPTER NINETEEN. A HYMN FROM THE BOOK OF SONGS - 1

Bring forth the instruments of music, let all voices be raised in thanksgiving to The
Lord of Our Lives. Be happy in heart and let joyfulness flow from your lips, but remain in stillness while the hands move. Peace and honour be Yours, O Great One, Shadow of Our Days, Comforter of Our Nights, to whom alone we pay homage. Long ago the skydoor opened and You appeared over the land in the days of our forefathers, shaking it with Your wrath, but now You are hidden, Your awesome glory is seen no more.

We, Your children, rejoice, for You bring peace and spread contentment and security over the whole face of the Earth. Heaven and Earth and all the spheres of the infinite spaces are filled with Your Spirit. The demons of darkness tremble before You. Yet to us You are truly The Mysterious Hidden One, The Guide of our fathers in the sad days of darkness when the face of the sun was veiled in gloom from the eyes of men.

You pour out goodness, bringing fresh water to the green pasturelands, bestowing life upon all beasts and living creatures therein. Through the blessing of Your bounty, even the parched lands drink unceasingly in then-season.

You are The Bestower of Bread, for you cause the corn to increase and the harvest to be plentiful. You are The Supplier of Reeds and The Provider of Fish. Every craftsman is prosperous and deft when under the guidance of Your hand. Your eye directs the hammers of the smith and Your hand covers the fingers of the potter.

Your creating breath is inhaled by the craftsman, so he is inspired to create an object of beauty. You whisper on the breeze and the hearts of men are filled with a gladness which issues from their mouths as joyous song. You move the brush of the painter and direct the pen of the writer. You are The Warden of Fishes within the waters and direct them into the nets of the fishermen. You are The Watchman who keeps the waterfowl away from the field sown at the rising of the bountiful waters.

You are The Lookoutman at the eye of the barge moving safely over the flowing waters. You are The Director of the energy-giving breezes which press against the sails. Your hand rolled the corn grains and Your life-giving breath sucks up the green growing shoots. Your fingers unfold the awakening buds. Your firm will holds stone in stability, so the great buildings endure through the ages. Nothing can escape Your Vigilance, and rest is unknown to You. Eternal activity is the essence of Your nature.

You are The Ever Watchful One, The Great Bearer of the Scales, The Unchanging Guardian of the Helpless and The Protector of the Poor. Those who fill these roles on Earth do them in You name, for You are the motivation and power behind their deeds. Were You non-existent men would devour one another like crocodiles, while justice and mercy would be things unknown. Something intangible and unseeable
flows out from You and rules the lives of men, causing men to deal justly with one another. For though injustice is part of the fabric of life, it is not dominant and Your power mitigates its effects. You caress the face of the land and at Your touch the womb of Earth is opened, green growth springs through the soil and reaches up towards the sun.

All creatures move about according to Your design, and by Your decree their lives are directed. You paint the patterns of life and design its destinies. Though the prince lay his head on a pillow of down and the beggar lay his on an unyielding stone, both sleep alike on Your bosom. The sleep of the rich man is no better than that of a poor man, while the sleep of a labourer is better than that of an idler. The Night frightener does not haunt the dreams of those who have paid their debts to the taskmaster of the day. Those who spend their days in idleness sleep in a restless bed. Thus, You have ordained that the scales of life be adjusted. All is balanced in Your hands. Your spirit moves over the Earth, instructing the bee in the gathering of its honey and the hornet in the making of its nest. It directs the ant in the complex design of its cavern and the swallow in its mud gathering. It guides the birds in their season and calls the locusts at the appointed times. All creatures have their unlearned wisdom, which is an outpouring force emanating from Your Spirit.

When You fill the Earth with the shining light which rules the day under Your command, all men rejoice, for by this all things are increased and food comes forth in abundance. When the Lady of the Night rules the darkness and all is hushed in mellow coolness, hearts are filled with tranquillity and content. You fulfil all the needs of men, for You are The Great Provider. Men labour in the fields and fill the storehouses with grain, but You provide the increase.

You are The Ever Bountiful One, yet with all You give never is Your substance lessened. You remain everlastingly the same. Man has nought but what originates with You. It is Your waters of life, everlastingly flowing, that sustain him. Eternal glory be Yours, my God and my Life. I sought You in many temples, only to discover that there was One God hidden behind all other gods. That You are indeed The Father of Gods, yet The Maker of none of them. You have illuminated the widespread universe with beauty and filled it with awesome, imperishable grandeur beyond description. So great are Your works above that they must be veiled, so we can comprehend them only dimly, lest we be overcome.

Beforetimes many great men have praised You in error; not knowing what was good for them they sought to attain the things which fed the flesh alone. O Great One, show such as these the error of their ways, giving them not the good things of life but making all better men, that they may be worthy of these. You have loved us with an exceedingly great love, having compassion on our many failings and weaknesses, knowing that men are but frail creatures prone to go astray. O God of Gods, for the sake of our fathers who placed their trust in You, to whom You gave the ordinances of life, be merciful to us. Instruct and guide us along the paths we should follow. Lead us through the many entanglements of earthly life, so we may finally come to rest in Your safekeeping.

CHAPTER TWENTY. A HYMN FROM THE BOOK OF SONGS - 2

O Great and Bountiful One who is the fountainhead of glory and the eternal spring of power; who sits enthroned in wisdom; whose counsel is the Law, great are the manifestations of Your wrath when it purges the land, even as it was done in the days of our fathers. Yet we, weak, wayward and wilful men, know in the depth of our hearts that whatever You do is done in justice and to our ultimate benefit. With inscrutable wisdom You prepared a compatible place for the spirits of men, a place encompassing the domain of man, a place wherein man rules under the decrees of Your everlasting and unchanging Law. You have set the boundaries and they are held back, neither troubling nor oppressing us beyond our endurance.

The spirits of men rule in the mysterious domains governing the sun and the moon, the stars and the nightwatchers, the mistmen and the hidden caves of power. They undertake their appointed tasks there and are wave wanderers of the watery wastes, guardians of the deep. You have created man in the likeness of an original conceived in Your mysterious abode, and the manner of his life is fixed according to Your plan. Great and wonderful is the ultimate destiny of man who, as yet, has progressed but a few steps along the road towards the goal of life.

Yet You have opened his ear to mysterious and wonderful things. You have revealed strange mysteries to his eye, he knows things unbelievable in olden times. This being on whom You have conferred so much is a thing of weakness and frailty. He was shaped from moistened clay and moulded in water, then set upon a mound in the midst of the great chaos. His eyes were shown the glory above but he wearied of looking, for such splendour was beyond his comprehension. Therefore, he sought his pleasures among the things from whence he came, and therein he now finds his delight. So he sits on a pedestal of shame down by the polluted spring. His repast comes from the pot of fornication and he is clad in the garments of wickedness. Great One. You who are all wise know the words which come forth from his lips. You know the fruit of his mouth, the pollen of his tongue. Be merciful to man and overlook his weaknesses, for he is as he was made and, perchance, so he was meant to be. Who can question the mystery? May Your will prevail!

CHAPTER TWENTY-ONE. THE SUNSETTING HYMN FROM THE BOOK OF SONGS

O Great God, unbounded by earthly limitations, Your Will is an eternal mystery and Your deeds confound the minds of men. Men worship You, the lesser gods pay due homage, while they who are between gods and men devote themselves to Your service. Highest of Gods, Lord of Men, Ancient Lord of Life and Light, Creator of the Tree of Life, who made the herb and fruit to nourish men and grass to feed the cattle; who perfumed the flowers and gave birds their gay plumage, Hail to The Supreme Power and Spirit! Maker of all that exists in all the spheres above and below, the essence of whose Spirit is in all things.

Ruler of all the regions of light and Master of the nether regions. Great Fountainhead of Wisdom whose abode is in Truth, who fashioned men so they accord with Your own nature; who gave rare abilities to animals and instilled cunning knowledge into insects; who chose the colours of the flowers and the songs of the birds. O Veiled One whose sanctuary is hidden in the breasts of men, whose temple is open to the Heavens and hung about with the stars.

O Mighty One, hear the cry of my spirit as it seeks nourishment from the divine source Hail to The Supreme Power and Spirit! Great Fashioner of Earthly Things, who came into being before all else, whose sacred name none can know, whose likeness is not displayed in writings and whose image is not carved in wood or stone; whose eyes were the pattern for the sight of men and whose sensitivity generated their touch; whose tongue gave speech to the little gods; who made the herbage for cattle and the waterweed for fish; who feeds even the worms and insects and quickens the life within the egg; who fashioned wild fruits for the birds and wild seed for the mice; who sustains the lifeforce within every living thing, up to the heights of Heaven, across the wide breadth of Earth, down to the very depths of the sea.

O save me from that which is beneath the Earth and from those upon the Earth who would work wickedness against me. Hear me, and, my God, I shall praise You, my voice will rise up to Heaven and roll right across the Earth. All those who ply the great mothering river shall hear its echoes. I will tell of Your goodness and greatness to my children and to their children. My words will resound down through the generations as yet unborn. Respond to me, O Great One, as I seek to commune in the silence. My desire is to learn, but You are too mysterious for men to understand. Hail to The Supreme Power and Spirit!

O help my soul to rectify its evil deed and balance them with good. Destroy every form of evil which clings to me, and let there be nothing in my soul to cause malformation and thus estrange me from my friends who have departed to dwell in the happy Land of Dawn. Let brightness be my new life's birthright and let my spirit be ever light. Hail to The Supreme Power and Spirit! The great dome of Heaven rises above and no man knows its limitations. The broad Earth is spread wide and no man knows its boundaries. Man cannot fathom it all,

O God who is great, have compassion on my littleness. Bear Patiently with my blunderings and overlook my ignorance. Your reach is so great and mine is so small, help me to know You for myself. I am helpless and lost. Hail to The Supreme Power and Spirit! O Great God, who brings comfort to the prisoner, peace to the tormented; who strengthens the fearful and adjust the scales between the weak and the strong. Strengthen my desire to understand Your great purpose.

O Sole God whose tears vitalize the hearts of men, in reverence and humility my spirit awaits Your command, my Creator and my Light. Hail to The Supreme Power and Spirit! O Great Craftsman, who fashioned man so wonderfully; who brought together the elements of the Earth and transmuted them so mysteriously; who created with such diversity that no two things are exactly alike, give your servant some task, that he may accomplish it to Your glory.

O Provident Benefactor, who provides sustenance for the beasts of the wilderness and fills the storehouses of men; who placed the great metals in the bosom of the Earth, that man might draw them forth, let not my body go naked, nor my sleeping place be destroyed. Accept my homage, O God of Truth, who lives down through the ages of time which make up the everlasting Circle of Eternity. Hail to The Supreme Power and Spirit!

O Powerful God, whose wrath lit up the vaults of Heaven and whose fire devoured the wicked in olden times; whose whirlwind swept clean the Earth; who lifted the seas and dashed them against the mountains. O let not the great forces of Earth afflict me. Hold them fast in Your hand, that they may not crush me as the chariot crushes the ant. Hail to The Supreme Power and Spirit! Having an affinity with You, my soul knows You and rejoices in the knowledge. It hears You and is at peace. It opens in response to Your warmth as the lotus, and awakens softly as the day opens its eye to the night. My soul knows what I know not. It sees into hidden places and understands deep mysteries. Let me know its nature better, that it may instruct me in wisdom. My soul swells with gratitude towards The Bounteous Being who causes all things to be which fulfil all desires.

My God is not graven in marble or stone. He is not shaped in wood or cast in copper. He has neither offerings nor ministrations. My God is a god of quiet places and silences. He is found where the wild winds blow and the gay flowers blossom, away from the habitations of men. He is not worshipped in temples and His praises are not sung by the unthinking multitude.

My God is a constant companion, He lives quietly in the homes and hearts of men. His true abode is unknown. He has no painted shrine, no building fashioned by the hands of men could contain Him. Hail to The Supreme Power and Spirit! O Ever Watchful God, The All Seeing One, if aught be done or concealed in the darkness of the night it shall be known to You.

O Supreme Power, who alone can deflect the Awesome Ones of Heaven from their path of destruction; who alone can turn aside the sky boulders and break the winds of the hurricane, I acknowledge You as my Sole God, The Guide of my ways and The Guardian of my Life. I will call upon You by Your names of Power. I give You Your degrees, O Lord Over the Thrones of Earth, Director of the Destinies of Nations, Ancient Dweller in the Heavens, Lord of Existence, Lord of Terrors, Master of the Hidden Spheres, Commander of the Universal Hosts, Lord of The Law wherein Your will is manifested.

Victor in the Skyfight, Creator of Hidden Desires of the Soul, Great One who mysteriously fashions His body as men fashion their souls. Giver of Life to souls, by whose breath they awaken. Selector of the Generative Substances, Transformer of Matter, Keeper of the Eternal Essences, Ruler of the Spirits in their Spheres. He who hears the prayer of the prisoner; who stands between the weak and the strong. Lord of Fertility for whom the great mothering river flows and the waters rise. Lord of the Tree of Life, Emperor of the Sacred Spheres, who dispenses the Celestial Substance, who directs the Thunderbolts; who pilots the stars in the skyways; who overlooks the Watchers in the Night, Great Guardian of Hidden Things and Master of the Divine Secrets, whose domain is shrouded in mystery; who makes tender the hearts of women and makes stern the faces of men.

Dweller in Deep Obscurity whose sanctuary is infinite; who died in the effort of creation and was reborn in the soul of man. Great God, whose face shall be revealed in the future, when all men are wise, grant me Your Truth and Peace Divine. Hail to The Supreme Power of Spirit! Though I falter on the way and fail at the task, despise me not. I try but success eludes me. I seek but cannot find. I am so small and You are so great that I cannot span the gulf between, unless You incline towards me. O Great Spirit, how near men are to You in reality! Through the darkness of ignorance greater than night they have groped a way to You. You alone are addressed in the prayers of men. To whatever men pray You alone hear their petitions, You alone can answer them. Only for You are their words of praise fitting. O Great One, enter into the hearts of men and renew the bond with their souls.

Hail to The Supreme Power and Spirit! O Mysterious God hidden in time, Great Ruler of the Ages, we who cannot know more than the smallest part of Your creation turn to You for help and enlightenment. If it be Your will that man should struggle towards understanding and strive for knowledge, then so be it. Man will do whatever he must do, but, O Great God, be patient with him in his failures and failings. Hail to The Supreme Power and Spirit!

CHAPTER TWENTY-TWO. THE HYMN OR PRAYER FROM THE BOOK OF SONGS - 3

O Great One in Heaven, whose thoughts probe the hearts of men, cast forth a small ray of illumination to light my way in the darkness of man's ignorance. Strengthen me by Your revelation, that for even a brief moment I may see Truth and know the mysteries of life. I ask not to see as the Great Ones have seen, but just for something within my understanding.

O Great God, send me one bright shaft of light, that I may see silhouetted as in a flash of lightning the forces that wage war for the possession of my soul. For what mortal unaided can understand or visualise the dark things that lurk to lure the soul along the path of horror, such as the demons waiting to twist the weak soul into coils of frightfulness before casting it into the abyss of terror? Lord of the Universe, take pity on me. Everything hes in Your Great Hand except the fate of each man, and men are frail and weak.

Many who have seen Truth revealed have quailed before the awful responsibilities of man and consoled themselves by fashioning unnatural gods before whom they quelled the fears in their hearts. I am not one worthy to gaze upon Truth, nor do I desire to do so lest I be overwhelmed, perhaps I ask too much from One who reads the hearts of men. O Great Luminated One, keep me from the final horror which has in wait to devour the souls of men. Help me in the dread hour when I come face to face with my own soul. O save it from the abode of the Dark Warden of Terrors!

What are the great mysteries of man's destiny so dimly perceived even by the Illuminated Ones? Have mercy on my dismal ignorance, or I am delivered into the toils of my own repulsiveness. What is the Great Secret whispered so fearfully among the great columns? What are the substances wherewith men may pass through the Great Portal and return to life? Is it true that the destiny of man is determined by man?

O what fearful responsibility, my heart is overwhelmed and my spirit becomes weak with dread. Is it for this that men shun the Truth and cast themselves at Your feet for mercy? I fear, for my soul is heavy with evil and the scales will bear down against me. Will it be stamped with the dread impress of condemnation by the forty-two seals? Place Your hand in mercy upon the balances and let my soul be made light.

O Great One, hidden within the eternal silence, who shines forth as a beacon of light to few men. O lighten our darkness and our fear-shadowed hearts! Lift the veil just slightly, that we may understand something of Your greatness. We are not uninstructed and know we can be granted no more than a glimpse of Your greatness, for to receive more would be too awesome for the frail constitution of man. This is why the ignorant doubt, for their very ignorance spawns the frailty which inhibits their enlightenment.

We hardly dare murmur these fervent words. O Great One, grant that the spirit within us may be helped to cleanse itself of the besmirching foulness spawned by our thoughts. Remove from us every trace of that which may pollute, and let us know timeless splendour in glory.

CHAPTER TWENTY-THREE. THE HYMN FROM THE BOOK OF SONGS - 4 THE HYMN OF REWA

I am here, I am Yours, I sing Your praises. Join the dance, O priests and priestesses. Join the dance, O Skytravellers, who cover the Earth with your rays of power. Join the dance, O strangers. Accept our offerings and salutations, accept our devotions and make them successfully beneficial. Move around moonwise, O priests and priestesses. Stamp on wickedness. Stamp on hypocrisy. Stamp your feet on malice and hatred. Sound the flutes, blow the pipes, shake the bells. Come, stamp on the head of pride, stamp on the Foul Fiend of Lust. Melody and music ring me about in a protecting wall. I am one who rises over the fallen.

Hail, O Overlooking, All seeing Power! I am Yours, I am a Chosen One. I am gifted with strength, I am thrice gifted with strength. I am filled with The Sacred Essence. I have partaken of the cup of joy. I am pure, I am pure, I am pure. I see the light of the East, the arrow of All Embracing Love. I see the light of the South, the arrow of All Comforting Benevolence. I see the light of the West, the arrow of Everlasting Hope. I see the light of the North, the arrow of All Consoling Comfort. Let the golden bow speed the arrows of my desire. I am still, I worship the Hallowed Limbs. The Heavenly Hosts gather, as swallows for the flight, as stormclouds for the downpour. Before the Sacred Shrine I renew my strength. I free myself from all earthly desires, from all bodily passions, of all soul-eating lusts, of all soul-destroying vices. Now I see the rainbow-hued radiance of the real within the unreal. Now I see true where before I saw what was not and heard what was not. I was deceived by my body, I was deluded by my feelings. Now I see things not seeable by unaided mortal eyes. I hear things beyond mortal hearing.

O Great One, O Radiant One, O Timeless Knower, O Limitless Viewer, O Majestic One with a form of indescribable beauty! I have seen You through the veil, I have glimpsed the reflection of eternity. I am free. I, Your son, bow humbly before You. Lord, my heart is pure. I proclaim my loyalty to my neighbour on my right and my neighbour on my left.
I see the meat. I see the tripod. I see the knife. All is ready. Come, benevolent spirits, gather about the flame. Hover over the bowl. To you in whom resides the power to appear in any form or shape desired, come, come as welcome guests. Before the Place of Awe I stand unafraid, for those who are damned to sorrow and horror cannot approach within the barrier. They await in jealous hate without, they who come up from the dismal depths. Away foul spirits of the damned! Away O self-destroyed ones!

O Great Representative, the court is purified, I now see the flame-like radiance. Brothers and sisters, do you see it too? I see the Radiant Risen Ones who have torn aside the veil for one brief moment. I see things of overwhelming splendour. Bring incense, bring water, bring salt and bring the offering flame.

CHAPTER TWENTY-FOUR. THE HYMN FROM THE BOOK OF SONGS - 5

I believe in You, Great God of Life, Lord of the Kingdom of Light, Dweller in the Eternal Silences. From the centre of Your domain there is an outflowing which sustains all life, and in You rest the hopes of all men. You are The Ruler of All Spheres and Your dominion is unchallengeable. Under Your benevolent guidance Earth continues to exist and hold together, changing for nought but the benefit of man. We are Your children and You are our Father.

I believe in the Sacred Spirit of Inspiration which enters the hearts of men, flowing out from You and joined with You and yet separate, the Spirit to whom our fathers of old gave the greatest reverence, the Beautiful One, the Gentle One, the Inspirational One who first taught men to love and who drew aside the veil to show them beauty.

I believe in the Great Kingdom Beyond Earth, where, in the Place of Light the souls of men, if worthy, find a perfection not known here. The light which is in the Region Beyond the Veil is not as earthly light, it has a sustaining quality, it is a vitalising light indescribable in earthly words. O Great Dweller in the vast silences which are not as the silence known on Earth, who attends this sacred place where men gather in devotion. We who are here see You revealed as a beacon light for those whose hearts dwell in the darkness of ignorance. We rejoice in the strengthening emanation which flows out towards those with the wisdom to attract and absorb it. Here, in the Hidden Place, we Your servants are gathered, and we bow before You, O Great One. We bow in humility, not in servility; we bow in recognition of our earthly limitations. We are overcome with awe and can but stand in worshipful silence before the vision of Your glory.

It shines before our eyes, and our mouths cannot open. Here, on this Sacred Ground, we hardly dare to utter the words of prayer, for the sentences formed by men are so unworthy of their purpose, when used and spoken before You. Man is limited in knowledge, in understanding and in ability, it is the recognition of this which makes him humble. O Great One, who understands even the speech of the dumb man, help us to expand our knowledge and understanding.

We, for our part, will not remain inactive but will ever sincerely struggle to reach out towards You, striving even to extend beyond our limitations. Were it otherwise we would be dishonest in seeking Your help. Help us to remove the disfiguring stains upon our everlasting spirit, and when earthly life is renewed in us let us not be too disadvantaged. Teach us to pray without prayerfulness, so that the taint of self-seeking is eliminated. When we petition, let this not be in the spirit of selfishness.

O enfolded, sleeping soul, unaware of the life fountain within from which you may drink, unfeeling of the throbbing life all about us, now is your hour. Prepare yourself for the great awakening. The bright light of wisdom awaits to encircle you, as you stand before the awful door within the Sacred Temple of Mystery. That the light of Truth may be a sure guide amidst the dark gloom of earthly life, a certain aid enabling you to find the way of your eternal spirit, you are not unknowing of your inner wisdom. It is the key to everlasting life in the glorious place beyond the Western veil.

O live my soul, awaken, hear me. Let not my love and my sacrifice be in vain, let not all my hopes turn to dust within the tomb. Can love become soil and hope become sand? Never, for the grave is not the destination of the sublime attributes which ennoble the nature of man. Man is as a flame burning in water, as it is written on the pillars without. His soul is as the rosebud awaiting the kiss of the sun to awaken it to bloom. His nature is as the day which is ever accompanied by the night.

I will praise The Nameless God who is The True God and The Knower of Every Name. Hail Great Overseer of Earth! The high Heavens will hear the sound of my voice and its loudness shall ring across the widespread land. It shall resound throughout the Red Land. My song shall ride on the wings of the wind and my gladness shall whisper into the ear of the air. Hail Great Overseer of Earth! I shall seek diligently for enlightenment and knowledge, that I may proclaim the ways of The True God among people, for they are mysterious ways not easily understood.

Man wallows in a quicksand of ignorance, and only by extreme effort can he extricate himself. Great Overseer, grant me the ability to understand. Hail Great Overseer of Earth! I say to the people, "Declare The Great One to your children, to the high born and to the lowly ones who dwell together under the same sun, to the generations as yet unborn. Sing songs that will echo down the corridors of time". Hail Great Overseer of Earth! "Sing His praises with the birds of the air, tell of Him to the fishes in the waters, to the creatures which hide in the ground and to the things which walk and crawl above it". Hail Great Overseer of Earth!

"Declare Him unto all, for He is The God of All, He is The Great Compassionate One whose wrath declines with the setting sun and in the morning departs with the dawnlight mists". Hail Great Overseer of Earth! Sometimes, in the lonely nightwatches, I wonder, have You turned Your face from me? What have I done that You are unresponsive? Have I ever lived otherwise than in accordance with Your word? O Great Overseer of Earth, what is Your will for me?

O Great One, everlastingly considerate of our needs, Overseer and Taskmaster of mankind, look down upon us with compassion and lay not too great a burden upon us, your dutiful servants. Labour we must, for thus we prepare for a higher state of being, but bear with us, for sometimes we grow weary and falter at the task. Here we have fallen victims of our own wiles, we have hopelessly snarled up the threads of our existence, so we know not how to loosen the knots we ourselves have tied and so free ourselves. We are entangled in a net of our own weaving. Let us, Your servants, look to You, The Great One, for aid. Our destinies are held in the hollow of your hands, while the future is visible to you as is writing upon an open scroll.

The Glorious Ones worship You with service and serve through following the words of guidance. Thus, the earthbound spirits worship You, the shades of the departed worship You and the whole of creation worships You. We, Your servants, offer our continual and everlasting devotion to Your service. We are not as others, O Great One, for we know well that worship and devotion mean service and expended effort, not mere words and ritual.

Your spirit governs the breezes that comfort mankind. You send the fertilising rains, Your Spirit quickens the seed within the womb of Earth. The songs of the birds are inspired by the knowledge of You and the wild beasts rejoice in the sustenance provided. You are The Universal Being, The Raincloud Overshadowing the Earth, The One Dwelling in the Cave of the Heart within all breathing creatures. You are The Weaver of the Warp and Woof of Life.

I praise The One Who Eats Evil, The Disposer of Earthly Residue. He who sustains the devoted followers of The Deathless One in whom all merge on leaving the body. For the day comes when we discard all that is of Earth, when we recognise and realise that all remaining is the pure and sacred spirit, boundless and free as the winds. I praise The One Who Eats Evil, The Disposer of Earthly Residue. He who sustains the devoted followers of The Deathless One; who is with us everywhere and in all things; in whom is all, though not Himself the all; who sees and hears all, who knows and understands all, but whom none tied to Earth can know; who projects His word of power, so that it is within all and holds all things together in stability.

I praise The One Who Eats Evil, The Disposer of Earthly Residue. He who sustains the devoted followers of The Deathless One; who created all things and thus became His Own Greater Self; who clothed Himself in the universe as with a garment.

O Great Spirit, I would see the vast face of the Earth as You behold it. I would know how the seed is quickened, so that it grows into the plant, and how the fowl comes forth from the egg. What is added to the egg to give it the power to reproduce life? I would touch Your Great Body born of the breath from The Eternal Source and watch Your thoughts creating and moulding all things to shape step by step. I would see the links of Heaven and Earth and rest one hand in each. I would see the thread that binds yesterday, today and tomorrow, so all are one and parts of the whole. I would see the appointed place of every living man and understand why. I would see the purpose of every beast and every plant, every tree and every thing that flies and crawls.

I would know gladness with the children, as they play and go singing on the way to their places of instruction. I would watch birth and death and solve their mysteries. I would know the depths of hatred and the heights of love. I would journey the adventurous path of love hand in hand with another. I would know its secret, its delights and their shadows, and the secrets of its silences. I would know the beginning and the end, and understand what links them. I would see the chain of the years and the necklace of the days. I would know the purpose of it all. Then, knowing all these, I would know You at last, O Great Spirit!

O True God, by whom the worthy are guided in all they undertake; who rises as a beacon in the darkness for the lowly. Grant us, Your servants who put their trust in You, strength to overcome all the doubts and uncertainties which rise in our hearts, as frightening shadows arise in the night. Let us sip the waters from the inexhaustible well of wisdom, that we may not move along false paths to encompass our own destruction. For we cannot see the way in the enveloping darkness, and confusing voices shout this way or that way. We are bewildered, for we know not which one is right. Can there be so many ways? We are not men of great learning or high position. We do not sit among princes, being among the lowliest in the land. Yet it is we who carry the burdens of the people, we feed the hungry and provide for the widow and orphan. Ours are the aching backs and weary feet, ours the naked body and empty bowl. Those who are concerned with higher things sit at tables of plenty, those seemingly unworthy rejoice amid prosperity and plenty. Those who take are given more, while those who give are mocked. We see these things and doubt enters our thoughts, we ask one another, "Why is this the order of things? Is it the will of our God? Then we seek for an answer in all sincerity and with productive effort, and The Great God Above All does not remain mute.

O God, hear my prayer, for I have gone into the great recess within me and await a response from out of the enveloping silence and tranquillity. The restlessness and discontent of life I have left at the portal. I have closed the door to the outer things of life. Give ear, O my soul, to the whispers from the silence. Close out the clamour of Earth and harken to the soft voice which echoes from the far reaches of eternity.
Hear without ears the wordless voice of Truth. Close the eyes of the flesh, that the greater eye may see in the inner darkness. Enter into the inner temple and await the revelation of heavenly secrets. Shut out the clamouring senses that demand expression in sensual pleasures. Then, when all outer doors are closed and all inner doors open, speak to me and I will hear your voice. Tell me the

secrets of the ages, and my spirit will dwell in contentment for ever. This alone I ask and no more, it is sufficient for one lifetime.

O Great One on High, have pity on us, for we are hopelessly ensnared by our complete lack of things needed to sustain the body. Without sustenance our spirits are restless, our hearts cannot find peace. We do not desire foolish things, or pleasurable or vain things, but just the things without which we cannot live. Though we lack all things we do not turn our faces from You, for we know well that in Your bounty all men are provided for and the Earth is full of richness. It is not You who take away the things needed to sustain our lives, but those made in our own likeness, our own brother men. They deny meat to the hungry and drink to the thirsty, though they themselves are gorged to fullness and bloated with good things. Be merciful to them, instruct and enlighten them with Your chastising afflictions. Thus they may come to know that man needs man and each man is brother to all others. Others have reaped where we have sown and others sleep where we have built, because of the statutes of men. Therefore, mete out nought but justice, that we may be fed and clothed and have a place to rest our heads.

O God, who teaches us in so many strange ways in this great place of instruction called Earth; who set us tasks to an end which we cannot foresee, and who tests us to measure our abilities and to try our courage and fidelity. Instruct us, so we may better understand the bitter lessons which purge from our natures all which is unwholesome to the spirit. Strengthen us, so we may bear all things without complaint and conduct ourselves manfully under the strict discipline of this unique place of instruction. Open the-eyes of understanding within us, that we may benefit by every experience and not waste time bewailing our lot. Tell us, so we may know. Instruct us in our duties in the battleline, so that when we are called upon to take our appointed place we shall not shirk the clash.
Toughen us on the training ground of adversity, so that we may be stronger for the fray. When the day of battle comes upon us and cowards flee before the strength of our adversary, when the valiant ones kiss the dust at the portals of glory, let our place be where the battle rages most fiercely and the blows fall the thickest. If we faint, may we still remain faithful. If we are

exhausted, may we remain dauntless. If our hour come and we fall before the onslaught, may it be with weapons in hand and face to the foe.

We fight the fight where the victor can be the vanquished and the vanquished the victor, for here the fight is the end and not the victory. He who serves the end well justly claims the fruits of victory. We cannot ask to win, but we can ask to be made strong if we struggle for strength. We cannot ask to remain unhurt, but we do ask for courage. We cannot ask to be supported in weakness, but we can ask for the fortitude to endure. We stand firmfooted, grim-faced to the foe. The ranks of wickedness encompass us about, but we will surge forward with closed ranks, carrying all before us until we come to rest in the presence of victory. O God, Supreme Among Spirits, watch over us in the struggle, for we are Your children.

This is my prayer, O Great Spirit, accept my prayer. O Dweller in the Pure Region of Truth, hear me. O Great Fountain of Wisdom, hear me. O Comforter and Companion of the Soul Silences, hear me. I, Your son, come into your presence with faith and humility. Grant that my spirit be admitted into the Glorious Audience Chamber between the two regions. I, Your son, come into Your presence with faith and humility. O Supreme Source of the form-holding rays, grant me a hearing. O Great One seated on The Celestial Throne behind The Great Solar Disk, hear me. All homage to you Great God, Master of the bodies of men. I, Your son, come into Your presence with faith and humility. My every thought and deed are dedicated to Your service. These things are written clearly in my heart and are not mere puffs of wind from my mouth.

Lord of my heart, hear me now as I stand in communicating silence before the listening shrine. You are The Great One who existed before the upheaval of the mountains; who tore apart the land and waters in the infant years of man. For in Your sight a thousand great years are as an hour in the heat of the day, or as a watch in the coolness of the night. You are The Timekeeper in Eternity and Warden of the Ages. You reap men as corn is reaped at the harvest and sweep them away as floodwaters cleanse the land. For man is like unto the grass of the field, in the morning it grows full of vigour, gaily bedecked with the gems of morning dew; in the eventide it is cut down, to wither in the night. The day is not important if men live by the hour, fulfilling in each its appointed task.

When the Dread Messenger calls for you, let him not find you ill-equipped and unprepared. In the final hour, which must surely come, there will be no opportunity for fine speech and nought can delay his imperious command. Then all the possessions you have cherished and stored will be as nought, and all you will be able to take with you will be that which you have fashioned within. Do not be numbered among the foolish who say, 'Time enough, for I am yet young". Death claims the breast-child as well as the aged, and on this you should ponder. Consider well your future estate. Here you are the architect of your future abode, the plans prepared here are carried out in another place. Earth is the place of sowing, Heaven is the place of reaping.

Here you are the sculptor who chisels the statue, the potter who fashions the pot, the woodworker who carves the pillar. What is there on Earth more deserving of your care and attention than your own future form and appearance? Do you recklessly hew or wilfully cut? Do you heedlessly pound the pliable clay and carelessly fashion the unfired pot? Do you mix the colours with proper thought? What manner of thing are you fashioning in this great workshop? A beauteous being arrayed in radiant splendour, or a hideously foul fiend which can do nought but squirm in the slime of its fitting abode? Whom will you praise for your prudence or curse for your lack of foresight? Who can force you to deal tenderly and responsibly with the slumbering child of your own self? Or prevent you from carelessly and wilfully shattering all hopes for its future wellbeing?

Rejoice all cities beside the waters, be joyful all people in the land, for great things have come to pass. Behold, the foe is scattered in confusion, they are no more, they are eaten up, victory is with us. All praise to our Commanding Lord. Hail The Great Leader, hail The Source of Power in the land, live forever in glory.

O Mighty Fighter, let us rest in the shade of Your greatness, let us dwell under Your shadow, under the protection of Your right arm. You have given us that which we never thought to know again. Men sit in peace, speaking freely one with another. They walk abroad with light steps and their heads are held high. Men look their fellowmen in the eye and there is none to josde them.

They are delivered from the shadow of fear, and confidence is renewed in them. The fortresses are no longer overflowing with fighting men and all throughout the land no well is forbidden to the thirsty, all may drink freely where there is water. Men come and go across the wilderness, carrying the burdens of trade and none falls upon them to plunder. Men journey peacefully along the lonely roads and none waylays them to rob. Traders cross the barren places and are unmolested, none rises against them. The bearers of messages no longer hasten about, pale of face and frightened, they no longer carry doleful tidings, they no longer bear words of fear. Their coming no longer causes the knees to tremble and the stomachs to fall. Now the messengers loiter in shady places, remaining there until the nightwatch calls, for there is no urgency in the words they carry.

The fighting men rest, their hazardous days have gone; the bow, the sword, the spear and the shield have been laid away in the weapon stores. Women walk freely, they talk gaily, for they are not overshadowed with fear, neither do they tremble for fear of molestation. The faces of the border guardians are no longer haggard with sleeplessness, nor are their eyes tired and strained with watchfulness. Throughout the whole land there is content and tranquillity. The herds are large and sleek, they are no longer tense and restless. The flocks graze contentedly in their green pastures. The fowls are no longer alert and noisy but squabble playfully, chasing one another through the dust.

The voices of men are no longer hoarsened with war cries, instead they can be heard singing as each goes about his appointed task. The doleful wailing of women who mourn their dead is no longer heard and widows no longer proclaim themselves. The husbandman sows contentedly, knowing that where he sows he shall also reap. He no longer doubts that he will enjoy his own harvest. The face of God is once more inclined favourably towards us, even the lesser gods look again upon the land with favour. The reign of Saku is over, he no longer overshadows the lives of men, all is well in the two lands.

We praise our own God with joyous and grateful hearts. He has shown Himself among us. He will come again in His season, all is well with us. His desire brings forth the green growing things and the land is clothed in its gay mantle. His hand guides the stars, His mind contains all things that fly above the Earth and all things that walk and crawl upon its face. We praise You, Great Eternal One whose forms are so many. We kiss the ground before You. All the sacred beings and sacred things men worship are but manifestations of their groping through the clouds of ignorance to understand You. Have pity on them, for they were born into darkness and mysteries, but their hearts are good. Each day You bring some new thing to the attention of men and place before them problems to unravel. The nature of men ever inclines them towards the path of ease and passiveness, therefore they tend to shun the things which are truly profitable. Therefore, deal with men in a manner best fitting for their progress towards Truth.

Neither life nor love ends at the Grim Portal. The strength of the invisible bond between two souls binds them even after death. That which binds strongest of all is the love which is sincere, true and constant. Such love endures through tribulations and trials. If one you love has departed through the Western Gates into the Great Halls of Eternity, then be comforted by the words of Truth. This you will then know: that the Guardian at the Grim Portal is no fearsome being but a compassionate attendant who tends you gently while asleep, until the morning of a more glorious day. Then you will be awakened to journey through a greater adventure with the companions of former times.
In death you are greater than ever you were on Earth, for now the companionable spirits lament for your sake. They strike their bare flesh for you and smite upon their forearms. They tear at their hair and cast dust on their heads. Yet if they be true to themselves, they are not cast down, they are not distressed. There is a voice speaking out of the silence, saying, "If he goes he shall come, if he sleeps he shall awaken, and if he dies he shall live". Can

you be gone from us forever? No, you are not dead or lost unto us, unless by our own deeds we depart to dwell in different regions. I am not cast down. You are now in the Great Place beyond the everlasting stars. You have passed over the horizon of immortality and now walk erect along the path of glory. May we meet there in days yet to come. Hail O Glorious One!

My side when I come before the Assessors, that when I hear the verdict I may not be alone. If my eyes cannot see, then tell me of the balances, do they bear down in my favour? O Guardian God, lighten the darkness for me and deliver me from the meshes of the net woven by my own deeds of wickedness and weakness. You are my strength and support, to You have I given my offerings, You I have honoured above all. There I may be in distress and have none to abide with me. I may have no comforter and may be alone, therefore desert me not in my time of trial. Stand by my side, O Guardian God. If I am numbered among the distressed ones, look upon me with compassion and mercy, and if I am deserted, then sustain me with water, bread and oil.

I sing words of glory unto my God who is the Great God Above All Gods, and the words which issue from my mouth shall be exalted above all things. With them I will praise Him in the Sacred Place, in the silence of His Hidden Sanctuary. They will glorify my God, so that His Majesty is not dishonoured and He is not deserted, until the day when He shall be declared before all men. With the ever loving thoughts of a devoted heart I praise Him. Even as the sun rises joyfully into the daysky, so does my heart rise towards He who gives me life and renews it day by day. He is Great, He is Mighty, He is Glorious. He made the great river to flow, that all men in the two lands might be fed. It never wearies, it never ceases its onward flowing. It is everlastingly renewed.
Even as the great river flows steadily and strongly through the barren wilderness and bestows verdant life on its way, so let the river of my life flow through the Earth and eat away the sands of wickedness. Release me from my mortal fetters. Loosen the heavy covering of flesh which imprisons me, which restrains me. Let me rise free into the glory above, as the falcon floats freely on the wing. Let not the melody of my song be cut off while I sing, nor the story end before its completion. Keep me, O my God, from the ways of darkness and let my spirit rejoice in the light of righteousness. Glory to You,

Great God, Lord of Truth, whose eternal throne is concealed behind man's limitations; who issued the command that brought things into being; who made man so wonderfully that man himself cannot understand his own nature; who hears with compassion the cry of the distressed and the moan of the captive.

All hail the everlasting spirit within, the real self, the seat of all thought inseparable from me. I am one who can truly call bis soul everlasting, for I am one of the Awakened Ones, one of the few who have at long last attained the Splendid Vision. I have seen the bright flash of Truth in the darkness of earthly existence, I am free, I am illuminated. I will sing, that you may be glorified in the solitudes of Your Hidden Places, where the eyes of the profane can never penetrate, where few men come as Chosen Ones. There we will sing songs of yore. We will sing of Your ways and of Your laws, which remain everlastingly unchangeable.

Heaven and the many Heavens beyond Heaven, Earth and the many Earths beyond Earth are held in the thoughts and power of God. They are as a monument to His everlasting glory. All things living that move and breathe have their place in the abode of life. Man finds the greatest joy in the Eternal Halls, therefore set not your heart on earthly possessions. Here a man may desire life for a hundred years and may even attain it, but what benefit are the extended years to him if they do not exalt the soul? There is a horror haunted region of darkness, and whosoever rejects the godward life on Earth will surely dwell therein. They will go down to partake of the nature of demons, down into the darkness of delusion and doom. The soul, without moving flies on wings swifter than thought. It stands behind and beyond the senses.
It is the Knower working within the things mat are known. The spirit of man is carried down the stream of action into the ocean of life. The spirit is everlasting, it is near and it is far, it is in all and it contains all. He who sees his own self in all things and all things in his own self is awakened. He is beyond delusion and outside the reach of futile sorrow.

I am Hahrew the Enlightened One, Hahrew the Twice Bom. Having crossed the dark waters myself, I carry the others across. Being free from fear, I free others from fear. Being unrestricted, I ease the restriction of others. Knowing the way, I show it to others. Having trodden the road, I now guide others along it. I am an Illuminated One, the open of ear, the keen of eye. I am one who knows the Law, I am a keeper of ordinances. I shall refresh all those whose bodies are bent with toil or sorrow. I shall come to the aid of those whose souls are withered and distorted, and give them strengthening sustenance. I shall open the eyes of many who are deluded in the heavy mists of threefold existence. Hear me, all who toil under the yoke of ignorance, who labour under the clouds of despair. I am the Forthcoming One, the Future One Turned Back. I am the Spirit Within The Law. I am the Voice of Enlightenment, one who proclaims the brotherhood of all men. I am to one as to another. I am Hahrew.

O life-giving Sun, handwork of God, projection of divine fire, heat of Heaven, light of the day, solitary glory of the daytime, let me behold the hidden form behind your brightness, for the spirit within you is even as my spirit. Thus, I may come to understand the nature of my God who commands you and to whom I pray. The fair face of the daughter of Truth remains hidden behind its mask of gold.

O spirit of light, draw aside the veil even slightly, that I may see. Who among men is wise enough to know his own wrongdoing, or to see clearly his own errors and follies? The eyes of men are dim and the road narrow, therefore it is not hard to wander from the way. Therefore, O my God, keep me from all hidden wrongdoing and errors, and keep me from the power of temptations to which I so readily succumb.

I know the rebellions of my heart, and my wickedness is ever before my eyes, yet how much more do I not see! I have chafed against the restrictions of Your decrees and the Law. I am a foolish one who does himself an injury. I am ashamed and blush for my folly. I am as a man who, when his arm does wrong, cuts off a finger. Help to make clean my heart and strengthen my spirit, that it may resist my own inflictions upon it. I believe I do right and do wrong, for I have not listened carefully and diligently to Your words written on the sacred scrolls.

O my God, whom I have long worshipped with devotion, incline from the great heights of Your splendour and stretch a helping hand down towards Your weary servant. Trusting in You I will depart from the pastures of sweet grass and the calm waters of restful repose, and go into the presence of the Everlasting Lords. I will pass out of the dark tomb, I will arise refreshed with the outpouring of Your Spirit. I will clasp Your mighty hand and be guided along the path of Truth. Thus, I cannot stray and the lonely places will not claim me. In confidence and trust I will take my place before the Court of Assessors. Guided by Your light I shall pass safely by the Place of Darkness, and those who lurk shall do me no harm. My trust is in You and I will come safely past the lurking ones. I shall be freed of all earthly weariness and my spirit shall shine forth in glory. I will stand in the Place of Brightness, and the Glorious Ones will come bringing refreshing waters. I will not lack sweet sustenance, and delicacies shall be poured forth for me in abundance.

CHAPTER TWENTY-SIX. FROM THE SCROLL OF SENMUT

The stonebearer measures the stone and it is trimmed and pushed into place. It is fitted and the overseer looks upon it and says, "This stone is well laid. It remains in its appointed place". Beside it other stones are fitted and set, each according to its own shape and design, each has its own place and position. Then upon it are placed other stones and so it becomes concealed from sight in the foundations of the structure. The building rises, firm and strong, to become the dwelling place of a prince. I am one of whom men say, "He establishes buildings which stand forever". I remember that stone deep below the ground in the base of the structure where no eye ever sees it. Men know it is there, it just remains in its place, fulfilling its appointed duty, a necessity for the upholding of the building. What difference whether that stone be set upon the pinnacle, shining in the sun, ever before the eyes of men, or hidden in the ground, unseen at the base? It does its duty by standing solidly in its rightful place and seeking not to change it. I, who establish great buildings which will stand forever, remember that stone.

CHAPTER TWENTY-SEVEN. THE SONGS OF NEFATARI ONE

I sing my song because the Earth sings; though the wind is hushed among the groves it still plays with soft melodic gaiety. The benevolent sky looks gently down, its breath stilled as it listens to the melody of the leaves. The dew smiles in the morning, for it has captured the light of love from the stars.

My song is beautiful because my heart dances gladly in my bosom, its joyfulness conveys gay music to my thoughts and places endearing words on my lips.

Because I am dedicated to love I have but one love, the beautiful container of my life. My heart is a lonely thing ever seeking companionship with yours. It is lost to you, so let it beat in your breast nestled against your heart, for there it surely belongs.

My love is wholesome, not tainted by any residue of past affections; it is gentle and pure, therefore treat it with manly tenderness, for it is a precious treasure. I give it gladly and can give no more. That which I give to you I can give to no other man. For you the lovely pearl, for others the empty shell. Let me live just for you, let me serve as your housewife. Let me hold your child to my breast, let my eyes be gladdened by your presence each night and in the morning. Let me bask continuously in the wonderful radiance of your presence. Never part me from the source of my joyfulness and gaiety, but let us go down the corridor of life together, your arm laid on my arm and my hand in your hand.

My heart is desolation, it is like a wilted flower. You are away, my love, and my eyes search the road for your coming. The caress of sleep eludes me, for your image is ever there beside me and I cannot find consolation with even the most comforting shadow. Come to me, my living love, that I may feel the warmth of your flesh and be at peace. While you are absent I concern myself no more with things which give pleasure to a woman's heart. I neglect my hair arrangement and my diadem hangs disregarded. My curls are laid aside, for I await your coming to put them on and greet you in my gaiety.

The song is silent on my lips, for my heart is without joy. While you are away my heart slumbers, my bosom is empty. Come quickly, my love, that my heart may awaken and beat gladly with the pulse of life. I await your coming as the dawn awaits the sun, as the parched lands await the rising waters. My eyes search the nightskies and see the mating dance of the stars, the Earth about me throbs with the pulse beat of love. The dark waters reflect the mystery of life, but I sit beside them desolate.

Come to me my love, for none but you can awaken my response. I stand alone on the shore of the sea of love, Come, O come, that we may enter the enchanted waters together. Does the night long for the day as I long for you? Does the thirsty wayfarer long for water as I yearn for you? If so, then truly they are to be pitied. O come, my living love, and fill my days with the sunshine of your love. It seems the ages of man have never been loveless.

CHAPTER TWENTY-EIGHT. THE SONGS OF NEFATARI TWO

Life is the bearer of the most wonderful gifts. You are a man and my man. Maker of my heart's butterfly flutter when my breath becomes a necklace of sighs. In your strong arms I melt as honey in the warm night waters. O man and my man, great one in my maidenly eyes. The light of my life, the sun of my days and the moon of my nights; the rock against which I confidently nestle, for to feel your protecting strength is my everlasting delight. My body yearns for you as the parched fields cry out for the caress of the fertilising waters. How delightful the gentle hour of love with you.

O that it might become an eternity wherein I might sleep with you as your wife, your lifelong companion in love. In this life always yours, to serve your pleasure and be ever with you; to stand at last, my hand in your hand, together before the dream goddess in the Halls of Eternal Joy. There, those who have loved wholesomely, such as we, find everlasting pleasures. I am yours, both here and there, escapable never, yours forever. Yours pure, untouched and unsullied. I am with you first, sister in love. If at times my tongue speaks with unmaidenly boldness, then let this be forgiven me, for I am pure of heart. The words pour forth from a heart overflowing with love and not from a tongue dipped into the shame of impure experience.

I come to you with maidenly pride, as a dew-bedecked garden of herbs, fair flowering, sweet smelling and refreshing. Peace and contentment are mine to gladly give. Upon you I gladly bestow all that is precious to a maiden. You share me with no other, I honour love by bestowing what is exclusively yours. Your brow becomes hot with the body passion of man burning within, and I cool it with my womanly hand as the cooling north wind tempers the heat of the burning sands. The strength of an ox and the gentleness of a kitten are united in love. We walk together in a land of beauty, a garden of loveliness fashioned thus by the dreams we share. Hand in hand in the kingdom of men, heart in heart in the kingdom of spirit. When hearts are bound together in a love exceeding all bounds, then bodies may unite with purity and peace.

We wander heedlessly about and my heart sings with joy, for we are together. Your voice is the food of my heart, your touch the life of my body. I see you and I am gay, you depart and I am sad. Your glance pierces me like an arrow of fire, your words carry me away like the surge of bitter waters over the beach. For the lovers' hour we sit beneath the wild fig tree, beneath its fruits of lovers' blood and its leaves of lovers' eyes. Hear it whisper to our hearts. I am a maiden reserved to you in love, you are my lord, the commander of my heart. I dwell beneath your shadow and within your shadow. O never leave me unshielded!

My nights are restless and hot, shall I give my love the apple of his desire, the first fruits of womanly love? Am I the wild bird snare awaiting the wild goose? O my heart, how have women beyond number decided before me which answer is the true one? O take me not in my weakness, lest you despise me after the manner of men and bring low the head of my father. Have manly compassion on the weaknesses made by my love. Degrade me not before my mother and let not the shadow of shame fall over my father's house. Let me ever keep faith with the Mother Guardian of Love, that when I am called before her I shall stand in unsullied radiance. Make me not a woman of the hedgerow. Let our love bear us up in glory, up into the revealing light where we may stand together, proud and unashamed. Let ours be a love that fulfils its appointed function in the great chain of life, something honoured by men and an inspiration to our children. Let it not become a flower of the field corner which withers in shame when the sunlight falls upon it. I wait, the day comes, its hours are long and extended, but with its declining you hasten to me, my man and my life. Sweet mistress of love, speed the fulfilling hour.

CHAPTER TWENTY-NINE. THE SONGS OF TANTALIP ONE

The night rolls back to reveal the promise of another day. The great sun comes up in the morning time and the lotus opens to reveal its shining heart displayed in devotion. You come and my heart leaps up from my breast to meet you. The wind blows and shakes the wild fig tree, you come and your delicate perfume enwraps my spirit, and my body is shaken. I become weak within the shadow of your presence. I feel a radiance about you which calls to something within me and I am awed by the wonder of a love which can subdue all base feelings. I have seen you. In the cool dewtime of the morning I passed on my way and you were bathing in the freshening waters. I saw your pure loveliness and all else faded and passed from me, the beauty of the morning was dimmed before the vision I had of you.

Modest maiden of mine, clad in a white garment which clutched your supple limbs, I saw you and my heart swelled up in joy. The breath was stopped within my throat. You looked up and smiled a chaste greeting, covering yourself in a garment expressing your maidenly modesty. Your delicate hand plucked a lily, and my heart left its cradle when you came up out of the waters and drew near. You embraced me with cool, glistening arms and open wet lips. I savoured the joys of the gods, with a greater promise of unutterable joys to come, before I continued on my way. Would that I were the fishes in the pool, that I might be so near to you twice daily. Yet I am a man and consumed in the fires of manhood in my need for you. Still you remain veiled in reserve and I pray to the great god for the assurance that some day my sister in love will be truly mine. Her reserve and modesty, treasured as gifts to be surrendered in love, mean more to me than gold and pearls or the treasures of kings. What is mine no king, no matter how great, can claim. It is love's mantle bestowed on manliness. The night comes and I dream it is our wedding night and you are beside me. My spirit rises on wings of joy, singing, "O let my love find its ultimate expression in this night of beauty!" Your breath caresses me with the fragrance of Heaven, your lips dispense the heavy wine of love. Our bodies meet in ecstasy and part, but our spirits remain mingled in the greater bond that knows no severance. Our united souls share together the destiny of eternity. I sleep at last in the gentle arms of contentment.

O Great Readers of the Souls of Men, see the strength of my love. Is it not untainted with base feelings? Is it not wholesome and undemanding? Is it not protective of womanly secrets? Let it endure on Earth, that it may blossom in glorious fullness throughout the great ages in everlasting splendour. May it shine forever in the unwalled Halls of Eternity. O grant me my heart's desire!

CHAPTER THIRTY. THE SONGS OF TANTALIP TWO

I am one on whom the fates smile. My sister in love is the light of my life. She is the promise of love enduring, the brazier of a love undying, the hope of joy throughout eternity. The night becomes silent, for its fragrance is as nothing to her sweetness. The brightness of the dawn fades before her loveliness and the dove hangs its head before her virtue. She breathes gently and caresses with her glance. Her skin exudes a sweet perfume and her hair is proud and confident, as becomes the guardian of secret mysteries of charm and delight. She is graceful, her robes are not stiffened, they are not of royal or white linen and caress her softly. Her sandals are daintily bedecked with beads and her lovely curls are clasped in a circlet of blue and red stones.

Her bosom is covered with cloth of Ithika and held by a clasp of silver. She flutters her fan with delicacy and grace. Her speech is gentle as the cool breeze. Her eyes sparkle as the moonlit waters, their deep pools enhanced with tinges of green and purple delicately applied. Men say, "Who is she who walks with graceful steps and lively air? The blush of the blood rose is on her cheeks, the perfume of morning sweetness breathes from her parted lips. High-spirited joy tempered with innocence and modesty sparkles in her eyes. Her voice tinkles like sweetly rippling waters, and from the gay cheerfulness of her tender heart she gladdens all nature with her gentle singing".

I say, "She is mine, my wife in waiting", and confidently know all her secret charms are for me alone. I shall be lifted in joy above all men or cast into the abyss of despair. I wonder about her in the manner of men and rebuke myself for my thoughts. Could such beauty ever betray love? I inhale the sweet breezes which once filled her mouth, and each day my thoughts recall her beauty. My heart longs for the sweetness of her lovely voice, fresh as the cool north wind. Her love strengthens my limbs, my heart rises from its place. Let me clasp once more the delicate hands that hold my heart. Let me feel her once again in warm embrace. I hear her name whispered on the cool nightwind, and never do I hear it without my spirit responding.
O my Lord God, who led me in the conquest, who directed my right arm in battle and chastened my pride in victory, help me now in the time of peace. Help me when the turmoil is over. I am well skilled in the ways of war, but am a ready victim for the snares and wiles of peaceful life. Give to me my heart's desire, to be the mother of my children and the companion of my life. I am burnt with passion and need the cool quenching waters of true love. My body cries out in the night towards one so distant from me. You made me as men are made, you gave me the craving, now grant me relief.

I am alone and one when I should be two. I speak and none answers, I eat and my food lacks flavour, I thirst and none brings water. I am a sword unused, let the sword not rust in the sheath. I await my other self, my right side desires union with my left, I wait and know that the waiting is not in vain. I await her coming, she is on her way, as she was from me beginning of time. She draws near and my spirit leaps from its seat and dances from the body to meet her. I see her, she is mine, fashioned for me by the ages, her body is made for mine and mine for hers. We are betrothed by eternity. I will keep her always for myself, I will never let her go hungry or let her live to lament her fate. We will share seven lives together and in each I will seek her anew.

Man is two, the life force and the life material. Love holds all things together and no man can know the joys of love who shares the secret charms of his beloved with another.

CHAPTER THIRTY-ONE. THE MARRIAGE SONG

O devotee of a love that rises above the mire of matter and flowers in realms where romantic love is glorified! O daughter of love and sweet mistress of life, now is the hour of your fulfilment. Prepare to accept the sceptre of womanhood as becomes a true maiden, prepare to accept the burdens and pleasures of motherhood as becomes a true woman. Verily you are a disciple of love. Earth knows no greater joy than that of contented wedded love. Such love is a beacon light to all mankind, it guides the caravan of its journeying with a pure and sacred flame. Sweet, hallowed love has a temple in the heart of every chaste maiden, and all men worship the mystery enshrined within.

O resolute priestess and guardian, you are now worthy of the white crown of love. Great has been your inspiration to man. Well have you fulfilled the duty of maidenhood, now step forward to accept the joyful burden of womanhood, the crown that proclaims you a wife. Marriage is sanctified by ancient tradition, for it has survived the tests of time and turmoil. It has ever been the anchor of society and the shield of the family.

Loveliness belongs to all women, for it is the heritage of womanhood. Beauty of face and form is carried away by the passing years, but the beauty of heart and thought grows as the waters rise and fall. The glorious channs of modesty and purity can be possessed by any woman. Weave a mantle of contentment around your chosen mate, O gentle bearer of womanly charms. Remember that you are the mother of generations yet unborn. Maidenhood, wifehood and motherhood, these are the phases of a woman's life. A chaste maiden becomes a good wife and a good wife becomes a good mother. Thus it is written. May The Great God whom you now worship spread His protecting wings over you, and may you enjoy the companionship of many children. May your life be enwrapped in peace and contentment, and may it be attended by the four bearers of prosperity.

O son of strength and goodness, remember always your obligations and duties as a husband and father. Love belongs nowhere but beside your own hearth, for what foolishness it would be for a man to expend it on one other than his wife! That which a man gives to his wife is his also, a love truly shared is joy multiplied. He who sows beside his own hearth reaps a manifold harvest. Be not harsh with your wife or impatient because of her weaknesses, for her ways are those of all women. Be gentle with her, remembering that the dart of love cannot penetrate a hard and inconsiderate heart. Love is a treasure unearthed by few. It is found by less than one in a thousand. Yet, where it is let it be held sacred, for it is the decree of a divine destiny uniting one to the other in ever increasing glory and beauty, as they rise from life to life.

Is not every part of the Earth paired with its mate? Even Heaven and Earth are mated, for does not Earth cherish and nourish whatever Heaven lets fall? When Earth lacks heat Heaven bestows it bountifully upon her, and when she loses her freshness and withers. Heaven restores her freshness with gentle soothing waters. Heaven daily goes about the task of sustaining Earth, she is never neglected. Therefore, take an example from the greater sphere of life, sustain and cherish your wife, that she never be neglected. He who sows seeds of discontent before his hearth reaps a full harvest of misery. Thus it is written by the Wise One in olden times, even so it is now and will always be.

CHAPTER THIRTY-TWO. THE LAMENT OF NEFATARI

They have placed my dear lord in the engulfing tomb, they have laid him to rest in eternal secure silence. We depart, we journey home but home is no more, it is rent apart and a place of dull shadows. Some with me are silent and solemn, some are weeping, some make show of weeping. Some suffer silently, some talk idly, some mask their sorrow with false mirth. It is a time of solitary heart pain. Some say it is finished and others that he sails the sky, but I ask my soul and it says this is not the end. It is not finished, this is the beginning, which all loving things must know as they awake to a new dawn. The years of earthly instruction are left behind, the last lesson is read, the pupil has departed to take up his appointed task. He has been born to life, and death has been left behind. There are no dead, just the departed living, death alone occupies the silent tomb.

Death is a pause at the beginning of life, a hesitation before the light of a greater day. Death is a deceiver, a non-existent thing of the shadows. From the creeping caterpillar comes the light-loving butterfly, and from the hard grain the full blooming barley. Who, looking at the date stone, can see therein the tree to be? Search the seed and the plant is nowhere to be found. Even so is it with the spirit. I trust in He who gave us life and love, but I suffer because of my loss. I am alone. Where is my lord, the one I loved, the sharer in my cup of joyfulness?

Where is the caressing hand, the touch that soothed, the voice that strengthened my heart in times of distress, the consoling counsel, the quiet laugh that dispelled God-given hurt? Though he has gone to glory, yet my heart shrinks, aching with solitary grief. I will keep him, that he wander not in the darkness; for he has been loved and cannot be alone for evermore. I will keep him, that he be not despaired and condemned to walk with himself; for he is a man who has loved beyond himself. He has stepped from his body as one steps from a mantle. He has left it as one leaves a discarded garment. His future is in my hands and I shall live in such wise that none can deny our reunion. There is a subtle something, I know that, that ties us together still. May I be given strength never to break the loving link which comforts me through the long night and sorrowful days.

CHAPTER THIRTY-THREE. THE SCROLL OF HERAKAT

Great God of Wisdom, help me in my transcription of these writings, that they may be a true record; for I am not learned in letters, as was Sopher. I am unskilled even as a scribe. Man is a battleground, he is torn apart in the struggle between his two selves. He dwells in the dark night of ignorance. From Ramakui of the seven cities, Land of Copper, came the People of the Light and they brought with them, out of their transparent temples, the light that shines, when darkness falls, without being lit. Led by the Old Bald-Headed One, he whose name is not spoken, they came out of the West at the sunsetting. They came from the place where now the sun goes down; in the days when the Western wilderness was green and sand had not replaced the waters; when the outlands nourished cattle and sheep fed where now there is nought but rock and stone.

The Tirdinians welcomed them not, but they passed safely through the westward places to the land of Ansibyah, and were succoured and fed. They brought to the people many things, for wise they were and learned. They were men of wisdom. Truth is not for the multitude, dirty hands despoil fine linen. The high born have their estates and the lowly ones have their appointed places.

Truth is not sold in the marketplace, nor can riches alone obtain it. Few entered the great chambers to die and to live. The temples were fine shells, but the kernel was dead inside. Men lacked the foods of life. The True God was guarded and hidden by the false gods. He spoke in the hearts of the wise, but the people heard the voice in the stone. Their ears were closed to all but the voices of men. Small places there were in olden times for all gods, the pillars were not yet stood up. The stones were not yet in their places and the House of Hidden Secrets was not yet in the land. Then temples were built in splendour and priests were comforted in mansions. Great gardens and fields were the property of the gods of men. They had great herds of cattle in their pastures. Within the worship and ritual, amid the pomp enshrining the little gods, shone the light of Truth which was the revelation of The True God.
It was known to few and fewer understood it. Seven years men being chosen waited and were called. Seven years they served and seven years they ministered at the feet of their Masters of Instruction. They were passed into bleak caverns to die and know God, and called forth with the sure knowledge of Truth. Thus, men were made servants of The One True God. Thus, they knew the Truth which may not be written, for many read who are not with us in God. There were writings which speak truly, but they are no longer with us. The Arisen Ones know the secrets of the lesser gods who are no more than these. The Great Scales weigh the soul by its appearance in the Netherworld, and this its place is appointed. Its virtues from its food, but no man eats the filth that is his.

He who devours souls is but the dark cave of horror which opens to receive dark souls into affinitive darkness. The Rakima watches in silence; patiently it sits, waiting for the day of the Destroyer. It will come in a hundred generations, as is written in the Great Vault. All men are not equal in heart and spirit.

Is the Southern Man learned, or the Ambric Man brave? The Land of Incense bestows all good things upon its inhabitants, yet they are not great. The Land of Bright Waters raises nothing but trees and grass, yet its people are strong and the lion does not equal them in courage. Above are the waters of Heaven and below are the waters of the Dark Region, yet there are not two waters but one. There is the fire above and the fire below, yet there are not two fires but one.

The Lady of Ladies is arrayed in a radiant garment, when it dims the great trial begins. Her footsteps do not waver, her path is straight, but beware when she wavers and is inconsistent. Great Mistress of the Stars, let us abide in peace, for we fear the revelation of your horns. Remain ever constant as a good wife to the Lord of the Day. When women are as men and inconsistent as women, the hour approaches when the Great Lady will wander. When man and woman meet as one in likeness, the Fiery Heralds will appear in the darkness of the sky vault. Man twirls the drill in his hand; he is the master of fire, but the day comes when fire will leap forth from the heart of the stone and consume him.

Men read the Great Book of the Master of the Hidden Temple. They die and take it with them, but there is no power in their words, and who but we, the Enlightened Ones, know the hidden meanings? It is not for those dead to the Earth, who step forth in the Netherworld, but for those who died and remain with us. Men make offerings for their fathers after the custom of their fathers. The motions are those of their fathers' fathers' fathers, but their hearts remain locked.

It is foolishness. In the First Book it is written: "Words that do not produce deeds are as thistledown on the wind. They were better never uttered". The soul of man is as a bird that knows of a place to which it must journey, but which it has never seen yet it departs on the appointed day. Men have gods in Heaven and gods on Earth, but Heaven is for gods and earth for men. Thus did we write our own doom. In the Secrets of the Soul it is written: "The soul of man is not a small thing inside him, but wraps him about. It is greater than the boundaries of the Lands of the Reed and the Lily, and reaches out beyond the stars". To live, man must believe in his soul. Belief comes not from outside teaching but from listening to its whispers, unbelief comes from stopping the ears to its murmurs. Read the Sacred Writings diligently and hear the voice of the Instructing Master with receptive heart, so you may furnish your soul with nourishment, and it shall not wither from any lack of sustenance.

The seed of Truth came to the black fertile land in olden times and was planted in well watered soil. Pontas was not yet born. It grew not in the light of the sun, for ignorant men would cut it down. In the dark places it flourished. Earth is a strange place and stranger the creature who rules it. Then came the dawn of a brighter day. The tree was goodly and its leaves filled both the Land of the White Crown and the Land of the Red Crown. In a day of darkness men came who exposed it, and the king said, "Cut it down, lest it choke us with wisdom". The tree died, but its seeds falling into the red soil lived and from them saplings grew. They were sheltered under the strong arm of the East. Then came one who was Lord of the Sweet Breeze, one who had sat beneath the Tree of Life, and he raised up a city to the Veiled Truth. Over the great road it was, by way of Lados it lay.

He revealed the Light of Truth darkly to the people, but they were people of the night and even its dim flame consumed them. The child of good intentions may be fair or dark. The Guardians of Truth covered the bright flame and even its glow was seen no more by the people. No unlearned man again saw the light. A treasure in the hands of a few is great to each. Shared among many it has little value for one. We had been told the ways of men from olden times, but we heeded not the warning. Now the Truth is scattered to the four quarters of the Earth. Thus it was foretold it should be, therefore it is appointed. A tree scatters its seeds by the thousand, yet but one may spring to life, and that may lay long in the soil. These writings have been re-written with diligent care. They have been transcribed exactly as they are and no thought or belief of mine has gone into them. May those to whom they come as a heritage be no less circumspect in dealing with them.

THE BOOK OF THE SONS OF FIRE
this being **THE FOURTH BOOK OF THE BRONZEBOOK** Being all that remains of the Sacred Writings formerly contained in the Great Book of the Sons of Fire

CHAPTER ONE. THE RECONSTRUCTED CHAPTER

We took refuge with the sons of Uteno whose fathers had been in the land many generations, for they had come out of Egypt in the days of Pharaoh Nafohia. There on the borderland, we dwelt in caves above Kathelim. We were without books or possessions, but we were diligent and laboured to make the land fruitful. We knew ourselves as The Brothers in Light, but others called us The Children of Light, even as we are called to this day.

This is a good and fertile land, it is a wide land of flowing streams where wheat and barley increase a hundredfold. Figs and pomegranates flourish here and it is a land of olive groves and vineyards. All the needs of life are supplied with an overflowing bounty. It is a land where sheep and cattle multiply without fear and a land where the sickle of famine never reaps. It is a land where even an effortless search is rewarded with the materials of copper, but it is not a manless land. We are not alone in this land and must live among people whose ways are not our ways. They have gods with many names and even now those beside the sea strive among themselves, for some say God is called Mamrah, while others say he is called Aneh.

All about us men are in dispute and the strife among them arises out of the bounty of the land. Gaining their livelihood with little effort they have much time for argument and strife. We must build, for these people, a court of peace, the four pillars whereof shall be Love, Consideration, Justice and Truth. The land of our fathers and our inheritance has been lost to us forever. Their homes have been returned to the sands and their altars where they worshipped cast down. Their temples have been destroyed and the forms of worship practiced there are no longer known.

The songs once sung are now mingled with the winds and the voices of the singers are silent. The wisdom once revered has departed, the illuminating flame no longer burns and the lamps lie broken in the dust. The honoured writings have been used for kindling and the sacred vessels turned into vain ornaments. The very names held sacred by our fathers are now defiled and held to represent wickedness. Those who would have been our brothers are sold and their leaders slain. Those who would have been our wives are violated and degraded in servitude.

Therefore, brothers, it is time the memory of these things was put aside and forgotten. What cause have we for sorrow? We are in a bountiful land, we have hope for the future and an unshakable faith. Better by far than all else, we have with us the key to the ancient Portal of Communication.

Our memories must replace the books, and decrees of former times. Let us, therefore, be thankful for our blessings and diligently preserve the flame from which the lamps of Truth will one day be relit. In days gone by you have had leaders to guide you, but before them were even greater leaders whom you have not known. The inspiration of their words is something that must never be lost, it must be preserved for all time. We must be like a man who has traveled far with a heavy burden. He rests and seeks among the things he carries to find what can be discarded, knowing he has still a long way to go. The choice you must make has to be made soon, for the years remaining to our father cannot be plentiful.

We must establish a community where men can live together and where they can enjoy the companionship of women. Men always benefit from united effort, but this is inseparable from necessary restrictions. Let the restrictions imposed be such that no man can feel resentment because of the restraints set upon him. Let the only ordinances and restrictions imposed be founded on the nature of man and upon spiritual and moral values. We must seek to assure freedom of action for every man and woman, so long as it does not prejudice the equal rights of others. We must work for the benefit of the many, but in doing so must not overlook the provision of rewards for those who serve best. The rewards must go to the men who are best in all ways and not to the worst. We must see that good lives are rewarded and evil ones punished. We must place the greatest value on things spiritual, and no man must be unduly rich or unduly poor. We must provide for the sick and helpless, for the old and incapable. We must assure the integrity of the family. The first objective must be the spiritual goal, which is the only proper one for all men. After that all instruction and law should be bent towards an increasingly harmonious relationship between every living being. The upbringing of children must have as its objective the attainment of well balanced manhood and womanhood.

We must make men high-minded and above all pettiness. They must be upright and rejoice in their manhood. They must possess courage and fortitude equal to any trial, for there will be many. They must be prepared to endure oppression and persecution with self-control and a calmness which no misfortune or calamity can shake. They must also be such men that good fortune and abundance does not weaken them.

We must teach men to be quick in decision and deliberate in judgement. Because in numbers we are like two grains of sand in the desert, we must seek converts diligently.

We must be a guiding light before the eyes of all men, leading them along the paths of honest labour rather than power.

We must teach men their duty towards others, so that no man ever says, "Unless I place my own welfare first no other will".

We must seek out and accept suitable converts and they must be particularly precious to us. We must hold them in high regard, not because they have accepted our beliefs, the good within them can be developed within their own, but because they assume willingly and cheerfully the great duties and obligations peculiar to us.

We must always remain a brotherhood engaged in an organized quest for Truth. We must ensure that the teachings we expound are valid everywhere and among all men as a code of goodness. If a brother become powerful he must not glory in that power, if wise in his wisdom or if rich in his riches. If a brother have to glory in something, then let it be in the fact that he is always the best of men. By this is not meant the victor in the earthly struggle, but he who best serves the purpose and good of mankind.

We found refuge in a place where men spoke our tongue, though now they are no more. The land of our fathers is denied to us, so we must seek another, for a man without a nation is more heavily afflicted than any orphan. Egypt was a land destined for greatness, its people should have led all others towards the Great Light.

Egypt failed in its destiny because those who were entrusted with power and position proved unworthy. Its kings, who should have reared families dedicated to goodness and inspiration, betrayed their trust to satisfy the weaknesses of men. The leaders to godhood were misled and became ensnared in the deserts of worldliness, and those who followed them were betrayed. The priesthood became corrupt when it offered a life of ease and abundance, instead of a life of service and austerity. The ideals of man were above reproach, but man himself was unworthy of them. We have no need to change ideals, but to attain them we must change men. The sacred lore of Egypt, enshrining the treasure of the ages, was possessed by only a select few who safeguarded it as nothing else has ever been guarded, because of its greatness. Not only this, but even a little knowledge of it could be dangerous in the hands of any who sought to utilize it improperly. Of all desirable things attainable by man, the assurance of his immortality, clear insight into the purpose behind his creation and true knowledge of the road towards the fulfillment of his destiny are the greatest. Those were the things so closely guarded, and just as they are the most desirable things on Earth, so are they the most highly priced and difficult to attain. Religion records the efforts of men, its doctrines and inspiration are the measure of its success or failure.

CHAPTER TWO. THE HIBSATHY

These things must not be entrusted to common folk, neither must they be degraded by disclosing them to such as would profane them. They were once reserved for those who were exalted in wisdom and virtue. In those days of Harempta, Mouth of God on Earth, they were hidden from those in high places. This is one among the Lesser Mysteries, the Ritual of the Twice Born. It is a ceremony to regain spiritual vigour and to restore spiritual power, whereby a Chosen One dies and rises again. It is a grim undertaking fraught with danger. It is not for the spiritually weak or for the faint-hearted. Not all survive to walk again upon the friendly ground of Earth. Only the older men who had completed the three cycles of seven years were accepted. They had to be men with wisdom and courage, with the strength and fortitude to survive. Other essentials were absolute purity and complete self-discipline. The ability for self-sacrifice and a strict sense of duty were demanded. Only men possessing all these qualities could cross the border in consciousness and return. To be deficient in any essential quality meant death.

The Tree of Life has many branches and that which is initiation bears the best fruit. It is about this that your brother writes. It began in that far away glorious period before the days of wickedness which caused men to walk in darkness, in the days when they walked in the light of Truth.

A House of Hidden Places was maintained, so that all who had any part in governing the lives of the people, whether as king or priest or official, could prove themselves worthy before becoming encumbered with the office. Later, it came about that the Hidden Places had to be further secured and only men long established in goodness could enter them. Those in high places and those with power shirked the austerities and dangers demanded, and thereby they cut themselves off from the light of Truth.

The kings and governors who ruled in Egypt, during all the many long generations of twilight and darkness, were born to the frailties of the flesh. Seeing only through earthly eyes they lacked the clear guidance of revelation and knowledge.
The Serif Egg remains, it will give up its secrets on the distant day when hatched under the breast of understanding. Then it will open its eyes, unfold and spread its wings to reveal the light of Truth.

The spirit of man is like an unweaned child which has wandered away and become lost among the rocks and cave. Unless it is found and given sustenance from the source of its life it will perish. The first Temple of the Shrine of the Hidden Places was built on the Scared Heights. It was a temple within an inner court where there were lesser temples and the rooms of priests and teachers. The whole was surrounded by a courtyard and gardens, and beneath the main temple were the three Caverns of Initiation.

Later the Temple of the Shrine of the Hidden Places was built during a time when the light was revealed throughout the land. Though previously the shrines of the Twice Born had been concealed in the smaller temples, when Ramsis built the Great Temple of Ramen it contained, within itself, both temple and shrine of the All Highest God. Also there were Caverns of Initiation underneath. In the hall of the temple which faced East and West, between pillars of pure stone, was the portal of the outer sanctuary.

As the sun rises in the East, to give life to the day, so was the Devoted Priest placed in the East of the sanctuary, to open the services of worship and to instruct, like a father, those who came to him with understanding. In the ceiling above the candidates was the symbol of the sun and from it extended seven hands. This represented the sun of life dispensing the vitalizing forces of life from their fount within the circle of creative consciousness.

Behind the priest were representations of the ten rays of power that flowed out from the All Highest God when He created Earth, and which became the attributes of His Spirit. They are: Love, Foresight, Wisdom, Insight, All Knowledge, Strength, Resolution, Justice, Mercy and Courage.

Between the Devoted Priest and the wall behind him was the triangular representation of the three Sublime Essences Supreme Spirit, Soul Spirit and Forming Spirit - the three parts of Spirit ever in unity. The entrance to the sanctuary was in the East and above this was a representation of the Great Eye, the secrets of which cannot be written. Before the Devoted Priests was a hidden doorway and this led down to the Marriage Chamber. In this chamber were performed the rites known as The Marriage of the Soul. Here, too, spiritual nourishment could be inhaled through fragrant smoke of incense prepared from secret essences and ingredients which activate life. Here was learned the profound Secret of the Soul, the secret that was in the silence. Behind the sacred place in the temple, behind the place of flame, was the Thrice Hidden Door and this led down to the Chambers of Darkness, which were before the Caverns of Initiation.

Before the first Chamber of Darkness there was an antechamber containing a small lamp and light. Cut on the walls were representations of Life and Spirit. The candidate had studied with the priests of the upper temple for seven years and been observed by one of the Twice Born for seven years. Now, here in the antechamber he became an Anointed One.

The Anointed One went into the first Chamber of Darkness for testing by one of the Twice Born of a lesser order. Here it was discovered whether he truly desired The Great Illumination and whether he had all earthly desires and ambitions under control. Here he was warned of the dangers he would have to face and was tested for courage and fortitude. Before him now there was only one choice, victory or death.

This was the Chamber of the Red Light. Now the candidate and he who attended upon him stood before the next door, and the priest said to one who stood there. "Having realized by his own preparation, that the external is unreal and having eliminated earthly desires and substituted spiritual ones, he who aspires stands ready. He has tamed the wild steed of his body, so that it is completely under his command. He has awakened the man within the man, and the eyes of inner vision are open. He has made the irrevocable decision and is one ready to go forward".

The Anointed One was admitted into the second Chamber of Darkness and here he was uncovered and placed within a bath of cold water where he remained for a period determined by the burning of a lamp. This was the Chamber of the Purple Light. From here the Anointed One passed into a small chamber which was the entrance to the Caverns of Initiation. He now stood before the Portal of Restuah and recited the Prayer Before the Portal, "O Unnamable God, give me a burden of suffering to bear and place about my shoulders the yoke of tribulation. O God, fill the empty spaces of my spirit with pain. O grant me such fortitude that even under an almost unendurable load of distress I may be willing to lighten the burden and suffering of another. Even as I stand prepared for the awaiting test, I ask that should I be returned to the light of Earth, I be granted a share in the afflictions of others, for I need the strength given by suffering and sorrow, and will welcome them for the benefits they bestow".

Then one who stood in this place gave the Anointed One water to drink and said this prayer, "O Unnamable God, hear the prayer of the Anointed One.

Strengthen him with such courage and fortitude that he will not fail in his hour of awful trial, but shall pass beyond the Place of Terror through the Portal of Death, and so may shine with the protecting radiance and therefore return unharmed in spirit and body".

The Anointed One entered the first Cavern of Initiation and was tested there in such manner that no ordinary mortal could endure it. After three days he came out saying to one who stood there, "O acceptable suffering, what has been decreed is indeed best". After passing through the first two Caverns of Initiation the candidate became an Enwrapped One, and in the last small Cavern of the Lord of the Twice Born released his spirit. The Enwrapped One was then placed within the Womb of Rebirth and there, within the tomb of stone, he was left seven days. Here came complete liberation of the spirit. It floated out through the confining stone and went as it willed. No words of men, however learned, can ever describe this experience. The spirit of the Enwrapped One returned to the body at the behest of the Lord of the Twice Born, and he who had survived became a Twice Born One.

When led forth into the Place of Glorification his face shines with an inner beauty indescribable. From that day onward his conduct and attitudes are changed and he is at peace with all men and with himself. He needs nothing from earthly life and seeks nothing. He accepts and enjoys whatever life offers, for he has learned the answer to the riddle of life and solved the Secret of the Ages.

Your brother was one who underwent the Initiation of the Twice Born, and he has drawn the curtain aside a little to reveal only what is permitted. It is little enough but sufficient for you to understand why, when kings and governors rose to position and power, they declined the ordeal. It is understandable, for the final ordeal brought earthly life as close as possible to extinction, without complete severance of the spiritual umbilical cord. Before this, went more than twenty years arduous preparation.

Yet long and terrible though it was, the time and austerity did not exceed the necessary limits by even one jot. In sorrow your brother must say that it was not an ordeal required to obtain something man has never possessed, it was to regain something he had lost. It was, however hard as it may seem, the lowest price payable for the Secret of the Ages. For long years he who aspired to become one of the Twice Born had to practise the awakening of his spirit and bring his body under complete control.

The first thing to overcome was met long before any threshold was approached, it was something which lurked in the uncontrolled thoughts of men. The frightening experiences during the years of preparation had to be modified and their effect channeled off, otherwise the awakening spirit would have been completely overwhelmed. As the material body of man cannot come too close to a blazing fire, so cannot the spirit approach too close to the sphere of divinity. Having arisen from the Womb of Rebirth, the spirit is completely freed from any doubt about the immortality of man. Can a man doubt the source of sunlight when he can see the sun arising in glory before his eyes?

Having joined the Twice Born each man has a choice, he can go on to higher development within the Realms of Light, or he can remain to help others. Your brother chose to remain. This wisdom of the Twice Born has spread to every corner of the Earth, and Caverns of Initiation are opened everywhere. But increasingly, through the years, men have declined to undergo the austerities and trials essential to bring them into the clear light of Truth.

Therefore, the places of initiation decay and their secrets are lost, men grope in the dark and try to open a door to which they have no key. If a man has not the courage or the time, the inclination or the ability to sail to a far distant land, then if he would know about that land he must listen to those who have made the journey. So it is with those who would know the Secret of the Ages. Men possess creed of little value because they are unwilling to pay the price of something better. Your brother has no way of explaining his ultimate experience to others. Although he has looked upon the face of Truth and now understands the purpose of life, what he has seen must remain locked within the heart. Though he no longer has to be satisfied with belief alone, he cannot extend his certainty to others.

Yet men forever seek him out hoping to share with him the wonderful knowledge which has so gloriously transformed his life. This he tries to do, within the limits imposed by his own expanded enlightenment, beyond that he cannot go. The spirit of the Twice Born can be liberated at will. How often have you seen your brother in a state of ecstasy which he cannot describe? It is a state beginning in quiet bliss, flowing outward in bright radiance from an inner light which can even illuminate the material darkness about him. He hears the music of the sacred spheres and sees the throbbing pulsations of life heaving about him, like waves upon the great seas. He becomes aware of an inflowing of unspoken knowledge from a surrounding power. It does not come from any one point, but appears to flow out of all things and to penetrate all things. Material objects lose their density and become visible within, they become as though compounded of ten thousand whirling spheres of brightness. Colours are no longer dull and restricted, they become infinite in depth and number. The spirit becomes lost in adoration and wonder at the beauty revealed in everything.

The soul is aware of something glorious within all this and knows it for the spirit outflowing from its source. There is a complete unconsciousness of others, for the greater sight transcends their material bodies. The spirits of men are seen in a harmony of colours and their bodies as whirling masses of power. The experiencing soul is lost in a sea of sensitivity and feeling. There is a swelling surge of harmony, a sounding of glorious chords. It is the sea that washes the shores of eternity lapping upon the nearer strand. It is an experience that no one can give to another or adequately describe to him. It is the earned reward of those who have paid the price. It is not he only reward, for throughout the life of one who is Twice Born there is boundless feeling of wellbeing, sickness and disease are unknown.

There is an abiding love for all men, a sense of brotherhood, and over all this the certain knowledge of the immortality of the soul and its unity with the source. The impressions received in moments of illumination are everlasting. They fill the spirit with a glorified splendour. There are flashes of inspired visions, and the future unrolls and can be read as the past. There is a form of joyous rapture experienced by those who have risen from the Womb of Rebirth, and when it comes it can no more be held back than the sun can be stayed in its rising. When the body of your brother lay enwrapped within the Womb of Rebirth, his spirit was carried out as on the wings of a serif and became lost in a sphere beyond understanding.

He knew not which way to go or what to seek. Then, like a roll of distant thunder, there was a swelling sound and there came an over dazzling light. It grew steadily more brilliant until your brother saw a beautiful form of divine glory arrayed in a splendour beyond all earthly bounds. The cumbersome words of Earth cannot do justice to what your brother wishes to describe. It is like trying to sew a silk garment with rope, or to eat sweetmeats with a spade. Words are wholly inadequate symbols. The vision of glory which had been granted passed away and your brother found himself in the familiar sphere of the Spirit. Once the mysterious border has been crossed it remains open ever after and can be recrossed almost at will.

You are told of these things because your brother knows that the age of the Twice Born draws to its close. Because of those who have devoted their lives to the discovery of Truth, there is progress in the sphere of the spirit. Nothing has been lost, nothing has been in vain; the Great Gates are still closed, but they are no longer bolted. Now they will open at a knock. The road is better marked and the way more clearly indicated. They who lit the path have departed from Earth, but their service has not ended. They serve still in another place. While life on Earth moves forward, life in the sphere of the spirit does not stand still.

CHAPTER THREE. THE BROTHERHOOD

Brothers in belief, there are two roads through life, the Road of Good and the Road of Evil; they are not clearly defined roads and often run side by side, and sometimes cross each other. Those who travel without a guide or in darkness often mistake one road for the other. We are those who have chosen to walk in light, a brotherhood of men who travel the Road of Good together in companionship. We are companions on the Great Path of the True Way, and when an instructing brother speaks of the Great Path of the True Way he speaks of a double path.

The Companions of the Right Hand are those who bear the burdens of earthly labour and advancement, for they require strength, dexterity and steadiness. The Companions of the Left Hand are those who bear the burdens of spiritual Labour and enlightenment, things closer to the heart of man. The brotherhood is separated into two parts. There is an Earthly Brotherhood, and though it may be small in numbers and have few possessions, this will not always be so. There is also a Heavenly Brotherhood comprising certain of the Twice Born and their followers who have gone before. Their task is to clear the Netherworld of demons and dark spirits and to prepare the way for those who follow. They are like men who enter a new country and must clear it of wild beasts and bring the land under control.

It is the task of those above and those below to build a road joining the two territories. Your brother is not well equipped to instruct in earthly matters, and therefore leaves it to another. The caravan moves quicker when each man rides his own camel. In spiritual matters the most important is that each man should awaken his own soul, a task far more difficult than it may appear, but for which Earth is the dedicated instrument. The first objective to attain towards this end is self-taming. Just as a horse has to be broken in before it can be of any service, so has the mortal body of man to be tamed and brought under control. To do this requires not only self-discipline, but also the ability to rise above earthly conditions. No easy task, for the Earth is a hard taskmaster and worthy adversary, and the mortal body of man an unruly steed.

The duties, the obligations and the restraints by which those who follow the Great Path of the True Way direct their steps are not imposed capriciously. They are, in fact, no more than the bare essentials covering the first steps. That is why everyone, before admittance to the brotherhood, must accept every obligation and decree covering our way of life. We do not claim to know the only path, undoubtedly there are others, but we can claim to know the best.

The top of the mountain may be reached by many paths, but the shortest one is always the hardest. Supreme personal spiritual experience is undoubtedly the best source for the foundation of true spiritual faith. It begins with the development of latent spiritual powers through meditation. When you are ready seek out a place of solitude, a place that is away from the abodes of men, a place that is restful and quiet. Take a skin and a little food and water, just sufficient for your needs. now turn your thoughts inwards, harmonizing them with the rhythm of the body. Let your spirit seek harmony with the spirit flowing about it, so that the two become one. While at your meditations, neither overeat nor undereat, for there must be harmony in your eating and sleeping, in your relaxation and activity.

To become one who knows the joys of spiritual self-consciousness, to have a Truth revealing vision transcending anything knowable by the senses, to rise above the bondage of pain and sorrow and to free the spirit from the shackles of the body at will, is something unattainable by spiritual meditation alone. Leading to this road is the path of moral self-discipline and courage. The creed that teaches spiritual things alone is as barren as one concerned only with earthly things.

Your brother will not set forth in writing all things concerning the awakening of the spirit, they would be of no use until the moral foundation is laid. Such teachings must remain within the higher circle of those who travel the Right Hand Path and not disclosed to the uninitiated. Let the prayer upon your admission be always fresh in your memories: "Great Supreme Creator, Craftsman of Earth and of the multiple spheres, grant that our brother may always remain loyal.

That he will, day by day, become ever more worthy and so dedicate and devote his life to the service of mankind and the completion of its purpose, that he shall forever walk in the light of Truth. Grant him the crown of wisdom, the garments of knowledge, and let him be shod with diligence. Grant him the strength to abide by our instruction and discipline, so that with these and by his own efforts he may awaken within him the true beauties of the spirit. Add your strength to his weakness, that he may overcome all selfish motives and unworthy desires. Help him in his self taming, so that he may combat the tendency inherent in men towards anger, greed and self-pity. Strengthen him, that he may overthrow the evils of talebearing, malice and jealousy. Grant him the ability to see with the eye of understanding the defects and shortcomings of his brothers and to emulate their goodness".

CHAPTER FOUR. AMOS

Amos led the congregation and the people down from the mountains and brought them into the land of Heth, a good land was opened up before them. But Amos warned the people that they were like gems among pebbles, therefore they were not to provoke the people who had accepted them because of their skill. Amos said, "We will build a city for ourselves and our children, and within it a temple for those who follow the light of the Right Hand Path. The temple will be like the pearl within an oyster, or the heart within the body."

The congregation with Amos were the Children of Light and the people were Kenim who worshipped Yawileth, and Galbenim who worshipped Eloah. But Amos taught the people to walk in the light of Truth and said, "To each of you his own god, but above any god which can be named is something that cannot be named and you shall know it as The Supreme Spirit".

The Galbenim built the city and the temple, while the Kenim set up forges among the sons of Heth, and Amos went among them and saw that all was well. The number of those who followed the Right Hand Path and resided about the temple was one hundred and forty-four, and it was never any more or any less. The number of those who laboured in and about the city and dug the soil or attended to sheep and cattle, was two thousand four hundred and thirty-five. The number of the Kenim who followed Amos was eight hundred and twenty, and the number of the Galbenim was three thousand and fifteen. These were the numbers of those who could labour or bear arms. As Amos went out among the sons of Heth he taught the way of light, but they would not listen to bis words. They were like men walking a circle in darkness, one behind the other, each having his hand on the shoulder of the man in front. Therefore, when the king of the sons of Heth came to buy what Kenim had made, Amos spoke to him about the way of light, and sometimes the king listened. When they came upon priests of the sons of Heth, Amos said, "What manner of men are these who prance about as though the ground were covered with hot cinders?

Before their altars they are like drunkards who go about shouting and singing. They leap like horses kicking at the wind".

"What manner of spirit possess them, is it a spirit of light or a spirit of darkness? We have seen this often among your people, it is seen even among the princes and those who sit in judgement. Who can understand the words that pour from their lips? This is not prophecy but a drug-induced delusion. The people who listen to their words are as misguided as those who resort to a tomb at night and sit within a vault. If a spirit comes, it is a restless one whose words have little value, for they are hollow, empty things".

"Surely the gods of such as these are demons in disguise, whose powers are a myth, for they are unhearing and unseeing things. They are unfeeling idols clothed in garments of delusion woven within the tormented thoughts of men". The king said, "I have seen your own holy men as they sat beneath their trees and they, too, acted in a manner strange to the eyes of ordinary men. Where is the difference?" Amos said, "Our holy men sit in quietude, at peace within themselves and if their mortal eyes are unseeing it is because their spirits roam freely as birds. There is a test whereby the difference can be made known, if you will agree to it".

The king gave the sign of consent. Then a place of absolute darkness was prepared, a place to which light could in no manner be admitted. Into it went two priests of the sons of Heth and two of the Holy Ones from the congregation, the king and two attendants, and Amos. Then, while the king and his attendants watched, they saw the Holy Ones radiate a light that lit up the whole darkness, so that the faces of all became visible. The priests of the sons of Heth remained in darkness, for their spirits were feeble things without power. This is the test of true illumination.

Because of this the king looked even more favourably upon Amos and his people, but he did not change his ways or seek to walk in the light. For Amos refused to perform acts of magic before his court or to foretell the future, and the king believed that magic could accomplish all things. He believed there was an effortless way to accomplish all things, if the secret were known, and could not understand that the secret was safeguarded behind the doors of austerity and self-discipline.

There was a city called Migdal within the kingdom and some of the Kenim laboured there for the temple. When Amos came to the city it was the festival of its great god and no man laboured, neither did the Kenim, for it was the day when their fires rested. When Amos sought the overseer of the Kenim, he could not find him and none of his people would say where he had gone. But Amos found him at the temple of Belath and awaited him in the courtyard outside, and was filled with anger against the overseer. When the overseer came out Amos chided him, but the overseer said, "What have I done wrong? This place provides the food I eat, and is its god not brother to mine? There was a decision to be made, should a door of brass be cast one way or another? I sought an answer from the god by means beyond the control of men". Amos said, "Might not even the god answer according to his own pleasure? By what means was the decision sought?" The overseer said, "By the ebin which only the god could control". Amos said, "You say this is beyond the control of men, it may be so, but there are men who are more than men, men even as this god whose smallness I will prove. Come, let us put this matter to the test".

Amos then sent an attendant in haste to bring back a Holy Man of the congregation, who was with his caravan. When the Holy Man came, Amos showed the overseer and the priests that such things were not beyond the control of enlightened men, for the Holy Man could foretell the issue, whatever was done with the ebin. When Amos left the temple he took with him a woman named Kedshot, whom he had won from the priests, and made her free. The degradation of women to serve the temples was common in the land of Heth and Amos raised his voice against it. When next in the presence of the king, he said, "The common feelings of all men condemn fornication, and it is not allowed by your own laws. Yet if fornication is sanctified to your god the priests permit it for their profit. Is it not true that this wickedness is now so common in the temples of Heth that the woman who seeks to sell the services of her body in the drinking booths can ask no more than a handful of meal? " The king said, "Such is the custom of Heth, which is of long standing and cannot be changed".

Amos said, "Does the long standing of a custom make it good?" Amos said, "If your desire is to walk in the light of Truth you must choose between your form of worship and righteousness. You must choose between your gods of this land, and Truth. If a nation sow the wind it must be prepared to reap the whirlwind, for no other crop can spring from such seed, except through violation of laws which are never inconsistent".

The king said, "I have long been patient with you, stranger with the unbridled tongue, but do not overvex me". Amos held his peace, for he had disregarded his own command to his people. Yet the king heard the words of Amos and was kindly towards him. When the king came to Lethsan to buy the wares of the Kenim, Amos was there with them and the king said to him, "The gods of Heth are many, added to those of other places the gods must be beyond counting. Why are there so many and which one is it most profitable to serve?

The priests say each has power in its own place, can this be so among gods?" Amos said, "There is only one God, but each man views Him from a different standpoint and in his own light. It is even so with lesser things of Earth, how much more so with the greater things of Heaven! A mountain rises up from a plain and men see it from all sides, and to each it appears different. Some see it in daylight and others in moonlight, some at dusk and some at dawn, it is never alike to all men. Even so do men view God in different aspects. As no man knows the whole mountain but sees it only in part, so men see God in part, and each man names the part he sees according to what he sees and his understanding. Therefore, though it seems that the gods are numerous because of their names and differences, each is no more than a part of the whole. There is, in Truth, only one God, but what mortal man can see Him in wholeness?"

The king said, "If this be so, as well it may be, my eyesight is as good as yours and I see just as far". Amos said, "He who has ridden around the mountain and climbed to its summit knows it best". The city built by the Children of Light grew in strength and the people prospered under Amos and forgot their trials in Enshamis.
When Amos led them into the land of Heth he was still a young man, but as the people became many and strong, so he became heavy in years. The king who knew Amos died and the young king did not look upon him with favour, for Amos did not forbid the Kenim to go out into other nations.

CHAPTER FIVE. THE LAWS OF AMOS

These are the decrees of Amos, which he made so that justice should prevail in the land of his people. That wickedness and wrongdoing should be destroyed and the strong prevented from oppressing the weak.

Amos said, "In the days that are yet to come and for all future, let these decrees remain as a memorial". "When they are used in judgment, let the judges have wisdom and give attention to the words that are written. Let every judge seek to root out the wicked and evildoers from the land and promote the welfare of the people. If he seek Truth and Justice among these words, when they are before him, let him remember that no written words can serve him fully. Truth and Justice are but dimly reflected in the writings and laws of men and must be made clearer by the light of righteousness within his own heart".

'The seats of judgement are to be raised above all small thoughts and unworthy aims. If petty-minded men are permitted to argue over the form of sentences or pick out particular words for attention, then there will be no end to pettiness. Let no deduction or interpretation be made from the decrees, which alters them".

"Judge every man with the scales weighed in his favour. Do not be hasty in rendering a decision, time will make it more just. Be patient and calm in speech, whatever the provocation. The impatient and bad-tempered judge is an unworthy judge who sits astride an untamed horse." "The words of a judge must be shaped to fit the ears of his listeners. They must be spoken at the right time and in the right manner. His speech should not be too long or too short and every word should be well chosen. "The frailties of men accompany judges to their seats, therefore no judge shall sit in judgement alone. Where no punishment is provided by decree, then the judges shall fix the punishment according to past judgements. Where the words of a decree refer to men, then women shall be treated in the same manner, unless it be otherwise stated elsewhere. A child is one whose body has not reached manhood or womanhood."

"When two persons stand before a judge he should look upon them as though both were likely to be in the wrong, and when they have gone, as though both may have been in the right. The motives of men are many and strange, and even though they bow to the judgement the dispute between them may not be settled with justice." "When a rich man and a poor man come before a judge for a decision between them, he cannot say in his heart, "How can I say the poor man is wrong and the rich man is right and add to the misery of the poor man?" Neither can he say in his heart, "How can I say the poor man is right and the rich man is wrong, when the rich man is powerful and I may be delivered into his hand?"

"If there is a dispute between men the judges shall not let one sit and the other stand, or be patient with one and impatient with the other. Both may sit or both may stand and unless one be afflicted they shall at all times be equal before the judges." "A judge shall never say anything that will indicate a way to win his favour or to obtain a favourable decision. If all men walked in righteousness there would be no need of judges to punish the wicked. Therefore, righteousness is more desirable than the laws of men. If all men walked in the light of Truth there would be no need of judges to settle disputes between them. But as men see only a pale reflection of Truth, and that distorted by their own understanding of it, there are times when two men in dispute each believes truly that he is right. It is then that they come before the judges, believing them able to see Truth more clearly. Let the judges be able to see Truth better than any who come before them."

"When a man comes before the judges, having his life or freedom at stake or the freedom of one of his family, then the judges shall first hear reasons why they should consider him innocent or in the right, and not why they should consider him guilty or in the wrong." "Every man who comes before the pillars of the judgement place to bear witness shall be given a drink from the cup of marat and shall swear the judgement oath before the shrine and fire. Every man shall be allowed two months to discover those who speak for him, and if he ask for another two months with reason it shall not be denied him".

These are the decrees of Amos for the Children of Light:

"It is decreed that no man shall worship in the temple of any god or stand in homage before any image or idol. No god shall be joined with The Supreme Spirit in worship and the whole of his devotion and worship shall be given to The Supreme Spirit."

"It is decreed that no man shall swear an oath in the name of The Supreme Spirit or in any other name which shall bind him to do anything against the Scriptures of The Supreme Spirit. Neither shall he swear an oath which will incline his loyalties and obligations away from those who walk in their light. But as kings and governors must be served, and loyalty and obligation together with duty are our declared principles, to swear to serve them well or be faithful to a trust or an obligation is not denied him. The only solemn oath binding upon a man shall be that sworn on his immortal soul, for to swear in the name of The Supreme Spirit is forbidden."

"It is decreed that no man shall sell or barter spiritual knowledge or knowledge of The Great Path of the True Way. He shall not come into a sacred place or enter into prayer while drunk. Neither shall he do these things when unwashed, unless he be a wayfarer or one who has come from a distant place on the same day. If water is unavailable to purify himself, clean sand is not to be despised."

"It is decreed that all those who truly follow the Great Path of the True Way and those who are of the Brotherhood of Men who serve The Supreme Spirit shall be called the Children of Light. If any among them shall turn from the Children of light through fear of others, then he is unworthy and shall be cast out. He shall not be numbered among them here or in Heaven, where there is a special place for the Children of Light. But those who remain loyal to the Children of Light, even though
they have to flee to strange places, if they continue to struggle there is no wrong in them."

"It is decreed that if a man hear anything about an evil deed or know something about it and fail to disclose the knowledge before a judge or to the judge's servant, he shall not go unpunished."

"It is decreed that if any man will not bear witness to murder, to theft or to adultery, he shall not go unpunished. If he bear false witness according to his own understanding, before the flame and shrine, if it be grievous he shall lose his tongue."

"It is decreed that if any man make a false accusation of adultery against his wife, without just cause and without her acting indiscreetly, he shall receive seventy lashes." "If any man slay another he shall die, unless it be done in his own defence or in defence of his house and family. He shall not die if he who is slain be an adulterer or a seducer of one within the household of the slayer."

"It is decreed that if any man slay another in anger, during an argument or dispute, and if the fight be fair and equal, then he shall be exiled. But if any man slay another by lying in wait, or by guile or by coming behind him, he shall not live."

"It is decreed that revengers of blood shall be appointed by the judges, and no man shall revenge another of his own blood unless he be appointed by the judges." "It is decreed that if a man slay another without intent to slay, without hatred or malice, then he shall not die for the slaying."

"It is decreed that no man shall be put to death by the word of one witness. If a wife cause the death of her husband through neglect or malice, she shall not live. The law of blood shedding is: a freeman for a freeman, a slave for a slave and a woman for a woman. The free can be enslaved to repay a death."

"It is decreed that when a man must die because of his deed, it shall be by the sword, by drowning or by entombment. A woman shall be smothered or entombed or drowned."

"It is decreed that if a man strike his father or his mother or curse them, he shall be seized and sold into slavery and the money received shall be given to his father and his brothers. But if a man stand between bis father and his mother and his sister because he fears for their lives, then he shall not be punished. In this case the matter shall not fail to come before the judges, for if the father be a man of such violence, how can he claim to be numbered among the Children of Light?"

"It is decreed that if a man seize upon another to sell him into captivity, he who seizes shall die. If a man smite another so that he lose an eye or a tooth or suffer any wound, and this without provocation, then he who committed the wrong shall make it good in kind, according to the judgement."

"It is decreed that if the beast of any man injure another man within its own place of confinement, then there shall be no blame upon the owner of the beast. But if the beast be outside its place of confinement and loose, he who owns the beast shall make restitution in kind. If the beast has been savage in times past and this made known to he who owns it, and it strays beyond the limits of its enclosure to harm a man, then who owns it shall make restitution to threefold the damage. The beast shall also be slain, but the carcass shall belong to he who owned the beast." "It is decreed that if a beast stray beyond the limits of its confines and being savage to the knowledge of he who owns it, if it cause the death of any man, then he who owns it shall die. But if it be so decreed by the judges his life may be ransomed."

"It is decreed that if a man shall cause death or injury to the beast of any man and the beast be within its proper place of confinement or upon the lands of its owner, then he who caused the death or injury shall make restitution to threefold its value. If the beast be outside the lands of he who owns it and be the cause of no danger or damage, then he who caused its death shall make restitution to its value. If it was seeming that the beast would be the cause of danger or much damage, then providing there was no choice but to slay it, there shall be no restitution, but the carcass shall be returned to the owner."

"It is decreed that if the beast of any man cause the death of another man's beast, then the beast causing death shall be sold and the money received divided between the owners. But if the beast causing the death was known to be savage and its owner informed, then he shall make restitution in full to the value of the dead beast, but the carcass shall be his."

"It is decreed that if a man shall cause anything growing within the pastures of another or upon his cultivated land, to be damaged by a negligent or purposeful deed, then he shall make restitution twofold its value. If a man find the beast of another man going astray, he shall not pass it unheeded but shall provide for its return to its owner. Having done this he shall not lose or go unrewarded, but if the owner of the beast be a poor man, then bear with him."

"It is decreed that if a man set off a fire he shall make restitution for whatever it consumes to a like value in kind. But if he be careless or seek to bide his deed, then he shall make restitution twofold. If a thing be scorched or there is a blackening of wood or stone, the amount to be paid for restitution shall be agreed by the judges. If the fire was caused by accident, then he who caused it shall make restitution to half the value of whatever it consumes. The fire a man handles is like the arrow he shoots, for the bowman is liable, no matter how far his arrow flies."

"It is decreed that if a man steal any beast or fowl and dispose of it so that it is not recovered, he shall make restitution of threefold its value and shall not go unpunished. But if the beast or fowl be recovered and restored, then he who stole it shall pay its value and shall not go unpunished."

"It is decreed that if a man give anything into the keeping of another and that thing be of gold or other metal, or of some other nature and it be stolen, then the thief, if caught, shall pay twice its value and the money shall be divided equally between he who owns it and he who held it. If the thing is not restored to its owner, then the thief, if caught, shall pay its value threefold and one part shall go to he who held it and two parts to he who owned it. The thief shall not go unpunished."

"It is decreed that if the thief is not found, then he who held the thing in safekeeping shall be brought before the judges and questioned about his integrity. If he took the thing for bis own use he shall restore its value twofold and shall not go unpunished. If he dealt with it carelessly, then he shall make restitution to its value, but if he was not careless he shall not be called upon to do so. But if he were paid for the safekeeping of the thing, then he shall restore its value."

"It is decreed that if a man give a beast or fowl into the safekeeping of another and it be stolen or injured and die, then if he in whose keeping it was be found careless in its keeping, he shall make restitution of its value. If he be not found careless, then he shall not be called upon to make restitution. If it be stolen from him and he be paid for its safekeeping, then he shall make restitution of its value. If the thief be found, he shall make restitution to threefold its value and shall not go unpunished."

"It is decreed that to take from a child, or from a man who is both deaf and dumb, or from a blind man, or from an idiot, is stealing and shall be punished as theft." "It is decreed that if a man steal the boat of another or push it into the water so that it goes away or loose any rope that holds it, so that it is lost, he shall restore its value twofold and shall not go unpunished."

"It is decreed that if any man steal from a house on fire or from a house abandoned by flood, he shall become enslaved to the owner."

"It is decreed that if a man steal from a temple or holy place he shall be whipped and sold into slavery and his price given to the temple or holy place."

"It is decreed that for all manner of disputes regarding beast or anything without life, whether it be lost or not, where different men make claim to own it the dispute shall be decided by the judges. He whom the judges decide to be wrong shall pay its value to he who was the true owner. If he who is wrong has been malicious or avaricious, then he shall not go unpunished."

"It is decreed that if a man borrow a beast or anything without life, the owner not being with it, and it be lost or damaged or injured or die, then he who borrowed it shall make good its value. If a man find a thing that was lost and keep it, or he withhold from another that which is rightly his, then he shall restore it and make payment of its value in kind. If he swear falsely about these things, then he shall make restitution to twofold its value. If the thing be not restored he shall also restore its value."

"It is decreed that if a man make a false report regarding another so that he be harmed in substance, then he who did the harming shall make restitution of twofold the amount of damage done, according to the decision of the judges. If he knew not that the report was false, then the judges shall judge him according to his dealings in the matter. If it be not done carelessly and with bad intent, then he shall make a smaller payment and shall go to the man he wronged and make amends with words. It is an obligation on every man hearing a report to discover its truth before letting go. Carelessness with words should not go unpunished."

"It is decreed that if any man bear false witness against another and he be not otherwise punished, or to a lesser extent, then he shall bear upon himself the punishment he would have brought down upon the other and shall also make payment as the judges decree."

"It is decreed that if a man take a bribe to turn a judgement, then he and the man who gave it shall make restitution twofold to he who was wronged, and neither shall go unpunished."

" It is decreed that no man who sits in judgement in any place shall take a gift or benefit from any man because of his position. If any man seeking a decision shall give a gift or benefit to another to speak words in his favour, or shall forbear to do anything that words may be turned, he shall not go unpunished."

"It is decreed that if a man take advantage of the ignorance of another, or gain advantage from his dealings with an idiot, he shall make threefold restitution. If a man deceive another to his loss, or take anything from him by violence or threats, he shall make threefold restitution."

"It is decreed that if a man declare a falsehood to the loss of another, the loss shall be made good in kind twice its value. If a man deceive another who has entrusted him with goods, he shall make twofold restitution. If a man deliver a beast or thing without life, making payment to another who deals with them, if the one who deals with them or carries them loses them or fails to deliver, he shall make restitution of their value. If he be found careless in his dealings by the judges he shall make restitution to twice their value, but if he be waylaid or struck by powers above man he shall not make payment."

"It is decreed that if a scribe alter a record or make a false writing he shall be punished with thirty lashes. If a man suffer loss because of the scribe, the loss shall be made good by twice its value. He who does wrong or causes any loss, be it done with purpose or without purpose, and seeks to blame another who is innocent, shall bear the guilt of his deed. He shall not go unpunished for his deceit and shall make payment to the man he sought to blame."

"It is decreed that if a man have a maidservant or slave and he seek to give her to his son in marriage, he shall deal with her as a daughter. If he smite a manservant or a maidservant so that they lose blood or cannot move about, or if they suffer pain for three days, he shall be brought before the judges and they shall decide upon his dealings and bring justice to the one injured. It shall be within the power of the judges to free a slave from an unworthy master and place him with another, either as a slave or a freeman."

"It is decreed that if a master die and all those of his blood be absent, his servant or slave shall send for them without delay. If the servant or slave steal anything with life or without life from the dead man, he shall be whipped. If a servant, he shall be made a slave. If one who is of the same blood as the dead man steal, he shall be denied his inheritance. If he would not have inherited, he shall make twofold restitution."

"It is decreed that a master shall not allow his servant or slave to remain unmarried if they wish to marry. No man or woman having a child above the age of marriage should forbid a marriage because of their selfishness. It is their duty to see that their child is not left without children. The duty of a child towards father and mother is great, but the duty to marry is greater. If a man have a slave who serves him loyally and is righteous, he should set him free to serve as a servant. Slavekeeping is not forbidden, but it is not goodness, the truly righteous man sustains the poor by finding work for their hands. When a land is divided into large portions worked by lowly men and slaves, it is in a weak condition and ripe for the plucking. It is a truth that if men are so oppressed with toil and servitude they lose the manliness which would make them rise against their oppressors, they will not have the stomach to withstand those who invade the land. But whether the land remains at peace or is invaded, it is no longer great."

"It is decreed mat the inheritance of a man shall not go to his sons alone, for the daughters are not to be denied their portion. If he have no sons it shall pass to his wives and daughters. If he have no wife or daughter it shall pass to his brothers. If he have no brother it shall pass to his sisters. If he have no sister it shall pass to his father's brothers. If his father have no brother it shall pass to the next nearest to him in blood, but not to a woman."

"It is decreed that if a son or daughter be adopted, they shall be as though they were of the same blood as he who adopted them. Those who stand together in blood shall not be given their portion by decree, for a man knows those of his own blood best. The portions a man declares shall be fair, when all his reasons are known. If it be not thought fair the judges can decide, but they must remember that a man knows those of his blood best."

"It is decreed that no woman having an inheritance shall marry a man who is not of the Children of light. If she does so her possessions shall not go with her. A man should not forget the portion for his father and mother." "It is decreed that if a man who bears witness to an inheritance and its portion shall change it so that a man suffer a loss, then he shall make twofold retribution and not go unpunished. If he who bears witness fear that he who died made an error and seek to adjust it, there shall be no blame if he deal justly."

"It is decreed that if a man die without wife or children his inheritance shall go to his mother and father, and when they die to his brothers and sisters. If he have wives but no children the inheritance shall be theirs, but if one die while his mother and father live, her portion shall go to them."

"It is decreed that no man shall be denied his portion, if he be worthy and righteous and not an idiot. A man's inheritance should be shared out fairly among all of his blood."

"It is decreed that if a wife die and have an inheritance, the portion of her husband shall be half and the other half she may leave to her mother or father, or to her brothers and sisters. But if she have children, then the other half shall be theirs."

"It is decreed that if a man die and have wife or children, they shall not be put out of their habitation. If a wife remarry and there are others of her husband's blood within the habitation who are not children, she shall not remain there."

"It is decreed that the wives of a man who has died shall be able to marry again after one year and no restraint shall be placed upon them against remarriage."

"It is decreed that no man shall cause his daughter or any other woman to remain a maiden under oath. Strife between the children of the same father to the same mother is worse than bloodshed. These things are the obligations of a father towards his son: to teach him a craft, to teach him to defend himself and his wife and children, to teach him the wisdom of the Sacred Books and to find him a wife.

These things are the obligations of a mother towards her daughter: to teach her housewifery and the care of children, to teach her the craft of clothes and to teach her the womanly virtues according to the Sacred Books. A father should never show favour to one son over another. A child should be instructed in the Sacred Books as soon as it is able to talk.

A wife should be able to prepare flour and bake bread, cook food and brew, gather herbs, wash and mend clothes, keep her dwelling neat and clean. She should be able to make all things and do all things for the comfort of her husband; to suckle his children and work in linen, wool, pottery, basketry and tapestry. If she brought one maidservant from her father's house, she should give her the least important of the tasks, but no matter how many maidservants accompanied her, she should never neglect the care and upbringing of her children or be idle. There is an excuse for the poor woman whose children are wilful and unruly, but none for the rich woman who has all the time to devote to them. They and her husband are her greatest obligations and her most important concern. The husband who permits his wife to be slothful or idle inclines her towards unfaithfulness. A man without a wife may not be man, but one with an unchaste wife certainly is not."

"It is decreed that a man shall not pledge his daughter in marriage while she is still young, but must wait until she can say "yes" or "no" to his choice. A worthless wife or one who is lewd, a wife who displays herself immodestly before other men, or is over wasteful, may be enslaved within her own household but cannot be sold outside of it.
A woman may become an inferior wife by decision of the judges. It is intended that the pledges of marriage shall be maintained until death."

It is decreed that if a man divorce his wife and she be of good character, he shall leave their dwelling or provide another suitable for her until she marry again. A man and wife shall not be intruded upon and their enjoyment of each other shall be unhampered by any other. Every child is entitled to proper shelter, bed, food, upbringing and instruction. If a child have no father or mother or if they be proven worthless, the judges shall appoint a guardian for it. If an unmarried woman become with child it shall be a disgrace upon her father who shall be called before the judges. If she have no father, then her mother or her brothers or the person having care of her. If a wife fear she cannot be trusted or remain faithful to her pledges she shall not deceive her husband but declare herself truly, and he shall decide whether to put her away or not. If he decide to keep her and she prove unworthy, her punishment shall be lessened. The punishment of an unfaithful wife is not only for the deed but for the deception."

"It is decreed that if a man divorce his wife they shall not come together again without renewing the pledges of marriage after they have the permission of the judges. If it be done it shall not go unpunished."

"It is decreed that if a wife fear for herself at the hands of her husband, she may come before the judges who will decide for her welfare. Men should treat their wives with kindness and generosity. It is the duty of a wife to be faithful to her husband; to be modest in the presence of others and to be prudent during her husband's absence. A wife must not only be faithful, but she must give her husband no cause to suspect her of unfaithfulness. A wife must never forget that marriage was ordained for the benefit and protection of women. Therefore, they have the greater obligation in upholding it. Wanton women for forncators and good women for good men, that is the rule! Thus shall the cause of mankind be advanced and calamity kept from the heart. The upright man who walks in the paths of duty and obligation is allowed all things wholesome and healthful. He should marry only a chaste woman who would be a good mother to his children.

He should live with her in cleanliness of heart and meet her without the stain of fornication. It is not wholly good to maintain a concubine, but an unchaste woman may be kept as one or lain with if a slave."

"It is decreed that before a man and woman come to judges seeking a divorcement, there shall have been a meeting between those of their blood. There shall be a man or woman of the wife's blood and a man or woman of the husband's blood who, between them, shall choose another not of their blood to deliberate with them. Let them try to reach agreement and strive to heal the breacn with goodwill, and if anyone have a grievance it should not be hidden."

"It is decreed that before every marriage there shall be an announcement of betrothals in a public place. If anyone have something to say regarding the man or the woman, not in their favour, he shall declare it to the nearest of their blood and one who witnesses. If any man hide within his breast something that should be declared, or speak about it after the marriage, he shall not go unpunished."

"It is decreed that if a man say a betrothed woman is unchaste, without proper cause, he shall be punished with twenty lashes and if a woman do so she shall be punished with twenty stripes. If a man know a betrothed woman to be unchaste and fail to make it known, he shall be punished with forty lashes and shall make repayment as the judges decide. If a woman, she shall receive thirty stripes. No marriage shall take place until seven weeks after the betrothal. No fornication shall be committed during this time, for it would be a betrayal of marriage, and your soul bears witness to your deeds."

"It is decreed that when a man takes to himself a wife and is newly married he shall not be called upon to take up weapons or to serve away from home for one year. If he is taken away he must not be separated from his wife. A marriage is the union of flesh with flesh and of spirit reaching out to spirit. It shall be witnessed by two men and two women and declared before men by the man giving the woman a ring and bangle and piece of silver, and by her giving him a lock of hair and piece of woven cloth."

"It is decreed that all women who are not unchaste are women reserved for marriage. They shall, be sought as wives with respectful conduct and without fornication or deceit. A man who seduces them shall not go unpunished. It is not wrong for a man to make a proposal of marriage to a woman within the time she is denied to him. A promise of marriage shall not be made in secret, for such promises often cover shame and deceit."

"It is decreed that if a man accuse his wife of adultery or lewdness and there be no other witness, he shall swear three times on his immortal soul that he speaks the truth. His words shall be accepted, for if he swear a falsehood he has condemned himself and his soul to most grievous punishment. But if the wife likewise swear three times that the words sworn to by the man were false, then it shall not before the judges to decide which has damned their soul. Both shall go their own ways and if one speak to the other, that one shall not go unpunished; if they both speak, then both shall be punished. The judges shall receive reports on both and if one of them cease to live a righteous life, that one shall be cast out."

"It is decreed that if a man divorce a woman who has done no grievous wrong, he shall support her in the household of one of her blood for six months. If the woman be with child and she hide it from the father, she shall not go unpunished, neither shall they with whom she dwells. If she be found with child, then she shall be treated with kindness and consideration and those of the child's blood may seek a reconciliation between its mother and father. Both must act fairly towards the other and in righteousness and good faith."

"It is decreed that a wife may be divorced once and taken back, but if she be divorced again she shall not be taken back. The things a man gives his wife during marriage remain hers. A woman who is divorced without committing any grievous wrong is to be treated kindly and generously by her husband. A woman shall not be divorced while carrying a child or suckling it, unless it be the child of adultery. If a man be called to high office with the Elect of the Children of Light and his wife prefer earthly things to spiritual things, then they may agree to a just and fair divorce. Such a woman would be a burden, for her soul is heavy with darkness."

"It is decreed that if a man divorce his wife he shall put no restraint upon her. She shall not take his heir with her and if children go with her their father shall sustain and clothe them. A true man makes fair provision."

"It is decreed that if a man seduce a maiden he shall endow her with goods as though she were his wife and bestow upon her all the benefits due to a wife. He shall do this even though her father keep her from him."

"It is decreed that if a man permit his wife to become a whore, he shall be declared unworthy of a wife and shall not marry. His wife shall be removed from him so that he has none, and he shall not go unpunished. If a man permit his daughter to become a whore he shall die."

"It is decreed that as a woman may be taken in lust with her consent, if it be done, both man and woman shall bear the guilt alike and neither be more deserving of punishment than the other. But if the woman be a child or an idiot, or if she be protected by the judges, it shall be as though she were ravished without consent. When a woman is taken with force it shall be punished with death. If the deed be done in the fields or in places where women go away from the abodes of men, or in a forest or uncultivated place, or where no man can hear her cry, then it shall be taken by the judges that the deed was done without her consent, unless otherwise proven. But the woman shall explain her presence alone. If it be done in the city, among habitations, and the woman made no call for help and did not cry out, it shall be taken that she consented, unless threatened with death or mutilation by a weapon.

Where there has been no struggle, then it was with her consent, for no man can take a woman without her consent while she is conscious."

"It is decreed that if a man commit adultery with his son's wife or his wife's mother, both shall die by stoning. If a married women commit adultery, both she and the man with whom she committed it shall die. A husband may ransom his wife, but if he does he shall be cast out from the people, lest he bring corruption upon them. When a woman is ransomed from adultery he who shared the blame with her shall not die, but he shall not go unpunished.
When judging the adulterer or adulteress, the whore and the whoremonger, deal with them strictly and without compassion, for they are the enemies of love. They place man back among the beasts. A fornicator should not marry a chaste woman, but it is not forbidden. A whore shall not marry among the Children of Light. The sins of whoredom are not unforgivable and those who truly show repentance over many years may be accepted back into the Children of Light. A woman who becomes a whore to feed a starving child has committed no great wrong. The wrongdoing is by the people."

"It is decreed that no man shall permit a female slave to engage in fornication and it is his duty to keep her modest and free from lewdness. If, after marriage, slaves commit adultery they shall not be punished to the extent of a free person, for they have been brought up as slaves. Though the punishment of a slave be less, the master may be punished, if the slave warranted punishment because of his neglect."

"It is decreed that a man shall not be guilty of adultery except with a married woman. If a woman have three witnesses against her for whoring, or she does not deny it, she shall be shut up in a place alone where no man can come at her. There, she shall weave or work for her sustenance, and if any man come to lie with her he shall be punished. If the judges decree and a man be found willing to take her, with obligations for her keeping, she may be enslaved to him. If a whore run away from her place of confinement or from her master she shall die."

"It is decreed that if a man have a woman slave who is a maiden and the intended wife of a freeman, he shall not lie with her. If a man he with a slave and she become with child, he shall not sell her or cease to support her. If a woman slave marry the slave of another master, then her master shall not restrain her unduly, but he shall meet with the master of her husband and make an arrangement concerning her that is fair and just."

"It is decreed that the punishment for whoring shall not be upward of two years. If a woman be accused of fornication and three bear witness against her, she shall be treated as a whore. A maiden cannot be guilty of whoring after a man."

"It is decreed that the Children of Light shall not deny their servants or their slaves, or the ignorant among them, their own gods, for they have no better light. Even as the dim glow of an ember comforts a child in darkness, so are they comforted. The gods Teloth, Yole, Yahwelwa, Bel, Behalim, Elim and all the lesser gods of light may have a shrine in the city and lands about it, to serve those who would be blinded by a greater light. Better the glow from rotted wood than no light at all. Negil, Mudu, Hani, Neflim and the gods of darkness shall not be permitted to the servants and to the slaves and to the ignorant. But the stranger shall not be denied his god, for the Children of Light are not denied their light and dwell in peace among strangers."

"It is decreed that if the tongue of the stranger stray to lewdness in the presence of women, or he cast lustful looks upon them, he shall be spoken to and warned. If the warning is not heeded he shall be dismissed, so that the women be established in their goodness and be honoured among men. In the lands of strangers, where deceit is considered a virtue and vanity a womanly charm, there is no understanding of women who are modest and restrained. Men treat women as they find them, therefore women should restrain their glances and conduct themselves with modesty. They should not display too much of their body or reveal clothes that are not overgarments. They should not reveal the nakedness of their bosoms. It shall not be wrong for woman to uncover before woman, or before young children who'will grow to be men but have not reached the age of full talking."

"It is decreed that if a wife be guilty of lewdness before the eyes of men, or provoke them to lust after her, she shall not go unpunished by her husband and can lose her rights of inheritance. If any man complain to the judges about her, then her husband shall be called before them to account for her. If a maiden be proven guilty of lewdness, then her father or guardian shall not go unpunished.
If a man be so punished he shall not revenge himself on the maiden or her mother, for the fault is not theirs alone and he must bear his burden manfully. It is well to deal with daughters kindly, so that they are not estranged. In chastising a daughter for something bad in her, do not overlook the good. If the wife of a man in high position be guilty of any lewdness or other unwomanly thing, her punishment shall be doubled, for she is unworthy of her trust."

"It is decreed that if a man slander a woman who is virtuous but careless, he shall come before judges to swear to the truth of his words. If he decline or his words be proven against him he shall not go unpunished. If the man swear, then the woman shall be brought before the judges to swear likewise that his words are false, and if she decline, his words are established. If both swear they shall go out, but one soul has condemned itself to punishment."

"It is decreed that when a woman is beyond the age of childbearing it shall not be wrong if she lay aside the garments of modesty, providing she does not degrade modesty or is unmarried. It shall not be done so that she display some part of her body not commonly displayed by women. Neither shall she display any ugliness, but what she does shall be done with decorum and grace. No woman slave shall be made to do any deed of lewdness and her modesty shall be honoured. If she be forced into lewdness or immodesty she shall bear no sin, but he who forced her shall not go unpunished. Lewd talk about women and foul speech shall not go unpunished,"

"It is decreed that the fat of a beast that has died of itself or been torn by another beast may be used, providing it is not eaten or placed upon the body in any way. The flesh may be given to another beast to eat, but if any part of it is given to a man without him knowing its nature, he who gave it shall not go unpunished. No man shall eat the flesh of the falcon, the vulture, the eagle, the crow, the raven, the ibis, the owl, the hawk, the pelican, or of any bird that wades in water and has legs greater than the height of its body.

These creeping things shall not be eaten: the beetle, the snail, the ant, the slug, the grasshopper, all manner of lice and all creeping things less in size than a finger joint, and everything that creeps upon the ground without legs. The cat, the dog, the mouse, the mole, the weasel and the fox shall not be eaten. To overeat is as harmful as to starve. To fast is not an empty deed and is healthful for both spirit and body. It teaches discipline and self-control as well as moderation and frugality. Food is never lacking in the places where justice holds sway. Consume food slowly and with content, for a restless stomach robs it of taste and goodness. The man who overeats is worse than the beast who knows no better. If any man pollute food he shall not go unpunished."

"It is decreed that if a man steal water from the land of another or cause it to run away, or if he pollute it, he shall not go unpunished. If there be loss, then he shall make threefold restitution. Water in which there is a carcass shall not be used to drink. A man may drink wine or beer, or anything that is not unwholesome, providing he maintains his self-control and decency, but no longer. He who causes strife or harm to another because of something he has put into his mouth, shall not go unpunished. Wine taken in moderation is not wrong, unless it lead the hand to wickedness. No fruitbearing tree shall be cut down until it ceases to bear or dies." "It is decreed that no man shall leave a dead beast undealt with. If he do so he shall not go unpunished, for if it be not eaten or used it must be buried. If a man place anything that is foul into a storage pit or among stored corn, he shall make fourfold restitution and shall not go unpunished."

"It is decreed that no man shall cut his flesh for adornment or make any mark upon it which cannot be removed, though the ears of men and women may be pierced. Circumcision such as the strangers practise is mutilation and is forbidden."

"It is decreed that no man shall engage in usury, but shall deal with men in fairness and moderation. Payments and punishments shall be decided by the judges."

"It is decreed that no man shall associate with another who deals with spells or calls up the spirits of the dead. If he do he shall not go unpunished and those who practise sorcery shall be cast out."

"It is decreed that no man shall cheat in weight or measure and he who does shall make threefold restitution and not go unpunished. No man shall take advantage of the misfortune of another of his own blood and shall not buy their house, their field, their beast or anything without life, to his own advantage. No man should lend upon interest to another of his own blood or to a friend, for this is the cause of much strife."

"It is decreed that if a man remove a beast or a fowl or a fish from a trap laid by another, he is stealing. If a man is collecting fruit from the top of a tree, it is stealing to take whatever falls to the ground. If a man borrow something and sell it, or sell something in his keeping belonging to another, it is stealing. If a man do any of these things he shall make restitution as though he had stolen them."

"It is decreed that if a man receive a beast or anything with life or without life from another, and the two do not have proper witnesses, whether it be sold or given the two shall be punished by making payment as the judges decide."

"It is decreed that no man shall cut the living flesh from any beast or remove a limb or a piece of hide while it lives, and if he do he shall not go unpunished. The law of life demands that men eat and that beasts be slain for food, but this should be done with least pain and distress to the beasts. No beast shall be tormented for the enjoyment of its suffering and shall not be confined with cruelty, and he who does so shall not go unpunished. A beast and its young shall not be slain within sight of each other, or where the blood of the other can be smelled. No man should partake of food or drink while beasts in his charge go unprovided and uncared for."

"It is decreed that if a man carry weapons without the right to do so, he shall be punished with thirty lashes. If another be hurt so that blood is drawn unjustly, restitution shall be made for any loss and payment made according to the decree of the judges. If a man who carries weapons without the right wound another grievously, he shall die. It is cowardly to slay a man who has cast down his weapons in surrender, or to slay a woman or child. It is cowardly to torture a man who is helpless in your power or a bound captive. These things are unworthy.

Treat a captive with firmness and dignity. When in battle raise your thoughts above the spoil, look to Heaven for your reward. Peace is the proper course for all men to follow, but peace at any price is a delusion. Therefore, it may better become a man of peace to stir up the righteous to fight. Ten courageous men can overcome a hundred of lesser courage. Prepare for war with peace in your heart and with regret, but for the sake of the cause press forward resolutely. Be at peace within yourself through gain or loss, advance or retreat, victory or defeat. The peaceful man who shouts "Peace at any price" does not prevent war, he only steps aside to put another to the fore who will slay and be slain. That is contemptible and worse than if he had stood his own ground."

"It is decreed that if a man or woman be bound to another for a debt or payment, they shall be fed, clothed and given shelter. They shall not be beaten or ill-treated, but they should do a full day's work. Their welfare shall be in the hands of the judges." "It is decreed that if two men enter upon the same wrongdoing together, or one against the other, both shall be punished alike, except if one be in the power of the other."

"It is decreed that games of chance played for money shall be undertaken only in moderation and if any man cheat or weigh the game unfairly, he shall not go unpunished."

"It is decreed that no man or woman who is of the Children of Light shall marry another who is not, for this is wrong against their children, whose upbringing is divided against itself.
A slavewoman who believes as her master is better for a mate than a freewoman who does not, even though the freewoman be more pleasing. No man shall permit his maiden daughter to marry a man who is not of the Children of Light. A slave who is righteous and walks in the light would be better, even though he be unacceptable to her father."

"It is decreed that if a man withhold from an orphan or anyone under his care that which is theirs, if it be done without cause or to his benefit, he shall not go unpunished and shall also make twofold restitution. He shall not deny them the right to marry, or if it be a man the right to his own livelihood. If a man or woman of a man's own blood be in his care because they are an idiot or incapable, then let not the burden of responsibility for their own sustenance fall upon them. Keep them from harm, support them with food and maintain them in clothes. The man who is rich and powerful has a duty to protect the destitute and ailing woman from the afflictions of life and from the wiles of men."

"It is decreed that if any man or woman die, those who stand next to them in blood shall be responsible for the disposal of the body. Those who declare the need to burn the body so that the departed one may use its essence in Heaven, indulge in a vain superstition."

"It is decreed that if anyone seek refuge within the sanctuary of the temple, it shall not be denied them, and if any violate this sanctuary they shall not go unpunished. The labours of the sanctuary shall not be diminished."

"It is decreed that the measure within a logua shall be equal to the water which can be contained in twelve blown eggs of the ground fowl. The weight of a silver shekel shall be the same as barleycorns numbered according to the days in the year. The length of a cubit shall be the same as forty-eight barleycorns. From these all things shall be weighed and measured."

"It is decreed that a man may be declared to be outside the law, and then though he be liable to all restrictions and penalties which it imposes, he can enjoy none of it benefits or its protection. If a man be declared fully beyond the law, no other shall speak to him or supply him with food or clothing or shelter. If a man be declared an outlaw, he is to be slain on sight. If exiled, he is to be slain if he return from his place of exile."

"It is decreed that no man shall make an image of any god or make anything in the likeness of a god, but all objects of beauty can be made. Anything can be made bearing the likeness or image of a man, woman or beast, providing it be done with good taste and without obscenity."

"It is decreed that if anyone attempt to slay another with poison, they shall die, even though they have not succeeded. All who aid them in the deed or seek to hide it shall also die."

"It is decreed that if anyone take their own life they shall not be buried or burnt for three days."

"It is decreed that if a man die having no son or daughter, and no one of his own blood who can claim, a son or daughter born to his wife after remarriage may become his heir."

"Justice and Truth are not in the safekeeping of the judges. They are, to those who sit in judgement, as the sun is to other men. Every man who comes before the judges should walk in the light of Truth and Justice, even though he speak against himself or against those of his own blood. The man who bears witness should take no heed whether he be on the side of the rich or the poor. He should not follow the road of passion or the paths of his own prejudices, lest he lose the guiding light of Truth. The man who hides within himself knowledge that would assist the cause of Justice and Truth inflicts an injustice upon his own soul."

"A too hasty decision by the judges often inclines towards injustice. Therefore, when the judges have heard all and every word has been spoken by those who have a right to speak, the judges shall retire and pray. Each should say, within his heart, "I will consider my words carefully before I speak and they will be uttered in the purity of Truth, untainted by falsity or hypocrisy. I will not be harsh in my judgement and it will be bent towards a benefit rather than a loss. My speech will be directed towards the safeguarding of others and be without any taint of malice or evil intent."

CHAPTER SIX. THE TALE OF HIRAM

Thute, the son of Pelath, a freeman of Elanmora in the land of the Hethim, wrote these things in the harvest years of his life, when his heart was filled with wisdom and understanding. He who reads them with the eyes alone will derive little benefit, but he who receives them with an enlightened and uplifted heart will find a response within the depths of his own spirit.

While Hiram Uribas, son of Hashem, was still a beardless youth taking his pleasure among the riches and splendour of his father's house, a wise man came from a faraway land. He came, not as a great man riding with a rich caravan but wearyfooted, begging water and food. These were not denied him and while he sat in the shade, slaking his thirst and satisfying his hunger, Hiram, the youth, came up to him with courteous greetings. The wise man was pleased and poured out words like jewels, so that the young man became filled with the desire for wisdom and Truth, swearing that from that day forward he would devote his life to the search for them. After the departure of the wise man, Hiram became restless under his father's roof and it was not long before he set off with a bundle of food and skin of water for Uraslim. Arriving there he slept in the house of Gabel, a servant at the temple of the Winged God of Fire, and from thence he journeyed towards Bethshemis, which lies past Tirgalud, on the road to Egypt.

Hiram was a young man of his people, tall of stature, with a darting brighteyed glance. His long, band-bound hair hung low on bis shoulders and his stride was wide and firm. He came upon Bethshemis close to nightfall, when it was not good to enter the city, and therefore as darkness closed about him he prepared to lay himself down beneath the wall of a vineyard. This was owned by a wealthy widow who, seeing the young man preparing for the night, sent men out to bring him into her guest house. The widow was neither old nor unbeautiful and when she saw the comeliness of the young man her heart was gladdened and she bade him welcome. Hiram did not depart with the light of the morning and it came to pass that the widow offered him a high place on her estates.

Hiram accepted, for he was young and pleased with the honour, but in the course of time the widow had become enamoured with him and sought to make him her husband. Hiram sought a way of release from this, for he had already heard tales of the woman's many lovers. The widow said to Hiram, "Be my husband, for the one I had has died and left no heir. Let us enjoy the fruits of your manhood, for I desire the seed of your body, so that I may have a splendid son. I will give you robes of blue and red and they will be laced with chains of gold. You shall ride in a high chariot wheeled with brass and poled with copper. Many servants will attend you and wise men brought from East and West will fill your heart with wisdom. You shall lack nothing that satisfies your desires."

Hiram was not at ease with himself, for he was young and lacked the wisdom to deal with the situation. He answered the widow hastily in these words, "You are a woman of beauty and this alone makes you a desirable treasure to men, but how would it fare with me in marriage? It is said that you have had many lovers and they find you as a smouldering fire in a cold room, a door restraining neither wind nor sand, a roof that falls in upon the sleeper beneath it, a boat that drowns the boatman, the crust over a quicksand, water that does not slake the thirst and food that sits heavily on the stomach. Which man did you ever love with constancy, so that he walked in the joy of contentment? Which man could ever call you his?" The words from his mouth stung the widow like hornets and she flew into a rage after the manner of women. She called upon her servants and they beat Hiram with sticks and drove him off her estate. With a little more wisdom in his heart, he continued on his way into Egypt and after many days he arrived at the city of On.

Hiram dwelt among the Southern Men on the outskirts of the city, for many had been captured during the wars and made slaves. When lustfully aroused the bodies of these men exude a sweet odour like honey, which no man can detect and it makes all women succumb to them. This is the manner in which the nation of Egypt sacrificed its purity. In the days when Hiram came to Egypt the Pharaoh Athmos ruled. In those days Egypt was at war with the

Abramites, for their great red-headed king had committed adultery with the wife of a prince of Paran.

The remorseful king reaped as he had sown, for his favourite daughter was ravished by her own brother and his wives were humiliated and ravished before the eyes of all men. Because of the war, there was much coming and going of strangers in the city of On and Hiram went unnoticed. Hiram dwelt long in Egypt and absorbed its wisdom, but the thing which delighted his heart the most was the tale of its long-hidden treasures. He learnt about the nestburning bird whose wondrous many-hued egg granted men the gift of eternal life. He heard about the serpent pearls and the bright jewels which glowed with the light of the sun even on the darkest night. All these things he desired to possess for himself.

The nesting place of the nest-burning bird was among the Mothbenim, eastward of Egypt, but among the treasures of Egypt was one of its eggs. The egg, the pearls and the jewels were safeguarded in a dark cave upon an island called Inmishpet, which was set in the middle of a lake called Sidana. In the waters of the lake were fearsome watermonsters, part beast, part fish. On the shores of the lake dwelt the shapeshifting priests, guardians of the treasures. Northward of the lake was a broad pastureland where the shepherd Naymin tended the temple flocks, but Naymin was old and had no son who would follow him. Therefore, he took Hiram into his household and Hiram became as a son to him, tending the sheep of the temple, and no Egyptian was with him. One day, while the sheep still suckled their lambs, Hiram was out in the pastures, sitting near the cool waters because of the heat. As he reclined in the shade he played gay shepherd tunes on his flute and in the many times he had been there no one had ever disturbed him. Yet not far away was the House of the Virgins of Elre, but the maidens who dwelt there rarely went abroad.

This day, however, Asu, daughter of the High Priest, walked abroad and hearing the melody of the flute drew near to listen, but Hiram did not see her because of the bush between them. The maiden sat down, taking the sandals of her feet. Hearing a cry from one of the sheep in the distance Hiram stopped playing and stood up, his back towards the maiden. She, seeing him standing up, sought to creep away before he saw her, but as she did so her foot was pierced by a thorn and she let out a cry of pain. Hiram turned and seeing her distress hastened to help her.

He withdrew the thorn tenderly and carried her down to the pool, so that she could bathe the foot in cool waters. While she did so he entertained her with sweet melodies on his flute. The maiden fell in love with Hiram and he with her, but because she was a dedicated virgin and daughter of the High Priest neither could open the doors of their heart. The maiden spent nights weeping, for she had a love for which there was no remedy.

Hiram took his flock to other pastures, but still their hearts drew them back to the place of meeting and they met again and yet again. Now, the wife of Naymin noticed that Hiram pined as with a sickness and she spoke to him about it, and he told her of Asu, the maiden from the House of the Virgins of Elre. The wife of Naymin spoke words of consolation for this hopeless love, knowing they helped but little. In the fullness of the year Hiram took his flock to distant pastures around the other side of the lake. While he was away the wife of Naymin took herself down to the place where he was wont to meet Asu, and one day Asu came. She was known to the wife of Naymin who was the gatherer of herbs for the temple. They spoke of many things, of Hiram and of the gods, of priests and their ways and of temples and those who served in them, of life and of man and of woman. Now, when Hiram returned it was nigh the feast of sheepslaying and at this time sacrifices of lambs were made to the watermonsters in the lake. While away Hiram had thought about Asu and about the treasure of Egypt, both seemingly equally unattainable.

The wife of Naymin spoke to him rarely and Hiram wondered, for this is not the way of women. On the eve of the feast of sheepslaying the lake boats were prepared for the annual pilgrimage to the island. Among these was the great boat of Erab, kept in memory of the day when the Scorcher of Heaven rose with the sun, and earth was overwhelmed. From this boat the sacrificial lambs were offered to the watermonsters and on it served Asu and eight virgins. There, too, the High Priest officiated. Hiram had conceived a plan within his mind whereby, at the risk of bis life, he might possess himself of the treasures of Egypt. This year, Naymin being now frail, he alone would be in charge of the sacrificial lambs, together with two boy priests to assist him.

They came from the Temple of the Lake dedicated to the Bright Bearded One who once saved Earth from destruction through fiery hail by making a third round. On the night before the festival, Hiram slept with his small flock beside the boats and at first light they were put aboard. As the sun rose upon high the High Priest came with many other priests and princes, and the virgins came also. They offered sacrifices at the Temple of Departure and then set out upon the waters. In another boat were Naymin and his wife and there were other boats filled with people. After making offerings upon the waters the boats arrived at the island and preparations were made for the Island Ceremony, which lasted throughout the night. The lambs were offered as darkness came and the waters became red with blood, and the watermonsters satiated with meat. Now, the cave on the island was protected from men by the Spirit of Mot, who had died there in days long forgotten, and the priests guarded its entrance. But Hiram did not fear the Spirit of Mot, for it could do no harm to one who carried upon his body the same bloodscar as Mot had borne.

Hiram the stranger had been so marked out from other men in his childhood. At the sixth hour of the night three virgins entered the cave to bring forth the treasures, and with them went a priest protected by sanctification in the blood of a lamb. Five priests who were Guardians of the Treasures and never left the island also went into the cave with them, garbed in skins and masked with the heads of beasts. The treasures were brought forth and placed upon the altar against the rock wall beside the cave, so that all might behold them. Over the altar was laid a cloth of linen and gold. While the people passed before the treasures and danced and sang, priests came and went in the cave. Before the cave and away from the road leading down to the lake, there was a pathway which went down to the Pool of Purification. Here, after the maidens had bathed, men and women came down one by one to be purified in its waters. They then went through an opening into the lake and, passing through the waters along the shore where they rose not much above the waist, ascended by steps through a small arched temple back on the road. If they were truly purified they were never touched by watermonsters. Never had a maiden been taken by the watermonsters, but on this awful night, while a

maiden passed between pool and temple, there was a loud cry of agony quickly stifled.
The island fell silent with forboding and as the night passed the name of Asu was whispered from mouth to mouth. The treasures were carried back in gloom and silence under a mantle of dread, and the head of the High Priest was bowed in sorrow and disgrace. When the boats departed none noticed that Hiram was missing, for his duty done he could return in any boat. And none was the strange craft that clove the waters of the lake of Sidana that night. Hiram returned to the shepherd hut of Naymin and nothing was said to him, for Naymin thought he had joined with the people sorrowing in the temples, and always many remained about for several days.

When Hiram had refreshed himself he left Naymin who was weary and weighed down with age and sorrow, and prepared to return to his flocks. In his grief, because of the death of Asu, he could find solace nowhere, except perhaps in the familiar solitude among his sheep. But the wife of Naymin said, "Let me walk with you a little way, for I, too, suffer and yet must seek herbs which are needed and not easy to find."

When they had gone some distance, she said, "I go this way, will you not accompany me and humour an old woman who may need your aid?" Hiram did so, for the woman was even as his own mother, though he could not understand her strange manner. She brought him to a place in a hollow enclosed by thickets, and lo there was Asu. When the embraces and the greetings were over and the explanations given, the wife of Naymin said, "Here you cannot remain. There are clothes and food and no pursuers will follow the maiden, and none will query your departure. Go this night, taking thought for nothing here, for you are young, with a lifetime of joy before you, after the pangs of parting have passed." Hiram said, "No gladness, no joy can ever surpass what I now feel, yet this thing increases a burden already upon me and is less simple than it appears. For this you must know, I have taken the treasures of Egypt and hidden them in a place where no man can find them. Who would suspect me if I went about my task without change, a shepherd with no thought beyond his sheep and flute? The cry may be raised even now, though I think another day will pass first. Then who could trace the

passage of every man who has departed, even though pursuit is made in all directions?
Why did you not tell me of your plot?" The wife of Naymin said, "How could you be told of something which might not have been or which you might have betrayed by glance or bearing? We, too, thought you no more than a simple shepherd with no thought beyond flute-playing, except love. What now will you flee with the maiden and abandon the treasures? Or shall she flee alone, for she is committed to flight." Hiram said, "I cannot abandon love for treasure, but neither can I abandon this treasure for life or let it corrupt. Therefore, let Asu, the maiden disguise herself and together we will depart to a safe place without the treasure, none suspecting she still lives. Then in the fullness of time I will return and recover the treasure, for no man can discover its hiding place. However, I will not depart in haste but wait and bid Naymin farewell and go in the fullness of time." Hiram left Asu and returned with the wife of Naymin.

Coming in to Naymin Hiram told him he had had a vision such as no man could disregard and must go to the land of his fathers, but would return before the coming again of the season. That night a great cry went up among the temples and in the light of the morning men came and questioned Naymin and those with him, but found them simple shepherds. Hiram departed, taking the ass of Naymin and with him went the wife of Naymin. They were joined by Asu, cloaked as a beggar girl who earned her food by ungainly dancing, whose face was unwashed and clothes unclean. They accompanied men who hunted for the stolen treasures and their possessions were open before the eyes of all men.

After seven days the wife of Naymin returned. Hiram and Asu went onwards until they came to Bethelim near Fenis. beyond the borders of Egypt, and they dwelt there among the Kerofim. In the fullness of time Hiram returned to Egypt and recovered the treasures, bringing them inside skins hidden within other skins filled with water and oil. Now, when Hiram had left Egypt and drawn nigh to Bethelim, he saw that the dwelling he had left no longer stood and the fields about it were overgrown with burning bushes. Within the burnt out ruins he found remains and bones and knew them for those of Asu and the Kerofim with whom she dwelt. He saw that they had died by the sword.

Hiram did not linger at the place of death and thought to take himself to a place of safety, but knowing the dangers of the land he sought a place where he hid the egg of the nest-burning bird and the pearls, all except two, and most of the jewels. Having secured them in safety, he went on his way. Hiram kept going until he came upon a small wooded place nearly two days journey away. Here, while he slept, two wild swine came and swallowed three of the jewels which he had tied in a piece of hide. Later he lost one while fording a river, and one was taken from him when he sought shelter in a temple. Two pearls and two jewels were taken from him by other priests who placed them in the treasury of their god. The remaining treasures which he had with him were lost when he was waylaid, and though his life was spared he was left bleeding and near to death.

As Hiram lay by the roadside he was succoured by wandering metalworkers and brought back to health by them, for they were men of his own blood. Hiram remained with the metalworkers for some years and learned their craft. He became skilled in the making of weapons and in their use. In the fullness of time he returned to the place where he had secreted the treasures and recovered them. He then went down to a city by the sea and took ship to a far off land. No man has seen him since, but it is said he married the daughter of a king and became a prince among foreign people. This is the tale of Hiram.

CHAPTER SEVEN. THE ROLLS OF RECORD - 1

By the hand of Raben, son of Hoskiah who was the Bowman of God and brought the Children of Light to the Land of Mists. Hoskiah was a mighty man whose bow shafts struck like the lightning flash, and his enemies went down like corn before the reapers. He was a Captain of Men in the War of Gods and those he slew where numbered like barley in the measure. His enemies were spread before him like a carpet at his feet and there was no other like him. He was a man who knew the Almight God and looked up to Him as the God of his fathers.

But Hoskiah worshipped Him after the customs of his people and therefore knew Truth only in part, for having stolen Him they were unable to know Him fully. Now the days of fighting were past and Hoskiah and those who remained alive with him slept in strange places, for they were sought by the king who had been victorious. His wives and his children and all his household dwelt at Kadesh, against the mountain, and awaited his coming there. But he came not while being sought by the king. So it came to pass that his brother Isias, who held stewardship over all his household and his possessions, seeing that Hoskiah could not come unto this place, possessed himself of them. Isias had the ear of those in high places, and Hoskiah lost his birthright.

So all that was Hoskiah's passed into the possession of his brother Isias. He took even the wives of Hoskiah, for such was the decree of the king. But Athelia, the first of the wives of Hoskiah, spurned Isais and called down the wrath of Helyawi upon his head. And Isais was afraid and did not possess her. When they saw this the other wives, being jealous of her, for she was ever in high favour with Hoskiah, stirred Isais up against her. They mocked him, saying, "Are you truly the master here, or are there fruits you cannot pluck?" So Isais sought to take Athelia by strength, but she strove against him and his manhood was hurt, so that did not take her. Then Isais had her bound and her hands were tied for seven days, so that she could not of herself either eat or drink or do the things required by her body. She was humiliated and her womanhood betrayed, for an idiot man attended her wants and he mocked her modesty, and she was tormented by her needs.

Then on the seventh day she was brought forth by Isias to trial, and she was stripped and lashed and her hair was burnt off. She was branded on the face and her lips and tongue were cut. She was given a robe and a pitcher of water, and dried fruits and flour. She was driven forth by Isias who said, "Go woman, and perhaps, should you even find him, Hoskiah will understand your babble."

Athelia went out into the wilderness to die and at night she fell in pain and weariness, under an elan tree and lay there. In anguish she cried out unto her God and cast her soul from her, that she might not feel pain. And her soul found Hoskiah. As it became light next day, Athelia awoke and praised God, saying, "I have slept amid my pain, for God is good and merciful. And I know that Hoskiah yet lives in a far off place, but my soul and my God will lead me to him." And she went, guided by her soul. On the same night, Hoskiah lay in a cavern amid mountains, but he slept not, for one had come bearing tidings of his brother, saying, "Isias has possessed himself of all that once was yours. Even your wives has he taken, and between you and he are many men who would slay you."

As Hoskiah lay thus in agony of spirit it came to pass that he felt the presence of Athelia's soul, and peace came upon him and he slept. And as he slept he dreamed, and in his dream Athelia stood at his feet, fairer than he had ever known her. And she said, "All is not lost unto you, for I come seeking you in the wilderness and I will find you, so be at peace." And Hoskiah awoke refreshed and strong in spirit. And he came down out of the mountains, and over the wilderness came to the Place of Bitter Waters where men find refuge. And men were hiding there from the wrath of the king. And Hoskiah enquired of them, saying, "You have come from many places, which of you has seen a woman seeking me?" They said, "No woman travels abroad on such a quest. Or has she many attendants, and what is her appearances?" And Hoskiah said, "She is fair as the dawning, with hair like the raven's wing and skin like fine oil. Her touch is like cool waters and her bearing like the gazelle." Then the men mocked him and talked much, saying, "How long would such a one as you describe travel alone? It is not in the nature of women to leave their household and come into the wilderness. Would any man pass her by? Who, then, now possesses her?

Seek her not in the wilderness, for is she not clad in fine linen and perfumed with sweet smelling oils?" Then Hoskiah took counsel with himself and said, "I am indeed a fool who chases dreams. This is no time for dreaming when there is a man's task at hand". So in the morning he said to those with him, "I go up against my brother". But they pleaded with him, saying, "Have you a host of men or even a company? Abandon such foolishness". Now, at that time Athelia dwelt beneath a mountain where there was a spring, for she was weary from many days journeying. And she was sick in spirit, for men, when she came among them, beat her with sticks and drove her from the place of their habitations. She offended their eyes and none desired her. No man came to the spring, for it was an accursed place where voices came from the rocks and the dead spoke.

Therefore, it is called the Audience Chamber of the Dead. And none but witches go there, for these the dead do not harm. Now, when night fell Hoskiah slept, and those with him were not watchful. And evil men said among themselves, "Let us slay Hoskiah in the night, for he has gold and silver and spoils of war with him. Let us cut off his head and carry it to his brother, that we may be rewarded and made welcome." So it came to pass that in the morning hours of the night men came to fall upon Hoskiah and those with him to slay them. But one among them was heavy-footed and Hoskiah awoke as they fell upon him, and he seized his sword and leaping up as a lion springs smote about him, and there was a slaughter. But he was without helmet and his head was bare, and so he was wounded. They who came against him died or fled, but of those with him just one remained, and he sorely wounded.

In the morning they left with their asses laden, and Hoskiah held his bow and none came near him. And as the sun mounted on high the sight departed from the eyes of Hoskiah and he became blind. So Hoskiah and he who was his companion abandoned hope, for there were men who would destroy them in front and behind, and the wilderness enclosed them. And they said, "Let us, therefore, go to the place called the Audience Chamber of the Dead, which is by our side. For are we not as those already dead? There we shall find water to quench our thirst and soothe our wounds as we end our days."

And as they entered the pass at the place where the waters entered the sand, the companion of Hoskiah died. Then Hoskiah heard voices of the dead calling him from among the mountains, and he arose and said, "I come, for this is my hour." And he passed up the watercourse. So it was that being blind he dashed against the rocks and fell to the ground, and lay there as one already dead. Now, on that day the soul of Athelia was troubled and she wandered abroad, straying from her tasks. And she looked up and saw a raven descending from out of the sky, and her soul said unto her, "Behold, it comes for the soul of Hoskiah, for he is near by and close to death." So Athelia sped away guided by the bird. She came upon Hoskiah as his soul was preparing to depart, and she took him in her arms and lifting his head gave him water. And her soul communed with his soul and bade it stay, and because of the bond between them it stayed. And she remained with him three days and built a bower and ministered to him, but he lay as one already dead.

On the third day, as the sun prepared to enter into his night kingdom, Hoskiah stirred. He groaned in anguish from his wounds and Athelia comforted him, and he slept in peace. When it became light next day he awoke and felt Athelia's touch upon him. And Hoskiah knew her and said, "Athelia are you here? How came you to this place and found me in my hour of need?" But Athelia answered not because of her tongue and she drew a veil around her face, for she knew not that Hoskiah was blind. She wept and her tears fell upon his face. And he held on to her, for her hands told him that she could not speak to him as once she did. And he said, "I am blind and cannot see", but she drew not the veil, for she feared for him when his hands sought to be his eyes.

Days passed and Hoskiah grew strong, and he knew the tale of his brother's deeds and swore vengeance in the name of his God. He said, "For this purpose life has been left to me". And Athelia grieved that he spoke thus, for he could not walk without her. The waters of the valley were cool and there were herbs and wild fruits, and goats upon the mountainside. So it came to pass that after

many days Hoskiah was whole and strong again. But he remained blind, so he could not see Athelia and therefore she remained fair in his eyes. But the soft speech was gone from her.
This, Hoskiah did not mind, for what he heard daily was the speech which greeted him as he lay in her arms before she knew he had come back to life. Hoskiah and Athelia were no longer troubled by the voices among the rocks, for no harm was done to them in this place. When Hoskiah became strong again he desired to go from that place and fretted to be gone, but Athelia bade him stay. She said, "You are blind and therefore like a child. And will we not die of hunger in the wilderness, or be slain by men who seek after you? Let us stay here." And Hoskiah listened to her words, for it was not unpleasant in this place.

And it came to pass that one day, as Athelia gathered herbs in the valley, she espied a stranger drinking at the waters and he was weak and weary from much journeying. And she took Hoskiah and together they went up to the stranger and Hoskiah greeted him, saying, "May the peace of God be with you, master, how may we serve you?" The stranger answered them saying, "I am Lokus, Son of the Fire Bird and physician to the king of Tyre. I have travelled from afar to this place, that I may hear the wisdom of the dead. I came to talk with my soul in solitude, for I am weary of the ways of men. I no longer seek to be the companion of those in high places who concern themselves overmuch with wars and the affairs of men". And Hoskiah knew Lokus for a magician of great renown. Hoskiah dwelt in a cave in the mountainside, by the waters of a spring which came forth from a smaller cave nearby. The land before the caves was flat and there were ancient gardens and enclosures. Beyond these were trees. When Lokus had been brought to the abode of Hoskiah, to the place where he camped, he was given food and rested.

Then Hoskiah said unto him, "You are great even among great magicians, for your magic is greater even than the magic of Egypt. I beg you, master, look with pity upon my blindness, for it makes me even as a child, I who am a man among men and have a man's task before me. Pray, therefore, cast magic with fire, that I may be made whole again." Lokus said unto Hoskiah, "Is this then the one desire of your heart, is there nought in Heaven or Earth you desire more?" Hoskiah said, "There is nought above this." Then Lokus spoke to Athelia, saying, "What is your desire, is it that you may be as you once were?" And Athelia said, 'This indeed I desire, especially for the sake of my lord. But, master, above all I desire that he may see again; but, oh, let not his eyes lead him from me to destruction." Lokus said to Athelia, "You know what his eyes will see." She answered him, "Let his eyes see what they will, but let them see." Lokus said unto her, "So it shall be, for you have but one desire between you. I will make a covenant with Hoskiah, so that his eyes may see again.

This is the covenant: That Hoskiah will stay in this place until Athelia has borne him a son and until six months after his son's weaning he will sit at my feet and absorb my instruction". Then Athelia said unto Lokus, "Master, when he is no longer blind and sees me as I am, will not the burden of the covenant be too great for him? Lokus answered, "He has more than two eyes." Lokus took Hoskiah and cast a spell upon him, so that he fell asleep. And Lokus opened his head and let out the evil which blinded him and encased his head in clay, that the demon might not resume its residence.

And Hoskiah was left asleep for six days and six nights. On the seventh day Hoskiah awoke, and behold, he was no longer blind. And he called for Athelia, but she came not unto him. Then Hoskiah cried, "I see, but the woman is not here, is this not a time for rejoicing? But lo, she stays away". Lokus said unto him, "It is the manner of women, let her be.". And when night had come Atheha came and sat at the feet of Hoskiah and said unto him, "It is well my lord, and my heart rejoices." And Hoskiah, stretching out his hand, caught hold of Atheha, saying unto Lokus, "Long have I been with this woman. And I was blinded that I could not see her face; now I say, bring me my torch quickly, that I may look upon the face I desire to see with all my heart." And Athelia, bowing her head, remained cold and still beside Hoskiah, the veil held before her face. And Lokus, placing the torch aside, drew the veil and lifted her head towards the light, and the woman looked up fearfully. Hoskiah looked long upon her in silence. Then he lifted her towards him and kissed her face, saying, "Wife of my bosom, the years have taken nothing from the loveliness of your youth". And Athelia fell before him in a swoon. Now, when morning came Lokus sat outside the cave and Athelia came, and kneeling before him said, "Great master, what magic have you wrought? The waters do not lie, yet my lord sees me not as they". And Lokus answered her, saying, "Nor does the soul he, but the eyes of men are deceivers and not to be trusted. One desire only have I granted, for my magic has not touched you. Hoskiah sees indeed, but if he sees not wholly with his eyes and in part with his heart, seeing not with the eyes of other men, then perhaps my magic is imperfect and I am not the greatest of magicians".

Unnumbered days passed and Athelia was first delivered of a daughter and then of a son. And Hoskiah sat before Lokus and received his instruction, and many books were opened unto him. He learned the Mysteries of the Secret Way and the Songs of the Fire. He knew the wisdom that had come down through the ages. So it came to pass that one day Hoskiah went unto Lokus and said, "All has been done that the covenant required." And Lokus answered him, saying, "It is well, prepare now to follow the path of your destiny." Then Hoskiah took Athelia and his son and his daughter, and with Lokus passed out into the wilderness. And when they came to the habitations of men Atheha was veiled. And Lokus journeyed as a great magician, following his stars, and Hoskiah served him as though bis slave.

Thus they came to the lands held by Isias and Lokus made masks of animal skins, with tree gum and clay, and gave them unto Hoskiah and Athelia. And he clothed them in strange garments and dyed their skins, saying, "Men expect all things of a magician and make no query concerning the strange things they see about him. Therefore, let not the men of this place be disappointed in my attendants". To Hoskiah he said, "Be as one dumb, for your tongue would betray you to those we come amongst in this place". And Hoskiah answered, "My tongue shall be dead in this place. "In this manner they came before Isias. Isias had looked well upon the fleshpots and his body was filled with fat. He was clad in fine linen from Egypt and perfumed. And Hoskiah said within himself, "Can this be the son of my father and the companion of my childhood? It is truly written, in the hands of a weakling gold turns to fat". Lokus spoke unto Isias, saying, "Lord I have come far and therefore beg that I and my servants be given food and drink and a place to lay our heads. I am a magician of magicians and a physician of physicians. Mayhap there are those within your household who are sick or possessed by demons, whom I may serve. Or may I enliven your leisure with wonders and magic and show you strange things beyond the understanding of men? Isias said unto Lokus, "Remain with us, for there is little pleasure here. If you enliven our days you serve us well." So it came to pass that Isias prepared a great feast to which came many lords with their households. The fame of Lokus had spread afar, for he had healed the sick and cast out demons and shown many wonders beyond the understanding of men. And among those who came were many who knew Hoskiah.

When the day of the great feast came there was much feasting and merrymaking, and Lokus worked great wonders, so that all men acclaimed his magic. And there were games and feats of strength and dancing. When night had fallen great fires were lit and many torches. Tables were spread with all manner of good things and the guests assembled within the great courtyard. Isias sat beneath the tall sycamore tree and before him was a table laden with every kind of meat. There were breads and sweet things and spices in abundance. And Isias was sitting among half men and wanton women and with him were gluttons and drunkards. There was much loud laughter in their company and many sly gestures. There were singing women and dancing girls. There were half men who performed as women, and the night was heavy with the scents of wickedness.

The feasting and dancing went on well into the night and Lokus displayed his powers before the assembly. When the clamour was at its height Isias spoke to Lokus, saying, "Show us now the greatest of your wonders which we have not yet seen. Let the night be more enlivened". So Lokus stood before them and lo, before their eyes he changed stones into gold, and a dog into an ass. He drew wine and milk from an empty pitcher and caused a rod to become a snake. Standing before a table that was bare he drew all manner of foods and wines out of the air and furnished it for a splendid repast. Then he called Hoskiah as his slave and stood a comely maiden before him. And Hoskiah shot arrows into her and they stood out from her body, so that there was not space for a man to place his hand.

And the blood flowed down her robe as though she stood in a rainstorm of blood, before she sank to the ground and lay there dead before them. Then Lokus went up to her and after wrenching the arrows from out of her body threw a cloak over it. The arrows he carried to Isias and those about him, saying, "See the blood of amaiden", and they held the arrows and looked at them. And behold, as they held the arrows and looked the blood went from them and the arrows were clean. And Lokus cried out in a loud voice, "Lo, the blood returns". Then, passing over unto the maiden, he lifted the cloak off her and behold, as he did so her robe became clean again. And Lokus took her by the hand and said unto her, "Arise", and she arose and stood before Isias.

And he was silent and those about him did not speak. Casting aside her garment, which was the outer robe, the maiden danced before the gathering, and all there wondered greatly, for her body was unmarked. Isias spoke to Lokus, saying, "How can such things be? What manner of magic is this?" Lokus answered him, saying, "Lord your eyes saw as I bid them see, for I am the master of men's hearts, not the master of flesh and wood. The eye is the greatest of deceivers. It is the magic of Egypt which undid the work of the Ethiopian's bow". And Isias said, "Who is this Ethiopian who stands there so strangely garbed? It is indeed a bowman among bowmen to loose his arrows so that one has scarcely struck ere another left the bow. Has Rasfamishel come among us? " Lokus answered him, saying, "Lord he comes from beyond the Land of Elephants, in the place where the Earth tips over. The magic is in his bow, which can shoot at a wild ass and bring down a lion." So saying Lokus took up a clay pot and stood it on a table, and Hoskiah, standing off, loosed an arrow at it. And the pot was shattered and as it fell apart lo and behold, a silver pot appeared in its place. And those who saw these things were amazed and spoke one to the other about the magic of Lokus.

One among the gathering, a speechmaker, stood up and spoke words praising the magic of Lokus, but Isias sat quiet, deep in thought. Then bidding Lokus come to his side, Isias said, "This night I have seen With my own eyes a maiden slain with arrows and raised from the sleep of death. I have seen the magic of the bow change clay to silver.

Is then your magic great enough to change age into youth and weakness into strength? It is said that the greatest of magicians can do even this." And Lokus lifted himself and said, "Even this I can do". Then there was much whispering back and forth and talk among those who sat about Isias. They that stood in the place of his favour said, "Master this is the hour, let the magic of this great magician cast the years from off your back and renew the vigour of youth". And while they spoke there was much whispering and sly laughter among the half men. Lokus stepped back from the presence of Isias and he raised his left hand, and there were loud thunders. He raised his right hand and fire leaped forth from the ground, and a great cloud of smoke went up. And he said unto Isias, "Great Isias, this is your hour. You are the lord of this land and place, therefore command as you will.

Already the night is more than half spent and speeds to its closing. Hear now my words, this I say unto you: Enter now into my magic tent which stands strangely adorned over against the edge of the feasting place. The tent wherefrom I issue forth my magic, to which I return to replenish my strength when it is done. Therein is the fount of my magic, the hub of the great circle of power. Remain in there until the first red glow from the fires of the underworld appears in the night sky. Then lord, I will come into the tent and, standing against it, will call forth the lord of this land and place, and behold, a new lord will stand before the gathering in manly strength and vigour.

A man among men and a fitting master for this household. He will be such a man that I, even I Lokus, the master of magic, will be the first to proclaim him." So Isias entered into the tent of Lokus the magician, and as he passed within, Lokus gave him the great bow of Hoskiah, saying, 'Take this with you, for its magic is great and may well be needed. It is a worthy weapon for the lord of this land." Then the gathering spoke amongst themselves and waited. Singing women whiled away the hours. And as the first arrows of morning light struck the night sky, Lokus arose and stood against the tent of magic. Lifting up the door he cried out in a loud voice, "Great Lord of these lands and place, come forth to your heritage, behold your lord." And as he spoke, lo,

Hoskiah stepped forth into the morning light, arrayed as a lord and girded about with belt and sword.

He wore a helmet and in his hand was the great bow. The sound of a great sigh passed through the gathering and men looked one at the other. They were bemused, not knowing what to do, for there was magic about them. And Lokus lifted up his voice in the silence and cried, "Behold, I have brought forth a man among men as lord of these lands and place. Will you not, therefore, receive him in a befitting manner?"

And men spoke among themselves, saying, "This is one having the appearance of Hoskiah whom we know, in truth the lord of these lands and place. He is a man indeed, if it be he; has magic drawn him back from the grave, or has the spirit of Isias clothed itself in the form of Hoskiah?" Then first one and then another hailed the man before them saying, "This is a man among men, if not our lord Hoskiah." Then a great shout of, "Hoskiah!" went up, and Hoskiah stood stern before them.

Now, there were those among the gathering who stood silent. The half men and wanton women who were about the table where Isias had been, sat pale and silent, clinging to each other. They said among themselves, "If indeed this be Hoskiah, where then is our lord Isias ?" And a man stood up among the gathering, shouting, "This is not Isias transformed by magic, but Hoskiah, who, with this evil magician, has worked a trick. Isias is not transformed but murdered. Let him be avenged". And reaching back he took a javelin and sought to hurl it at Hoskiah. But the bow in the hand of Hoskiah bent, and before the javelin could be sped an arrow pierced the man's throat. Then the bow sang twice more before the enemies of Hoskiah departed.

Now, it came to pass that those remaining gathered about Hoskiah and rejoiced, saying, "Hoskiah is indeed the rightful lord and none but he ever bent bow as we have seen a bow bent this dawning". And Hoskiah passed through them to the seat of Isias. And those gathered there shrank from him, and he swept the table clean and drove away those who stood about it, saying, "Begone, lest I have you seized and beaten, for you befoul the Earth and serve

neither God nor man." They departed, saying, 'This is indeed Hoskiah and not Isias."
And Isias was seen no more by the eyes of men. Now, after three days had passed Lokus said to Hoskiah, "The time has come when I must depart. I shall go unto my king who is now your king and speak with him concerning you. It is well that I go now and dally not unduly here, for mayhap as things are he will lend a willing ear to my words. But if I dally here with you, others will gain his ear with another account." So Lokus departed and Hoskiah was grieved. Before he left, Lokus was given horses and servants, also slaves and asses with food for the journey. And Lokus said to Hoskiah, "We shall meet again, for it is decreed in the Book of Heaven."

Athelia came before Hoskiah many times and said, "Lord let me depart from your residence and dwell in a place not too far off." And Hoskiah was perplexed within himself because of her manner of speech, for he did not understand what she wanted. He said, "Have no fear for the women of my household, for there is none I desire but you". And it came to pass that on his way to the king, Lokus was stricken with a sickness and lay as one already dead, and for many days his soul was prepared for departure. And while he lay sick the power that bound the eyes of Hoskiah became weakened and the eyes of Hoskiah were no longer bound. Now, Hoskiah purged his household and spent the days dealing with his estates, and his lands flourished. His servants no longer bickered among themselves as before and contentment reigned within his shadow.

So when many days had passed and all things were ordered, Hoskiah called his steward and said unto him, "Let a feast be prepared. As the land has given generously to me, so will I give no less generously." Hoskiah said this and it was done. Now, there was a woman called Mirim of the household of Isias, who was fair to behold and she sought the favour of Hoskiah. And among the women there was much talk of Athelia who remained ever veiled, for there were those among the women who knew her. But none spoke to Hoskiah, for he was a man who talked little with women and Athelia stood first in his eyes. Mirim had not seen the degradation of Athelia, nor had she seen her unveiled.

But it came to pass that she spied upon Athelia one day, while she was about her toilet, and seeing her unveiled Mirim took counsel with herself.

Now, the day of feasting came and many were the guests, but of half men and wanton women there were none. And among the women Athelia sat apart, and among the men there was much talk of riches and battles, and of spoils of war and husbandry. Among the guests was a young lord who sought the favours of Mirim. And while the feasting and dancing were at their height, they came one to the other. And as they dallied beyond the torchlight Mirim said unto him, "Am I fair indeed?" And he answered her, saying, "You are fair even among the fairest". Then she said unto him, "Yet there is one more fair by far, so fair that she needs go veiled before men. She is Athelia, wife of Hoskiah, who keeps her thus. He fears for himself and does not trust her, for this is his weakness".

And Mirim moved away from the young lord, saying, "Go look upon her face, and if you can then say I am the fairest of the fair, I shall know that your heart speaks sincerely of itself and not at the behest of your body." The young lord returned to the feasting and sat in a place nearby to Hoskiah and spoke to those about him, saying, "Have any among you seen a woman here who rivals the fairest bearers of myrtle and palm?" And the men rebuked him, saying, "It is not meet to talk thus about the women of a household wherein you are a guest. Are they to be judged as are women of the night?" But the tongue of the young lord was not stayed and he replied, saying, 'That which causes talk will be talked about?"

And Hoskiah heard him and was angry and said, "What, in my household, moves foolish tongues to gossip?" The young lord said, "That which a man tries to conceal ever arouses the interests of others. Does any man conceal that of which he is proud?" And Hoskiah looked about him, saying, "This talk I do not understand". The young lord said, "My lord, men talk of what lies beneath the veil of the woman you brought here, is she indeed as fair as men say, or is there truth even in the gossip of women?" And those who knew about the degradation of Athelia muttered among themselves, for her secret could not be kept hidden. They said, "This is loose talk and wicked, let the evil which belongs to the past remain buried. Does this concern any man but

Hoskiah? Are we among women that the talk should be thus? Is our custom to be lightly set aside? Let the veil remain".

But Hoskiah, hearing the muttering, thought wrongly of what was said. And he spoke to the young lord, saying, "This woman is fair as few women are fair, should I not know? This you shall indeed see for yourself". And Hoskiah said within himself, "Long enough have I indulged Athelia her whims, does a pearl give pleasure withinits shell?" And Hoskiah sent his attendant for her. So Athelia came with her hand maiden, and Mirim came too and stood close behind them. And Athelia stood before Hoskiah and said, "My lord what is your wish?" And he said to her, "Woman, rcmove your veil." And Athelia put her hand to the veil and pleaded with him, saying, "My lord there are many men here and strangers. There is a custom of my people by which I abide." And men, hearing her voice, looked one at another and the oldest among them said to Hoskiah, "Let the woman be, for this is of no importance and of no interest to us. Allow her the whim, for such is the nature of women. Shall we deny them their small pleasures?" Athelia inclined her head towards the man who spoke and as she did so Mirim stepped forward and caught hold of the veil, snatching it aside. And the stricken face of Athelia was revealed to the gathering.

All men were silent and still, like statues. And Hoskiah looked at Athelia and she at him. And Hoskiah saw her as she was, and Athelia knew what he saw. Then came the voice of the young lord, saying, "Behold the pearl of Hoskiah." And Hoskiah turned upon him in rage and slew him.

And Hoskiah turned to Athelia who stood still and alone, saying, "What evil has been wrought here? Begone, take your face from me." And Athelia went out between the gathering. And passing into her bedchamber she took a draught of poison. And her handmaiden sped to Hoskiah, saying, "Come my lord, my mistress dies." Then Hoskiah, his heart filled with remorse, sped to Athelia. And as he came unto her she died. And Hoskiah wept over her and his heart was filled with grief. And he looked upon the body of Athelia and said, "I have slain the life within my own heart. I have slain the one who cherished me in my blindness, the one who loved beyond the bounds of love." In his anguish the eye of his soul was opened and saw the soul of Athelia standing nearby. And Hoskiah was dazzled by the vision of her beauty, for she was radiant as the sun.

He stretched out his hands towards her, but could not touch her, for she was beyond the reach of earthly things. And she shook her head at him and raising her hand departed to the Antechamber of Eternity. Hoskiah raised himself up and strode out from the chamber, but he returned not again to the place of feasting. He sorrowed many days. Now, while Hoskiah still sorrowed, word came to him that a company of men was coming against him. And he sent out his servants with laden asses and went forth himself. And with his true men he prepared a place on the heights above the road, to meet those who came to take him. And Hoskiah met them with arrows and with stones and left them with their dead. And Hoskiah and those with him passed out into the wilderness and lived there many days.

And it came to pass that word came to him of Lokus and he arose and went into the land of the Sons of Fire, passing into Tyre as a merchant from Kithim. So it came about that Hoskiah came with sons of the Children of Light on ships of Arad, by way of Hawnibo and Mesilonas, where there are many temples. The ships made one harvest towards the Land of Trees, where the great river flows to the West. And his sons he left in Tyre, that they might receive instruction in the household of Lokus. Hoskiah governed many years in the Land of Mists and made laws, and died in his old age. And he was buried by the river where the ground rises, beneath stones and soil carried in many baskets. A fence was made and trees, which still grow, set about the place. When Hoskiah came here he had been forty and four years on Earth, and two score and five years passed before he died. May his God fulfil his hopes! Raben, the son of Hoskiah, was born of a daughter from the house of Lokus in this land.

CHAPTER EIGHT. THE ROLLS OF RECORD - 2

Lothan, Captain of Men of Valour, Victorious over the Sons of the New Moon and Guardian of the Hidden Wisdom. Maker of Roads in the Red Lands and Builder of the Secret Fort. By Abisobel, once Scribe of the God Eloah in Ladosa, Keeper of Records in the New Temple, to his Fathers in Wisdom at the Temple of Iswarah, Greetings. May you live long on Earth in prosperity, peace and health, and depart in knowledge. We left the good land, hearts heavy-laden with grief. The ships were five and I looked to mine and found it good. It was built of alonwood and stout-masted. All about it, casks were lashed. Along the planking the cords that moved were free, but all clear spaces were filled with things wrapped about and bound. There was much leather for the sails and leathern scoops. There were half a score of large buckets of wood hooped about and handled with plaited leather.

Between the eyes of the ship the guide pole was raised, beneath which were stored all kinds of unusual things made of wood and cordage used by men of the sea. There was a machine for slinging stones and another for hurling fire. There were high shieldguards which could be strapped to the side. A store contained every kind of weapon and much armour. There were pots for cooking and braziers. There was a store behind the mast and in it were over five score jars of oil and not less of wine and vinegar. Casks of food there were and more stored in baskets. Many large pitchers were lashed about and dried meat stored in cloth. Dried dates and figs and small fruits there were in large quantities. Water was not lacking, nor the dishes for eating. There were nets for fishing and hooks for catching birds. The chief among the men of the sea was skilled in the notched stick called 'thumb of the night', which guided him across the widths of the sea. We brought up against Keftor, where Nebam departed, for they were troublesome.

Men of Melkat came who had been wrecked, and we took a score who were men of valour. We passed many lands by the sea, where once broad sea-girt Posidma reigned, before blown apart by underworld fires. By the lands of

Hogburim we went over the wide sea to the gate of Athlesan and beyond it across the sea of Tapuim.

One ship and forty men and the households of six men were lost on the way. Three ships have I left, with one brought up on the land. Twelve men have I lost in battle and ten have gone with sickness. There are, with me, two hundred fighting men. One hundred and ten men of skill and one hundred bondsmen. Sixty households with their cattle and sheep and corn and tools and wagons. All things with us are numbered and the tally grows daily. The encampment is well made and encircled with a wall where water does not lie. Trees and soil are the material of its construction. Great trees are about us, but no stone for building, for the soil is deep. The waters rise not over the fields where men have cut water passages, but there is much rain. Wild men are in the land, who write on their skins.

They are hairy ones whose gods are the plants of the field. Their quarters are like baskets over the ground and they are unwashed. The women are like hellcats, uttering wild cries among the trees, but the men are quiet and come in silence. They have temples of poles, roofed over in part and encircled by great logs, with logs laid over. Skins and painted leather are hung about, but no cloth. They place plants on altars, that their high gods may consume the essence of life within them and draw it back into themselves.

Virgins they keep in cages, why I know not, but the women in cages are virgins and well cared for. Is virginity uncaged like a hound unleashed? The wild men are unlearned and without soft speech. They are cousins to the wild dog, yet with children they are gentle. The children of Fikol, the stoneworker, were lost among the trees and wild beasts beset them at night. The wild men found them there and carried them away and fed them. Then came the searchband of men of valour upon the place, and the children, seeing them, ran away from the wild men. The men of valour slew the wild men, thinking they had taken the children, for they knew not their speech. Since then we have seen their ways. One hundred and ten of the wild people we have as bondsmen and bondswomen. The men work with the soil and wood about the encampment. The wall I caused to be built out into the water and it encloses a pier against the bank, where ships can moor. Within the wall and circle of water I have built the temple, but not all go in there with me.

We are not one people. The gates of the temple are on pillars of wood and turn on a stone, and wooden are the pillars within. Great beams support the roof, and the walls are of wood and mud brick. The floor is of sand finely raked, and before the heir the altar rests on stones. There are no images designed to confuse men, for though the temple is poor it does not enshrine ignorance. We have no evil men with us. There are men of valour and men of skill, men of the land and men of the sea, no more. Beneath the altar is the Grave of Life, kept dry with mortar. In its place is the Great Chest of Mysteries and in the Urns of Life are the records. Well kept they are and safe from the unlearned, all the records of the Eastern Quarter. Thus all things have been done according to your divining, and it is good.

(Between that just copied and that which follows there was a full plate, but the writing upon it was ineffective.) In the land at the edge of the Earth there is little sun and the people grow sick with water. The dampness causes a sickness among us, where the teeth become loose in the gums and skin peels. Flesh puffs up and holds the marks of fingers. The people of the land beset us and we cannot find them among the trees. Lothan was slain, with twelve men of valour, three days journey inland among the trees. He died in the night. Two men were caught by the wild men who burnt them in cages.

Men have come in ships from the Land of the Sons of Fire, who are our brothers. Alman, the scribe, and Kora, the builder, came. Hoskiah who is a man mighty in battle, having gone from us brought them here by Kedaris. Of the Sons of Fire there are four hundred, but few are fighting men. They are not men of valour. They are men of the sea and cultivators and men who trade. There are builders among them and men skilled in the ways of wood and stone, for they came to establish a city in this place. This, the Kingdom of the Trees, is no place for a city. Trees shut us in and hold us captive. They conceal those who lie in wait to do us harm. A house is built and trees take over the roof, and plants creep over the walls. Corn is planted and rots, while weeds smother other growing food. Greyness is everywhere, even the face of the sun is pale here. Men shiver without heat and the air is not pure and mixed with water. Wild dogs lurk among the trees, to tear the unwary to pieces. There are few stones and they are covered with slime.

The wild fruits and herbs are poisonous and men have died eating them. The wild men in this place eat their own children and anoint their bodies with the fat of the dead. There is a race of men with great hairy bodies and the heads of dogs, who carry children off to feast on them. Arutha, wife of Amora, died in the embrace of one. They have hides that no arrow can pierce. The Book of Heaven is open to the Sons of Fire, in it they found the road across the waters. They are filled with the wisdom of wanderers. As we came by the sea in the hands of seafarers, so shall we go out. We long for the welcome omens of the shining arrows of the night. Our people are weary and there is muttering among the men of valour, for they fear the Spirit of the Trees. His breath surrounds us. His grey fingernails corrupt our possessions. He has caused our cattle to die and our crops to wither.

Against him we are powerless. He was robbed of this land hewn out from among the trees, he will never forget. The Great Secrets and Sacred Wisdom are secured for our children. We place them and ourselves in the hands of the Sons of Fire. We shall leave this place and sail towards Hireh, towards the West, where lies the Land of White Stone. There we may build with stone and brick. Here is the tally of our departure: Of those who came with Lothan, ninety men of valour and the households of thirty-five. There are seventy men of valour who came later, and those of the Sons of Fire. Eighty-two men of skill and eight households newly formed. There are the men of valour who came with Hoskiah and the households among them. There are nine households which came later. There are two hundred and forty bondsmen. Of these one hundred and ten carry slings and clubs. Some have fighting axes of stone and stave shod with metal, but there is no sharpened weapon among them. One hundred and four among all the households are children and unmarried women, for many have died of the sickness belonging to this place. There are slaves, but most have died or perished among the trees. The cattle are gone and there are a few sheep and goats. There are, for each man of valour, two measures of corn at morning and for others one measure. Of corn there are sixty great baskets. Of herbs dried by fire, forty-five ankrim. There is fish fried by fire and some meat.

There are a hundred and ten baskets of cuped nuts, which are bitter and go sour. The Men of the Trees eat them and for such people it is proper food. There are narah nuts which grow in this place, sweet but not stomach filling, and nuts which are good for cakes in quantities. There is much weapon metal melted down and gold and silver in pieces. There are all kinds of tools for the men of skill and much pottery in the households. But much has gone to the Men of the Trees, and of cloth there is little, and men are clothed in skins and the woven fibre of plants. The Harbour of Sorrow we leave behind and with four ships sail towards the sunsetting. One ship goes to the Land of the Sons of Fire. Spirit of Lothan, remain among us as we go far away among men who are strangers to us!

THE BOOK OF MANUSCRIPTS
incorporating THE TREASURY OF LIFE Compiled from writings preserved by Amos, an Egyptian; Claudius Linus, a Roman; and Vitico, a Gaul.
CHAPTER ONE. THE SCROLL OF EMOD

The writings from olden days tell of strange things and of great happenings in the times of our fathers who lived in the beginning. All men can know of such times is declared in the Book of Ages, but the gods had their birth in events and things which were in the beginning. It is told, in the courtyards, that there was a time when Heaven and Earth were not apart. Truth echoes even there, for Heaven and Earth are yet joined in men. It is written that God once walked the earth with man and dwelt within a cave above a garden where man laboured. God encompasses all that is and cannot be contained in a cave.

Look to the Sacred Writings for Truth. It is told that woman made God angry and He took Himself into the sky, removing Heaven from man because of his disgust for woman. It is also told that man offended God by imitating Him. These are tales made by man. This is not wisdom, for the Sacred Writings reveal the Plans of God and these things cannot be as told. It is the talk of the courtyard, it is the knowledge of the outerplace. Men talk of the land of Oben, from whence they came. Not from Oben towards the South came men, for the great land of Ramakui first felt his step. Out by the encircling waters, over at the rim it lay. There were mighty men in those days, and of their land the First Book speaks thus: Their dwelling places were set in the swamplands from whence no mountains rose, in the land of many waters slow-flowing to the sea. In the shallow lakelands, among the mud, out beyond the Great Plain of Reeds. At the place of many flowers bedecking plant and tree. Where trees grew beards and had branches like ropes, which bound them together, for the ground would not support them. There were butterflies like birds and spiders as large as the outstretched arms of a man. The birds of the air and fishes of the waters had hues which dazzled the eyes, they lured men to destruction. Even insects fed on the flesh of men. There were elephants in great numbers,

with mighty curved tusks. The pillars of the Netherworld we unstable. In a great night of destruction the land fell into an abyss and was lost forever.
When the Earth became light, next day, man saw man driven to madness. All was gone. Men clothed themselves with the skins of beasts and were eaten by wild beasts, things with clashing teeth used them for food. A great horde of rats devoured everything, so that man died of hunger. The Braineaters hunted men down and slew them.

Children wandered the plainland like wild beasts, for men and women became stricken with a sickness the passed over the children. An issue covered their bodies which swelled up and burst, while flame consumed their bellies. Every man who had an issue of seed within him and every woman who had a flow of blood died. The children grew up without instruction, and having no knowledge turned to strange ways and beliefs. They became divided according to their tongues. This was the land from whence man came, the Great One came from Ramakui and wisdom came from Zaidor. The people who came with Nadhi were wise in the ways of the seasons and in the wisdom of the stars. They read the Book of Heaven with understanding. They covered their dead with potter's clay and hardened it, for it was not their custom to place their dead in boxes. Those who came with the Great One were cunning craftsmen in stone, they were carvers of wood and ivory.

The High God was worshipped with strange light in places of great silences. They paid homage to the huge sleeping beast in the depths of the sea, believing it to bear the Earth on its back; they believed its stirrings plunged lands to destruction. Some said it burrowed beneath them. In Ramakui there was a great city with roads and waterways, and the fields were bounded with walls of stone and channels. In the centre of the land was the great flat-topped Mountain of God. The city had walls of stone and was decorated with stones of red and black, white shells and feathers. There were heavy green stones in the land and stones patterned in green, black and brown. There were stones of saka, which men cut for ornaments, stones which became molten for cunning work. They built walls of black glass and bound them with glass by fire. They used strange fire from the Netherworld which was but slightly separated from them, and foul air from the breath of the damned rose in their midst. They made eye reflectors of glass stone, which cured the ills of men.

They purified men with strange metal and purged them of evil spirits in flowing fire. We dwell in a land of three peoples, but those who came from Ramakui and Zaidor were fewer in numbers. It was the men of Zaidor who built the Great Guardian whichever watches, looking towards the awakening place of God. The day He comes not its voice will be heard. In olden times, when men lived in the ground, there came the Great One whose name is hidden. Son of Hem, Son of the Sun, Chief of the Guardians of Mysteries, Master of Rites and Spoken Word. Judge of Disputes, Advocate of the Dead, Interpreter of the Gods and Father of Fishermen. From the West, from beyond Mandi, came the Great One arrayed in robes of black linen and wearing a head-dress of red. Who taught men the secret of writing and numbers, and measurement of the years? Who taught the ways of the days and months, who read the meaning of clouds and writing of the nightlights? Who taught the preservation of the body? That the soul might commune with the living, and that it might be a doorway to the Earth? Who taught that light is Life?

Who taught the words of God, which spoke to men and hid things from them, which stood in the place of Truth for those with understanding? Which spoke to the priests, the scribes and the people differently according to their enlightenment. Who taught that beyond the visible is the invisible, beyond the small the smaller and beyond the great the greater, and all things are linked together in one? Who taught the song of the stars, which now no man knows, and the words of the waters, which are lost? Who taught men to grow corn and to spin, to make bricks and fashion stone after a cunning manner? Who taught men the rituals of sea shells, and the reading of their mysteries and the manner of their speech? Who taught men the nature and knowledge of God, but in the years left to him could not bring them to understanding? Who, then, veiled the great secrets in simple tales which they could remember and in signs which would not be lost to their children's children? Who brought the Sacred Eye from the distant land and the Stone of Light made of water, by which men see God, and the firestone which gathers the light of the sun before the Great Shrine? He died in the manner of men, though his likeness is that of god. Then they cut him apart, that his body might make fertile the fields, and took away his head, that it might bring them wisdom.

His bones they did no paint red, for they were not as those of others. These are the words of the Scared Writings, recorded after the old custom. As they are, so let them be; for that which is recorded remains with you. The stone of Light and the firestone were stolen in the days of disaster and none now knows their resting place, therefore the land is empty.

CHAPTER TWO. THE SCROLL OF KAMUSHAHRE

In this fertile black land there are those who worship the sun and they call it the greatest and the most bountiful among all gods, the Seer of Heaven, the of the squalid manner in which men dwelt before the Golden One led his people hence. He came to this fertile land. Now it is a pleasant place with many great cities and contented villages; there is the great broad river of fresh water which rises and falls in its due seasons. Channels there are and waterways which lead the fertilising waters unto the growing things, the herbage and the trees. There are flocks of sheep and herds of cattle on the green pastures. It was not ever thus. In the days before Harekta came all was barren and desolate. Nought divided the wilderness from the swamplands filled with reeds. Then there were no cattle or sheep and the land knew not the hand of man, it lay untilled and unwatered.

No land was sown, for they who dwelt in it knew not the making of waterways, nor did they know how to command the water and make it flow at their behest. There were no cities and men dwelt in holes in the ground or in places where the rock was cleft. They walked in their nakedness or clothed themselves with leaves or bark, while at night they covered themselves with the skin of wild beasts. They fought with the jackal for food and snatched dead things from the lion. They pulled roots from out of the ground and sought for sustenance among things that grew in the mud. They had none to rule over them, nor had they leaders to guide. They knew not obligation or duty. None spoke to them about their manner of life and none knew the way of Truth. They were truly unenlightened in those days.

Then came the servant of the Sun and he it was who brought the people together and put rulers over them. He set Ramur up as king over the whole land. He showed them, man and woman, how to dwell together in contentment as husband and wife, and he divided their tasks between them. He instructed men in the sowing of corn and the growing of herbs. He instructed them in the tilling of the ground and the manner of cutting the waterways and channels. He it was who showed men the ways of the beasts of the field. He instructed men in the working of gold and silver and the making of vessels from clay.

He instructed men in the hewing and cutting of stone and the building of temples and cities. The making of linen and the dying of cloth that forms garments ever pleasing to the eyes, he did not teach. Neither did he instruct them in the making of bricks or the working of copper. Then, when he departed he bade the people not to weep, for though he went to his father, the sun would adopt them as his children and all could become sons of the sun. Thus many became sons and servants of the sun and they believed what they had heard, that the sun was their father and the light of goodness overlooking the whole land.

It is this light that sustains all living things, but within it is the greater light which sustains the spirit. It is the light that enlightens the hearts of men. There are lesser lights that guide men about their daily tasks and shield them from harm, there are unseen lights that influence men for good or ill, but it is the Great Light that banishes coldness and makes all men warm. The warmth it bestows ripens the harvests of man and makes his herds yield their increase. It oversees the whole activity of men on Earth as it journeys the skies from one end to the other, thus it knows the needs of all men. Therefore, be like the sun, be far-seeing and foresighted, be regular in your comings and goings while about your daily tasks.

When their guide and leader left, the people knew themselves as children of the sun. They were warlike and subdued other people in its name, and brought them under its rule. Then great temples were raised up to it and for a time it displaced the greater gods which the people of this land had set up in their ignorance. The One True God it never displaced, for the True God was ever hidden from the eyes of the profane and ignorant. Then some priests among those who followed the rule of the sun stole its spirit and brought it down, so that it enlivened the statues and images of their gods. Thus the spirit which enlivens all the lesser gods is but the one spirit held in captivity, and not many as the people think.

Then came the Wise Ones from the East and they caused the people to have other thoughts. They were men who knew the ways of Heaven and asked of the people, "Is the sun spirit indeed supreme, is this not a thing requiring much thought?

Consider its movements, are they not more like those of one who is directed in his comings and goings? Does it move about freely as it wills, or is it restricted and held to its appointed path, like a yoked ox, or as the ass treading out corn? Does it rise up from the Netherworld as it wills or go down into the cavern of darkness by its own decree? Is its path not more like that of a stone hurled forth by the hand of man? Is it not like a boat controlled by the will of a man, rather than a free-ranging god? Is it not more like a slave under the direction of a master?"

These things disturbed the hearts of people, some pondered upon them, but others, in the manner of men, cried death to those who deny the truth of these things. However, because of the things said the worship of the older gods grew in strength, for the people had never turned from Usira who was with them before the first water channel was cut. He was not the god of the high born but of the lowly people. Thisis a land of two peoples, of two nations, two priesthoods, two streams of wisdom and two hierarchies of gods. It is a land where the light of Truth burns brightly, thought hidden away from the eyes of all but a few. It is the Land of Dawning on Earth.

CHAPTER THREE. THE DESTROYER - PART 1 FROM THE GREAT SCROLL

Men forget the days of the Destroyer. Only the wise know where it went and that it will return in its appointed hour. It raged across the Heavens in the days of wrath, and this was its likeness: It was as a billowing cloud of smoke enwrapped in a ruddy glow, not distinguishable in joint or limb. Its mouth was an abyss from which came flame, smoke and hot cinders. When ages pass, certain laws operate upon the stars in the Heavens. Their ways change, there is movement and restlessness, they are no longer constant and a great light appears redly in the skies. When blood drops upon the Earth, the Destroyer will appear and mountains will open up and belch forth fire and ashes.

Trees will be destroyed and all living things engulfed. Waters will be swallowed up by the land and seas will boil. The Heavens will burn brightly and redly, there will be a copper hue over the face of the land, followed by a day of darkness. A new moon will appear and break up and fall. The people will scatter in madness. They will hear the trumpet and battle cry of the Destroyer and will seek refuge in the den in the Earth. Terror will eat away their hearts and their courage will flow from them like water from a broken pitcher. They will be eaten up in the flames of wrath and consumed by the breath of the Destroyer. Thus in the Days of Heavenly Wrath, which have gone, and thus it will be in the Days of Doom when it comes again.

The times of its coming and going are known unto the wise. These are the signs and times which shall precede the Destroyer's return: A hundred and ten generations shall pass into the West and nations will rise and fall. Men will fly in the air as birds and swim in the seas as fishes. Men will talk peace one with another, hypocrisy and deceit shall have their day. Women will be as men and men as women, passion will be a plaything of man. A nation of soothsayers shall rise and fall and their tongue shall be the speech learned. A nation of law givers shall rule the Earth and pass away into nothingness. One worship will pass into the four quarters of the Earth, talking peace and bringing war. A nation of the seas will be greater than any other, but will be as an apple rotten at the core and will not endure.

A nation of traders will destroy men with wonders and it shall have its day. Then shall the high strive with the low, the North with the South, the East with the West, and the light with the darkness. Men shall be divided by their races and the children will be born as strangers among them. Brother shall strive with brother and husband with wife. Fathers will no longer instruct their sons and their sons will be wayward.

Women will become the common property of men and will no longer be held in regard and respect. Then men will be ill at ease in their hearts, they will seek they know not what, and uncertainty and doubt will trouble them. They will possess great riches but be poor in spirit. Then will the Heavens tremble and the Earth move, men will quake in fear and while terror walks with them the Heralds of Doom will appear. They will come softly, as thieves to the tombs, men will no know them for what they are, men will be deceived, the hour of the Destroyer is at hand. In those days men will have the Great Book before them, wisdom will be revealed, the few will be gathered for the stand, it is the hour of trial. The dauntless ones will survive, the stout-hearted will not go down to destruction. Great God of All Ages, alike to all, who sets the trials of man, be merciful to our children in the Days of Doom. Man must suffer to be great, but hasten not his progress unduly. In the great winnowing, be not too harsh on the lesser ones among men. Even the son of a thief has become Your scribe.

CHAPTER FOUR. THE DESTROYER - PART 2 FROM THE GREAT SCROLL

O Sentinels of the Universe who watch for the Destroyer, how long will your coming vigil last? O mortal men who wait without understanding, where will you hide yourselves in the Dread Days of Doom, when the Heavens shall be torn apart and the skies rent in twain, in the days when children will turn grey-headed? This is the thing which will be seen, this is the terror your eyes will behold, this is the form of destruction that will rush upon you: There will be the great body of fire, the glowing head with many mouths and eyes ever changing.

Terrible teeth will be seen in formless mouths and a fearful dark belly will glow redly from fires inside. Even the most stout-hearted man will tremble and his bowels be loosened, for this is not a thing understandable to men. It will be a vast sky-spanning form enwrapping Earth, burning with many hues within wide open mouths. These will descend to sweep across the face of the land, engulfing all in the yawning jaws. The greatest warriors will charge against it in vain. The fangs will fall out, and lo, they are terror-inspiring things of cold hardened water. Great boulders will be hurled down upon men, crushing them into red powder.

As the great salt waters rise up in its train and roaring torrents pour towards the land, even the heroes among mortal men will be overcome with madness. As moths fly swiftly to their doom in the burning flame, so will these men rush to their own destruction. The flames going before will devour all the works of men, the waters following will sweep away whatever remains. The dew of death will fall softly, as grey carpet over the cleared land. Men will cry out in their madness, "O whatever Being there is, save us from this tall form of terror, save us from the grey dew of death."

CHAPTER FIVE. THE DESTROYER - PART 3 FROM THE SCROLL OF ADEPHA

The Doomshape, called the Destroyer, in Egypt, was seen in all the lands whereabouts. In colour it was bright and fiery, in appearance changing and unstable. It twisted about itself like a coil, like water bubbling into a pool from an underground supply, and all men agree it was a most fearsome sight. It was not a great comet or a loosened star, being more like a fiery body of flame. Its movements on high were slow, below it swirled in the manner of smoke and it remained close to the sun whose face it hid. There was a bloody redness about it, which changed as it passed along its course. It caused death and destruction in its rising and setting.

It swept the Earth with grey cinder rain and caused many plagues, hunger and other evils. It bit the skin of men and beast until they became mottled with sores. The Earth was troubled and shook, the hills and mountains moved and rocked. The dark smoke-filled Heavens bowed over Earth and a great howl came to the ears of men, borne to them upon the wings of the wind. It was the cry of the Dark Lord, the Master of Dread. Thick clouds of fiery smoke passed before him and there was an awful hail of hot stones and coals of fire. The Doomshape thundered sharply in the Heavens and shot out bright lightings. The channels of water were turned back unto themselves when the land tilted, and great trees were tossed about and snapped like twigs. Then a voice like ten thousand trumpets was heard over the wilderness, and before its burning breath the flames parted.

The whole of the land moved and mountains melted. The sky itself roared like ten thousand lions in agony, and bright arrows of blood sped back and forth across its face. Earth swelled up like bread upon the hearth. This was the aspect of the Doomshape called the Destroyer, when it appeared in days long gone by, in olden times. It is thus described in the old records, few of which remain. It is said that when it appears in the Heavens above, Earth splits open from the heat, like a nut roasted before the fire. Then flames shoot up through the surface and leap about like fiery fiends upon black blood.

The moisture inside the land is all dried up, the pastures and cultivated places are consumed in flames and they and all trees become white ashes. The Doomshape is like a circling ball of flame which scatters small fiery offspring in its train. It covers about a fifth part of the sky and sends writhing snakelike fingers down to Earth. Before it the sky appears frightened, and it breaks up and scatters away. Midday is no brighter than night. It spawns a host of terrible things. These are things said of the Destroyer in the old records, read them with a solemn heart, knowing that the Doomshape has its appointed time and will return. It would be foolish to let them go unheeded. Now men say, "Such things are not destined for our days". May the Great God above grant that this be so. But come, the day surely will, and in accordance with his nature man will be unprepared.

CHAPTER SIX. THE DARK DAYS

The dark days began with the last visitation of the Destroyer and they were foretold by strange omens in the skies. All men were silent and went about with pale faces. The leaders of the slaves which had built a city to the glory of Thom stirred up unrest, and no man raised his arm against them. They foretold great events of which the people were ignorant and of which the temple seers were not informed. These were days of ominous calm, when the people waited for they knew not what. The presence of an unseen doom was felt, the hearts of men were stricken. Laughter was heard no more and grief and wailing sounded throughout the land. Even the voices of children were stilled and they did not play together, but stood silent. The slaves became bold and insolent and women were the possession of any man. Fear walked the land and women became barren with terror, they could not conceive, and those with child aborted.

All men closed up within themselves. The days of stillness were followed by a time when the noise of trumpeting and shrilling was heard in the Heavens, and the people became as frightened beasts without a herdsman, as asses when lions prowl without their fold. The people spoke of the god of the slaves, and reckless men said. "If we knew where this god were to be found, we would sacrifice to him". But the god of the slaves was not among them. He was not to be found within the swamplands or in the brickpits. His manifestation was in the Heavens for all men to see, but they did not see with understanding. Nor would any god listen, for all were dumb because of the hypocrisy of men.

The dead were no longer sacred and were thrown into the waters. Those already entombed were neglected and many became exposed. They lay unprotected against the hands of thieves. He who once toiled long in the sun, bearing the yoke himself, now possessed oxen. He who grew no grain now owned a storehouse full. He who once dwelt at ease among his children now thirsted for water. He who once sat in the sun with crumbs and dregs was now bloated with food, he reclined in the shade, his bowls overflowing.

Cattle were left unattended to roam into strange pastures, and men ignored their marks and slew the beasts of their neighbours. No man owned anything. The public records were cast forth and destroyed, and no man knew who were slaves and who were masters. The people cried out to the Pharaoh in their distress, but he stopped his ears and acted like a deaf man. There were those who spoke falsely before Pharaoh and had gods hostile towards the land, therefore the people cried out for their blood to appease it. But it was not these strange priests who put strife in the land instead of peace, for one was even of the household of Pharaoh and walked among the people unhampered. Dust and smoke clouds darkened the sky and coloured the waters upon which they fell with a bloody hue. Plague was throughout the land, the river was bloody and blood was everywhere. The water was vile and men's stomachs shrank from drinking. Those who did drink from the river vomited it up, for it was polluted. The dust tore wounds in the skin of man and beast. In the glow of the Destroyer the Earth was filled with redness. Vermin bred and filled the air and face of the Earth with loathsomeness.

Wild beasts, afflicted with torments under the lashing sand and ashes, came out of their lairs in the wastelands and caveplaces and stalked the abodes of men. All the tame beasts whimpered and the land was filled with the cries of sheep and moans of cattle. Trees, throughout the land, were destroyed and no herb or fruit was to be found. The face of the land was battered and devastated by a hail of stones which smashed down all that stood in the path of the torrent. They swept down in hot showers, and strange flowing fire ran along the ground in their wake. The fish of the river died in the polluted waters; worms, insects and reptiles sprang up from the Earth in huge numbers. Great gusts of wind brought swarms of locusts which covered the sky. As the Destroyer flung itself through the Heavens, it blew great gusts of cinders across the face of the land. The gloom of a long night spread a dark mantle of blackness which extinguished every ray of light.

None knew when it was day and when it was night, for the sun cast no shadow. The darkness was not the clean blackness of night, but a thick darkness in which the breath of men was stopped in their throats. Men gasped in a hot cloud of vapour which enveloped all the land and snuffed out all lamps and fires.

Men were benumbed and lay moaning in their beds. None spoke to another or took food, for they were overwhelmed with despair. Ships were sucked away from their moorings and destroyed in great whirlpools. It was a time of undoing. The Earth turned over, as clay spun upon a potter's wheel. The whole land was filled with uproar from the thunder of the Destroyer overhead and the cry of the people. There as the sound of moaning and lamentation on every side. The Earth spewed up its dead, corpses were cast up out of their resting places and the embalmed were revealed to the sight of all men. Pregnant women miscarried and the seed of men was stopped. The craftsman left his task undone, the potter abandoned his wheel and the carpenter his tools, and they departed to dwell in the marshes.

All crafts were neglected and the slaves lured the craftsmen away. The dues of Pharaoh could not be collected, for there was neither wheat nor barley, goose nor fish. The rights of Pharaoh could not be enforced, for the fields of grain and the pastures were destroyed. The highborn and the lowly prayed together that life might come to an end and the turmoil and thundering cease to beat upon their ears. Terror was the companion of men by day and horror their companion by night. Men lost their senses and became mad, they were distracted by frightfulness.

On the great night of the Destroyer's wrath, when its terror was at its height, there was a hail of rocks and the Earth heaved as pain rent her bowels. Gates, columns and walls were consumed by fire and the statues of gods were overthrown and broken. People fled outside their dwellings in fear and were slain by the hail. Those who took shelter from the hail were swallowed when the Earth split open. The habitations of men collapsed upon those inside and there was panic on every hand, but the slaves who lived in huts in the reedlands, at the place of pits, were spared. The land burnt like tinder, a man watched upon his rooftops and the Heavens hurled wrath upon him and he died. The land writhed under the wrath of the Destroyer and groaned with the agony of Egypt. It shook itself and the temples and palaces of the nobles were thrown down from their foundations.

The highborn ones perished in the midst of the ruins and all the strength of the land was stricken. Even the great one, the first born of Pharaoh, died with the highborn in the midst of the terror and falling stones. The children of princes were cast out into the streets and those who were not cast out died within their abodes. There were nine days of darkness and upheaval, while a tempest raged such as never had been known before. When it passed away brother buried brother throughout the land. Men rose up against those in authority and fled from the cities to dwell in tents in the outlands. Egypt lacked great men to deal with the times. The people were weak from fear and bestowed gold, silver, lapis lazuli, turquoise and copper upon the slaves, and to their priests they gave chalices, urns and ornaments. Pharaoh alone remained calm and strong in the midst of confusion. The people turned to wickedness in their weakness and despair. Harlots walked through the streets unashamed. Women paraded their limbs and flaunted their womanly charms.

Highborn women were in rags and the virtuous were mocked. The slaves spared by the Destroyer left the accursed land forthwith. Their multitude moved in the gloom of a half dawn, under a mantle of fine swirling grey ash, leaving the burnt fields and shattered cities behind them. Many Egyptians attached themselves to the host, for one who was great led them forth, a priest prince of the inner courtyard. Fire mounted up on high and its burning left with the enemies of Egypt. It rose up from the ground as a fountain and hung as a curtain in the sky. In seven days, by Remwar the accursed ones journeyed to the waters. They crossed the heaving wilderness while the hills melted around them; above, the skies were torn with lightning. They were sped by terror, but their feet became entangled in the land and the wilderness shut them in. They knew not the way, for no sign was constant before them.

They turned before Noshari and stopped at Shokoth, the place of quarries. They passed the waters of Maha and came by the valley of Pikaroth, northward of Mara. They came up against the waters which blocked their way and their hearts were in despair. The night was a night of fear and dread, for there was a high moaning above and black winds from the underworld were loosed, and fire sprang up from the ground.

The hearts of the slaves shrank within them, for they knew the wrath of Pharaoh followed them and that there was no way of escape. They hurled abuse on those who led them, strange rites were performed along the shore that night. The slaves disputed among themselves and there was violence. Pharaoh had gathered his army and followed the slaves. After he departed there were riots and disorders behind him, for the cities were plundered. The laws were cast out of the judgement halls and trampled underfoot in the streets. The storehouses and granaries were burst open and robbed. Roads were flooded and none could pass along them. People lay dead on every side. The palace was split and the princes and officials fled, so that none was left with authority to command. The lists of numbers were destroyed, public places were overthrown and households became confused and unknown.

Pharaoh pressed on in sorrow, for behind him all was desolation and death. Before him were things he could not understand and he was afraid, but he carried himself well and stood before his host with courage. He sought to bring back the slaves, for the people said their magic was greater than the magic of Egypt. The host of Pharaoh came upon the slaves by the saltwater shores, but was held back from them by a breath of fire. A great cloud was spread over the hosts and darkened the sky. None could see, except for the fiery glow and the unceasing lightnings which rent the covering cloud overhead.

A whirlwind arose in the East and swept over the encamped hosts. A gale raged all night and in the red twilit dawn there was a movement of the Earth, the waters receded from the seashore and were rolled back on themselves. There was a strange silence and men, in the gloom, it was seen that the waters had parted, leaving a passage between. The land had risen, but it was disturbed and trembled, the way was not straight or clear. The waters about were as if spun within a bowl, the swampland alone remained undisturbed. From the horn of the Destroyer came a high shrilling noise which stopped the ears of men. The slaves had been making sacrifices in despair, their lamentations were loud. Now, before the strange sight, there was hesitation and doubt; for the space of a breath they stood still and silent. Then all was confusion and shouting, some pressing forward into the waters against all who sought to flee back from the unstable ground.

Then, in exaltation, their leader led them into the midst of the waters through the confusion. Yet many sought to turn back into the host behind them, while others fled along the empty shores. All became still over the sea and upon the shore, but behind, the Earth shook and boulders split with a great noise. The wrath of Heaven was removed to a distance and stood upwards of the two hosts.

Still the host of Pharaoh held its ranks, firm in resolve before the strange and awful happenings, and undaunted by the fury which raged by their side. Stern faces were lit darkly by the fiery curtain. Then the fury departed and there was silence, stillness spread over the land while the host of Pharaoh stood without movement in the red glow. Then, with a shout, the captains went forward and the host rose up behind them. The curtain of fire had rolled up into a dark billowing cloud which spread out as a canopy. There was a stirring of the waters, but they followed the evildoers past the place of the great whirlpool. The passage was confused in the midst of the waters and the ground beneath unstable. Here, in the midst of a tumult of waters, Pharaoh fought against the hindmost of the slaves and prevailed over them, and there was a great slaughter amid the sand, the swamp and the water.

The slaves cried out in despair, but their cries were unheeded. Their possessions were scattered behind them as they fled, so that the way was easier for them than for those who followed. Then the stillness was broken by a mighty roar and through the rolling pillars of cloud the wrath of the Destroyer descended upon the hosts. The Heavens roared as with a thousand thunders, the bowels of the Earth were sundered and Earth shrieked its agony. The cliffs were torn away and cast down. The dry ground fell beneath the waters and great waves broke upon the shore, sweeping in rocks from seaward. The great surge of rocks and waters overwhelmed the chariots of the Egyptians who went before the footmen. The chariot of the Pharaoh was hurled into the air as if by a mighty hand and was crushed in the midst of the rolling waters. Tidings of the disaster came back by Rageb, son of Thomat, who hastened on ahead of the terrified survivors because of his burning. He brought reports unto the people that the host had been destroyed by blast and deluge. The captains had gone, the strong men had fallen and none remained to command.

Therefore, the people revolted because of the calamities which had befallen them. Cowards slunk from their lairs and came forth boldly to assume the high offices of the dead. Comely and noble women, their protectors gone, were their prey. Of the slaves the greater number had perished before the host of Pharaoh. The broken land lay helpless and invaders came out of the gloom like carrion.

A strange people came up against Egypt and none stood to fight, for strength and courage were gone. The invaders, led by Alkenan, came up out of the Land of Gods, because of the wrath of Heaven which had laid their land waste. There, too, had been a plague of reptiles and ants, signs and omens and an earthquake. There, also, had been turmoil and disaster, disorder and famine, with the grey breath of the Destroyer sweeping the ground and stopping the breath of men. Anturah gathered together the remnants of his fighting men and the fighting men who were left in Egypt, and set forth to meet the Children of Darkness who came out of the eastern mountains by way of the wilderness and by way of Yethnobis. They fell upon the stricken land from behind the grey cloud, before the lifting of the darkness and before the coming of the purifying winds.

Rageb went with Pharaoh and met the invaders at Herosher, but the hearts of the Egyptians were faint within them. Their spirits were no longer strong and they fell away before the battle was lost. Deserted by the gods above and below, their dwellings destroyed, their households scattered, they were as men already half dead. Their hearts were still filled with terror and with the memory of the wrath which had struck them from out of Heaven. They were still filled with the memory of the fearsome sight of the Destroyer and they knew not what they did. Pharaoh did not return to his city. He lost his heritage and was seized by a demon for many days. His women were polluted and his estates plundered. The Children of Darkness defiled the temples with rams and ravished women who were crazed and did not resist. They enslaved all who were left, the old, young men and boys. They oppressed the people and their delight was in mutilation and torture. Pharaoh abandoned his hopes and fled into the wilderness beyond the province of the lake, which is in the West towards the South. He lived a goodly life among the sand wanderers and wrote books.

Good times came again, even under the invaders, and ships sailed upstream. The air was purified, the breath of the Destroyer passed away and the land became filled again with growing things. Life was renewed throughout the whole land. Kair taught these things to the Children of Light in the days of darkness, after the building of the Rambudeth, before the death of the Pharaoh Anked. This is written in this land and in our tongue by Leweddar who, himself, chose it for saving. It was not seen until the latter days.

Papyrus of Ani Egyptian Book of the Dead

240 BC THE PAPYRUS OF ANI (THE EGYPTIAN BOOK OF THE DEAD)
Translated by E.A. Wallis Budge HYMN TO OSIRIS

"Homage to thee, Osiris, Lord of eternity, King of the Gods, whose names are manifold, whose forms are holy, thou being of hidden form in the temples, whose Ka is holy. Thou art the governor of Tattu (Busiris), and also the mighty one in Sekhem (Letopolis). Thou art the Lord to whom praises are ascribed in the name of Ati, thou art the Prince of divine food in Anu. Thou art the Lord who is commemorated in Maati, the Hidden Soul, the Lord of Qerrt (Elephantine), the Ruler supreme in White Wall (Memphis). Thou art the Soul of Ra, his own body, and hast thy place of rest in Henensu (Herakleopolis). Thou art the beneficent one, and art praised in Nart. Thou makest thy soul to be raised up.

Thou art the Lord of the Great House in Khemenu (Hermopolis). Thou art the mighty one of victories in Shas-hetep, the Lord of eternity, the Governor of Abydos. The path of his throne is in Ta-tcheser (a part of Abydos). Thy name is established in the mouths of men. Thou art the substance of Two Lands (Egypt). Thou art Tem, the feeder of Kau (Doubles), the Governor of the Companies of the gods. Thou art the beneficent Spirit among the spirits. The god of the Celestial Ocean (Nu) draweth from thee his waters. Thou sendest forth the north wind at eventide, and breath from thy nostrils to the satisfaction of thy heart. Thy heart reneweth its youth, thou producest the.... The stars in the celestial heights are obedient unto thee, and the great doors of the sky open themselves before thee. Thou art he to whom praises are ascribed in the southern heaven, and thanks are given for thee in the northern heaven. The imperishable stars are under thy supervision, and the stars which never set are thy thrones. Offerings appear before thee at the decree of Keb. The Companies of the Gods praise thee, and the gods of the Tuat (Other

World) smell the earth in paying homage to thee. The uttermost parts of the earth bow before thee, and the limits of the skies entreat thee with supplications when they see thee.
The holy ones are overcome before thee, and all Egypt offereth thanksgiving unto thee when it meeteth Thy Majesty. Thou art a shining Spirit-Body, the governor of Spirit-Bodies; permanent is thy rank, established is thy rule. Thou art the well-doing Sekhem (Power) of the Company of the Gods, gracious is thy face, and beloved by him that seeth it. Thy fear is set in all the lands by reason of thy perfect love, and they cry out to thy name making it the first of names, and all people make offerings to thee. Thou art the lord who art commemorated in heaven and upon earth. Many are the cries which are made to thee at the Uak festival, and with one heart and voice Egypt raiseth cries of joy to thee.

"Thou art the Great Chief, the first among thy brethren, the Prince of the Company of the Gods, the stablisher of Right and Truth throughout the World, the Son who was set on the great throne of his father Keb. Thou art the beloved of thy mother Nut, the mighty one of valour, who overthrew the Sebau-fiend. Thou didst stand up and smite thine enemy, and set thy fear in thine adversary. Thou dost bring the boundaries of the mountains. Thy heart is fixed, thy legs are set firm. Thou art the heir of Keb and of the sovereignty of the Two Lands (Egypt). He (Keb) hath seen his splendours, he hath decreed for him the guidance of the world by thy hand as long as times endure. Thou hast made this earth with thy hand, and the waters, and the winds, and the vegetation, and all the cattle, and all the feathered fowl, and all the fish, and all the creeping things, and all the wild animals thereof. The desert is the lawful possession of the son of Nut. The Two Lands (Egypt) are content to crown thee upon the throne of thy father, like Ra. "Thou rollest up into the horizon, thou hast set light over the darkness, thou sendest forth air from thy plumes, and thou floodest the Two Lands like the Disk at daybreak.

Thy crown penetrateth the height of heaven, thou art the companion of the stars, and the guide of every god. Thou art beneficent in decree and speech, the favoured one of the Great Company of the Gods, and the beloved of the Little Company of the Gods. His sister [Isis] hath protected him, and hath repulsed the fiends, and turned aside calamities (of evil). She uttered the spell with the magical power of her mouth. Her tongue was perfect, and it never halted at a word.

Beneficent in command and word was Isis, the woman of magical spells, the advocate of her brother. She sought him untiringly, she wandered round and round about this earth in sorrow, and she alighted not without finding him. She made light with her feathers, she created air with her wings, and she uttered the death wail for her brother. She raised up the inactive members of whose heart was still, she drew from him his essence, she made an heir, she reared the child in loneliness, and the place where he was not known, and he grew in strength and stature, and his hand was mighty in the House of Keb. The Company of the Gods rejoiced, rejoiced, at the coming of Horus, the son of Osiris, whose heart was firm, the triumphant, the son of Isis, the heir of Osiris."

A HYMN OF PRAISE TO RA WHEN HE RISETH IN THE EASTERN PART OF HEAVEN:
Behold, the Osiris Ani, the scribe of the holy offerings of all the gods, saith:

Homage to thee, O thou who hast come as Khepera, Khepera the creator of the gods, Thou art seated on thy throne, thou risest up in the sky, illumining thy mother [Nut], thou art seated on thy throne as the king of the gods. [Thy] mother Nut stretcheth out her hands, and performeth an act of homage to thee. The domain of Manu receiveth thee with satisfaction. The goddess Maat embraceth thee at the two seasons of the day. May Ra give glory, and power, and thruth-speaking, and the appearance as a living soul so that he may gaze upon Heru-khuti, to the KA of the Osiris the Scribe Ani, who speaketh truth before Osiris, and who saith: Hail, O all ye gods of the House of the Soul, who weigh heaven and earth in a balance, and who give celestial food [to the dead].

Hail, Tatun, [who art] One, thou creator of mortals [and] of the Companies of the Gods of the South and of the North, of the West and of the East, ascribe ye praise to Ra, the lord of heaven, the KING, Life, Strength, and Health, the maker of the gods. Give ye thanks unto him in his beneficent form which is enthroned in the Atett Boat; beings celestial praise thee, beings terrestial praise thee. Thoth and the goddess Maat mark out thy course for thee day by day and every day. Thine enemy the Serpent hath been given over to the fire. The Serpent- fiend Sebau hath fallen headlong, his forelegs are bound in chains, and his hind legs hath Ra carried away from him. The Sons of Revolt shall never more rise up. The House of the Aged One keepeth festival, and the voices of those who make merry are in the Great Place. The gods rejoice when they see Ra crowned upon his throne, and when his beams flood the world with light. The majesty of this holy god setteth out on his journey, and he goeth onwards until he reacheth the land of Manu; the earth becometh light at his birth each day; he proceedeth until he reacheth the place where he was yesterday.

O be thou at peace with me. Let me gaze upon thy beauties. Let me journey above the earth. Let me smite the Ass. Let me slit asunder the Serpent-fiend Sebau. Let me destroy Aepep at the moment of his greatest power. Let me behold the Abtu Fish at his season, and the Ant Fish with the Ant Boat as it piloteth it in its lake. Let me behold Horus when he is in charge of the rudder [of the Boat of Ra], with Thoth and the goddess Maat on each side of him. Let me lay hold of the tow-rope of the Sektet Boat, and the rope at the stern of the Matett Boat. Let Ra grant to me a view of the Disk (the Sun), and a sight of Ah (the Moon) unfailingly each day. Let my Ba- soul come forth to walk about hither and thither and whithersoever it pleaseth. Let my name be called out, let it be found inscribed on the tablet which recordeth the names of those who are to receive offerings. Let meals from the sepulchral offerings be given to me in the presence [of Osiris], as to those who are in the following of Horus. Let there be prepared for me a seat in the Boat of the Sun on the day wheron the god saileth. Let me be received in the presence of Osiris in the Land of Truth-speaking- the Ka of Osiris Ani.

APPENDIX (From the Papyrus of Nekht, Brit. Mus. No. 10471, Sheet 21) NEKHT, THE CAPTAIN OF SOLDIERS, THE ROYAL SCRIBE, SINGETH A HYMN OF PRAISE TO RA, and saith:-

Homage to thee, O thou glorious Being, thou who art dowered [with all sovereignty]. O Tem-Heru-Khuti (Tem- Harmakhis), when thou risest in the horizon of heaven a cry of joy goeth forth to thee from all people. O thou beautiful Being, thou dost renew thyself in thy season in the form of the Disk, within thy mother Hathor. Therefore in every place every heart swelleth with joy at thy rising for ever. The regions of the South and the North come to thee with homage, and send forth acclamations at thy rising on the horizon of heaven, and thou illuminest the Two Lands with rays of turquoise-[coloured] light. O Ra, who art Heru-Khuti, the divine man-child, the heir of eternity, self-begotten and self-born, king of the earth, prince of the Tuat (the Other World), governor of Aukert, thou didst come from the Water-god, thou didst spring from the Sky-god Nu, who doth cherish thee and order thy members.

O thou god of life, thou lord of love, all men live when thou shinest; thou art crowned king of the gods. The goddess Nut embraceth thee, and the goddess Mut enfoldeth thee at all seasons. Those who are in thy following sing unto thee with joy, and they bow down their foreheads to the earth when they meet thee, the lord of heaven, the lord of the earth, the King of Truth, the lord of eternity, the prince of everlastingness, thou sovereign of all the gods, thou god of life, thou creator of eternity, thou maker of heaven wherin thou art firmly stablished. The Company of the Gods rejoice at thy rising, the earth is glad when it beholdeth thy rays; the people who have been long dead come forth with cries of joy to behold thy beauties every day. Thou goest forth each day over heaven and earth, and thou art made strong each day be thy mother Nut. Thou passest over the heights of heaven, thy heart swelleth with joy; and the Lake of Testes (the Great Oasis) is content thereat. The Serpent-fiend hath fallen, his arms are hewn off, the Knife hath severed his joints. Ra liveth by Maat (Law), the beautiful! The Sektet Boat advanceth and cometh into port.

The South and the North, and the West and East, turn to praise thee. O thou First, Great God (PAUTA), who didst come into being of thine own accord,

Isis and Nephthys salute thee, they sing unto thee songs of joy at thy rising in the boat, they stretch out their hands unto thee. The Souls of the East follow thee, and the Souls of the West praise thee. Thou art the Ruler of all the gods. Thou in thy shrine hast joy, for the Serpent-fiend Nak hath been judged by the fire, and thy heart shall rejoice for ever. Thy mother Nut is esteemed by thy father Nu.

HYMN TO OSIRIS UN-NEFER A Hymn of Praise to Osiris Un-Nefer, the great god who dwelleth in Abtu, the king of eternity, the lord of everlastingness, who traverseth millions of years in his existence. Thou art the eldest son of the womb of Nut. Thou was begotten by Keb, the Erpat. Thou art the lord of the Urrt Crown. Thou art he whose White Crown is lofty. Thou art the King (Ati) of gods [and] men.

Thou hast gained possession of the sceptre of rule, and the whip, and the rank and dignity of thy divine fathers. Thy heart is expanded with joy, O thou who art in the kingdom of the dead. Thy son Horus is firmly placed on thy throne. Thou hast ascended thy throne as the Lord of Tetu, and as the Heq who dwelleth in Abydos. Thou makest the Two Lands to flourish through Truth-speaking, in the presence of him who is the Lord to the Uttermost Limit. Thou drawest on that which hath not yet come into being in thy name of "Ta-her-sta-nef." Thou governest the Two Lands by Maat in thy name of "Seker." Thy power is wide-spread, thou art he of whom the fear is great in thy name of "Usar" (or "Asar"). Thy existence endureth for an infinite number of double henti periods in thy name of "Un-Nefer." Homage to thee, King of Kings, and Lord of Lords, and Prince of Princes. Thou hast ruled the Two Lands from the womb of the goddess Nut. Thou hast governed the Lands of Akert. Thy members are of silver-gold, thy head is of lapis-lazuli, and the crown of thy head is of turquoise. Thou art An of millions of years. Thy body is all pervading,

O Beautiful Face in Ta-tchesert. Grant thou to me glory in heaven, and power upon earth, and truth-speaking in the Divine Underworld, and [the power to] sail down the river to Tetu in the form of a living Ba-soul, and [the power to] sail up the river to Abydos in the form of a Benu bird, and [the power to] pass in through and to pass out from, without obstruction, the doors of the lords of the Tuat. Let there be given unto me bread-cakes in the House of Refreshing, and sepulchral offerings of cakes and ale, and propitiatory offerings in Anu, and a permanent homestead in Sekhet-Aaru, with wheat and barley therein-to the Double of the Osiris, the scribe Ani.

THE CHAPTERS OF COMING FORTH BY DAY HERE BEGIN THE CHAPTERS OF COMING FORTH BY DAY, AND THE SONGS OF PRAISING AND GLORIFYING WHICH ARE TO BE RECITED FOR

"COMING FORTH" AND FOR ENTERING INTO KHERT-NETER, AND THE SPELLS WHICH ARE TO BE SAID IN BEAUTIFUL AMENTET. THEY SHALL BE RECITED ON THE DAY OF THE FUNERAL, ENTERING IN AFTER COMING FORTH.

The Osiris Ani, the Osiris the scribe Ani saith:- Homage to thee, O Bull of Amentet, Thoth the king of eternity is with me. I am the great god by the side of the divine boat, I have fought for thee, I am one of those gods, those divine chiefs, who proved the truth-speaking of Osiris before his enemies on the day of the weighing of words. I am thy kinsman Osiris. I am [one of] those gods who were the children of the goddess Nut, who hacked in pieces the enemies of Osiris, and who bound in fetters the legion of Sebau devils on his behalf. I am thy kinsman Horus, I have fought on thy behalf, I have come to thee for thy name's sake. I am Thoth who proved the truth of the words of Osiris before his enemies on the day of the weighing of words in the great House of the Prince, who dwelleth in Anu. I am Teti, the son of Teti. My mother conceived me in Tetu, and gave birth to me in Tetu.

I am with the mourners [and with] the women who tear out their hair and make lament for Osiris in Taui-Rekhti, proving true the words of Osiris before his enemies. Ra commanded Thoth to prove true the words of Osiris before his enemies; what was commanded [for Osiris], let that be done for me by Thoth. I am with Horus on the day of dressing Teshtesh. I open the hidden water-springs for the ablutions of Urt-ab. I unbolt the door of the Shetait Shrine in Ra-stau. I am with Horus as the protector of the left shoulder of Osiris, the dweller in Sekhem. I enter in among and I come forth from the Flame-gods on the day of the destruction of the Sebau fiends in Sekhem. I am with Horus on the day[s] of the festivals of Osiris, at the making of offerings and oblations, namely, on the festival which is celebrated on the sixth day of the month, and on the day of the Tenat festival in Anu. I am the UAB priest (libationer) in Tetu, Rera, the dweller in Per-Asar.

I exalt him that is upon the high place of the country. I look upon the hidden things (the mysteries) in Ra-stau. I recite the words of the liturgy of the festival of the Soul- god in Tetu. I am the SEM priest, and [perform] his duties. I am the UR-KHERP-HEM priest on the day of placing the Henu Boat of Seker upon its divine sledge. I have taken in my hand the digging tool on the day of digging up the earth in Hensu.

Hail, O ye who make perfect souls to enter into the House of Osiris, make ye the well-instructed soul of the Osiris the scribe Ani, whose word is true, to enter in and to be with you in the House of Osiris. Let him hear even as ye hear; let him have sight even as ye have sight; let him stand up even as ye stand up; let him take his seat even as ye take your seats.

Hail, O ye who give cakes and ale to perfect souls in the House of Osiris, give ye cakes and ale twice each day (in the morning and in the evening) to the soul of the Osiris Ani, whose word is true before the gods, the Lords of Abydos, and whose word is true with you.

Hail, O ye who open up the way, who act as guides to the roads [in the Other World] to perfect souls in the House of Osiris, open ye up for him the way, and act ye as guides to the roads to the soul of the Osiris, the scribe, the registrary of all the offerings made to the gods, Ani, [whose word is true] with you. May he enter the House of Osiris with boldness, and may he come forth therefrom in peace. May there be no opposition made to him, and may he not be sent back [therefrom]. May he enter in under favour [of Osiris], and may he come forth gratified [at the acceptance of] his true words. May his commands be performed in the House of Osiris, may his words travel with you, may he be glorious as ye are. May he be not found to be light in the Balance, may the Balance dispose of his case. (In the Turin Papyrus, ed. Lepsius, this Chapter ends with the following.) Permit thou not me to be judged according to the mouths of the multitude. May my soul lift itself up before [Osiris], having been found to have been pure when on earth.

May I come into thy presence, O Lord of the gods; may I arrive at the Nome of Maati (Truth); may I rise up on my seat like a god endowed with life; may I give forth light like the Company of the Gods who dwell in heaven; may I become like one of you; may I lift up my footsteps in the town of Kher-Aha; may I look upon the Sektet Boat of the god, Saah, the holy one, as it passeth across the sky; may I not be repulsed; may I look upon the Lords of the Tuat, or, according to another reading, the Company of the Gods; may I smell the savour of the divine food of the Company of the Gods; may I sit down with them; may my name be proclaimed for offerings by the KHER-HEB priest at the sacrificial table; may I hear the petitions which are made when offerings are presented; may I draw nigh unto the Neshem Boat; and may neither my Heart-soul nor its lord be repulsed. Homage to thee, O Chief of Amentet, thou god Osiris, who dwellest in the town of Nifu-ur.

Grant thou that I may arrive in peace in Amentet. May the Lords of Ta-Tchesert receive me, and may they say unto me: "Hail, hail; welcome, welcome!" May they make ready for me a seat by the side of the President of the Chiefs; may the Nursing-goddesses receive me at the seasons, and may I come forth into the presence of Un-Nefer true of word. May I be a Follower of Horus in Ra-stau, and of Osiris in Tetu; and may I perform all the transformations which my heart may desire to make in every place wherein my Double (KA) wisheth to be. RUBRIC: If this text be known [by the deceased] upon earth or if he causeth it to be done in writing upon [his] coffin, then will he be able to come forth on any day he pleaseth, and to enter into his habitation unrepulsed. Cakes and ale and joints of meat from those which are on the altar of Ra shall be given unto him, and his homestead shall be among the fields of the Field of Reeds (Sekhet-Aaru), and wheat and barley shall be given unto him therein, and he shall flourish there even as he flourished upon earth.

APPENDIX (From the Papyrus of Nekhtu-Amen, ed. Naville, I, 5) THE CHAPTER OF MAKING THE SAHU TO ENTER THE TUAT ON THE DAY OF THE FUNERAL, WHEN THE FOLLOWING WORDS ARE TO BE SAID:

Homage to thee, O thou who dwellest in the Holy Hill (Set-Tchesert) of Amentet! the Osiris, the royal scribe, Nekhtu-Amen, whose word is true, knoweth thee, he knoweth thy name. Deliver thou him from the worms which are in Ra-stau, which live upon the bodies of men and women, and feed upon their blood, for Osiris, the favoured servant of the god of his city, the royal scribe Nekhtu-Amen, knoweth you, and he knoweth your names. Let the order for his protection be the first command of Osiris, the Lord to the Uttermost Limit, who keepeth his body hidden. May he give him release from the Terrible One who dwelleth at the bend of the River of Amentet, and may he decree the acts that will make him to rise up. Let him pass on to him whose throne is placed within the darkness, who giveth light in Ra-stau.

O thou Lord of Light, come thou and swallow up the worms which are in Amentet. Let the Great God who dwelleth in Tetu, and who is himself unseen, hear his prayers, and let those who cause afflictions hold him in fear as he cometh forth with the sentence of their doom to the Divine Block. I the Osiris, the royal scribe, Nekhtu-Amen, come, bearing the decree of Neb-er-tcher, and I am the Horus who taketh possession of his throne for him. His father, the lord of all those who are in the Boat of his Father Horus, hath ascribed praise unto him. He cometh bearing tidings.......let him see the town of Anu. Their chief shall stand on the earth before him, the scribes shall magnify him at the doors of their assemblies, and thy shall swathe im with swathings in Anu. He hath led heaven captive, and he hath seized the earth in his grasp. Neither the heavens nor the earth can be taken away from him, for, behold, he is Ra, the firstborn of the gods. His mother shall nurse him, and shall give him her breast on the horizon.

RUBRIC: The words of this Chapter shall be said after [the deceased] is laid to rest in Amentet; by means of them the region Tenn-t shall be contented with her lord. And the Osiris, the royal scribe, Nekhtu-Amen, whose word is truth, shall come forth, and he shall embark in the Boat of Ra, and [his] body upon its bier shall be counted up, and he shall be established in the Tuat.

THE CHAPTER OF GIVING A MOUTH TO THE OSIRIS ANI, THE SCRIBE, AND TELLER OF THE OFFERINGS WHICH ARE MADE TO ALL THE GODS, WHOSE WORD IS TRUE, WHO SAITH:-

I rise up out of the Egg in the Hidden Land. May my mouth be given unto me that I may speak therewith in the presence of the Great God, the Lord of the Tuat. Let not my hand and my arm be repulsed in the presence of the Chiefs

(Tchatchau) of any god. I am Osiris, the Lord of Ra-stau. May I, the Osiris, the scribe Ani, whose word is true, have my portion with him who is on the top of the Steps (Osiris). According to the desire of my heart I have come forth from the Island of Nesersert, and I have extinguished the fire.

THE CHAPTER OF GIVING A MOUTH TO THE OSIRIS, THE SCRIBE ANI, WHO SAITH: Homage to thee, O thou lord of brightness, Governor of the Temple, Prince of the night and of the thick darkness. I have come unto thee. I am shining, I am pure. My hands are about thee, thou hast thy lot with thy ancestors. Give thou unto me my mouth that I may speak with it. I guide my heart at its season of flame and of night. RUBRIC: If this Chapter be known by the Osiris the scribe Ani, upon earth, [or if it be done] in writing upon [his] coffin, he shall come forth by day in every form which he pleaseth, and he shall enter into [his] abode, and shall not be repulsed. And cakes, and ale, and joints of meat [from those which are on] the altar of Osiris shall be given unto him; and he shall enter in peace into Sekhet-Aaru, conformably to the decree of the Dweller in Busiris. Wheat and barley (dhura) shall be given unto him therein, and he shall flourish there just as he did upon earth; and he shall do whatsoever it pleaseth him to do, even as do the Company of the Gods who are in the Tuat, regularly and continually, for millions of times.

(From the Paprys of Nebseni, Sheet 3) THE CHAPTER OF COMING FORTH BY DAY AND OF OPENING UP A WAY THROUGH THE AMEHET: Behold, the scribe Nebseni, whose word is truth, saith:-

Homage to you, O ye Lords of Kau, ye who are without sin, and who live for the endless and infinite aeons of time which make up eternity. I have opened up a way for myself to you. I have become a spirit in my forms, I have gotten the mastery over my words of magical power, and I am adjudged a spirit; therefore deliver ye me from the Crocodile [which liveth in] this Country of

Truth. Grant ye to me my mouth that I may speak therewith, and cause ye that sepulchral offerings shall be made unto me in your presence, for I know you, and I know your names, and I know also the name of the mighty god before whose face ye set your celestial food. His name is "Tekem."

[When] he openeth up his path on the eastern horizon of heaven, [when] he alighteth towards the western horizon of heaven, may he carry me along with him, and may I be safe and sound. Let not the Mesqet make an end of me, let not the Fiend (Sebau) gain the mastery over me, let me not be driven away from the doors of the Other World, let not you doors be shut in my face, for my cakes are in the city of Pe, and my ale is in the city of Tep.

And there, in the celestial mansions of heaven which my divine father Tem hath stablished, let my hands lay hold upon the wheat and the barley, which shall be given unto me therein in abundant measure, and may the son of my own body make ready for me my food therein. And grant ye unto me when I am there sepulchral meals, and incense, and unguents, and all the pure and beautiful things whereon the god liveth, in every deed for ever, in all the transformations which it pleaseth me [to perform], and grant unto me the power to float down and to sail up the stream in the Field of Reeds (Sekhet-Aaru), [and may I reach Sekhet-hetepet (the Field of Offerings)]. I am the twin Lion-gods (Shu and Tefnut).

TEXTS RELATING TO THE WEIGHING OF THE HEART OF ANI THE NAMES OF THE GODS OF THE GREAT COMPANY:- 1. Ra Harmakhis, the Great God in his boat. 2. Temu. 3. Shu. 4. Tefnut. 5. Keb. 6. Nut, the Lady of Heaven. 7. Isis. 8. Nephthys. 9. Horus, the Great God. 10. Hathor, Lady of Amentet. 11. Hu. 12. Sa. **THE PRAYER OF ANI:-**

My heart, my mother; my heart, my mother! My heart whereby I came into being! May nought stand up to oppose me at [my] judgment, may there be no opposition to me in the presence of the Chiefs (Tchatchau); may there be no parting of thee from me in the presence of him that keepeth the Balance! Thou art my KA, which dwelleth in my body; the god Khnemu who knitteth together and strengtheneth my limbs. Mayest thou come forth into the place of happiness whither we go. May the Sheniu officials, who make the conditions of the lives of men, not cause my name to stink, and may no lies be spoken against me in the presence of the God. [Let it be satisfactory unto us, and let the Listener god be favourable unto us, and let there be joy of heart (to us) at the weighing of words. Let not that which is false be uttered against me before the Great God, the Lord of Amentet. Verily, how great shalt thou be when thou risest in triumph.]

THE SPEECH OF THOTH:- Thoth, the judge of right and truth of the Great Company of the Gods who are in the presence of Osiris, saith: Hear ye this judgment. The heart of Osiris hath in very truth been weighed, and his Heart-soul hath borne testimony on his behalf; his heart hath been found right by the trial in the Great Balance. There hath not been found any wickedness in him; he hath not wasted the offerings which have been made in the temples; he hath not committed any evil act; and he hath not set his mouth in motion with words of evil whilst he was upon earth.

SPEECH OF THE DWELLER IN THE EMBALMMENT CHAMBER (ANUBIS):- Pay good heed, O righteous Judge to the Balance to support [the testimony] thereof. Variant: Pay good heed to the weighing in the Balance of the heart of the Osiris, the singing-woman of Amen, Anhai, whose word is truth, and place thou her heart in the seat of truth in the presence of the Great God.

THE SPEECH OF THE GODS:- The Great Company of the Gods say to Thoth who dwelleth in Khemenu: That which cometh forth from thy mouth shall be declared true. The Osiris the scribe Ani, whose word is true, is holy and righteous. He hath not committed any sin, and he hath done no evil against us. The devourer Am-mit shall not be permitted to prevail over him. Meat offerings and admittance into the presence of the god Osiris shall be granted unto him, together with an abiding habitation in the Field of Offerings (Sekhet-hetepet), as unto the Followers of Horus.

THE SPEECH OF HORUS TO OSIRIS IN INTRODUCING ANI TO HIM:- Horus, the son of Isis, saith: I have come to thee, O Un-Nefer, and I have brought unto thee the Osiris Ani. His heart is righteous, and it hath come forth from the Balance; it hath not sinned against any god or any goddess. Thoth hath weighed it according to the decree pronounced unto him by the Company of the Gods, and it is most true and righteous. Grant thou that cakes and ale may be given unto him, and let him appear in the presence of the god Osiris, and let him be like unto the Followers of Horus for ever and ever.

THE SPEECH OF ANI:- And the Osiris Ani saith: Behold, I am in thy presence, O Lord of Amentet. There is no sin in my body. I have not spoken that which is not true knowingly, nor have I done anything with a false heart. Grant thou that I may be like unto those favoured ones who are in thy following, and that I may be an Osiris greatly favoured of the beautiful god, and beloved of the Lord of the Two Lands, I who am a veritable royal scribe who loveth thee, Ani, whose word is true before the god Osiris. **DESCRIPTION OF THE BEAST AM-MIT:-** Her forepart is like that of a crocodile, the middle of her body is like that of a lion, her hind quarters are like those of a hippopotamus.

HERE BEGIN THE PRAISES AND GLORIFYINGS OF COMING OUT FROM AND OF GOING INTO THE GLORIOUS KHERT-NETER, WHICH IS IN THE BEAUTIFUL AMENTET, OF COMING FORTH BY DAY IN ALL THE FORMS OF EXISTENCE WHICH IT MAY PLEASE THE DECEASED TO TAKE, OF PLAYING AT DRAUGHTS, OF SITTING IN THE SEH HALL, AND OF APPEARING AS A LIVING SOUL:

The Osiris the scribe Ani saith after he hath arrived in his haven of rest- now it is good for [a man] to recite [this work whilst he is] upon earth, for then all the words of Tem come to pass"I am the god Tem in rising. I am the Only One. I came into existence in Nu. I am Ra who rose in the beginning, the ruler of this [creation]." Who is this? "It is Ra, when at the beginning he rose in the city of Hensu, crowned like a king for his coronation. The Pillars of the god Shu were not as yet created, when he was upon the steps of him that dwelleth in Khemenu.

"I am the Great God who created himself, even Nu, who made his names to become the Company of the Gods as gods." Who is this? "It is Ra, the creator of the names of his limbs, which came into being in the form of the gods who are in the train of Ra. "I am he who cannot be repulsed among the gods." Who is this? "It is Temu, the dweller in his disk, but others say that it is Ra when he riseth in the eastern horizon of the sky.

"I am Yesterday, I know To-day." Who is this? "Yesterday is Osiris, and To-day is Ra, when he shall destroy the enemies of Neb-er-tcher (the lord to the uttermost limit), and when he shall establish as prince and ruler his son Horus. "Others, however, say that To-day is Ra, on the day when we commemorate the festival of the meeting of the dead Osiris with his father Ra, and when the battle of the gods was fought, in which Osiris, the Lord of Amentet, was the leader." What is this? "It is Amentet, [that is to say] the creation ofthe souls of the gods when Osiris was leader in Set-Amentet. "Others, however, say that it is the Amentet which Ra hath given unto me; when any god cometh he must rise up and fight for it.

"I know the god who dwelleth therein." Who is this? "It is Osiris. Others, however, say that his name is Ra, and that the god who dwelleth in Amentet is the phallus of Ra, wherewith he had union with himself. "I am the Benu bird which is in Anu. I am the keeper of the volume of the book (the Tablet of Destiny) of the things which have been made, and of the things which shall be made." Who is this? "It is Osiris. "Others, however, say that it is the dead body of Osiris, and yet others say that it is the excrement of Osiris. The things which have been made, and the things which shall be made [refer to] the dead body of Osiris. Others again say that the things which have been made are Eternity, and the things which shall be made are Everlastingness, and that Eternity is the Day, and Everlastingness the Night.

"I am the god Menu in his coming forth; may his two plumes be set on my head for me." Who is this? "Menu is Horis, the Advocate of his father [Osiris], and his coming forth means his birth. The two plumes on his head are Isis and Nephthys, when these goddesses go forth and set themselves thereon, and when they act as his protectors, and when they provide that which his head lacketh. "Others, however, say that the two plumes are the two exceedingly large uraei which are upon the head of their father Tem, and there are yet others who say that the two plumes which are upon the head of Menu are his two eyes. "The Osiris the scribe Ani, whose word is true, the registrar of all the offerings which are made to the gods, riseth up and cometh into his city." What is this [city]? "It is the horizon of his father Tem.

"I have made an end of my shortcomings, and I have put away my faults." What is this? "It is the cutting of the navel string of the body of the Osiris the scribe Ani, whose word is true before all the gods, and all his faults are driven out. What is this? "It is the purification [of Osiris] on the day of his birth. "I am purified in my great double nest which is in Hensu on the day of the offerings of the followers of the Great God who dwelleth therein." What is the "great double nest"? "The name of one nest is 'Millions of years,' and 'Great Green [Sea]' is the name of the other, that is to say 'Lake of Natron' and 'Lake of Salt.' "Others, however, say the name of the one is 'Guide of Millions of Years,' and that 'Great Green Lake' is name of the other.

Yet others say that 'Begetter of Millions of Years' is the name of one, and 'Great Green Lake' is the name of the other. Now, as concerning the Great God who dwelleth therein, it is Ra himself. "I pass over the way, I know the head of the Island of Maati." What is this? "It is Ra-stau, that is to say, it is the gate to the South of Nerutef, and it is the Northern Gate of the Domain (Tomb of the god). "Now, as concerning the Island of Maati, it is Abtu. "Others, however, say that it is the way by which Father Tem travelleth when he goeth forth to Sekhet-Aaru, [the place] which produceth the food and sustenance of the gods who are [in] their shrines. "Now the Gate Tchesert is the Gate of the Pillars of Shu, that is to say, the Northern Gate of the Tuat.

"Others, however, say that the Gate of Tchesert is the two leaves of the door through which the god Tem passeth when he goeth forth to the eastern horizon of the sky. "O ye gods who are in the presence [of Osiris], grant to me your arms, for I am the god who shall come into being among you." Who are these gods? "They are the drops of blood which came forth from the phallus of Ra when he went forth to perform his own mutilation. These drops of blood sprang into being under the forms of the gods Hu and Sa, who are in the bodyguard of Ra, and who accompany the god Tem daily and every day.

"I, Osiris the scribe Ani, whose word is truth, have filled for thee the utchat (the Eye of Ra, or of Horus), when it had suffered extinction on the day of the combat of the Two Fighters (Horus and Set)." What was this combat? It was the combat which took place on the day when Horus fought with Set, during which Set threw filth in the face of Horus, and Horus crushed the genitals of Set. The filling of the utchat Thoth performed with his own fingers. "I remove the thunder-cloud from the sky when there is a storm with thunder and lightning therein." What is this? "This storm was the raging of Ra at the thunder-cloud which [Set] sent forth against the Right Eye of Ra (the Sun). Thoth removed the thunder- cloud from the Eye of Ra, and brought back the Eye living, healthy, sound, and with no defect in it to its owner.

"Others, however, say that the thunder-cloud is caused by sickness in the Eye of Ra, which weepeth for its companion Eye (the Moon); at this time Thoth cleanseth the Right Eye of Ra. "I behold Ra who was born yesterday from the thighs of the goddess Mehurt; his strength is my strength, and my strength is his strength." Who is this? "Mehurt is the great Celestial Water, but others say that Mehurt is the image of the Eye of Ra at dawn at his birth daily. "[Others, however, say that] Mehurt is the utchat of Ra. "Now Osiris the scribe Ani, whose word is truth, is a very great one among the gods who are in the following of Horus; they say that he is the prince who loveth his lord." Who are the gods who are in the train of Horus? "[They are] Kesta, Hapi,

Taumutef, and Qebhsenuf. "Homage to you, O ye lords of right and truth, ye sovereign princes (Tchatcha) who [stand] round about Osiris, who do away utterly sins and offences, and who are in the following of the goddess Hetepsekhus, grant ye that I may come unto you. Destroy ye all the faults which are within me, even as ye did for the Seven Spirits who are among the followers of their lord Sepa. Anpu (Anubis) appointed to them their places on the day [when he said unto them], "Come ye hither." Who are the "lords of right and truth"?

"The lords of right and truth are Thoth and Astes, the Lord of Amentet. "The Tchatcha round about Osiris are Kesta, Hapi, Tuamutef, and Qebhsenuf, and they are also round about the Constellation of the Thigh (the Great Bear), in the northern sky. "Those who do away utterly sins and offences, and who are in the following of the goddess Hetepsekhus, are the god Sebek and his associates who dwell in the water. "The goddess Hetepsekhus is the Eye of Ra. "Others, however, say that it is the flame which accompanieth Osiris to burn up the souls of his enemies. "As concerning all the faults which are in Osiris, the registrar of the offerings which are made unto all the gods, Ani, whose word is truth, [these are all the offences which he hath committed against the Lords of Eternity] since he came forth from his mother's womb. "As concerning the Seven Spirits who are Kesta, Hapi, Tuamutef, Qebhsenuf, Maa-atef, Kheribeqef and Heru-khenti-en-ariti, these did Anubis appoint to be protectors of the dead body of Osiris.

"Others, however, say that he set them round about the holy place of Osiris. "Others say that the Seven Spirits [which were appointed by Anubis] were Netcheh-netcheh, Aatqetqet, Nertanef-besef-khenti-hehf, Aq-her-ami- unnut-f, Tesher-ariti-ami-Het-anes, Ubes-her-per-em-khetkhet, and Maaem- kerh-annef-em-hru. "The chief of the Tchatcha (sovereign princes) who is in Naarutef is Horus, the Advocate of his father. "As concerning the day wherein [Anubis said to the Seven Spirits], 'Come ye hither,' [the allusion here] is to the words 'Come ye hither,' which Ra spake unto Osiris." Verily may these same words be said unto me in Amentet. "I am the Divine Soul which dwelleth in the Divine Twin-gods." Who is this Divine Soul? "It is Osiris. [When] he goeth into Tetu, and findeth there the Soul of Ra, the one god embraceth the other, and two Divine Souls spring into being within the Divine Twin-gods.

(From the Papyrus of Nebseni, Brit. Mus. No. 9900, Sheet 14, ll. 16ff.) "As concerning the Divine Twin-gods they are Heru-netch-her-tefef and Heru-khent-en-Ariti (Horus the Advocate of his father [Osiris], and Horus the sightless). "Others say that the double Divine Soul which dwelleth in the Divine Twin-gods is the Soul of Ra and the Soul of Osiris, and yet others say that it is the Soul which dwelleth in Shu, and the Sould which dwelleth in Tefnut, and that these two Souls form the double Divine Soul which dwelleth in Tetu.

"I am the Cat which fought near the Persea Tree in Anu on the night when the foes of Neb-er-tcher were destroyed." Who is this Cat? "This male Cat is Ra himself, and he was called 'Mau' because of the speech of the god Sa, who said concerning him: 'He is like (mau) unto that which he hath made'; therefore, did the name of Ra become 'Mau.' "Others, however, say that the male Cat is the god Shu, who made over the possessions of Keb to Osiris. "As concerning the fight which took place near the Persea Tree in Anu [these words have reference to the slaughter] of the children of rebellion, when righteous retribution was meted out to them for [the evil] which they had done. "As concerning the 'night of the battle,' [these words refer to] the invasion of the eastern portion of the heaven by the children of rebellion, whereupon a great battle arose in heaven and in all the earth.

"O thou who art in thine egg (Ra,) who showest from thy Disk, who risest on thy horizon, and dost shine with golden beams in the height of heaven, like unto whom there is none among the gods, who sailest above the Pillars of Shu, who sendest forth blasts of fire from thy mouth, [who illuminest the Two Lands with thy splendour, deliver] thou Nebseni, the lord of fealty [to Osiris], from the god whose form is hidden, and whose eyebrows are like unto the two arms of the Balance on the night when the sentences of doom are promulgated." Who is this invisible god? "It is An-a-f (he who bringeth his arm.).

"As concerning 'the night when the sentences of doom are promulgated,' it is the night of the burning of the damned, and of the overthrow of the wicked at the Block, and of the slaughter of souls." Who is this [slaughterer of souls]? "It is Shesmu, the headsman of Osiris. "[Concerning the invisible god] some say that he is Aapep when he riseth up with a head bearing upon it [the feather of] Maat (Truth). But others say that he is Horus when he riseth up with two heads, whereon one beareth [the feather of] Maat, and the other [the symbol of] wickedness. He bestoweth wickedness on him that worketh wickedness, and right and truth upon him that followeth righteousness and truth.

"Others say that he is Heru-ur (the Old Horus), who dwelleth in Sekhem; others say that he is Thoth; others say that he is Nefer-Tem; and others say that he is Sept who doth bring to nought the acts of the foes of Nebertcher. "Deliver thou the scribe Nebseni, whose word is truth, from the Watchers, who carry murderous knives, who possess cruel fingers, and who would slay those who are in the following of Osiris." May these Watchers never gain the mastery over me, and may I never fall under their knives! Who are these Watchers? "They are Anubis and Horus, [the latter being] in the form of Horus the sightless. Others, however, say that they are the Tchatcha (sovereign princes of Osiris), who bring to nought the operations of their knives; and others say that they are the chiefs of the Sheniu chamber. "May their knives never gain the mastery over me. May I never fall under the knives wherewith they inflict cruel tortures. For I know their names, and I know the being, Matchet, who is among them in the House of Osiris.
He shooteth forth rays of light from his eye, being himself invisible, and he goeth round about heaven robed in the flames which come from his mouth, commanding Hapi, but remaining invisible himself. May I be strong on earth before Ra, may I arrive safely in the presence of Osiris. O ye who preside over your altars, let not your offerings to me be wanting, for I am one of those who follow after Nebertcher, according to the writings of Khepera. Let me fly like a hawk, let me cackle like a goose, let me lay always like the serpent-goddess Neheb- ka."

Who are those who preside over their altars? "Those who preside over their altars are the similitude of the Eye of Ra, and the similitude of the Eye of Horus. "O Ra-Tem, thou Lord of the Great House [in Anu], thou Sovereign (life, strentgh, health [be to thee]) of all the gods, deliver thou the scribe Nebseni, whose word is truth, from the god whose face is like unto that of a greyhound, whose brows are like those of a man, who feedeth upon the dead, who watcheth at the Bend of the Lake of Fire, who devoureth the bodies of the dead, and swalloweth hearts, and who voideth filth, but who himself remaineth unseen." Who is this greyhound-faced god? "His name is 'Everlasting Devourer,' and he liveth in the Domain [of Fire] (the Lake of Unt).

"As concerning the Domain of Fire, it is that Aat which is in Naarutef, and is near the Sheniu chamber. The sinner who walketh over this place falleth down among the knives [of the Watchers]. "Others, however, say that the name of this god is 'Mates,' and that he keepeth watch over the door of Amentet; others say that his name is 'Beba,' and that he keepeth watch over the Bend [of the stream] of Amentet, and yet others say that his name is 'Herisepef.' "Hail, Lord of Terror, Chief of the Lands of the South and North, thou Lord of the Desert, who dost keep prepared the block of slaughter, and who dost feed on the intestines [of men]!" Who is this Lord of Terror? "It is the Keeper of the Bend [of the stream] of Amentet." Who is this Keeper? "It is the Heart of Osiris, which is the devourer of all slaughtered things. "The Urrt Crown hath been given unto him, with gladness of heart, as Lord of Hensu." Who is this? "He to whom the Urrt Crown hath been given with gladness of heart as Lord of Hensu is Osiris. He was bidden to rule among the gods on the day of the union of earth [with earth] in the presence of Nebertcher." Who is this?
"He who was bidden to rule among the gods is the son of Isis (Horus), who was appointed to rule in the room of his father Osiris. "As concerning [the words] 'day of the union of earth with earth,' they have reference to the union of earth with earth in the coffin of Osiris, the Soul that liveth in Hensu, the giver of meat and drink, the destroyer of wrong, and the guide to the everlasting paths." Who is this? "It is Ra himself." "[Deliver thou the Osiris the scribe Ani, whose word is truth] from the great god who carrrieth away

souls, who eateth hearts, who feedeth upon offal, who keepeth watch in the darkness, who dwelleth in the Seker Boat; those who live in sin fear him."

Who is this? "It is Suti, but others say that it is Smamur, the soul of Keb. "Hail, Khepera in thy boat, the two Companies of the Gods are in thy body. Deliver thou the Osiris the scribe Ani, whose word is truth, from the Watchers who pass sentences of doom, who have been appointed by the god Nebertcher to protect him, and to fasten the fetters on his foes, and who slaughter in the torture chambers; there is no escape from their fingers. May they never stab me with their knives, may I never fall helpless into their chambers of torture. I have never done the things which the gods hate. I am he who is pure in the Mesqet chamber. And saffron cakes have been brought unto him in Tannt."

Who is this? "It is Khepera in his boat; it is Ra himself. "As concerning the Watchers who pass sentences of doom, they are the Apes Isis and Nephthys. "As concerning the things which the gods hate, they are acts of deceit and lying. He who passeth through the place of purification within the Mesqet chamber is Anpu (Anubis), who is hard by the coffer which containeth the inward parts of Osiris. He to whom saffron cakes have been brought in Tannt is Osiris. "Others, however, say that the saffron cakes in Tannt represent heaven and earth, and others say that they represent Shu, the strengthener of the Two Lands in Hensu; and others say that they represent the Eye of Horus, and that Tannt is the burial-place of Osiris. "Tem hath built thy house, and the double Lion-god hath laid the foundations of thy habitation. Lo! medicaments have been brought. Horus purifieth Set and Set strengtheneth, and Set purifieth and Horus strengtheneth.
"The Osiris the scribe Ani, whose word is truth before Osiris, hath come into this land, and he hath taken possession thereof with his two feet. He is Tem, and he is in the city. "Turn thou back, O Rehu, whose mouth shineth, whose head moveth, turn thou back before his strength." Another reading is, 'Turn thou back from him who keepeth watch, and is himself unseen.' Let the Osiris Ani be safely guarded. He is Isis, and he is found with her hair spread over him; it is shaken out over his brow. He was conceived by Isis, and engendered by Nephthys, and they have cut away from him the things which should be cut from him.

"Fear followeth after thee, terror is about thine arms. Thou hast been embraced for millions of years by arms; mortals go round about thee. Thou smitest down the mediators of thy foes, and thou seizest the arms of the power of darkness. Thy two sisters (Isis and Nephthys) are given to thee for thy delight. Thou hast created that which is in Kher-aha, and that which is Anu. Every god feareth thee, for thou art exceedingly great and terrible; thou [avengest] every god on the man who curseth him, and thou shootest arrows at him. Thou livest according to thy will. Thou art Uatchet, the Lady of Flame, evil befalleth those who set themselves up against thee." What is this? "'Hidden in form, given of Menhu,' is the name of the "tomb. 'He who seeth what is on his hand' is the name of Qerau, or, as others say, it is the name of the Block. "Now, he whose mouth shineth and whose head moveth is the phallus of Osiris, but others say it is [the phallus] of Ra. 'Thou spreadest thy hair, and I shake it out over his brow" is said concerning Isis, who hideth in her hair, and draweth it round about her. "Uatchet, the Lady of Flames, is the Eye of Ra."

THE SEVEN ARITS

The First Arit.
The name of the Doorkeeper is Sekhet-her-asht-aru. The name of the Watcher is Smetti. The name of the Herald is Hakheru. The Osiris Ani, whose word is truth, shall say when he cometh unto the First Arit: "I am the mighty one who createth his own light. I have come unto thee, O Osiris, and, purified from that which defileth thee, I adore thee. Lead on. Name not the name of Ra-stau

to me. Homage to thee, O Osiris, in thy might and in thy strength in Ra-stau. Rise up and conquer, O Osiris, in Abtu. Thou goest round about heaven, thou sailest in the presence of Ra, thou lookest upon all the beings who have knowledge.

Hail, Ra, thou who goest round about in the sky, I say, O Osiris in truth, that I am the Sahu (Spirit-body) of the god, and I beseech thee not to let me be driven away, nor to be cast upon the wall of blazing fire. Let the way be opened in Ra-stau, let the pain of the Osiris be relieved, embrace that which the Balance hath weighed, let a path be made for the Osiris in the Great Valley, and let the Osiris have light to guide him on his way."

The Second Arit.
The name of the Doorkeeper is Unhat. The name of the Watcher is Seqt-her. The name of the Herald is Ust. The Osiris Ani, whose word is truth, shall say [when he cometh to this Arit]: "He sitteth to carry out his heart's desire, and he weigheth words as the Second of Thoth. The strength which protecteth Thoth humbleth the hidden Maati gods, who feed upon Maat during the years of their lives. I offer up my offerings [to him] at the moment when he maketh his way. I advance, and I enter on the path. O grant thou that I may continue to advance, and that I may attain to the sight of Ra, and of those who offer up [their] offerings."

The Third Arit.
The name of the Doorkeeper is Unem-hauatu-ent-pehui. The name of the Watcher is Seres-her. The name of the Herald is Aa. The Osiris the scribe Ani, whose word is truth, shall say [when he cometh to this Arit]: "I am he who is hidden in the great deep. I am the Judge of the Rehui, I have come and I have done away the offensive thing which was upon Osiris. I tie firmly the place on which he standeth, coming forth from the Urt. I have stablished things in Abtu, I have opened up a way through Ra-stau, and I have relieved the pain

which was in Osiris. I have balanced the place whereon he standeth, and I have made a path for him; he shineth brilliantly in Ra-stau."

The Fourth Arit.
The name of the Doorkeeper is Khesef-her-asht-kheru. The name of the Watcher is Seres-tepu. The name of the Herald is Khesef-at. The Osiris the scribe Ani, whose word is truth, shall say [when he cometh to this Arit]: "I am the Bull, the son of the ancestress of Osiris. O grant ye that his father, the Lord of his god-like companions, may bear witness on his behalf. I have weighed the guilty in judgment. I have brought unto his nostrils the life which is ever lasting. I am the son of Osiris, I have accomplished the journey, I have advanced in Khert-Neter."

The Fifth Arit.
The name of the Doorkeeper is Ankhf-em-fent. The name of the Watcher is Shabu. The name of the Herald is Teb-her-kha-kheft. The Osiris the scribe Ani, whose word is truth, shall say [when he cometh to this Arit]: "I have brought unto thee the jawbone in Ra-stau. I have brought unto thee thy backbone in Anu. I have gathered together his manifold members therein. I have driven back Aapep for thee. I have spit upon the wounds [in his body]. I have made myself a path among you. I am the Aged One among the gods. I have made offerings to Osiris. I have defended him with the word of truth. I have gathered together his bones, and have collected all his members."

The Sixth Arit.
The name of the Doorkeeper is Atek-tau-kehaq-kheru. The name of the Watcher is An-her. The name of the Herald is Ates-her-[ari]-she. The Osiris the scribe Ani, whose word is truth, shall say [when he cometh to this Arit]: "I have come daily, I have come daily. I have made myself a way. I have advanced over that which was created by Anpu (Anubis). I am the Lord of the Urrt Crown. I am the possessor [of the knowledge of] the words of magical power, I am the Avenger according to law, I have avenged [the injury to] his

Eye. I have defended Osiris. I have accomplished my journey. The Osiris Ani advanceth with you with the word which is truth."

The Seventh Arit:
The name of the Doorkeeper is Sekhmet-em-tsu-sen. The name of the Watcher is Aa-maa-kheru. The name of the Herald is Khesef-khemi. The Osiris the scribe Ani, whose word is truth, shall say [when he cometh to this Arit]: "I have come unto thee, O Osiris, being purified from foul emissions. Thou goest round about heaven, thou seest Ra, thou seest the beings who have knowledge. [Hail], thou, ONE! Behold, thou art in the Sektet Boat which traverseth the heavens. I speak what I will to his Sahu (Spirit-body). He is strong, and cometh into being even [as] he spake. Thou meetest him face to face. Prepare thou for me all the ways which are good [and which lead] to thee." RUBRIC: If [these] words be recited by the spirit when he shall come to the Seven Arits, and as he entereth the doors, he shall neither be turned back nor repulsed before Osiris, and he shall be made to have his being among the blessed spirits, and to have dominion among the ancestral followers of Osiris. If these things be done for any spirit he shall have his being in that place like a lord of eternity in one body with Osiris, and at no place shall any being contend against him.

THE PYLONS OF THE HOUSE OF OSIRIS The following shall be said when one cometh to the FIRST PYLON. The Osiris the scribe Ani, whose word is truth, saith: "Lady of tremblings, high-walled, the sovereign lady, the lady of destruction, who uttereth the words which drive back the destroyers, who delivereth from destruction him that cometh."

The name of her Doorkeeper is Neruit. The following shall be said when one cometh to the SECOND PYLON. The Osiris the scribe Ani, whose word is truth, saith: "Lady of heaven, Mistress of the Two Lands, devourer by fire, Lady of mortals, who art infinitely greater than any human being."

The name of her Doorkeeper is Mes-Ptah. The following shall be said when one cometh to the THIRD PYLON. The Osiris the scribe Ani, whose word is truth, saith: "Lady of the Altar, the mighty lady to whom offerings are made, greatly beloved one of every god sailing up the river to Abydos."

The name of her Doorkeeper is Sebqa. The following shall be said when one cometh to the FOURTH PYLON. The Osiris the scribe Ani, whose word is truth, saith: "Prevailer with knives, Mistress of the Two Lands, destroyer of the enemies of the Still-Heart (Osiris), who decreeth the release of those who suffer through evil hap."

The name of her Doorkeeper is Nekau. The following shall be said when one cometh to the FIFTH PYLON. The Osiris the scribe Ani, whose word is truth, saith: "Flame, Lady of fire, absorbing the entreaties which are made to her, who permitteth not to approach her the rebel."

The name of her Doorkeeper is Henti-Reqiu. The following shall be said when one cometh to the SIXTH PYLON. The Osiris the scribe Ani, whose word is truth, saith: "Lady of light, who roareth mightily, whose breadth cannot be comprehended. Her like hath not been found since the beginning. There are serpents over which are unknown. They were brought forth before the Still-Heart."

The name of her Doorkeeper is Semati. The following shall be said when one cometh to the SEVENTH PYLON. The Osiris the scribe Ani, whose word is truth, saith: "Garment which envelopeth the helpless one, which weepeth for and loveth that which it covereth." The name of her Doorkeeper is Saktif. The following shall be said when one cometh to the EIGHTH PYLON. The Osiris the scribe Ani, whose word is truth, saith: "Blazing fire, unquenchable, with far-reaching tongues of flame, irresistible slaughterer, which one may not pass through fear of its deadly attack."

The name of her Doorkeeper is Khutchetef. The following shall be said when one cometh to the NINTH PYLON. The Osiris the scribe Ani, whose word is truth, saith: "Chieftainess, lady of strength, who giveth quiet of heart to the offspring of her lord. Her girth is three hundred and fifty khet, and she is clothed with green feldspar of the South. She bindeth up the divine form and clotheth the helpless one. Devourer, lady of all men."

The name of her Doorkeeper is Arisutchesef. The following shall be said when one cometh to the TENTH PYLON. The Osiris the scribe Ani, whose word is truth, saith: "Goddess of the loud voice, who maketh her suppliants to mourn, the awful one who terrifieth, who herself remaineth unterrified within."

The name of her Doorkeeper is Sekhenur. Nu, the steward of the keeper of the seal, saith when he cometh to the ELEVENTH PYLON of Osiris: "I have made my way, I know you, and I know thy name, and I know the name of her who is within thee: She who slayeth always, consumer of the fiends by fire, mistress of every pylon, the lady who is acclaimed on the day of darkness" is thy name. She inspecteth the swathing of the helpless one. The Osiris Nu, the steward of the keeper of the seal, saith when he cometh to the TWELFTH PYLON of Osiris: "I have made my way, I know you, and I know thy name, and I know the name of her who is within thee: Invoker of thy Two Lands, destroyer of those who come to thee by fire, lady of spirits, obeyer of the word of thy Lord" is thy name. She inspecteth the swathing of the helpless one.

The Osiris Nu, the steward of the keeper of the seal, saith when he cometh to the THIRTEENTH PYLON of Osiris: "I have made my way, I know you and I know thy name, and I know the name of her who is within thee: Osiris foldeth his arms about her, and maketh Hapi (the Nile-god), to emit splendour out of his hidden places" is thy name. She inspecteth the swathing of the helpless one. The Osiris Nu, the steward of the keeper of the seal, saith when he cometh to the FOURTEENTH PYLON of Osiris: "I have made my way, I know thee, and I know thy name, and I know the name of her who is within thee.

Lady of might, who trampleth on the Red Demons, who keepeth the festival of Haaker on the day of the hearing of faults" is thy name. She inspecteth the swathing of the helpless one. THE FIFTEENTH PYLON. The Osiris Heru-em-khebit, whose word is truth, shall say when he cometh to this pylon: "Fiend, red of hair and eyes, who appeareth by night, and doth fetter the fiend in his lair. Let her hands be given to the Still-Heart in his hour, let her advance and go forward" is thy name. She inspecteth the swathing of the helpless one.

THE SIXTEENTH PYLON. The Osiris Heru-em-khebit, whose word is truth, shall say when he cometh to this pylon: "Terrible one, lady of the rain- storm, destroyer of the souls of men, devourer of the bodies of men, orderer, producer, and maker of slaughter" is thy name. She inspecteth the swathing of the helpless one. THE SEVENTEENTH PYLON. The Osiris Heru-em-khebit, whose word is truth, shall say when he cometh to this pylon: "Hewer-in-pieces in blood, Ahibit, lady of hair" is thy name. She inspecteth the swathing of the helpless one.

THE EIGHTEENTH PYLON. The Osiris Heru-em-khebit, whose word is truth, shall say when he cometh to this pylon: "Fire-lover, pure one, lover of slaughterings, cutter off of heads, devoted one, lady of the Great House, slaughterer of fiends at eventide" is thy name. She inspecteth the swathing of the helpless one. THE NINETEENTH PYLON. The Osiris Heru-em-khebit, whose word is truth, shall say when he cometh to this pylon: "Light-giver for life, blazing all the day, lady of strength [and of] the writings of the god Thoth himself" is thy name. She inspecteth the swathings of the White House.
THE TWENTIETH PYLON. The Osiris Heru-em-khebit, whose word is truth, shall say when he cometh to this pylon: "Dweller in the cavern of her lord, her name is Clother, hider of her creations, conqueror of hearts, swallower [of them]" is thy name. She inspecteth the swathings of the White House. THE TWENTY-FIRST PYLON. The Osiris Heru-em-khebit, whose word is truth, shall say when he cometh to this pylon: "Knife which cutteth when [its name] is uttered, slayer of those who approach thy flame" is thy name. She possesseth hidden plans.

THE OSIRIS AUFANKH, WHOSE WORD IS TRUTH, SAITH: Hail, saith Horus, O Twenty-first pylon of the Still-Heart! I have made the way. I know thee. I know thy name. I know the name of the goddess who guardeth thee. "Sword that smiteth at the utterance of its own name, stinking face, overthrower of him that approacheth her flame" is thy name. Thou keepest the hidden things of the avenger of the god, thou guardest them.

Amam is his name. He maketh the ash trees (cedars) not to grow, and the shenu trees (acacias) not to blossom, and preventeth copper from being found in the mountain. The Tchatcha (Chiefs) of this Pylon are Seven Gods. Tchen, or Anthch (At), is the name of the one at the door. Hetepmes is the name of another there. Messep is the name of another there. Utchara is the name of another there. Beq is the name of another there. Anp (Anubis) is the name of another there. I have made the way. I am Menu-Heru, the avenger of his father, the heir of his father Un-Nefer.

I have come. I have given [offerings] to my father Osiris. I have overthrown all his enemies. I have come daily with the word of truth, the lord of fealty, in the house of my father Tem, the Lord of Anu, I, the Osiris Auf-ankh, whose word is truth in the southern heaven. I have done what is right for him that made the right, I have celebrated the Haker festival to the lord thereof. I have acted as the leader of the festivals. I have given cakes to the Lords of the Altar. I have been the leader of the propitiatory offerings, cakes, ale, oxen, geese, to my father Osiris Un-Nefer. I am the protector of the Ba- soul, I have made the Benu bird to appear [by my] words. I have come daily into the house of the god to make offerings of incense. I have come with the shenti tunic. I have set the Neshem Boat afloat on the water.

I have made the word of Osiris Khenti Amenti to be truth before his enemies. I have carried away in a boat all his enemies to the slaughter-house of the East, and they shall never escape from the wardship of the god Keb who dwelleth therein. I have made the Kefaiu gods of Ra to stand up, I have made his word to be truth. I have come as a scribe. I have explained [the writings]. I have made the god to have power over his legs. I have come into the house of him that is upon his mountain (Anubis). I have seen the Chief of the Seh hall. I have entered into Ra-stau. I have made myself invisible. I have found for myself the boundary. I have approached Nerutef. I have clothed the naked. I have sailed up the river to Abydos. I have performed the ceremonies of Hu and Sa. I have entered the house of Astes. I have made supplication to the Khati gods and to Sekhmet in the temple of Net (Neith), or the Aged Ones. I have entered Ra-stau. I have made myself invisible. I have found the frontier. I have approached Nerutef. I have clothed the naked. I have sailed up the river to Abydos.

I have performed the ceremonies of Hu and Sa. I have received. I have risen like a king crowned. I fill my seat on the throne in the place of my father, the God Who was at the beginning. I have praised the Meskhen of Ta-tchesert. My mouth is full of Maat (Truth). I have overwhelmed the Akhekhau serpents. I have come into the Great House with [my] body in a flourishing condition. I have caused myself to travel in the Boat of Hai. The myrrh unguent of..... is in the hair of men (Rekhit). I have entered into the House of Astes. I have approached with worship the two Khati gods and Sekhmet, who are in the temple of the Aged One [in Anu]. [And the god Osiris saith:] "Thou hast come, thou shalt be a favoured one in Tetu, O Osiris Auf-ankh, whose word is truth, the son of the lady Shert-en-Menu, whose word is truth."

THE PRIESTS ANMUTEF AND SAMEREF THE SPEECH OF THE PRIEST ANMUTEF.

I have come unto you, O ye great Tchatcha Chiefs who dwell in heaven, and upon earth, and in Khert-Neter, and I have brought unto you the Osiris Ani. He hath not committed any act which is an abomination before all the gods. Grant ye that he may live with you every day. The Osiris the scribe Ani adoreth Osiris, Lord of Rasta, and the Great Company of the Gods who live in Khert-Neter. He saith: "Homage to thee, Khenti Amenti, Un-Nefer, who dwellest in Abtu.

I come to thee. My heart holdeth Truth. There is no sin in my body. I have not told a lie wittingly, I have not acted in a double manner. Grant thou to me cakes, let me appear in the presence, at the altar of the Lords of Truth, let me go in and come forth from Khert-Neter [at will], let not my Heart-soul be driven away [from me]; and grant me a sight of the Disk and the beholding of the Moon for ever and ever.

THE SPEECH OF THE PRIEST SAMEREF.

I have come unto you, O ye Tchatcha Chiefs who dwell in Rasta, and I have brought unto you the Osiris Ani, grant ye unto him cakes, and water, and air, and a homestead in Sekhet-hetep as to the followers of Horus. The Osiris the scribe Ani, whose word is truth, adoreth Osiris, the Lord of everlastingness, and the Tchatcha Chiefs, the Lords of Rasta. He saith: "Homage to thee, O King of Khert-Neter, thou Governor of Akert! I have come unto thee. I know thy plans, I am equipped with the forms which thou takest in the Tuat. Give thou to me a place in Khert-Neter, near the Lords of Truth. May my homestead be lasting in Sekhet-hetep, may I receive cakes in thy presence." THE JUDGES IN ANU Hail, Thoth, who madest to be true the word of Osiris against his enemies, make thou the word of the scribe Nebseni to be true against his enemies, even as thou didst make the word of Osiris to be true against his enemies, in the presence of the Tchatcha Chiefs who are with Ra and Osiris in Anu, on the night of the "things of the night," and the night of battle, and of the fettering of the Sebau fiends, and the day of the destruction of the enemies of Neb-er-tcher.
Now the great Tchatcha Chiefs in Anu are Tem, Shu, Tefnut, [Osiris and Thoth]. Now the "fettering of the Sebau fiends" signifieth the destruction of the Smaiu fiends of Set, when he wrought iniquity a second time. Hail, Thoth, who didst make the word of Osiris to be true against his enemies, make thou the word of the Osiris Ani to be true against his enemies, with the great Tchatcha Chiefs who are in Tetu, on the night of setting up the Tet in Tetu.

Now the great Tchatcha Chiefs who are in Tetu are Osiris, Isis, Nephthys, and Horus the avenger of his father. Now the "setting up of the Tet in Tetu" signifieth [the raising up of] the shoulder of Horus, the Governor of Sekhem. They are round about Osiris in the band [and] the bandages. Hail, Thoth, who didst make the word of Osiris to be true against his enemies, make thou the word of the Osiris Ani to be true against his enemies, with the great Tchatcha Chiefs who are in Sekhem, on the night of the "things of the night" in Sekhem.

Now the great Tchatcha Chiefs who are in Sekhem are Heru-khenti-en-ariti and Thoth who is with the Tchatcha Chiefs of Nerutef. Now the night of the "things of the night festival" signifieth the dawn on the sarcophagus of Osiris. Hail, Thoth, who didst make the word of Osiris to be true against his enemies, make thou the word of the Osiris the scribe Ani to be true against his enemies, with the great Tchatcha Chiefs who are in the double town Pe-Tep, on the night of setting up the "Senti" of Horus, and of establishing him in the inheritance of the possessions of his father Osiris.

Now the great Tchatcha Chiefs who are in Pe-Tep are Horus, Isis, Kesta (Mesta) and Hapi. Now the "setting up of the 'Senti' of Horus" hath reference to the words which Set spake to his followers, saying "Set up the Senti." Hail, Thoth, who didst make the word of Osiris to be true against his enemies, make thou the word of the Osiris the scribe Ani to be true, in peace, against his enemies, with the great Tchatcha Chiefs who are in the Lands of the Rekhti (Taiu-Rekhti), in the night when Isis lay down, and kept watch to make lamentation for her brother Osiris.

Now the great Tchatcha Chiefs who are in Taiu-Rekhti are Isis, Horus, Kesta (Mesta) [Anpu and Thoth]. Hail, Thoth, who didst make the word of Osiris true against his enemies, make thou the word of Osiris the scribe Ani, whose word is truth, in peace, to be true against his enemies, with the great Tchatcha Chiefs who are in Abtu, on the night of the god Haker, when the dead are separated, and the spirits are judged, and when the procession taketh place in Teni.

Now the great Tchatcha Chiefs who are in Abtu are Osiris, Isis, and Up-uat. Hail, Thoth, who didst make the word of Osiris to be true against his enemies, make thou the word of the Osiris, the scribe and assessor of the sacred offerings which are made to all the gods, Ani, to be true against his enemies, with the Tchatcha Chiefs who examine the dead on the night of making the inspection of those who are to be annihilated.

Now the great Tchatcha Chiefs who are present at the examination of the dead are Thoth, Osiris, Anpu and Asten (read Astes). Now the inspection (or, counting) of those who are to be annihilated signifieth the shutting up of things from the souls of the sons of revolt. Hail, Thoth, who didst make the word of Osiris true against his enemies, make thou the word of the Osiris the scribe Ani to be true against his enemies, with the great Tchatcha Chiefs who are present at the digging up of the earth [and mixing it] with their blood, and of making the word of Osiris to be true against his enemies. As concerning the Tchatcha Chiefs who are present at the digging up of the earth in Tetu: When the Smaiu fiends of Set came [there], having transformed themselves into animals, these Tchatcha Chiefs slew them in the presence of the gods who were there, and they took their blood, and carried it to them. These things were permitted at the examination [of the wicked] by those [gods] who dwelt in Tetu. Hail, Thoth, who didst make the word of Osiris to be true against his enemies, make thou the word of the Osiris [the scribe] Ani to be true against his enemies, with the great Tchatcha Chiefs who are in Nerutef on the night of the "Hidden of Forms."

Now the great Tchatcha Chiefs who are in Nerutef are Ra, Osiris, Shu and Bebi. Now, the night of the "Hidden of Forms" referreth to the placing on the sarcophagus [of Osiris] the arm, the heel, and the thigh of Osiris Un-Nefer. Hail, Thoth, who didst make the word of Osiris true against his enemies, make thou the word of the Osiris, whose word is truth, to be true against his enemies, with the great Tchatcha Chiefs who are in Rasta, on the night when Anpu lay with his arms on the things by Osiris, and when the word of Horus was make to be true against his enemies. The great Tchatcha Chiefs who are in Rasta are Horus, Osiris, and Isis. The heart of Osiris is happy, the heart of Horus is glad, and the two halves of Egypt (Aterti) are well satisfied thereat. Hail, Thoth, who didst make the word of Osiris true against his enemies, make thou the word of the Osiris the scribe Ani, the assessor of the holy offerings made to all the gods, to be true against his enemies, with the Ten great Tchatcha Chiefs who are with Ra, and with Osiris, and with every god, and with every goddess, in the presence of the god Nebertcher. He hath destroyed his enemies, and he hath destroyed every evil thing which appertained to him.

RUBRIC: If this Chapter be recited for, or over, the deceased, he shall come forth by day, purified after death, according to the desire of his heart. Now if this Chapter be recited over him, he shall progress over the earth, and he shall escape from every fire, and none of the evil things which appertain to him shall ever be round about him; never, a million times over, shall this be.

THE CHAPTER OF OPENING THE MOUTH OF THE OSIRIS ANI. To be said:- The god Ptah shall open my mouth, and the god of my town shall unfasten the swathings, the swathings which are over my mouth. Thereupon shall come Thoth, who is equipped with words of power in great abundance, and shall untie the fetters, even the fetters of the god Set which are over my mouth. And the god Tem shall cast them back at those who would fetter me with them, and cast them at him. Then shall the god Shu open my mouth, and make an opening into my mouth with the same iron implement wherewith he opened the mouth of the gods.

I am the goddess Sekhmet, and I take my seat upon the place by the side of Amt-ur the great wind of heaven. I am the great Star-goddess Saah, who dwelleth among the Souls of Anu. Now as concerning every spell, and every word which shall be spoken against me, every god of the Divine Company shall set himself in opposition thereto.

THE CHAPTER OF BRINGING WORDS OF POWER TO THE OSIRIS ANI, who saith:-

I am Tem-Khepera who produced himself on the thighs of his divine mother. Those who dwell in Nu have been made wolves, and those who are among the Tchatcha Chiefs have become hyenas. Behold, I will gather together to myself this charm from the person with whom it is [and from the place] wherein it is [and it shall come to me] quicker than a greyhound, and swifter that light. Hail, thou who bringest the Ferry- Boat of Ra, thou holdest thy course firmly and directly in the north wind as thou sailest up the river towards the Island of Fire which is in Khert-Neter.

Behold, thou shalt gather together to thee this charm from wheresoever it may be, and from whomsoever it may be with [and it shall come to me] quicker than a greyhound, and swifter than light. It (the charm) made the transformations of Mut; it fashioned the gods [or] kept them silent; by it Mut gave the warmth [of life] to the gods. Behold, these words of power are mine, and they shall come unto me from wheresoever they may be, or with whomsoever they may be, quicker than greyhounds and swifter than light, or, according to another reading, "swifter than shadows." APPENDIX THE CHAPTER WHICH MAKETH A MAN TO REMEMBER HIS NAME IN KHERT-NETER. [The deceased] saith:- Let my name be given to me in the Great House (Per-ur), and let me remember my name in the House of Fire (Per Neser), on the night wherein the years are counted up, and the number of the months is told. I am dwelling with the Divine One, I take my seat on the eastern side of the sky. If any god cometh after me, I shall be able to declare his name forthwith.

THE CHAPTER OF GIVING A HEART TO THE OSIRIS ANI IN KHERT-NETER. He saith:- Let my heart be with me in the House of Hearts. Let my heart- case be with me in the House of heart-cases. Let my heart be with me, and let it rest in [me or] I shall not eat the cakes of Osiris in the eastern side of the Lake of Flowers, nor have a boat wherein to float down the river, nor a boat to sail up the river to thee, nor be able to embark in a boat with thee. Let my mouth be to me that I may speak therewith. Let my legs be to me that I may walk therewith. Let my arms be to me that I may overthrow the foe therewith. Let the two doors of the sky be opened to me. May Keb, the Erpat of the gods, open his jaws to me. May he open my two eyes which are blinded by swathings. May he make me to lift up my legs in walking which are tied together. May Anpu make my thighs to become vigorous. May the goddess

Sekhmet raise me, and lift me up. Let me ascend into heaven, let that which I command be performed in Het-ka-Ptah. I know how to use my heart. I am master of my heart-case. I am master of my hands and arms. I am master of my legs. I have the power to do that which my KA desireth to do. My Heart-soul shall not be kept a prisoner in my body at the gates of Amentet when I would go in in peace and come forth in peace.

THE CHAPTER OF NOT LETTING THE HEART OF THE OSIRIS, THE ASSESSOR OF THE DIVINE OFFERINGS OF ALL THE GODS, ANI, WHOSE WORD IS TRUTH BEFORE OSIRIS, BE DRIVEN BACK FROM HIM IN KHERT-NETER. He saith:- My heart of my mother. My heart of my mother. My heart-case of my transformations. Let not any one stand up to bear testimony against me. Let no one drive me away from the Tchatcha Chiefs. Let no one make thee to fall away from me in the presence of the Keeper of the Balance. Thou art my KA, the dweller in my body, the god Khnemu who makest sound my members. Mayest thou appear in the place of happiness whither we go. Let not make my name to stink Shenit Chiefs, who make men to be stable. [Let it be satisfactory unto us, and let the listening be satisfactory unto us, and let there be joy of heart to us at the weighing of words. Let not lies be told against me before the Great God, the Lord of Amentet. Verily, how great shalt thou be when thou risest up in triumph!]

RUBRIC I: These words are to be said over a scarab of green stone encircled with a band of refined copper, and [having] a ring of silver; which shall be placed on the neck of the Khu (the deceased), etc. RUBRIC II (From the Papyrus of Nu, Sheet 21): If this Chapter be known [by the deceased] he shall be declared a speaker of the truth both upon earth and in Khert-Neter, and he shall be able to perform every act which a living human being can perform. Now it is a great protection which hath been given by the god. This Chapter was found in the city of Khemenu upon the slab of ba, which was inlaid with [letters of] genuine lapis-lazuli, and was under the feet of [the statue] of the god, during the reign of His Majesty, the King of the South and North, Menkaura (Mycerinus), true of word, by Prince Herutataf, who found it during a journey which he made to inspect the temples. One Nekht was with him who was diligent in making him to understand it, and he brought it to the king as a wonderful object when he perceived that it was a thing of great mystery, [the like of] which had never [before] been seen or looked upon. This Chapter shall be recited by a man who is ceremonially clean and pure, who hath not eaten the flesh of animals, or fish, and who hath not had intercourse with women. And behold, thou shalt make a scarab of green stone, with a rim [plated] with gold, which shall be placed above the heart of a man, and it shall perform for him the "opening of the mouth." And thou shalt anoint it with myrrh unguent, and thou shalt recite over it the following words of magical power. [Here follows the text of the Chapter of Not Letting the Heart of Ani Be Taken from Him.]

THE CHAPTER OF NOT LETTING THE HEART-SOUL OF A MAN BE SNATCHED AWAY FROM HIM IN KHERT-NETER. The Osiris the scribe Ani saith:--I, even I, am he who cometh forth from the Celestial Water (Akeb). He (Akeb) produced abundance for me, and hath the mastery there in the form of the River. (This is a portion of a longer Chapter which is included in the appendix.)

APPENDIX (The following is from the Papyrus of Nefer-uben-f, Naville, op. cit., I, Bl. 72.) THE CHAPTER OF DRINKING WATER IN KHERT-NETER. The am khent priest, Nefer-uben-f, whose word is truth, saith:- I, even I, am he who cometh forth from the god Keb. The water-flood is given to him, he hath become the master thereof in the form of Hapi.
I, the am khent Nefer-uben-f, open the doors of heaven. Thoth hath opened to me the doors of Qebh (the Celestial Waters). Lo, Hepi Hepi, the two sons of the Sky, mighty in splendour, grant ye that I may be master over the water, even as Set had dominion over his evil power on the day of the storming of the Two Lands. I pass by the Great Ones, arm to shoulder, even as they pass that Great God, the Spirit who is equipped, whose name is unknown. I have passed by the Aged One of the shoulder. I am Nefer-uben-f, whose word is truth. Hath opened to me the Celestial Water Osiris. Hath opened to me the Celestial Water Thoth-Hapi, the Lord of the horizon, in his name of "Thoth, cleaver of the earth." I am master of the water, as Set is master of his weapon. I sail over the sky, I am Ra, I am Ru. I am Sma. I have eaten the Thigh, I have seized the bone and flesh. I go round about the Lake of Sekhet-Ar. Hath been

given to me eternity without limit. Behold, I am the heir of eternity, to whom hath been given everlastingness.

(The following two Chapters are from the Papyrus of Nu, Sheets 7 and 12) THE CHAPTER OF DRINKING WATER AND OF NOT BEING BURNT UP BY FIRE [IN KHERT-NETER]. Nu saith:- Hail, Bull of Amentet! I am brought unto thee. I am the paddle of Ra wherewith he transported the Aged Gods. Let me neither be burnt up nor destroyed by fire. I am Beb, the firstborn son of Osiris, to whom every god maketh an offering in the temple of his Eye in Anu. I am the divine Heir, the Mighty One, the Great One, the Resting One. I have made my name to flourish. Deliverer, thou livest in me [every day].

THE CHAPTER OF NOT BEING BOILED IN FIRE. Nu saith:- I am the paddle which is equipped, wherewith Ra transported the Aged Gods, which raised up the emissions of Osiris from the Lake of blazing fire, and he was not burned. I sit down like the Light-god, and like Khnemu, the Governor of lions. Come, cut away the fetters from him that passeth by the side of this path, and let me come forth therefrom.

THE CHAPTER OF GIVING AIR IN KHERT-NETER. The Osiris Ani saith:- I am the Egg which dwelt in the Great Cackler. I keep ward over that great place which Keb hath proclaimed upon earth. I live; it liveth. I grow up, I live, I snuff the air. I am Utcha-aab. I go round about his egg [to protect it]. I have thwarted the moment of Set. Hail, Sweet one of the Two Lands! Hail, dweller in the tchefa food! Hail, dweller in the lapis-lazuli! Watch ye over him that is in his cradle, the Babe when he cometh forth to you.

APPENDIX (From the Papyrus of Nu, Sheet 12) THE CHAPTER OF GIVING AIR TO NU IN KHERT-NETER. He saith:- Hail, thou God Temu, grant thou unto me the sweet breath which dwelleth in thy nostrils! I am the Egg which is in Kenken-ur (the Great Cackler), and I watch and guard that mighty thing which hath come into being, wherewith the god Keb hath opened the earth. I live; it liveth; I grow, I live, I snuff the air. I am the god Utcha-aabet, and I go about his egg. I shine at the moment of the mighty of strength, Suti. Hail, thou who makest sweet the time of the Two Lands! Hail, dweller among the celestial food. Hail, dweller among the beings of blue (lapis-lazuli), watch ye to protect him that is in his nest, the Child who cometh forth to you.

THE CHAPTER OF GIVING AIR IN KHERT-NETER. Nu saith:- I am the jackal of jackals. I am Shu. I draw air from the presence of the Light-god, from the uttermost limits of heaven, from the uttermost limits of earth, from the uttermost limits of the pinion of Nebeh bird. May air be given unto this young divine Babe. [My mouth is open, I see with my eyes.]

THE CHAPTER OF SNUFFING THE AIR WITH WATER IN KHERT-NETER. Hail, Tem. Grant thou unto me the sweet breath which dwelleth in thy nostrils. I am he who embraceth that great throne which is in the city of Unu. I keep watch over the Egg of Kenken-ur (the Great Cackler). I grow and flourish as it groweth and flourisheth. I live as it liveth. I snuff the air as it snuffeth the air.

THE CHAPTER OF NOT LETTING THE HEART OF A MAN BE SNATCHED AWAY FROM HIM IN KHERT-NETER. The Osiris Ani, whose word is truth, saith:- Get thee back, O messenger of every god! Art thou come to [snatch away] my heart-case which liveth? My heart-case which liveth shall not be given unto thee. [As] I advance, the gods hearken unto my propitiation [prayer] and they fall down on their faces [whilst] they are on their own land.

APPENDIX (From the Papyrus of Nu) THE CHAPTER OF NOT ALLOWING THE HEART.... TO BE CARRIED AWAY DEAD IN KHERT-NETER.
[Nu, whose word is truth, saith]:- My heart is with me, and it shall never come to pass that it be carried away. I am the Lord of Hearts, the slayer of the heart-case. I live in truth, I have my being therein. I am Horus, the Dweller in Hearts, [I am] in the Dweller in the body. I have life by my word, my heart

hath being. My heart-case shall not be snatched away from me, it shall not be wounded, it shall not be put in restraint if wounds are inflicted upon me. [If] one take possession of it I shall have my being in the body of my father Keb and in the body of my mother Nut. I have not done that which is held in abomination by the gods. I shall not suffer defeat [for] my word is truth.

THE CHAPTER OF NOT LETTING THE HEART-CASE OF A MAN BE TAKEN AWAY FROM HIM IN KHERT-NETER. The Osiris Ani saith:- Hail, ye who steal and crush heart-cases [and who make the heart of a man to go through its transformations according to his deeds: let not what he hath done harm him before you]. Homage to you, O ye Lords of Eternity, ye masters of everlastingness, take ye not this heart of Osiris Ani into your fingers, and this heart-case, and cause ye not things of evil to spring up against it, because this heart belongeth to the Osiris Ani, and this heart-case belongeth to him of the great names (Thoth), the mighty one, whose words are his members. He sendeth his heart to rule his body, and his heart is renewed before the gods. The heart of the Osiris Ani, whose word is truth, is to him; he hath gained the mastery over it. He hath not said what he hath done. He hath obtained power over his own members. His heart obeyeth him, he is the lord thereof, it is in his body, and it shall never fall away therefrom.
I command thee to be obedient unto me in Khert-Neter. I, the Osiris Ani, whose word is truth, in peace; whose word is truth in the Beautiful Amentet, by the Domain of Eternity.

APPENDIX (From the Papyrus of Nu, Sheet 5) THE CHAPTER OF NOT LETTING THE HEART OF NU, WHOSE WORD IS TRUTH, BE CARRIED AWAY FROM HIM IN KHERT-NETER. He saith:- Hail, thou Lion-god! I am Unb (the Blossom). That which is held in abomination to me is the block of slaughter of the god. Let not this my heart-case be carried away from me by the Fighting Gods in Anu. Hail, thou who dost wind bandages round Osiris, and who hast seen Set. Hail, thou who returnest after smiting and destroying him before the mighty ones! This my heart weepeth over itself before Osiris; it hath made supplication for me. I have given unto him and I have dedicated unto him the thoughts of the heart in the House of the god (Usekh-her), have brought unto him sand at the entry to Khemenu. Let not this my heart-case be carried away from me. I make you to ascend his throne, to fetter heart-cases for him in Sekhet-hetep, [to live] years of strength away from things of all kinds which are abominations to him, to carry off food from among the things which are thine, and which are in thy grasp through thy strength. And this my heart-case is devoted to the decrees of the god Tem, who guideth me through the caverns of Suti, but let not this my heart, which hath performed its desire before the Tchatcha Chiefs who are in Khert-Neter, be given to him. When they find the leg and the swathings they bury them.

THE CHAPTER OF NOT LETTING THE HEART OF NU, WHOSE WORD IS TRUTH, BE DRIVEN AWAY FROM HIM IN KHERT-NETER. He saith:- My heart of my mother. My heart of my mother. My heart-case of my existence upon the earth. Let no one stand up against me when I bear testimony in the presence of the Lords of Things. Let it not be said against me and of that which I have done "He hath committed acts which are opposed to what is right and true," and let not charges be brought up against me in the presence of the Great God, the Lord of Amentet. Homage to thee, O my heart (ab).

Homage to thee, O my heart-case. Homage to you, O my reins. Homage to you, O ye gods, who are masters of [your] beards, and who are holy by reason of your sceptres. Speak ye for me words of good import to Ra, and make ye me to have favour in the sight of Nehebkau.

THE CHAPTER OF BREATHING THE AIR AND OF HAVING POWER OVER WATER IN KHERT-NETER. The Osiris Ani saith:- Open to me! Who art thou? Whither goest thou? What is thy name? I am one of you. Who are these with you? The two Merti goddesses (Isis and Nephthys). Thou separatest head from head when [he] entereth the divine Mesqen chamber. He causeth me to set out for the temple of the gods Kem-heru. "Assembler of souls" is the name of my ferry-boat. "Those who make the hair to bristle" is the name of the oars. "Sert" ("Goad") is the name of the hold. "Steering straight in the middle" is the name of the rudder; likewise, [the boat] is a type of my being borne onward in the lake. Let there be given unto me vessels of milk, and cakes, and loaves of bread, and cups of drink, and flesh, in the Temple of Anpu. RUBRIC: If the deceased knoweth this Chapter, he shall go into, after coming forth from Khert-Neter of [the Beautiful Amentet].

THE CHAPTER OF SNUFFING THE AIR, AND OF HAVING POWER OVER THE WATER IN KHERT-NETER. The Osiris Ani saith:- Hail, thou Sycamore tree of the goddess Nut! Give me of the [water and of the] air which is in thee. I embrace that throne which is in Unu, and I keep guard over the Egg of Nekek-ur. It flourisheth, and I flourish; it liveth, and I live; it snuffeth the air, and I snuff the air, I the Osiris Ani, whose word is truth, in [peace].

THE CHAPTER OF NOT DYING A SECOND TIME IN KHERT-NETER. The Osiris Ani saith:My hiding place is opened, my hiding place is opened. The Spirits fall headlong in the darkness, but the Eye of Horus hath made me holy, and Upuati hath nursed me. I will hide myself among you, O ye stars which are imperishable. My brow is like the brow of Ra. My face is open. My heart-case is upon its throne, I know how to utter words. In very truth I am Ra himself. I am not a man of no account. I am not a man to whom violence can be done.
Thy father liveth for thee, O son of Nut. I am thy son, O great one, I have seen the hidden things which are thine. I am crowned upon my throne like the king of the gods. I shall not die a second time in Khert-Neter.

THE CHAPTER OF NOT ROTTING IN KHERT-NETER. The Osiris Ani saith:- O thou who art motionless, O thou who art motionless, O thou whose members are motionless, like unto those of Osiris. Thy members shall not be motionless, they shall not rot, they shall not crumble away, they shall not fall into decay. My members shall be made [permanent] for me as if I were Osiris. RUBRIC: If this Chapter be known by the deceased he shall never see corruption in Khert-Neter.

APPENDIX (From the Papyrus of Nu, Sheet 18) THE CHAPTER OF NOT LETTING THE BODY PERISH. The Osiris Nu saith:- Homage to thee, O my divine father Osiris! I come to embalm thee. Do thou embalm these my members, for I would not perish and come to an end [but would be] even like unto my divine father Khepera, the divine type of him that never saw corruption. Come then, strengthen my breath, O Lord of the winds, who dost magnify these divine beings who are like unto thyself. Stablish me, stablish me, and fashion me strongly, O Lord of the funeral chest.

Grant thou that I may enter into the land of everlastingness, according to that which was done for thee, along with thy father Tem, whose body never saw corruption, and who himself never saw corruption. I have never done that which
thou hatest, nay, I have acclaimed thee among those who love thy KA. Let not my body become worms, but deliver thou me as thou didst deliver thyself. I pray thee, let me not fall into rottenness, as thou lettest every god, and every goddess, and every animal, and every reptile, see corruption, when the soul hath gone out of them, after their death. And when the soul hath departed, a man seeth corruption, and the bones of his body crumble away and become stinking things, and the members decay one after the other, the bones crumble into a helpless mass, and the flesh turneth into foetid liquid.

Thus man becometh a brother unto the decay which cometh upon him, and he turneth into a myriad of worms, and he becometh nothing but worms, and an end is made of him, and perisheth in the sight of the god of day (Shu), even as do every god, and every goddess, and every bird, and every fish, and every creeping worm, and every reptile, and every beast, and every thing whatsoever. Let [all the Spirits fall] on their bellies [when] they recognize me, and behold, the fear of me shall terrify them; and thus also let it be with every being that hath died, whether it be animal, or bird, or fish, or worm, or reptile. Let life [rise out of] death. Let not the decay caused by any reptile make an end [of me], and let not [enemies] come against me in their various forms. Give thou me not over to the Slaughterer in this execution-chamber, who killeth the members, and maketh them rot, being [himself] invisible, and who destroyeth the bodies of the dead, and liveth by carnage. Let me live, and perform his order; I will do what is commanded by him. Give me not over to his fingers, let him not overcome me, for I am under thy command, O Lord of the Gods.

Homage to thee, O my divine father Osiris, thou livest with thy members. Thou didst not decay, thou didst not become worms, thou didst not wither, thou didst not rot, thou didst not putrefy, thou didst not turn into worms. I am the god Khepera, and my members shall have being everlastingly. I shall not decay, I shall not rot, I shall not putrefy, I shall not turn into worms, and I shall not see corruption before the eye of the god Shu. I shall have my being, I shall have by being; I shall live, I shall live; I shall flourish, I shall flourish, I shall flourish, I shall wake up in peace, I shall not putrefy, my intestines shall not perish, I shall not suffer injury. My eye shall not decay. The form of my face shall not disappear. My ear shall not become deaf. My head shall not be separated from my neck. My tongue shall not be removed. My hair shall not be cut off. My eyebrows shall not be shaved away, and no evil defect shall assail me. My body shall be stablished. It shall neither become a ruin, nor be destroyed on this earth.

THE CHAPTER OF NOT PERISHING AND OF BEING ALIVE IN KHERT-NETER. The Osiris Ani saith:- Hail ye children of the god Shu. The Tuat hath gained the mastery over his diadem. Among the Hamemet Spirits may I arise, even as did arise Osiris.

THE CHAPTER OF NOT GOING IN TO THE BLOCK OF THE GOD. The Osiris Ani saith:- My head was fastened on my body in heaven, O Guardian of the Earth, by Ra. [This] was granted [to me] on the day of my being stablished, when I rose up out of a state of weakness upon [my] two feet. On the day of cutting off the hair Set and the Company of the Gods fastened my head to my neck, and it became as firm as it was originally. Let nothing happen to shake it off again! Make ye me safe from the murderer of my father. I have tied together the Two Earths. Nut hath fastened together the vertebrae of my neck, and [I] behold them as they were originally, and they are seen in the order wherein they were when as yet Maat was not seen, and when the gods were not born in visible forms. I am Penti. I am the heir of the great gods, I the Osiris the scribe Ani, whose word is truth.

THE CHAPTER OF NOT BEING TRANSPORTED TO THE EAST IN KHERT-NETER. The Osiris Ani saith:- Hail, Phallus of Ra, which advanceth and beateth down opposition. Things which have been without motion for millions of years have come into life through Baba. I am stronger thereby than the strong, and I have more power thereby than the mighty. Now, let me not be carried away in a boat, or be seized violently and taken to the East, to have the festivals of Sebau Devils celebrated on me. Let not deadly wounds be inflicted upon me, and let me not be gored by horns. Thou shalt neither fall [nor] eat fish made by Tebun. Now, no evil thing of any kind whatsoever shall be done unto me by the Sebau Devils. [I shall not be gored by] horns. Therefore the Phallus of Ra, [which is] the head of Osiris, shall not be swallowed up. Behold, I shall come into me fields and I shall cut the grain. The gods shall provide me with food. Thou shalt not then be gored, Ra-Khepera. There shall not be then pus in the Eye of Tem, and it shall not be destroyed.

Violence shall not be done unto me, and I shall not be carried away in [my] boat to the East to have the festivals of the Sebau Devils celebrated on me in evil fashion. Cruel gashes with knives shall not be inflicted upon me, and I shall not be carried away in [my] boat to the East. I the Osiris, the assessor of the holy offerings of all the gods, Ani, whose word is truth, happily, the lord of fealty [to Osiris].

THE CHAPTER OF NOT LETTING THE HEAD OF A MAN BE CUT OFF FROM HIS BODY IN KHERT-NETER. The Osiris Ani saith:- I am a Great One, the son of a Great One. [I am] Fire, the son of Fire, to whom was given his head after it had been cut off. The head of Osiris was not removed from his body, and the head of Osiris Ani shall not be removed from his body. I have knitted myself together, I have made myself whole and complete. I shall renew my youth. I am Osiris Himself, the Lord of Eternity.

THE CHAPTER OF MAKING THE SOUL TO BE JOINED TO ITS BODY IN KHERT- NETER. The Osiris Ani saith:- Hail, thou god Aniu! Hail, thou god Pehreri, who dwellest in thy hall, the Great God. Grant thou that my soul may come to me from any place wherein it may be. Even if it would tarry, let my soul be brought unto me from any place wherein it may be. Thou findest the Eye of Horus standing by thee like unto those beings who resemble Osiris, who never lie down in death. Let not the Osiris Ani, whose word is truth, lie down dead among those who lie in Anu, the land wherein [souls] are joined to their bodies in thousands. Let me have possession of my Ba-soul and of my Spirit-soul, and let my word be truth with it (the Ba-soul) in every place wherein it may be. Observe then, O ye guardians of Heaven, my soul [wherever it may be]. Even if it would tarry, cause thou my Ba-soul to see my body. Thou shalt find the Eye of Horus standing by thee like [the Watchers]. Hail, ye gods who tow along the boat of the Lord of Millions of Years, who bring it over the sky of the Tuat, who make it to journey over Nent, who make Ba-souls to enter into their Spirit-bodies, whose hands hold the steering poles and guide it straight, who grasp tightly your paddles, destroy ye the Enemy; thus shall the Boat rejoice, and the Great God shall travel on his way in peace.

Moreover, grant ye that the Ba-soul of the Osiris Ani, whose word is truth before the gods, may come forth with your navel cords in the eastern part of the sky, and that it may follow Ra to the place where he was yesterday, and may set in peace, in peace in Amentet. May it gaze upon its earthly body, may it take up its abode and its Spirit-body, may it neither perish nor be destroyed for ever and for ever. RUBRIC: These words shall be said over a model of the Ba-soul made of gold, and inlaid with precious stones, which shall be placed on the breast of the Osiris.

THE CHAPTER OF NOT LETTING THE SOUL OF A MAN BE HELD CAPTIVE IN KHERTNETER. The Osiris Ani saith:- Hail, thou who art exalted! Hail, thou who art adored! Hail, Mighty One of Souls, thou divine Soul who inspirest great dread, who dost set the fear of thyself in the gods, who are enthroned upon thy mighty seat. Make thou a path for the Spirit-soul and the Ba-soul of the Osiris Ani. I am equipped with [words of power]. I am a Spirit-soul equipped with [words of power]. I have made my way to the place where are Ra and Hathor.

RUBRIC: If this Chapter be known by the deceased he shall be able to transform himself into a Spirit-soul who shall be equipped with [his soul and his shadow] in Khert-Neter, and he shall not be shut up inside any door in Amentet, when he is coming forth upon the Earth, or when he is going back into [Khert-Neter.]

THE CHAPTER OF OPENING THE TOMB TO THE BA-SOUL AND THE SHADOW, AND OF COMING FORTH BY DAY, AND OF HAVING MASTERY OVER THE TWO LEGS. The Osiris the scribe Ani, whose word is truth, saith:- The place which is closed is opened, the place which is shut (or sealed) is sealed. That which lieth down in the closed place is opened by the Ba-soul which is in it. By the Eye of Horus I am delivered. Ornaments are stablished on the brow of Ra. My stride is made long. I lift up my two thighs [in walking]. I have journeyed over a long road. My limbs are in a flourishing condition. I am Horus, the Avenger of his Father, and I bring the Urrt Crown [and set it on] its standard. The road of souls is opened. My twin soul seeth the Great God in the Boat of Ra, on the day of souls. My soul is in the front thereof with the counter of the years. Come, the Eye of Horus hath delivered for me my soul, my ornaments are stablished on the brow of Ra.

Light is on the faces of those who are in the members of Osiris. Ye shall not hold captive my soul. Ye shall not keep in durance my shadow. The way is open to my soul and to my shadow. It seeth the Great God in the shrine on the day of counting souls. It repeateth the words of Osiris. Those whose seats are invisible, who fetter the members of Osiris, who fetter Heart-souls and Spirit-souls, who set a seal upon the dead, and who would do evil to me, shall do no evil to me. Haste on the way to me. Thy heart is with thee. My Heart-soul and my Spirit-soul are equipped; they guide thee. I sit down at the head of the great ones who are chiefs of their abodes.

The wardens of the members of Osiris shall not hold thee captive, though they keep ward over souls, and set a seal on the shadow which is dead. Heaven shall not shut thee in.

RUBRIC: If this Chapter be known by the deceased he shall come forth by day, and his soul shall not be kept captive.

APPENDIX (From the Papryus of Nebseni, Sheet 6) That which was shut hath been opened [that is] the dead. That which was shut fast hath been opened by the command of the Eye of Horus, which hath delivered me. Established are the beauties on the forehead of Ra. My steps are long. My legs are lifted up. I have performed the journey, my members are mighty and are sound. I am Horus, the Avenger of his Father. I am he who bringeth along his father, and his mother, by means of his staff. The way shall be opened to him that hath power over his feet, and he shall see the Great God in the Boat of Ra, when souls are counted therein at the bows, and when the years also are counted up. Grant that the Eye of Horus, which maketh the adornments of splendour to be firm on the forehead of Ra, may deliver my soul for me, and let darkness cover your faces, O ye who would imprison Osiris. O keep not captive my soul. O keep not ward over my shadow, but let a way be opened for my soul and my shadow, and let them see the Great God in the shrine on the day of the counting of souls, and let them hold converse with Osiris, whose habitations are hidden, and those who guard the members of Osiris, and who keep ward over the Spirit-souls, and who hold captive the shadows of the dead, and who would work evil against me, so that they shall [not] work evil against me.

A way shall be for KA with thee, and thy soul shall be prepared by those who keep ward over the members of Osiris, and who hold captive the shadows of the dead. Heaven shall not keep thee fast, the earth shall not hold thee captive. Thou shalt not live with the beings who slay, but thou shalt be master of thy legs, and thou shalt advance to thy body straightway in the earth, [and to] those who belong to the shrine of Osiris and guard his members.

THE CHAPTER OF LIFTING UP THE FEET, AND OF COMING FORTH ON THE EARTH. The Osiris Ani saith:- Perform thy work, O Seker, perform thy work, O Seker, O thou who dwellest in thy circle, and who dwellest in my feet in Khert-Neter. I am he who sendeth forth light over the Thigh of heaven. I come forth in heaven. I sit down by the Light-god (Khu). O I am helpless. O I am helpless. I would walk. I am helpless. I am helpless in the regions of those who plunder in Khert-Neter, I the Osiris Ani, whose word is truth, in peace.

THE CHAPTER OF FORCING A WAY INTO AMENTET [AND OF COMING FORTH] BY DAY. The Osiris Ani saith:- The town of Unu is opened. My head is sealed up, Thoth. Perfect is the Eye of Horus. I have delivered the Eye of Horus which shineth with splendours on the brow of Ra, the Father of the gods, [I am] that self-same Osiris, [the dweller in] Amentet. Osiris knoweth his day, and he knoweth that he shall live through his period of life; I shall have by being with him. I am the Moon-god Aah, the dweller among the gods. I shall not come to an end. Stand up therefore, O Horus, for thou art counted among the gods.

APPENDIX (Naville, op. cit., I, Bl. X) THE CHAPTER OF FORCING A WAY INTO THE TUAT. The Am Khent priest Nefer- uben-f, whose word is truth, saith:- Hail, Soul, thou mighty one of terror. Behold, I have come unto thee. I see thee. I have forced a way through the Tuat. I see my father Osiris. I drive away the darkness. I love him. I have come. I see my father Osiris. He hath counted the heart of Set. I have made offerings for my father Osiris. I have opened all the ways in heaven and on earth. I love him. I have come. I have become a Spirit-body and a Spirit-soul, who is equipped. Hail, every god and every Spirit-soul, I have made the ways. I am Thoth....
ANOTHER CHAPTER OF THE TUAT AND OF COMING FORTH BY DAY. Open is the land of Unu. Shut is the head of Thoth. Perfect is the Eye of Horus. I have delivered the Eye of Horus, the shining one, the ornament of the Eye of Ra, the Father of the Gods. I am that same Osiris who dwelleth in Amentet. Osiris knoweth his day, which cometh to an end. I am Set, the Father of the Gods. I shall never come to an end.

THE CHAPTER OF COMING FORTH BY DAY AND OF LIVING AFTER DEATH. The Osiris Ani saith:- Hail, thou One, who shinest from the moon. Hail, thou One, who shinest from the moon. Grant that this Osiris Ani may come forth among thy multitudes who are at the portal. Let him be with the Light-God. Let the Tuat be opened to him. Behold, the Osiris Ani shall come forth by day to perform everything which he wisheth upon the earth among those who are living [thereon].

APPENDIX (From the Papyrus of Nu, Sheet 13) Hail, thou god Tem, who comest forth from the Great Deep, who shinest gloriously under the form of the twin Lion-gods, send forth with might thy words unto those who are in thy presence, and let the Osiris Nu enter into their assembly. He hath performed the decree which hath been spoken to the mariners at eventide, and the Osiris Nu, whose word is truth, shall live after his death, even as doth Ra every day. Behold, most certainly Ra was born yesterday, and the Osiris Nu was born yesterday. And every god shall rejoice in the life of the Osiris Nu, even as they rejoice in the life of Ptah, when he appeareth from the Great House of the Aged One which is in Anu.

THE CHAPTER OF COMING FORTH BY DAY AFTER FORCING AN ENTRANCE THROUGH THE AAMHET. The Osiris Ani saith:- Hail, Soul, thou mighty one of terror! Verily, I am here. I have come. I behold thee. I have passed through the Tuat. I have seen Father Osiris. I have scattered the gloom of night. I am his beloved one. I have come, I have seen my Father Osiris. I have stabbed the heart of Suti. I have made offerings to my Father Osiris. I have opened every way in heaven and on the earth. I am the son who loveth his Fathers (sic) Osiris. I am a Spirit-body. I am a Spirit-soul. I am equipped.
Hail, every god and every Spirit-soul. I have made the way [to Osiris]. I the Osiris the scribe Ani, whose word is truth.

THE CHAPTER OF MAKING A MAN TO RETURN TO LOOK UPON HIS HOUSE ON EARTH. The Osiris Ani saith:- I am the Lion-god who cometh forth with long strides. I have shot arrows, and I have wounded my prey. I have shot arrows, and I have wounded my prey. I am the Eye of Horus, I traverse the Eye of Horus at this season. I have arrived at the domains. Grant that the Osiris Ani may come in peace.

ANOTHER CHAPTER OF THE COMING FORTH OF A MAN BY DAY AGAINST HIS ENEMIES IN KHERT-NETER. [The Osiris Ani saith:-] I have divided the heavens. I have cleft the horizon. I have traversed the earth [following in] his footsteps. I have conquered the mighty Spirit-souls because I am equipped for millions of years with words of power. I eat with my mouth. I evacuate with my body. Behold, I am the God of the Tuat! Let these things be given unto me, the Osiris Ani, in perpetuity withou fail or diminution.

APPENDIX (From the Papyrus of Nu, Sheet 21) THE CHAPTER OF COMING FORTH AGAINST ENEMIES IN KHERT-NETER. The Osiris Nu saith:- Hail, Am-a-f (Eater of his arm), I have passed over the road. I am Ra. I have come forth from the horizon against my enemies. I have not permitted him to escape from me. I have stretched out my hand like that of the Lord of the Urrt Crown. I have lifted up my feet even as the Uraei-goddesses lift themselves up. I have not permitted the enemy [to be saved] from me. As for mine enemy, he hath been given to me, and he shall not be delivered from me. I stand up like Horus. I sit down like Ptah. I am strong like Thoth. I am mighty like Tem. I walk with my legs. I speak with my mouth. I chase my enemy. He hath been given unto me, and he shall not be delivered from me.

A HYMN OF PRAISE TO RA WHEN HE RISETH UPON THE HORIZON, AND WHEN HE SETTETH IN THE LAND OF LIFE.

Osiris the scribe Ani saith:- Homage to thee, O Ra, when thou risest as Tem-Heru-Khuti. Thou art to be adored. Thy beauties are before mine eyes, [thy] radiance is upon my body. Thou goest forth to thy setting in the Sektet Boat with [fair] winds, and thy heart is glad; the heart of the Matet Boat rejoiceth. Thou stridest over the heavens in peace, and all thy foes are cast down; the stars which never rest sing hymns of praise unto thee, and the stars which are imperishable glorify thee as thou sinkest to rest in the horizon of Manu, O thou who art beautiful at morn and at eve, O thou lord who livest, and art established, O my Lord! Homage to thee, O thou who art Ra when thou risest, and who art Tem when thou settest in beauty. Thou risest and thou shinest on the back of thy mother [Nut], O thou who art crowned the king of the gods! Nut welcometh thee, and payeth homage unto thee, and Maat, the everlasting and never-changing goddess, embraceth thee at noon and at eve.

Thou stridest over the heavens, being glad at heart, and the Lake of Testes is content. The Sebau-fiend hath fallen to the ground, his fore-legs and his hind-legs have been hacked off him, and the knife hath severed the joints of his back. Ra hath a fair wind, and the Sektet Boat setteth out on its journey, and saileth on until it cometh into port. The gods of the South, the gods of the North, the gods of the West, and the gods of the East praise thee, O thou Divine Substance, from whom all living things came into being.

Thou didst send forth the word when the earth was submerged with silence, O thou Only One, who didst dwell in heaven before ever the earth and the mountains came into being. Hail, thou Runner, Lord, Only One, thou maker of the things that are, thou hast fashioned the tongue of the Company of the Gods, thou hast produced whatsoever cometh forth from the waters, thou springest up out of them above the submerged land of the Lake of Horus. Let me breathe the air which cometh forth from thy nostrils, and the north wind which cometh forth from thy mother Nut.
Make thou my Spirit-soul to be glorious, O Osiris, make thou my Heart-soul to be divine. Thou art worshipped as thou settest, O Lord of the gods, thou art exalted by reason of thy wondrous works. Shine thou with the rays of light upon my body day by day, upon me, Osiris the scribe, the assessor of the divine offerings of all the gods, the overseer of the granary of the Lords of Abydos, the real royal scribe who loveth thee, Ani, whose word is truth, in peace.

Praise be unto thee, O Osiris, the Lord of Eternity, Un-Nefer, Heru- Khuti (Harmakhis), whose forms are manifold, whose attributes are majestic [Praise be unto thee], O thou who art Ptah-Seker-Tem in Anu, thou Lord of the hidden shrine, thou Creator of the House of the KA of Ptah (Het-ka-Ptah) and of the gods [therein], thou Guide of the Tuat, who art glorified when thou settest in Nu (the Sky). Isis embraceth thee in peace, and she driveth away the fiends from the entrances of thy paths. Thou turnest thy face towards Amentet, and thou makest the earth to shine as with refined copper. Those who have lain down in death rise up to see thee, they breathe the air, and they look upon thy face when the disk riseth on the horizon. Their hearts are at peace since they behold thee, o thou who art Eternity and Everlastingness.

THE SOLAR LITANY Homage to you, O ye gods of the Dekans in Anu, and to you, O ye Hememet-spirits in Kher Aha, and to thee, O Unti, who art the most glorious of all the gods who are hidden in Anu, O grant thou unto me a path whereover I may pass in peace, for I am just and true; I have not spoken falsehood wittingly, nor have I done aught with deceit. Homage to thee, O An in Antes, Heru-khuti, who dost with long strides march across the heavens, O grant thou unto me a path whereover I may pass in peace, for I am just and true; I have not spoken falsehood wittingly, nor have I done aught with deceit. Homage to thee, O Everlasting Soul, thou Soul who dwellest in Tetu, Un-Nefer, the son of Nut, who art the Lord of Akert, O grant thou unto me a path whereover I may pass in peace, for I am just and true; I have not spoken falsehood wittingly, nor have done aught with deceit.

Homage to thee in thy dominion over Tetu, upon whose brow the Urrt Crown is established, thou One who createst the strength to protect thyself, and who dwellest in peace, O grant thou unto me a path whereover I may pass in peace, for I am just and true; I have not spoken falsehood wittingly, nor have I done aught with deceit. Homage to thee, O Lord of the Acacia Tree, whose Seker Boat is set upon its sledge, who turnest back the Fiend, the Evildoer, and dost cause the Eye of Ra (utchat) to rest upon its seat, O grant thou unto me a path whereover I may pass in peace, for I am just and true; I have not spoken falsehood wittingly, nor have I done aught with deceit. Homage to thee, O thou who art mighty in thine hour, thou great and mighty Prince who dost dwell in Anrutef, thou Lord of Eternity and Creator of the Everlastingness, thou Lord of Hensu, O grant thou unto me a path whereover I may pass in peace, for I am just and true; I have not spoken falsehood wittingly, nor have I done aught with deceit. Homage to thee, O thou who restest upon Truth, thou Lord of Abtu, whose limbs form the substance of Ta-tchesert, unto whom fraud and deceit are abominations, O grant thou unto me a path whereover I may pass in peace, for I am just and true; I have not spoken falsehood wittingly, nor have I done aught with deceit. Homage to thee, O thou who dwellest in thy boat, who dost bring Hapi (the Nile) forth from his cavern, whose body is the light, and who dwellest in Nekhen, O grant thou unto me a path whereover I may pass in peace, for I am just and true; I have not spoken falsehood wittingly, nor have I done aught with deceit. Homage to thee, O thou Creator of the gods, thou King of the South and North, Osiris, whose word is truth, who rulest the world by thy gracious goodness, thou Lord of the Atebui, O grant thou unto me a path whereover I may pass in peace, for I am just and true; I have not spoken falsehood wittingly, nor have I done aught with deceit.

APPENDIX (From the Saite Recension, ed. Lepsius, Bl. V) Homage to thee, O thou who comest as Tem, who didst come into being to create the Company of the Gods. Homage to thee, O thou who comest as the Soul of Souls, the Holy One in Amentet. Homage to thee, O President of the Gods, who illuminest the Tuat with thy beauties. Homage to thee, O thou who comest as the Light-god, who travellest in thy Disk.

Homage to thee, O thou greatest of all gods, who are crowned King in heaven, Governor in the Tuat. Homage to thee, O thou who makest a way through the Tuat, who dost lead the way through all doors. Homage to thee, O thou who art among the gods, who dost weigh words in Khert-Neter. Homage to thee, O thou who dwellest in thy secret places, who dost fashion the Tuat with thy might. Homage to thee, O great one, O mighty one, thine enemies have fallen in places where they were smitten. Homage to thee, O thou who hast hacked the Sebau-fiends in pieces, and hast annihilated Aapep. Grant thou the sweet breeze of the north wind to the Osiris Auf-ankh, whose word is truth.

A HYMN OF PRAISE TO RA WHEN HE RISETH IN THE EASTERN PART OF HEAVEN. Those who are in his following rejoice, and the Osiris, the scribe Ani, whose word is truth, saith: Hail, thou Disk, thou lord of rays, who risest on the horizon day by day. Shine thou with thy beams of light upon the face of the Osiris Ani, whose word is truth, for he singeth hymns of praise to thee at dawn, and he maketh thee to sit at eventide [with words of adoration]. May the soul of the Osiris Ani, whose word is truth, come forth with thee into heaven! May he set out with thee in the Matet Boat [in the morning], may he come into port in the Sektet Boat [in the evening], and may he cleave his path among the stars of heaven which never rest. The Osiris Ani, whose word is truth, being at peace [with his god], maketh adoration to his Lord, the Lord of Eternity, and saith:-

Homage to thee, O Heru-khuti, who art the god Khepera, the self-created. When thou risest on the horizon and sheddest thy beams of light upon the Lands of the South and of the North, thou art beautiful, yea beautiful, and all the gods rejoice when they behold thee, the king of heaven. The goddess, the Lady of the Hour, is stablished upon thy head, her Uraei of the South and of the North are upon thy brow, and she taketh up her place before thee. The god Thoth is stablished in the bows of thy boat to destroy utterly all thy foes. Those who dwell in the Tuat come forth to meet thee, and they bow to the earth in homage as they come towards thee, to look upon thy beautiful Form. And I, Ani, have come into thy presence, so that I may be with thee, and may behold thy Disk every day. Let me not be kept captive [by the tomb], and let me not be turned back [on my way].
Let the members of my body be made new again when I contemplate thy beauties, even as are the members of all thy favoured ones, because I am one of those who worshipped thee upon earth. Let me arrive in the Land of Eternity, let me enter into the Land of Everlastingness. This, O my Lord, behold thou shalt ordain for me. AND MOREOVER, THE OSIRIS ANI, WHOSE WORD IS TRUTH, IN PEACE, THE TRUTH-SPEAKER, SAITH:-

Homage to thee, O thou who risest on thy horizon in the form of Ra, who restest upon Law, [which can neither be changed nor altered]. Thou passest over the sky, and every face, watcheth thee and thy course, for thou thyself art hidden from their gaze. Thou dost show thyself [to them] at dawn and at eventide each day. The Sektet Boat, wherein Thy Majesty dwelleth, setteth forth on its journey with vigour. Thy beams [fall] upon all faces, thy light with its manifold colours is incomprehensible [to man], and thy brilliant rays cannot be reported. The Lands of the Gods see thee, they could write [concerning thee]; the Deserts of Punt could count thee. Thy creation is hidden. It is one by the opening of thy mouth. Thy form is the head of Nu. May he (Ani) advance, even as thou dost advance, without cessation, even as Thy Majesty [ceaseth not to advance] even for a moment. With great strides thou dost in one little moment pass over limitless distances which would need millions and hundreds of thousands of years [for a man to pass over; this] thou doest, and then thou sinkest to rest. Thou bringest to an end the hours of the night, even as thou stridest over them. Thou bringest them to an end by thine own ordinance, and dawn cometh on the earth. Thou settest thyself before thy handiwork in the form of Ra, and thou rollest up on the horizon.......

Thou sendest forth light when thy form raiseth itself up, thou ordainest the increase of thy splendours. Thou mouldest thy limbs as thou advancest, thou bringest them forth, thou who wast never brought forth, in the form of Ra, who rolleth up into the height of heaven. Grant thou that I may reach the heaven of eternity, and the region where thy favoured ones dwell. May I unite with those holy and perfect Spirit-souls of Khert-Neter. May I come forth with them to behold thy beauties as thou rollest on at eventide, as thou journeyest to thy mother Nut (the Night-sky), and dost place thyself at the right hand (in the West).

My two hands are raised to thee in praise and thanksgiving when thou settest in life. Behold, thou art the Creator of Eternity, who art adored when thou settest in Nu. I have set thee in my heart, without wavering, O thou who art more divine than the gods. The Osiris Ani, whose word is truth, saith:- Praise and thanksgiving be unto thee, O thou who rollest on like unto gold, thou Illuminer of the Two Lands on the day of thy birth. Thy mother brought thee forth on her hand, and thou didst light up with splendour the circle which is travelled over by the Disk. O Great Light who rollest across Nu, thou dost raise up the generations of men from the deep source of thy waters, and dost make to keep festivals all districts and cities, and all habitations. Thou protectest [them] with thy beauties. Thy KA riseth up with the celestial food hu and tchefau.

O thou mightily victorious one, thou Power of Powers, who makest strong thy throne against the sinful ones, whose risings on thy throne in the Sektet Boat are mighty, whose strength is widespread in the Atett Boat, make thou the Osiris Ani to be glorious by virtue of his word, which is truth, in Khert-Neter. Grant thou that he may be in Amentet free from evil, and let [his] offences be [set] behind thee. Grant thou that he may [live there] a devoted slave of the

Spirit-souls. Let him mingle among the Heart-souls who live in Ta-tchesert (the Holy Land). Let him travel about in the Sekhet-Aaru (the Elysian Fields), conformably to [thy] decree with joy of heart- him the Osiris Ani, whose word is truth. [And the god maketh answer]:--Thou shalt come forth into heaven, thou shalt sail over the sky, and thou shalt hold loving intercourse with the Star-gods. Praises shall be made to thee in the Boat. Thy name shall be proclaimed in the Atett Boat. Thou shalt look upon Ra within his shrine. Thou shalt make the Disk to set [with prayer] every day. Thou shalt see the Ant Fish in his transformations in the depths of the waters of turquoise. Thou shalt see the Abtu Fish in his time. It shall be that the Evil One shall fall when he deviseth a plan to destroy thee, and the joints of his neck and back shall be hacked asunder. Ra saileth with a fair wind, and the Sektet Boat progresseth and cometh into port. The mariners of Ra rejoice, and the heart of the Lady of the Hour is glad, for the enemy of her Lord hath been cast to the ground. Thou shalt behold Horus standing on the pilot's place in the Boat, and Thoth and Maat shall stand one on each side of him.

All the gods shall rejoice when they behold Ra coming in peace to make the hearts of the Spirit- souls to live, and the Osiris Ani, whose word is truth, the assessor of the holy offerings of the Lords of Thebes, shall be with them!

THE CHAPTER OF THE NEW MOON THE FOLLOWING IS TO BE RECITED ON THE DAY OF THE MONTH (NEW MOON DAY). The Osiris the scribe Ani, whose word is truth, in peace, whose word is truth, saith:- Ra ascendeth his throne on his horizon, and the Company of his Gods follow in his train. The God cometh forth from his hidden place, [and] tchefau food falleth from the eastern horizon of heaven at the word of Nut. They (the gods) rejoice over the paths of Ra, the Great Ancestor [as] he journeyeth round about. Therefore art thou exalted, O Ra, the dweller in thy Shrine.

Thou swallowest the winds, thou drawest into thyself the north wind, thou eatest up the flesh of thy seat on the day when thou breathest truth. Thou dividest [it among] the gods who are [thy] followers. [Thy] Boat saileth on travelling among the Great Gods at thy word. Thou countest thy bones, thou gatherest together thy members, thou settest thy face towards Beautiful Amentet, and thou comest there, being made new every day. Behold, thou art that Image of Gold, thou hast the unitings of the disks of the sky, thou hast quakings, thou goest round about, and art made new each day. Hail! There is rejoicing in the horizon!

The gods who dwell in the sky descend the ropes [of thy Boat] when they see the Osiris Ani, whose word is truth, they ascribe praise unto him as unto Ra. The Osiris Ani is a Great Chief. [He] seeketh the Urrt Crown. His provisions are apportioned to him- the Osiris Ani, whose word is truth. [His] fate is strong from the exalted body of the Aamu gods, who are in the presence of Ra. The Osiris Ani, whose word is truth, is strong on the earth and in Khert-Neter. O Osiris Ani, whose word is truth, wake up, and be strong like unto Ra every day. The Osiris Ani, whose word is truth, shall not tarry, he shall not remain motionless in this land for ever. Right well shall he see with his two eyes, right well shall he hear with his two ears, the things which are true, the things which are true.

The Osiris Ani, whose word is truth, is in Anu, the Osiris Ani, whose word is truth, is as Ra, and he is exalted by reason of [his] oars among the Followers of Nu. The Osiris Ani, whose word is truth, cannot tell what he hath seen [or] narrate [what he hath heard] in the House of the God of Mysteries. Hail! Let there be shouts of acclamation of the Osiris Ani, whose word is truth, the divine body of Ra in the Boat of Nu, who beareth propitiatory offerings for the KA of the god of that which he loveth. The Osiris Ani, whose word is truth, in peace, whose word is truth, is like Horus, the mighty one of transformations.

RUBRIC: This Chapter is to be recited over a boat seven cubits long, made of green stone of the Tchatchau. Make a heaven of stars, and purify it and cleanse it with natron and incense. Make then a figure of Ra upon a tablet of new stone in paint, and set it in the bows of the boat. Then make a figure of the deceased whom thou wilt make perfect, [and place it] in the boat. Make it to sail in the Boat of Ra, and Ra himself shall look upon it. Do not these things in the presence of any one except thyself, or thy father, or thy son. Then let them keep guard over their faces, and they shall see the deceased in Khert-Neter in the form of a messenger of Ra.

A HYMN TO RA [WHICH IS TO BE SUNG] ON THE DAY OF THE MONTH (THE DAY OF THE NEW MOON) [WHEN] THE BOAT OF RA SAILETH. [The Osiris the scribe Ani, whose word is truth, saith:-] Homage to thee, O thou who dwellest in thy Boat. Thou rollest on, thou rollest on, thou sendest forth light, thou sendest forth light. Thou decreest rejoicing for [every] man for millions of years unto those who love him. Thou givest [thy] face to the Hememet spirits, thou god Khepera who dwellest in thy Boat. Thou hast overthrown the Fiend Aapep. O ye Sons of Keb, overthrow ye the enemies of the Osiris Ani, whose word is truth, and the fiends of destruction who would destroy the Boat of Ra. Horus hath cut off your heads in heaven. Ye who were in the forms of geese, your navel strings are on the earth. The animals are set upon the earth..... in the form of fish. Every male fiend and every female fiend shall be destroyed by the Osiris Ani, whose word is truth.

Whether the fiends descend from out of heaven, or whether they come forth from the earth, or whether they advance on the waters, or whether they come from among the Star-gods, Thoth, [the son of Aner], coming forth from Anerti shall hack them to pieces. And the Osiris Ani shall make them silent and dumb. And behold ye, this god, the mighty one of slaughters, the terror of whom is most great, shall wash himself clean in your blood, and he shall bathe in your gore, and ye shall be destroyed by the Osiris Ani in the Boat of his Lord Ra- Horus. The heart of the Osiris Ani, whose word is truth, shall live. His mother Isis giveth birth to him, and Nephthys nurseth him, just as Isis gave birth to Horus, and Nephthys nursed him.

[He] shall repulse the Smait fiends of Suti. They shall see the Urrt Crown stablished upon his head, and they shall fall down upon their faces [and worship him]. Behold, O ye Spirit-souls, and men, and gods, and ye dead, when ye see the Osiris Ani, whose word is truth, in the form of Horus, and the favoured one of the Urrt Crown, fall ye down upon your faces. The word of the Osiris Ani is truth before his enemies in heaven above, and on earth beneath, and before the Tchatchau Chiefs of every god and of every goddess.

RUBRIC: This Chapter shall be recited over a large hawk standing upright with the White Crown upon his head, [and over figures of] Tem, Shu, Tefnut, Keb, Nut, Osiris, Isis, [Suti] and Nephthys. And they shall be painted in colour upon a new tablet, which shall be placed in a boat, together with a figure of the deceased. Anoint them with heken oil, and offer unto them burning incense, and geese, and joints of meat roasted. It is an act of praise to Ra as he journeyeth in his boat, and it will make a man to have his being with Ra, and to travel with him wheresoever he goeth, and it will most certainly cause the enemies of Ra to be slain. And the Chapter of travelling shall be recited on the sixth day of the festival.

APPENDIX (From the Turin Papyrus) ANOTHER CHAPTER WHICH IS TO BE RECITED WHEN THE MOON RENEWETH ITSELF ON THE DAY OF THE MONTH [WHEREON IT DOETH THIS]. Osiris unfettereth the storm-cloud in the body of heaven, and is unfettered himself; Horus is made strong happily each day. He whose transformations are many hath had offerings made unto him at the moment, and he hath made an end of the storm which is in the face of the Osiris, Auf-ankh, whose word is truth. Verily, he cometh, and he is Ra in journeying, and he is the four celestial gods in the heavens above. The Osiris Auf-ankh, whose word is truth, cometh forth in his day, and he embarketh among the tackle of the boat.

RUBRIC: If this Chapter be known by the deceased he shall become a perfect Spirit-soul in Khert-Neter, and he shall not die a second time, and he shall eat his food side by side with Osiris. If this Chapter be known by the deceased upon earth, he shall become like unto Thoth, and he shall be adored by those who live. He shall not fall headlong at the moment of the intensity of the royal flame of the goddess Bast, and the Great Prince shall make him to advance happily.

THE CHAPTER OF ADVANCING TO THE TCHATCHAU CHIEFS OF OSIRIS. The Osiris Ani, whose word is truth, saith:- I have built a house for my Ba-soul in the sanctuary in Tetu. I sow seed in the town of Pe (Buto). I have ploughed the fields with my labourers. My palm tree [standeth upright and is] like Menu upon it. I abominate abominable things. I will not eat the things which are abominations unto me. What I abominate is filth: I will not eat it. I shall not be destroyed by the offerings of propitiation and the sepulchral meals. I will not approach filth [to touch it] with my hands, I will not tread upon it with my sandals. For my bread shall be made of the white barley, and my ale shall be made from the red grain of the god Hapi (the Nile-god), which the Sektet Boat and the Atett Boat shall bring [unto me], and I will eat my food under the leaves of the trees whose beautiful arms I myself do know. O what splendour shall the White Crown make for me which shall be lifted up on me by the Uraei-goddesses! O Doorkeeper of Sehetep-taui, bring thou to me that wherewith the cakes of propitiation are made. Grant thou to me that I may lift up the earth.

May the Spirit-souls open to me [their] arms, and let the Company of the Gods hold their peace whilst the Hememet spirits hold converse with the Osiris Ani. May the hearts of the gods lead him in his exalted state into heaven among the gods who appear in visible forms. If any god, or any goddess, attack the Osiris Ani, whose word is truth, when he setteth out, the Ancestor of the year who liveth upon hearts [Osiris] shall eat him when he cometh forth from Abydos, and the Ancestors of Ra shall reckon with him, and the Ancestors of Light shall reckon with him. [He is] a god of splendour [arrayed in] the apparel of heaven, and he is among the Great Gods.

Now the subsistence of the Osiris Ani, whose word is truth, is among the cakes and the ale which are made for your mouths. I enter in by the Disk, I come forth by the god Ahui. I shall hold converse with the Followers of the Gods. I shall hold converse with the Disk. I shall hold converse with the Hememet-spirits. He shall set the terror of me in the thick darkness, in the inside of the goddess Mehurt, by the side of his forehead. Behold, I shall be with Osiris, and my perfection shall be his perfection among the Great Gods. I shall speak unto him with the words of men, I shall listen, and he shall repeat to me the words of the gods. I, the Osiris Ani, whose word is truth, in peace, have come equipped. Thou makest to approach [thee] those who love thee. I am a Spirit-soul who is better equipped than any [other] Spirit-soul.

THE CHAPTER OF MAKING THE TRANSFORMATION INTO A SWALLOW. The Osiris Ani, whose word is truth, saith:- I am a swallow, [I am] a swallow. [I am] that Scorpion, the daughter of Ra. Hail, O ye gods whose odour is sweet. Hail, O ye gods whose odour is sweet. Hail, Flame, who comest forth from the horizon. Hail, thou who art in the city. I have brought the Warder of his corner there. Give me thy two hands, and let me pass my time in the Island of Flame. I have advanced with a message, I have come having the report thereof [to make]. Open to me. How shall I tell that which I have seen there? I am like Horus, the governor of the Boat, when the throne of his father was given unto him, and when Set, that son of Nut, was [lying] under the fetters which he had made for Osiris. He who is in Sekhem hath inspected me. I stretch out my arms over Osiris.

I have advanced for the examination, I have come to speak there. Let me pass on and deliver my message. I am he who goeth in, [I am] judged, [I] come forth magnified at the Gate of Nebertcher. I am purified at the Great Uart. I have done away my wickednesses. I have put away utterly my offences. I have put away utterly all the taints of evil which appertained to me [upon the earth]. I have purified myself, I have made myself to be like a god. Hail, O ye Doorkeepers, I have completed my journey. I am like unto you. I have come forth by day. I have advanced on my legs. I have gained the master over [my] footsteps. [Hail, ye] Spirit-souls! I, even I, do know the hidden roads and the Gates of Sekhet Aaru. I live there. Verily, I, even I, have come, I have overthrown my enemies upon the earth, although my body lieth a mummy in the tomb.

APPENDIX RUBRIC: (Naville, op. cit., II, Bl. 202) If this Chapter be known by the deceased, he shall enter in after he hath come forth by day. RUBRIC: (Saite Recension) If this Chapter be known by the deceased, he shall come forth by day from Khert-Neter, and he shall go [again] after he hath come forth. If this Chapter be not known [by the deceased], he shall not go in again after he hath come forth [and he] shall not know [how] to come forth by day.

[THE CHAPTER] OF MAKING THE TRANSFORMATION INTO A HAWK OF GOLD. The Osiris Ani saith:- I have risen up out of the seshett chamber, like the golden hawk which cometh forth from his egg. I fly, I alight like a hawk with a back of seven cubits, and the wings of which are like unto the mother-of-emerald of the South. I have come forth from the Sektet Boat, and my heart hath been brought unto me from the mountain of the East. I have alighted on the Atet Boat, and there have been brought unto me those who dwelt in their substance, and they bowed in homage before me. I have risen, I have gathered myself together like a beautiful golden hawk, with the head of the Benu, and Ra hath entered in [to hear my speech]. I have taken my seat among the great gods, [the children of] Nut. I have settled myself, the Sekhet-hetepet (the Field of Offerings) is before me. I eat therein, I become a Spirit-soul therein, I am supplied with food in abundance therein, as much as I desire. The Grain-god (Nepra) hath given unto me food for my throat, and I am master over myself and over the attributes of my head.

[THE CHAPTER OF] MAKING THE TRANSFORMATION INTO A DIVINE HAWK. The Osiris Ani saith:- Hail, thou Great God, come thou to Tetu. Make thou ready for me the ways, and let me go round [to visit] my thrones. I have laboured. I have made myself perfect. O grant thou that I may be held in fear. Create thou awe of me. Let the gods of the Tuat be afraid of me, and let them fight for me in their halls. Permit not thou to come nigh unto me him that would attack me, or would injure me in the House of Darkness. Cover over the helpless one, hide him. Let do likewise the gods who hearken unto the word [of truth], the Khepriu gods who are in the following of Osiris. Hold ye your peace then, O ye gods, whilst the God holdeth speech with me, he who listeneth to the truth. I speak unto him my words. Osiris, grant thou that that which cometh forth from thy mouth may circulate to me. Let me see thine own Form. Let thy Souls envelop me. Grant thou that I may come forth, and that I may be master of my legs, and let me live there like Nebertcher upon his throne. Let the gods of the Tuat hold me in fear, and let them fight for me in their halls. Grant thou that I may move forward with him and with the Ariu gods, and let me be firmly stablished on my pedestal like the Lord of Life.

Let me be in the company of Isis, the goddess, and let [the gods] keep me safe from him that would do an injury unto me. Let none come to see the helpless one. May I advance, and may I come to the Henti boundaries of the sky. Let me address words to Keb, and let me make supplicaion to the god Hu with Nebertcher. Let the gods of the Tuat be afraid of me, and let them fight for me in their halls. Let them see that thou hast provided me with food for the festival. I am one of those Spirit-souls who dwell in the Light-god. I have made my form in his Form, when he cometh to Tetu. I am a Spirit-body among his Spirit- bodies; he shall speak unto thee the things [which concern] me. Would that he would cause me to be held in fear! Would that he would create [in them] awe of me! Let the gods of the Tuat be afraid of me, and let them fight for me [in their halls]. I, even I, am a Spirit-soul, a dweller in the Light-god, whose form hath been created in divine flesh. I am one of those Spirit-souls who dwell in the Light-god, who were created by Tem himself, and who exist in the blossoms of his Eye. He hath made to exist, he hath made glorious, and he hath magnified their faces during their existence with him.

Behold, he is Alone in Nu. They acclaim him when he cometh forth from the horizon, and the gods and the Spirit-souls who have come into being with him ascribe fear unto him. I am one of the worms which have been created by the Eye of the Lord One. And behold, when as yet Isis had not given birth to Horus, I was flourishing, and I had waxed old, and had become pre-eminent among the Spirit-souls who had come into being with him. I rose up like a divine hawk, and Horus endowed me with a Spirit-body with his soul, so that [I] might take possession of the property of Osiris in the Tuat. He shall say to the twin Lion-gods for me, the Chief of the House of the Nemes Crown, the Dweller in his cavern: Get thee back to the heights of heaven, for behold, inasmuch as thou art a Spirit-body with the creations of Horus, the Nemes Crown shall not be to thee: [but] thou shalt have speech even to the uttermost limits of the heavens. I, the warder, took possession of the property of Horus [which belonged] to Osiris in the Tuat, and Horus repeated to me what his father Osiris had said unto him in the years [past], on the days of his burial.

Give thou to me the Nemes Crown, say the twin Lion-gods for me. Advance thou, come along the road of heaven, and look upon those who dwell in the uttermost limits of the horizon. The gods of the Tuat shall hold thee in fear, and they shall fight for thee in their halls. The god Auhet belongeth to them. All the gods who guard the shrine of the Lord One are smitten with terror at [my] words. Hail, saith the god who is exalted upon his coffer to me! He hath bound on the Nemes Crown, [by] the decree of the twin Lion-gods. The god Aahet hath made a way for me. I am exalted [on the coffer], the twin Lion-gods have bound the Nemes Crown on me and my two locks of hair are given unto me.

He hath established for me my heart by his own flesh, and by his great, two-fold strength, and I shall not fall headlong before Shu. I am Hetep, the Lord of the two Uraei-goddesses who are to be adored. I know the Light-god, his winds are in my body. The Bull which striketh terror [into souls] shall not repulse me. I come daily into the House of the twin Lion-gods. I come forth therefrom into the House of Isis. I look upon the holy things which are hidden. I see the being who is therein. I speak to the great ones of Shu, they repulse him that is wrathful in his hour.
I am Horus who dwelleth in his divine Light. I am master of his crown. I am master of his radiance. I advance towards the Henti boundaries of heaven. Horus is upon his seat. Horus is upon his thrones. My face is like that of a divine hawk. I am one who is equipped [like] his lord. I shall come forth to Tetu. I shall see Osiris. I shall live in his actual presence.... Nut. They shall see me. I shall see the gods [and] the Eye of Horus burning with fire before my eyes. They shall reach out their hands to me. I shall stand up. I shall be master of him that would subject me to restraint. They shall open the holy paths to me, they shall see my form, they shall listen to my words. [Homage] to you, O ye gods of the Tuat, whose faces are turned back, whose powers advance, conduct ye me to the Star-gods which never rest. Prepare ye for me the holy ways to the Hemat house, and to your god, the Soul, who is the mighty one of terror.

Horus hath commanded me to lift up your faces; do ye look upon me. I have risen up like a divine hawk. Horus hath made me to be a Spirit-body by means of his Soul, and to take possession of the things of Osiris in the Tuat. Make ye for me a path. I have travelled and I have arrived at those who are chiefs of their caverns, and who are guardians of the House of Osiris. I speak unto them his mighty deeds. I made them to know concerning his victories. He is ready [to butt with his] two horns at Set. They know him who hath taken possession of the god Hu, and who hath taken possession of the Powers of Tem.

Travel thou on thy way safely, cry out the gods of the Tuat to me. O ye who make your names pre-eminent, who are chiefs in your shrines, and who are guardians of the House of Osiris, grant, I pray you, that I may come to you. I have bound up and I have gathered together your Powers. I have directed the Powers of the ways, the wardens of the horizon, and of the Hemat House of heaven. I have stablished their fortresses for Osiris. I have prepared the ways for him. I have performed the things which [he] hath commanded. I come forth to Tetu. I see Osiris. I speak to him concerning the matter of his Great Son, whom he loveth, and concerning [the smiting of] the heart of Set. I look upon the lord who was helpless. How shall I make them to know the plans of the gods, and that which Horus did without the knowledge of his father Osiris?

Hail, Lord, thou Soul, most awful and terrible, behold me. I have come, I make thee to be exalted! I have forced a way though the Tuat. I have opened the roads which appertain to heaven, and those which appertain to the earth, and no one hath opposed me therein. I have exalted thy face, O Lord of Eternity.

APPENDIX (In the Papyrus of Nu, Sheet 14, the Chapter ends with the following.) Exalted art thou on thy throne, O Osiris! Thou hast heard fair things, O Osiris! Thy strength is vigorous, O Osiris! Thy head is fastened on thy body, O Osiris! Thy neck is made firm, O Osiris! Thy heart is glad, [O Osiris!]. Thy speech is made effective, O Osiris! Thy princes rejoice Thou art established the Bull in Amentet. Thy son Horus hath ascended thy trrone, and all life is with him. Millions of years minister unto him, and millions of years hold him in fear. The Company of the Gods are his servants, and they fold him in fear. The god Tem, the Governor, the only One among the gods, hath spoken, and his word passeth not away. Horus is both the divine food and the sacrifice. He made haste to gather together [the members of] of his father. Horus is his deliverer. Horus is his deliverer. Horus hath sprung from the essence of his divine father and from his decay. He hath become the Governor of Egypt. The gods shall work for him, and they shall toil for him for million of years. He shall make millions of years to live through his Eye, the only one of its lord, Nebertcher.]

(From the Turin Papyrus, Bl. XXX) Exalted is thy throne, O Osiris. Thou hearest well, O Osiris. Thy strength flourisheth, O Osiris. I have fastened thy head [on thy] body for thee. I have stablished thy throat, the throne of the joy of thy heart. Thy words are stable. Thy shenit princes are glad. Thou art stablished as the Bull of Amentet. Thy son Horus hath ascended thy throne. All life is with him. Millions of years work for him. The Company of the Gods fear him. Tem, the One Power of the Gods, hath spoken, and what he hath said is not changed, Hetu Aabi. Horus hath stood up. I have gone about collecting his father. Horus hath delivered his father. Horus hath delivered [his mother]. My mother is Horus. My brother is Horus. My uncle is Horus. I have come. Horus followeth his father.... there the dirt of his head. The gods shall serve him. Millions of years...... in his Eye, the Only One of its Lord, Neb-er-tcher.

THE CHAPTER OF BEING TRANSFORMED INTO THE PRINCE OF THE TCHATCHAU CHIEFS.

The Osiris Nu, whose word is truth, saith:- I am the god Tem, the maker of the sky, the creator of the things which are, who cometh forth from the earth, who made the seed of man to come into being, the Lord of things, who fashioned the gods, the Great God, who created himself, the Lord of Life, who made to flourish the Two Companies of the Gods. Homage to you, O ye divine Lords of things, ye holy beings, whose seats are veiled! Homage to you, O ye Lords of Eternity, whose forms are concealed, whose sanctuaries are mysteries, whose places of abode are not known! Homage to you, O ye gods, who dwell in the Tenait (Circle of Light)! Homage to you, O ye gods of the Circle of the country of the Cataracts! Homage to you, O ye gods who dwell in Amentet! Homage to you, O ye gods who dwell within Nut!

Grant ye to me that I may come before you, I am pure, I am like a god. I am endowed with a Spirit-soul. I am strong. I am endowed with a Heart-soul. I bring unto you incense, and spice, and natron. I have done away with the chidings of your mouths. I have come, I have done away the evil which was in your hearts, and I have removed the offences which appertained to you [against me]. I bring to you deeds of well-doing, and I present before you truth. I know you. I know your names. I know your forms which are not known. I come into being among you. My coming is like unto that god who eateth men, and who feedeth upon the gods. I am strong before you even like that god who is exalted upon his pedestal, unto whom the gods come with rejoicing, and the goddesses make supplication when they see me. I have come unto you. I have ascended my throne like your Two Daughters.

I have taken my seat in the horizon. I receive my offerings of propitiation upon my altars. I drink my fill of seth wine every evening. I come to those who are making rejoicings, and the gods who live in the horizon ascribe unto me praises, as the divine Spirit-body, the Lord of mortals. I am exalted like that holy god who dwelleth in the Great House. The gods rejoice greatly when they see my beautiful appearances from the body of the goddess Nut, and when the goddess Nut bringeth me forth.

[THE CHAPTER OF] MAKING THE TRANSFORMATION INTO THE SERPENT SATA. The Osiris Ani, whose word is truth, saith:- I am the serpent Sata whose years are infinite. I lie down dead. I am born daily. I am the serpent Sa-en-ta, the dweller in the uttermost parts of the earth. I lie down in death. I am born, I become new, I renew my youth every day.

[THE CHAPTER OF] MAKING THE TRANSFORMATION INTO THE CROCODILE-GOD. The Osiris Ani, whose word is truth, saith:- I am the Crocodile-god (Sebak) who dwelleth amid his terrors. I am the Crocodile-god and I seize [my prey] like a ravening beast. I am the great Fish which is in Kamui. I am the Lord to whom bowings and prostrations are made in Sekhem. And the Osiris Ani is the lord to whom bowings and prostrations are made in Sekhem. (From the Papyrus of Nebseni) Behold, I am the dweller in his terrors, I am the crocodile, his firstborn. I bring (prey) from a distance. I am the Fish of Horus, the Great One in Kamui. I am the lord of bowings in Sekhem.

THE CHAPTER OF MAKING THE TRANSFORMATION INTO PTAH.

The Osiris Ani [whose word is truth, saith]:- I eat bread. I drink ale. I gird up my garments. I fly like a hawk. I cackle like the Smen goose. I alight upon that place hard by the Sepulchre on the festival of the Great God. That which is abominable, that which is abominable I will not eat. [An abominable thing] is filth, I will not eat thereof. That which is an abomination unto my KA shall not enter my body. I will live upon that whereon live the gods and the Spirit-souls. I shall live, and I shall be master of their cakes. I am master of them, and I shall eat them under the trees of the dweller in the House of Hathor, my Lady. I will make an offering. My cakes are in Tetu, my offerings are in Anu. I gird about myself the robe which is woven for me by the goddess Tait. I shall stand up and sit down in whatsoever place it pleaseth me to do so. My head is like unto that of Ra. I am gathered together like Tem. Here offer the four cakes of Ra, and the offerings of the earth. I shall come forth. My tongue is like that of Ptah, and my throat is like unto that of Hathor, and I remember the words of Tem, of my father, with my mouth. He forced the woman, the wife of Keb, breaking the heads near him; therefore was the fear of him there. [His] praises are repeated with vigour.

I am decreed to be the Heir, the lord of the earth of Keb. I have union with women. Keb hath refreshed me, and he hath caused me to ascend his throne. Those who dwell in Anu bow their heads to me. I am [their] Bull, I am stronger than [the Lord] of the hour. I unite with women. I am master for millions of years.

[THE CHAPTER OF] MAKING THE TRANSFORMATION INTO THE SOUL OF TEM.

The Osiris Ani, whose word is truth, saith:- I shall not enter into the place of destruction, I shall not perish, I shall not know [decay]. I am Ra, who came forth from Nu, the Soul of the God who created his own members. What I abominate is sin; I will not look thereon. I cry not out against truth, nay, I live therein. I am the god Hu, the imperishable god, in my name of "Soul." I have created myself with Nu, in the name of "Khepera." I exist in them like Ra. I am the Lord of Light.

APPENDIX (From the Papyrus of Nu) That which is an abomination unto me is death; let me not go into the chamber of torture which is in the Tuat. I am the delight of the Khu of Osiris. I make to be content the heart[s] of those who dwell among the divine things which are beloved [by me]. They cause the fear of me [to abound], they create the awe of me to be in those divine beings who dwell in their own circles. Behold, I am exalted on my own standard, and upon my throne, and upon my seat which is assigned [to me]. I am the god Nu, and those who commit sin shall not destroy me. I am the firstborn of the primeval god, and my soul is the Souls of the Eternal Gods, and my body is Everlastingness.

My created form is [that of] the god Eternity, the Lord of Years, and the Prince of Everlastingness. I am the Creator of the Darkness, who maketh his seat in the uttermost limits of the heavens, [which] I love. I arrive at their boundaries. I advance upon my two legs. I direct my resting place. I sail over the sky. I fetter and destroy the hidden serpents which are about my footsteps [in going to] the Lord of the Two Arms. My soul is the Souls of the Eternal Gods, and my body is Everlastingness. I am the exalted one, the Lord of the Land of Tebu. I am the Child in the city: "Young man in the country" is my name. "Imperishable one" is my name. I am the Soul Creator of Nu. I make my habitation in Khert-Neter. My nest is invisible, my egg is not broken. I have done away the evil which is in me.
I shall see my Father, the Lord of the Evening. His body dwelleth in Anu. I am made to be the Light-god, a dweller in the Light-god, over the Western Domain of the Hebt bird.

[THE CHAPTER OF] MAKING THE TRANSFORMATION INTO THE BENU BIRD. The Osiris, the scribe Ani, whose word is truth, saith:- I flew up out of primeval matter. I came into being like the god Khepera. I germinated like the plants. I am concealed like the tortoise [in his shell]. I am the seed of every god. I am Yesterday of the Four [Quarters of the Earth, and] the Seven Uraei, who came into being in the Eastern land. [I am] the Great One (Horus) who illumineth the Hememet spirits with the light of his body. [I am] that god in respect of Set. [I am] Thoth who [stood] between them (Horus and Set) as the judge on behalf of the Governor of Sekhem and the Souls of Anu. [He was like] a stream between them. I have come. I rise up on my throne. I am endowed with Khu. I am mighty. I am endowed with godhood among the gods. I am Khensu, [the lord] of every kind of strength.

RUBRIC: [If] this Chapter [be known by the deceased], he shall come forth pure by day after his death, and he shall perform every transformation which hs soul desireth to make. He shall be among the Followers of Un-Nefer, and he shall satisfy himself with the food of Osiris, and with sepulchral meals. He shall see the Disk [of the Sun], he shall be in good case upon earth before Ra, and his word shall be truth in the sight of Osiris, and no evil thing whatsoever shall have dominion over him for ever and ever.

[THE CHAPTER OF] MAKING THE TRANSFORMATION INTO A HERON. The Osiris the scribe Ani, whose word is truth, saith:- I am the master of beasts brought for sacrifice, [and] of the knives which are [held] at their heads [and] their beards; those who dwell in their emerald [fields], the Aged Gods, and the Spirit-souls, are ready at the moment for the Osiris Ani, whose word is truth, in peace. He maketh slaughter on the earth, and I make slaughter on the earth. I am strong. I follow the heights unto heaven. I have made myself pure.

I walk with long strides to my city. I have become an owner of land there. I advance to Sepu...... is given to me in Unu. I have set the gods upon their roads. I have made splendid the houses and towns of those who are in their shrines. I know the stream of Nut. I know Tatun. I know Teshert. I have brought along their horns. I know Heka. I have hearkened to this words. I am the Red Bull-calf which is marked with markings. The gods shall say when they hear [of me]: Uncover your faces. His coming is to me. There is light which ye know not. Times and seasons are in my body. I do not speak [lies] in the place of truth, daily. The truth is hidden on the eyebrows. [By] night [I] sail up the river to keep the feast of him that is dead, to embrace the Aged God, and to guard the earth, I the Osiris Ani, whose word is truth.
APPENDIX (From the Saite Recension)

RUBRIC: If this Chapter be known [by the deceased], he will live like a perfect Spirit-soul in Khert-Neter; no evil thing whatsoever shall overthrow him.

[THE CHAPTER OF] MAKING THE TRANSFORMATION INTO THE LOTUS. The Osiris Ani, whose word is truth, saith:- I am the holy lotus that cometh forth from the light which belongeth to the nostrils of Ra, and which belongeth to the head of Hathor. I have made my way, and I seek after him, that is to say, Horus. I am the pure lotus that cometh forth from the field [of Ra]. APPENDIX (Naville, op. cit., I, Bl. XCIII) Chapter of making the transformation into a lotus. The Osiris, the lady of of the house, Aui, whose word is truth, in peace, saith:- Hail, thou Lotus, thou type of the god Nefer-Temu! I am the man who knoweth your names. I know your names among the gods, the lords of Khert-Neter. I am one among you. Grant ye that I may see the gods who are the Guides of the Tuat. Grant ye to me a seat in Khert-Neter, near the Lords of Amentet. Assign to me a habitation in the land of Tchesert. Receive ye me in the presence of the Lords of Eternity. Let my soul come forth in whatsoever place it pleaseth. Let it not be rejected in the presence of the Great Company of the Gods.

[THE CHAPTER OF] MAKING THE TRANSFORMATION INTO THE GOD WHO LIGHTENETH THE DARKNESS. The Osiris the scribe Ani, whose word is truth, saith:- I am the girdle of the garment of the god Nu, which giveth light, and shineth, and belongeth to his breast, the illuminer of the darkness, the uniter of the two Rehti deities, the dweller in my body, through the great spell of the words of my mouth. I rise up, but he who was coming after me hath fallen. He who was with him in the Valley of Abtu hath fallen. I rest. I remember him.

The god Hu hath taken possession of me in my town. I found him there. I have carried away the darkness by my strength, I have filled the Eye [of Ra] when it was helpless, and when it came not on the festival of the fifteenth day. I have weighed Sut in the celestial houses against the Aged One who was with him. I have equipped Thoth in the House of the Moon-god, when the fifteenth day of the festival come not. I have taken possession of the Urrt Crown. Truth is in my body; turquoise and crystal are its months. My homestead is there among the lapis-lazuli, among the furrows thereof. I am Hem-Nu, the lightener of the darkness. I have come to lighten the darkness; it is light. I have lightened the darkness. I have overthrown the ashmiu- fiends. I have sung hymns to those who dwell in the darkness. I have made to stand up the weeping ones, whose faces were covered over; they were in a helpless state of misery. Look ye then upon me. I am Hem-Nu. I will not let you hear concerning it. [I have fought. I am Hem-Nu. I have lightened the darkness. I have come. I have made an end to the darkness which hath become light indeed.]

THE CHAPTER OF NOT DYING A SECOND TIME. The Osiris Ani, whose word is truth, saith:Hail, Thoth! What is it that hath happened to the children of Nut? They have waged war, they have upheld strife, they have done evil, they have created the fiends, they have made slaughter, they have caused trouble; in truth, in all their doings the strong have worked against the weak. Grant, O might of Thoth, that that which the god Tem hath decreed [may be done!] And thou regardest not evil, nor art thou provoked to anger when they bring their years to confusion, and throng in and push in to disturb their months. For in all that they have done unto thee they have worked iniquity in secret.
I am they writing- palette, O Thoth, and I have brought unto thee thine ink-jar. I am not of those who work iniquity in their secret places; let not evil happen unto me. The Osiris, the scribe Ani, whose word is truth, saith:- Hail, Temu! What manner of land is this unto which I have come? It hath not water, it hath not air; it is depth unfathomable, it is black as the blackest night, and men wander helplessly therein. In it a man cannot live in quietness of heart; nor may the longings of love be satisfied therein. But let the state of the Spirit-souls be given unto me instead of water and air, and the satisfying of the longings of love, and let quietness of heart be given unto me instead of cakes and ale. The god Tem hath decreed that I shall see thy face, and that I shall not suffer from the things which pain thee. May every god transmit unto thee his throne for millions of years. Thy throne hath descended unto thy son Horus, and the god Tem hath decreed that thy course shall be among the holy

princes. In truth he shall rule from thy throne, and he shall be heir to the throne of the Dweller in the fiery Lake [Neserser].

In truth it hath been decreed that in me he shall see his likeness, and that my face shall look upon the face of the Lord Tem. How long then have I to live? It is decreed that thou shalt live for millions of years, a life of millions of years. Let it be granted to me to pass on to the holy princes, for indeed, I have done away all the evil which I committed, from the time when this earth came into being from Nu, when it sprang from the watery abyss even as it was in the days of old. I am Fate and Osiris, I have made my transformations into the likeness of divers serpents. Man knoweth not, and the gods cannot behold the two-fold beauty which I have made for Osiris, the greatest of the gods. I have given unto him the region of the dead. And, verily, his son Horus is seated upon the throne of the Dweller in the fiery Lake [of Neserser], as his heir. I have made him to have his throne in the Boat of Millions of Years. Horus is stablished upon his throne [among his] kinsmen, and he hath all that is with him. Verily, the Soul of Set, which is greater than all the gods, hath departed. Let it be granted to me to bind his soul in fetter in the Boat of the God, when I please, and let him hold the Body of the God in fear. O my father Osiris, thou hast done for me that which thy father Ra did for thee. Let me abide upon the earth permanently. Let me keep possession of my throne.

Let my heir be strong. Let my tomb, and my friends who are upon the earth, flourish. Let my enemies be given over to destruction, and to the shackles of the goddess Serq. I am thy son. Ra is my father. On me likewise thou hast conferred life, strength, and health. Horus is established upon his tomb. Grant thou that the days of my life may come unto worship and honour. APPENDIX (From the Leyden Papyrus of Ra) RUBRIC: This Chapter shall be recited over a figure of Horus, made of lapis-lazuli, which shall be placed on the neck of the deceased. It is a protection upon earth, and it will secure for the deceased the affection of men, gods, and the Spirit-souls which are perfect. Moreover it acteth as a spell in Khert-Neter, but it must be recited by thee on behalf of the Osiris Ra, regularly and continually millions of times.

[THE CHAPTER OF] ENTERING INTO THE HALL OF MAATI TO PRAISE OSIRIS KHENTI-AMENTI. The Osiris the scribe Ani, whose word is truth, saith:- I have come unto thee. I have drawn nigh to behold thy beauties (thy beneficient goodness). My hands are [extended] in adoration of thy name of "Maat." I have come. I have drawn nigh unto [the place where] the cedar-tree existeth not, where the acacia tree doth not put forth shoots, and where the ground produceth neither grass nor herbs. Now I have entered into the habitation which is hidden, and I hold converse with Set. My protector advanced to me, covered was his face.... on the hidden things. He entered into the house of Osiris, he saw the hidden things which were therein. The Tchatchau Chiefs of the Pylons were in the form of Spirits. The god Anpu spake unto those about him with the words of a man who cometh from Ta-mera, saying, "He knoweth our roads and our towns. I am reconciled unto him. When I smell his odour it is even as the odour of one of you." And I say unto him: I the Osiris Ani, whose word is truth, in peace, whose word is truth, have come. I have drawn nigh to behold the Great Gods. I would live upon the propitiatory offerings [made] to their Doubles. I would live on the borders [of the territory of] the Soul, the Lord of Tetu. He shall make me to come forth in the form of a Benu bird, and to hold converse [with him.] I have been in the stream [to purify myself]. I have made offerings of incense. I betook myself to the Acacia Tree of the [divine] Children.

I lived in Abu in the House of the goddess Satet. I made to sink in the water the boat of the enemies. I sailed over the lake [in the temple] in the Neshmet Boat. I have looked upon the Sahu of Kamur.

I have been in Tetu. I have held my peace. I have made the god to be master of his legs. I have been in the House of Teptuf. I have seen him, that is the Governor of the Hall of the God. I have entered into the House of Osiris and I have removed the head-coverings of him that is therein. I have entered into Rasta, and I have seen the Hidden One who is therein. I was hidden, but I found the boundary. I journeyed to Nerutef, and he who was therein covered me with a garment. I have myrrh of women, together with the shenu powder of living folk. Verily he (Osiris) told me the things which concerned himself. I said: Let thy weighing of me be even as we desire. And the Majesty of Anpu shall say unto me, "Knowest thou the name of this door, and canst thou tell it?" And the Osiris the scribe Ani, whose word is truth, in peace, whose word is truth, shall say, "Khersek-Shu" is the name of this door. And the Majesty of the god Anpu shall say unto me, "Knowest thou the name of the upper leaf, and the name of the lower leaf?" [And the Osiris the scribe Ani] shall say: "Neb-Maat-heri-retiu- f" is the name of the upper leaf and "Neb-pehti-thesu-menment" [is the name of the lower leaf. And the Majesty of the god Anpu shall say], "Pass on, for thou hast knowledge, O Osiris the scribe, the assessor of the holy offerings of all the gods of Thebes Ani, whose word is truth, the lord of loyal service [to Osiris]."

APPENDIX (From the Papyrus of Nu, Brit. Mus. No. 10477, Sheet 22) [THE FOLLOWING] WORDS SHALL BE SAID BY THE STEWARD OF THE KEEPER OF THE SEAL, NU, WHOSE WORD IS TRUTH, WHEN HE COMETH FORTH TO THE HALL OF MAATI, SO THAT HE MAY BE SEPARATED FROM EVERY SIN WHICH HE HATH COMMITTED, AND MAY BEHOLD THE FACES OF THE GODS. The Osiris Nu, whose word is truth, saith: Homage to thee, O great God, Lord of Maati! I have come unto thee, O my Lord, and I have brought myself hither that I may behold thy beauties. I know thee, I know thy name, I know the names of the Forty-two Gods who live with thee in this Hall of Maati, who live by keeping ward over sinners, and who feed upon their blood on the day when the consciences of men are reckoned up in the presence of the god Un- Nefer. In truth thy name is "Rehti-Merti-Nebti-Maati." In truth I have come unto thee, I have brought Maati (Truth) to thee. I have done away sin for thee.
I have not committed sins against men. I have not opposed my family and kinsfolk. I have not acted fraudulently in the Seat of Truth. I have not known men who were of no account. I have not wrought evil. I have not made it to be the first [consideration daily that unnecessary] work should be done for me. I have not brought forward my name for dignities. I have not [attempted] to direct servants [I have not belittled God]. I have not defrauded the humble man of his property. I have not done what the gods abominate. I have not vilified a slave to his master. I have not inflicted pain. I have not caused anyone to go hungry. I have not made any man to weep. I have not committed murder. I have not given the order for murder to be committed. I have not caused calamities to befall men and women. I have not plundered the offerings in the temples. I have not defrauded the gods of their cake-offerings. I have not carried off the fenkhu cakes [offered to] the Spirits. I have not committed fornication. I have not masturbated [in the sanctuaries of the god of my city].

I have not diminished from the bushel. I have not filched [land from my neighbour's estate and] added it to my own acre. I have not encroached upon the fields [of others]. I have not added to the weights of the scales. I have not depressed the pointer of the balance. I have not carried away the milk from the mouths of children. I have not driven the cattle away from their pastures. I have not snared the geese in the goose-pens of the gods. I have not caught fish with bait made of the bodies of the same kind of fish. I have not stopped water when it should flow. I have not made a cutting in a canal of running water. I have not extinguished a fire when it should burn. I have not violated the times [of offering] the chosen meat offerings. I have not driven away the cattle on the estates of the gods. I have not turned back the god at his appearances. I am pure. I am pure. I am pure. My pure offerings are the pure offerings of that great Benu which dwelleth in Hensu. For behold, I am the nose of Neb-nefu (the lord of the air), who giveth sustenance unto all mankind, on the day of the filling of the Utchat in Anu, in the second month of the season Pert, on the last of the month, [in the presence of the Lord of this earth]. I have seen the filling of the Utchat in Anu, therefore let not calamity befall me in this land, or in this Hall of Maati, because I know the names of the gods who are therein, [and who are the followers of the Great God].

THE NEGATIVE CONFESSION Hail, Usekh-nemmt, who comest forth from Anu, I have not committed sin. Hail, Hept-khet, who comest forth from Kher-aha, I have not committed robbery with violence. Hail, Fenti, who comest forth from Khemenu, I have not stolen. Hail, Am-khaibit, who comest forth from Qernet, I have not slain men and women. Hail, Neha-her, who comest forth from Rasta, I have not stolen grain. Hail, Ruruti, who comest forth from heaven, I have not purloined offerings. Hail, Arfi-em-khet, who comest forth from Suat, I have not stolen the property of God.

Hail, Neba, who comest and goest, I have not uttered lies. Hail, Set-qesu, who comest forth from Hensu, I have not carried away food. Hail, Utu-nesert, who comest forth from Het-ka-Ptah, I have not uttered curses. Hail, Qerrti, who comest forth from Amentet, I have not committed adultery, I have not lain with men. Hail, Her-f-ha-f, who comest forth from thy cavern, I have made none to weep. Hail, Basti, who comest forth from Bast, I have not eaten the heart. Hail, Ta-retiu, who comest forth from the night, I have not attacked any man.

Hail, Unem-snef, who comest forth from the execution chamber, I am not a man of deceit. Hail, Unem-besek, who comest forth from Mabit, I have not stolen cultivated land. Hail, Neb-Maat, who comest forth from Maati, I have not been an eavesdropper. Hail, Tenemiu, who comest forth from Bast, I have not slandered [no man].

Hail, Sertiu, who comest forth from Anu, I have not been angry without just cause. Hail, Tutu, who comest forth from Ati (the Busirite Nome), I have not debauched the wife of any man. Hail, Uamenti, who comest forth from the Khebt chamber, I have not debauched the wife of [any] man. Hail, Maa-antuf, who comest forth from Per-Menu, I have not polluted myself. Hail, Her-uru, who comest forth from Nehatu, I have terrorized none. Hail, Khemiu, who comest forth from Kaui, I have not transgressed [the law].

Hail, Shet-kheru, who comest forth from Urit, I have not been wroth. Hail, Nekhenu, who comest forth from Heqat, I have not shut my ears to the words of truth. Hail, Kenemti, who comest forth from Kenmet, I have not blasphemed. Hail, An-hetep-f, who comest forth from Sau, I am not a man of violence. Hail, Sera-kheru, who comest forth from Unaset, I have not been a stirrer up of strife. Hail, Neb-heru, who comest forth from Netchfet, I have not acted with undue haste. Hail, Sekhriu, who comest forth from Uten, I have not pried into matters.

Hail, Neb-abui, who comest forth from Sauti, I have not multiplied my words in speaking. Hail, Nefer-Tem, who comest forth from Het-ka-Ptah, I have wronged none, I have done no evil. Hail, Tem-Sepu, who comest forth from Tetu, I have not worked witchcraft against the king. Hail, Ari-em-ab-f, who comest forth from Tebu, I have never stopped [the flow of] water. Hail, Ahi, who comest forth from Nu, I have never raised my voice. Hail, Uatch-rekhit, who comest forth from Sau, I have not cursed God. Hail, Neheb-ka, who comest forth from thy cavern, I have not acted with arrogance. Hail, Neheb-nefert, who comest forth from thy cavern, I have not stolen the bread of the gods. Hail, Tcheser-tep, who comest forth from the shrine, I have not carried away the khenfu cakes from the Spirits of the dead. Hail, An-af, who comest forth from Maati, I have not snatched away the bread of the child, nor treated with contempt the god of my city. Hail, Hetch-abhu, who comest forth from Ta-she (the Fayyum), I have not slain the cattle belonging to the god.

APPENDIX (From the Papyrus of Nebseni) Hail, Usekh-nemmt, who comest forth from Anu, I have not committed sin. Hail, Hept-Shet, who comest forth from Kher-aha, I have not robbed with violence. Hail, Fenti, who comest forth from Khemenu, I have done no violence. Hail, Am-khaibitu, who comest forth from Qerrt, I have not stolen. Hail, Neha-hau, who comest forth from Rasta, I have not slain men. Hail, Ruruti, who comest forth from heaven, I have not made light the bushel. Hail, Arti-f-em-tes, who comest forth from Sekhem, I have not acted deceitfully. Hail, Neba, who comest and goest, I have not stolen the property of the god. Hail, Set-qesu, who comest forth from Hensu, I have not told lies. Hail, Uatch-nesert, who comest forth from Het-ka-Ptah, I have not carried away food. Hail, Qerti, who comest forth from Amenti, I have not uttered evil words.
Hail, Hetch-abhu, who comest from Ta-she, I have attacked no man. Hail, Unem-snef, who comest forth from the execution chamber, I have not salin a bull which was the property of the god. Hail, Unem-besku, who comest [forth from the Mabet chamber], I have not acted deceitfully. Hail, Neb-maat, who comest forth from Maati, I have not pillaged the lands which have been ploughed. Hail, Thenemi, who comest forth from Bast, I have never pried into matters [to make mischief]. Hail, Aati, who comest forth from Anu, I have not set my mouth in motion.

Hail, Tutuf, who comest from from A, I have not been wroth except with reason. Hail, Uamemti, who comest forth from the execution chamber, I have not debauched the wife of a man. Hail, Maa-anuf, who comest forth from Per-Menu, I have not polluted myself. Hail, Heri-uru, who comest forth from [Nehatu], I have terrorized no man. Hail, Khemi, who comest forth from Ahaui, I have not made attacks. Hail, Shet-kheru, who comest forth from Uri, I have not been a man of anger.

Hail, Nekhem, who comest forth from Heq-at, I have not turned a deaf ear to the words of truth. Hail, Ser-Kheru, who comest forth from Unes, I have not stirred up strife. Hail, Basti, who comest forth from Shetait, I have made none to weep. Hail, Her-f-ha-f, who comest forth from thy cavern, I have not committed acts of sexual impurity, or lain with men. Hail, Ta-ret, who comest forth from Akhkhu, I have not eaten my heart.

Hail, Kenmti, who comest forth from Kenmet, I have cursed no man. Hail, An-hetep-f, who comest forth from Sau, I have not acted in a violent or oppressive manner. Hail, Neb-heru, who comest forth from Tchefet, I have not acted [or judged] hastily. Hail, Serekhi, who comest forth from Unth, I have not.... my hair, I have not harmed the god. Hail, Neb-abui, who comest forth from Sauti, I have not multiplied my speech overmuch.

Hail, Nefer-Tem, who comest forth from Het-ka-Ptah, I have not acted with deciet, I have not worked wickedness. Hail, Tem-Sep, who comest forth from Tetu, I have not done things to effect the cursing of [the king]. Hail, Ari-em-ab-f, who comest forth from Tebti, I have not stopped the flow of water.
Hail, Ahi-mu, who comest forth from Nu, I have not raised my voice. Hail, Utu-rekhit, who comest forth from thy house, I have not curse God.

Hail, Neheb-Nefert, who comest forth from the Lake of Nefer, I have not acted with insufferable insolence. Hail, Neheb-kau, who comest forth from [thy] city, I have not sought to make myself unduly distinguished. Hail, Tcheser-tep, who comest forth from thy cavern, I have not increased my wealth except through such things are [justly] my own possessions. Hail, An-a-f, who comest forth from Auker, I have not scorned [or treated with contempt] the god of my town.

ADDRESS TO THE GODS OF THE TUAT (From the Papyrus of Nu, Brit. Mus. No. 10477, Sheet 24) THE FOLLOWING ARE THE WORDS WHICH THE HEART OF TRUTH THAT IS SINLESS SHALL SAY WHEN HE COMETH WITH THE WORD OF TRUTH INTO THE HALL OF MAATI; THEY SHALL BE SAID WHEN HE COMETH TO THE GODS WHO DWELL IN THE TUAT; AND THEY ARE THE WORDS WHICH ARE [TO BE SAID] AFTER [HE COMETH FORTH FROM] THE HALL OF MAATI.

Nu, the steward of the keeper of the seal, whose word is truth, saith:- Homage to you, O ye gods who dwell in your Hall of Maati! I know you, I know your names. Let me not fall under your knives of slaughter, and bring ye not forward my wickedness to this god in whose following ye are. Let not evil hap come upon me through you. Speak ye the truth concerning me in the presence of Neb-er-tcher, for I have done what is right and just in Ta-Mera. I have not cursed the god, and my evil hap did not come upon him that was king in his day. Homage to you, O ye who dwell in your Hall of Maati, who have nothing false in your bodies, who live upon Truth, who feed yourselves upon Truth in the presence of Horus who dwelleth in his Disk, deliver ye me from Beba, who feedeth upon the livers of the great ones on the day of the Great Judgment.

Grant ye that I may come before you, for I have not committed sin, I have done no act of deceit, I have done no evil thing, and I have not borne [false] witness; therefore let nothing [evil] be done to me. I have lived upon truth, I have fed upon truth, I have performed the ordinances of men, and the things which gratify the gods. I have propitiated the god by doing his will, I have given bread to the hungry man, and water to him that was athirst, and apparel to the naked man, and a ferry-boat to him that had no boat. I have made propitiatory offerings and given cakes to the gods, and the "things which appear at the word" to the Spirits. Deliver then ye me, protect then ye me, and make ye no report against me in the presence [of the Great God].

I am pure in respect of my mouth, and I am clean in respect of my hands, therefore let it be said unto me by those who shall behold me: "Come in peace, Come in peace." For I have heard that great word which the Sahu spake to the CAT, in the House of Hapt-ra. I have borne witness to Her-f-ha-f, and he hath given a decision [concerning me]. I have seen the things over which the Persea tree which is in Rasta, spreadeth its branches. I have made petitions to the gods, [and I] know the things [which appertain to] their bodies. I have come, travelling a long road, to bear righteous testimony, and to set the Balance upon its supports within Aukert. Hail, thou who art exalted high upon thy standard, thou Lord of the Atef Crown, who dost make thy name to be "Lord of the Winds," deliver thou me from thy divine Envoys who punish and afflict according to [thy] decrees, and who make calamities to arise, and whose faces are without coverings, for I have done what is right and true for the Lord of Truth. I am pure.

My breast is purified by libations, and my hinder parts are made clean with the things which make clean, and my inner parts have been dipped in the Lake of Truth. There is no single member of mine which lacketh truth. I have washed myself clean in the Lake of the South. I have rested myself in the City of the North, which is in Sekhet Sanhemu (the Field of the Grasshoppers), where the mariners of Ra wash themselves clean at the second hour of the night, and at the third hour of the day.

The hearts of the gods are gratified when they have passed over it, whether it be by night or whether it be by day, and they say unto me, "Let thyself advance." They say unto me, "Who art thou?" And they say unto me, "What is thy name?" [And I reply], "Sept-kheri-nehaitammi-beq-f" is my name. Then they say unto me, "Advance straightway on the city which is to the North of the Olive Tree. What dost thou see there?" The Leg and the Thigh. What dost thou say unto them? Let me see rejoicings in these lands of the Fenkhu. What do they give unto thee? A flame of fire and a sceptre-amulet [made] of crystal. What dost thou do with them? I bury them on the furrow of M'naat, as things for the night. What dost thou find on the furrow of Maat? A sceptre of flint, the name of which is "Giver of winds."

What now didst thou do with the flame of fire and the sceptre-amulet [made] of crystal, after thou didst bury them? I said a spell over them, and I dug them up. I quenched the flame of fire and I broke the sceptre-amulet, and I made a lake of water. [Then shall the Two and forty gods say unto me]: "Come now, pass in over the threshold of this door of the Hall of Maati, for thou hast knowledge of us." "We will not allow thee to enter in over us," say the bars of this door, "unless thou tellest us our names." [And I reply], "Tekh-bu- maa" is your name. The right lintel of this door saith: "I will not allow thee to pass over me unless thou tellest me my name." [And I reply], "Henku-en-fat-maat" is thy name. The left lintel of this door saith: "I will not allow thee to pass over me unless thou tellest me my name." [And I reply], "Henku-en-arp" is thy name. The ground of this door saith: "I will not allow thee to pass over me unless thou tellest me my name." [And I reply], "Aua-en-Keb" is thy name. And the bolt of this door saith: "I will not open the door to thee unless thou tellest me my name." [And I reply], "Saah-en-mut-f" is thy name. The socket of the fastening of this door saith: "I will not open unto thee unless thou tellest my name." [And I reply], "The Living Eye of Sebek, the Lord of Bakhau," is thy name. The Doorkeeper of this door saith: "I will not open to thee, and I will not let thee enter by me unless thou tellest my name." [And I reply], "Elbow of the god Shu who placeth himself to protect Osiris" is thy name. The posts of this door say: "We will not let thee pass in by us unless thou tellest our name." [And I reply], "Children of the uraei-goddesses" is your name.

The Doorkeeper of this door saith: "I will not open to thee, and I will not let thee enter in by me unless thou tellest my name. [And I reply], "Ox of Keb" is thy name. [And they reply], "Thou knowest us, pass in therefore by us." The ground of this Hall of Maati saith: "I will not let thee tread upon me [unless thou tellest me my name], for I am silent. I am holy because I know the names of two feet wherewith thou wouldst walk upon me. Declare, then, them to me." [And I reply], "Besu-Ahu" is the name of my right foot, and "Unpet-ent-Het-Heru" is the name of my left foot. [The ground replieth]: "Thou knowest us, enter in therefore over us." The Doorkeeper of this Hall of Maati saith: "I will not announce thee unless thou tellest my name." [And I reply], "Discerner of hearts, searcher of bellies" is thy name.
[The Doorkeeper saith]: "Thou shalt be announced." [He saith]: "Who is the god who dwelleth in his hour? Speak it" [And I reply], "Au-taui." [He saith]: "Explain who he is." [And I reply], "Au-taui" is Thoth. "Come now," saith Thoth, "for what purpose hast thou come?" [And I reply]: "I have come, and have journeyed hither that my name may be announced [to the god]." [Thoth saith]: "In what condition art thou?" [And I reply], "I, even I, am purified from evil defects, and I am wholly free from the curses of those who live in their days, and I am not one of their number." [Thoth saith]: "Therefore shall [thy name] be announced to the god." [Thoth saith]: "Tell me, who is he whose heaven is of fire, whose walls are living serpents, and whose ground is a stream of water? Who is he?" [And I reply], "He is Osiris." [Thoth saith]: "Advance now, [thy name] shall be announced to him. Thy cakes shall come from the Utchat (Eye of Horus or Ra), thy ale shall come from the Utchat, and the offerings which shall appear to thee at the word upon earth [shall proceed] from the Utchat." This is what Osiris hath decreed for the steward of the overseer of the seal, Nu, whose word is truth.

RUBRIC: THE MAKING OF THE REPRESENTATION OF WHAT SHALL HAPPEN IN THIS HALL OF MAATI. This Chapter shall be said by the deceased when he is cleansed and purified, and is arrayed in linen apparel, and is shod with sandals of white leather, and his eyes are painted with antimony, and his body is anointed with unguent made of myrrh. And he shall present as offerings oxen, and feathered fowl, and incense, and cakes and ale, and garden herbs. And behold, thou shalt draw a representation of this in colour upon a new tile moulded from earth upon which neither a pig nor any other animal hath trodden. And if this book be done [in writing, the deceased] shall flourish, and his children shall flourish, and [his name] shall never fall into oblivion, and he shall be as one who filleth the heart of the king and of his princes. And bread, and cakes, and sweetmeats, and wine, and pieces of flesh shall be given unto him [from among those which are] upon the altar of the Great God. And he shall not be driven back from any door in Amentet, and he shall be led along with the kings of the South and the kings of the North, and he shall be among the bodyguard of Osiris, continually and regularly for ever. [And he shall come forth in every form he pleaseth as a living soul for ever, and ever, and ever.]

THE CHAPTER OF THE DEIFICATION OF THE MEMBERS The hair of the Osiris Ani, whose word is truth, is the hair of Nu. The face of the Osiris Ani, whose word is truth, is the face of Ra. The eyes of the Osiris Ani, whose word is truth, are the eyes of Hathor. The ears of the Osiris Ani, whose word is truth, are the ears of Up- uatu. The lips of the Osiris Ani, whose word is truth, are the lips of Anpu. The teeth of the Osiris Ani, whose word is truth, are the teeth of Serqet. The cheeks of the Osiris Ani, whose word is truth, are the cheeks of Isis. The arms of the Osiris Ani, whose word is truth, are the arms of Ba- neb-Tetu. The neck of the Osiris Ani, whose word is truth, is the neck of Uatchit. The throat of the Osiris Ani, whose word is truth, is the throat of Mert. The breast of the Osiris Ani, whose word is truth, is the breast of the Lady of Sais. The backbone of the Osiris Ani, whose word is truth, is the backbone of Set. The trunk of the Osiris Ani, whose word is truth, is the trunk of the Lords of Kher-aha. The flesh of the Osiris Ani, whose word is truth, is the flesh of Aa- shefit. The belly of the Osiris Ani, whose word is truth, is the belly of Sekhmet. The buttocks of the Osiris Ani, whose word is truth, are the buttocks of the Eye of Horus. The phallus of the Osiris Ani, whose word is truth, is the phallus of Osiris. The thighs of the Osiris Ani, whose word is truth, are the thighs of Nut. The feet of the Osiris Ani, whose word is truth, are the feet of Ptah. The fingers of the Osiris Ani, whose word is truth, are the fingers of Saah. The toes of the Osiris Ani, whose word is truth, are the toes of the Living Uraei.

APPENDIX (From the Pyramid of Pepi I, ll. 565ff.) The head of this Meri-Ra is the head of Horus; he cometh forth therefore and ascendeth into heaven. The skull of this Pepi is the Dekan star of the god; he cometh forth therefore and ascendeth into heaven. The brow of this Meri-Ra is the brow of..... and Nu; he cometh forth therefore and ascendeth into heaven. The face of this Pepi is the face of Up-uatu; he cometh forth therefore and ascendeth into heaven. The eyes of this Meri-Ra are the eyes of the Great Lady, the first of the Souls of Anu; he cometh forth therefore and ascendeth into heaven. The nose of this Pepi is the nose of Thoth; he cometh forth therefore and ascendeth into heaven. The mouth of this Meri-Ra is the mouth of Khens-ur; he cometh forth therefore, and ascendeth therefore, and ascendeth therefore into heaven. The tongue of this Pepi is the tongue of Maaa (Truth) in the Maat Boat; he cometh forth therefore and ascendeth into heaven.

The teeth of this Pepi are the teeth of the Souls of [Anu]; he cometh forth therefore and ascendeth into heaven. The lips of this Meri-Ra are the lips of.........; he cometh forth therefore and ascendeth into heaven. The chin of this Pepi is the chin of Nest-khent-Sekhem (the throne of the First Lady of Sekhem); he cometh forth therefore and ascendeth into heaven. The thes bone of this Pepi is the thes bone of the Bull Sma; he cometh forth therefore and ascendeth into heaven. The soulders of this Pepi are the shoulders of Set; he cometh forth therefore and ascendeth into heaven. [The...... of this Pepi].........; he cometh forth therefore and ascendeth into heaven. [The......of this Pepi] ....of Baabu; he cometh forth therefore and ascendeth into heaven. The breast of this Meri-Ra is the breast of Bast; he cometh forth therefore and ascendeth into heaven. The belly of this Meri-Ra is the belly of Nut; he cometh forth therefore and ascendeth into heaven. [The........of this Pepi] ....; he cometh forth therefore and ascendeth into heaven. [The........of this Pepi] ....of the two Companies of the gods; he cometh forth therefore and ascendeth into heaven. The two thighs of this Pepi are the two thighs of Heqet; he cometh forth therefore and ascendeth into heaven. The buttocks of this Meri-Ra are like the Semktet Boat and the Mantchet Boat; he cometh forth therefore and ascendeth into heaven. The phallus of this Pepi is the phallus of the Hep Bull; he cometh forth therefore and ascendeth into heaven. The legs of this Meri-Ra are the legs of Net (Neith) and Serqet; he cometh forth therefore and ascendeth into heaven.

The knees of this Meri-Ra are the knees of the twin Souls who are at the head of the Sekhet-Tcher; he cometh forth therefore and ascendeth into heaven. The soles of this Meri-Ra are like the Maati Boat; he cometh forth therefore and ascendeth into heaven. The toes of this Pepi are the toes of the Souls of Anu; he cometh forth therefore and ascendeth into heaven. Now this Pepi is a god, the son of a god; he cometh forth therefore and ascendeth into heaven. This Pepi is the son of Ra, who loveth him; he cometh forth therefore and ascendeth into heaven. Ra hath sent forth Meri-Ra; he cometh forth therefore and ascendeth into heaven. Ra hath begotten [this] Pepi; he cometh forth therefore and ascendeth into heaven.

Ra hath given birth to Pepi; he cometh forth therefore and ascendeth into heaven. This spell therefore is in the body of Meri-Ra; he cometh forth therefore and ascendeth into heaven. This Meri-Ra is the Power, the Great Power, among the Great Council of Chiefs in Anu; he cometh forth therefore and ascendeth into heaven. He worketh the boat; Pepi cometh forth therefore and ascendeth into heaven. [Pepi is] Horus, the nursling, the child; Meri-Ra cometh forth therefore and ascendeth into heaven. Pepi hath not had union with Nut, she hath not given her hands to him; he cometh forth therefore and ascendeth into heaven. Keb hath not removed the obstacles in his path; he cometh forth therefore and ascendeth into heaven. No god hath smitten the steps of this Meri-Ra; he come forth therefore and ascendeth into heaven. [Though] Pepi is not censed is not mourned, hath not washed himself in the vessel, hath not smelt the haunch, hath not carried the meat- offering, hath not ploughed the earth, hath not dedicated an offering, he cometh forth therefore and ascendeth into heaven. Behold, it is not this Pepi who hath said these things to you, O ye gods, it is Heka who hath said these things to you, O ye gods, and this Meri-Ra is the support which is under Heka; he cometh forth therefore and ascendeth into heaven. Every god smiteth the feet of Pepi; he cometh forth therefore and ascendeth into heaven. He plougheth the earth, he dedicateth an offering, he bringeth the vessel of [blood], he smelleth the haunch, and he bringeth the meat offering; he cometh forth therefore and ascendeth into heaven. Every god graspeth the hand of Meri-Ra in heaven, He conducteth him to the House of Horus in the sky. The word of his Double is truth before Keb.

THE CHAPTER OF REPULSING SLAUGHTER IN HENSU (From the Papyrus of Nu, Sheet 6) THE CHAPTER OF DRIVING BACK THE SLAUGHTERS WHICH ARE PERFORMED IN HENSU.

The Osiris Nu, whose word is truth, saith:- O thou land of the Sceptre! O thou White Crown of the divine form! O thou rest of the ferry-boat! I am the Child. (Repeat four times). Hail, Abu-ur! Thou sayest daily: "The slaughter-block is made ready as thou knowest, and thou hast come to destruction." I am Ra, who stablisheth those who praise him. I am the Knot of the god in the Aser tree, the twice beautiful one, who is more splendid to-day than yesterday. (Repeat four times). I am Ra, who stablisheth those who praise him. I am the Knot of the god within the Aser tree, and my appearance is the appearance [of Ra] on this day. My hair is the hair of Nu. My face is the face of the Disk. My eyes are the eyes of Hathor. My ears are the ears of Up-uat. My nose is the nose of Khenti-Khabas. My lips are the lips of Anpu. My teeth are the teeth of Serqet. My cheeks are the cheeks of the goddess Isis. My hands are the hands of Ba-neb-Tet. My forearms are the forearms of Neith, the Lady of Sais.

My backbone is the backbone of Suti. My phallus is the phallus of Beba. My reins are the reins of the Lords of Kher-aha. My chest is the chest of Aa-shefit. My belly and back are the belly and back of Sekhmet. My buttocks are the buttocks of the Eye of Horus. My hips and legs are the hips and legs of Nut. My feet are the feet of Ptah. [My fingers] and my toes are the [fingers and] toes of the Living gods. There is no member of my body which is not the member of a god. Thoth protecteth my body altogether, and I am Ra day by day. I shall not be dragged back by my arms, and none shall lay violent hold upon my hands. And shall do me hurt neither men, nor gods, nor the Spirit-souls, nor the dead, nor any man, nor any pat-spirit, nor any rekhit-spirit, nor any hememet-spirit. I am he who cometh forth advancing, whose name is unknown. I am Yesterday. "Seer of Millions of Years" is my name. I pass along, I pass along the paths of the divine celestial judges. I am the Lord of Eternity: I decree and I judge like Khepera. I am the Lord of the Urrt Crown. I am he who dwelleth in the Utchat and in the Egg, and it is granted unto me to live therein.

I am he who dwelleth in the Utchat when it closeth, and I exist by the strength thereof. I come forth and I shine; I enter in and I come to life. I am in the Utchat, my seat is upon my throne, and I sit in the tent chamber before it. I am Horus. [I] traverse millions of years. I have decreed [the stablishing] of my throne, and I am the ruler thereof; and in very truth my mouth keepeth an even balance both in speech and in silence. In very truth my forms are inverted. I am Un-Nefer, from one period even unto another, and what I have is within me. I am the only One, who proceedeth from an only One, who goeth round about in his course. I am he who dwelleth in the Utchat.

No evil thing of any shape or kind shall spring up against me, and no baleful object, and no harmful thing, and no disastrous thing shall happen unto me. I open the door in heaven. I rule my throne. I open the way for the births which take place on this day. I am the child who traverseth the road of Yesterday. I am To-day for untold nations and peoples. I am he who protecteth you for millions of years. Whether ye be denizens of heaven, or of the earth, or of the South, or of the North, or of the East, or of the West, the fear of me is in your bodies. I am he whose being hath been wrought in his eye. I shall not die again. My moment is in your bodies, but my forms are in my place of habitation. I am "He who cannot be known." The Red Fiends have their faces directed against me. I am the unveiled one. The period when the heavens were created for me and were enlarged the bounds of earth, and multiplied the progeny thereof, cannot be found out. They shall fail and not be united again. By reason of the speech which I address to you, my name setteth itself apart from all things evil which are in the mouths of men. I am he who riseth and shineth, a wall which cometh out of a wall, an only One who proceedeth from an only One. There is never a day that passeth without the things which appertain unto him being therein; passing, passing, passing, passing.

Verily I say unto thee, I am the Plant which cometh forth from Nu, and my mother is Nut. Hail, my creator, I am he who hath no power to walk, the Great Knot who dwelleth in Yesterday. The might of my strength is within my hand, I am not known [by thee], but I am he who knoweth thee. I cannot be held in the hand, but I am he who can hold thee in his hand.
Hail, O Egg! Hail, O Egg! I am Horus who liveth for millions of years, whose flame shineth upon you, and bringeth your hearts unto me. I am master of my throne. I advance at this season. I have opened a path. I have delivered myself from all evil things. I am the golden dog-headed ape, three palms and two fingers [high], which hath neither arms nor legs, and which dwelleth in Het-ka-Ptah. I go forth as goeth forth the dog-headed ape who dwelleth in Het-ka-Ptah.

RUBRIC: Behold the Osiris Ani, whose word is truth, arrayed in fine linen, and shod with sandals of white [leather], and anointed with the very finest myrrh unguent. There are offered unto him a fine bull, and incense, and ra geese, and flowers, and ale, and cakes, and garden herbs. And behold, thou shalt draw a representation of a table of offerings on a clean tile with pure colours, and thou shalt bury it in a field whereon no swine hath trodden. And if a copy of this book be written upon it, he shall rise [again], and his children's children shall flourish and prosper, like unto Ra, without cessation. He shall be in high favour with the king, and with the shenit nobles of his court, and there shall be given unto him cakes and cups of drink, and portions of flesh, upon the altar-table of the Great God. He shall not thrust aside at any door in Amentet; he shall travel in the train of the Kings of the South and the Kings of the North, and he shall abide with the followers of Osiris near Un-Nefer, for ever, and for ever, and for ever.

Vignette (From the Papyrus of Nu, Sheet 24) The steward of the overseer of the seal, Nu, whose word is truth, begotten of the steward of the overseer of the seal, Amen-hetep, whose word is truth, saith:- Hail, ye Four Apes who sit in the bows of the Boat of Ra, who convey truth to Nebertcher, who sit in judgment on the oppressed man and on [his] oppressor, who make the gods to be contented by means of the flame of your mouths, who offer holy offerings to the gods, and sepulchral meals to the Spirit-souls, who live upon truth, and who feed upon truth of heart, who are without deceit and fraud, and to whom wickedness is an abomination, do ye away with my evil deeds, and put ye away my sins [which deserved stripes upon earth, and destroy ye every evil thing which appertaineth to me], and let there be no obstacle whatsoever on my part towards you.

O grant ye that I may make my way through the Amehet, let me enter into Rasta, let me pass through the hidden pylons of Ament. O grant that there may be given unto me shens cakes, and ale, and persen cakes, even as to the living Spirit-souls, and grant that I may enter into and come forth from Rasta. [The Four Apes make answer, saying]: Come thou, for we have done away with thy wickedness, and we have put away thy sin, along with thy sins upon earth which deserved stripes, and we have destroyed every evil thing which appertained to thee upon earth. Enter, therefore, unto Rasta, and pass through the hidden pylons of Amentet, and there shall be given unto thee shens cakes, and ale, and persen cakes, and thou shalt come forth and shalt enter in at thy desire, even as do those who are favoured [of the God], and thou shalt be called [to partake of offerings] each day in the horizon.

THE CHAPTER OF A TET OF GOLD. The Osiris Ani, whose word is truth, saith:- Thou risest up for thyself, O Still-heart! Thou shinest for thyself, O Still-heart! Place thou thyself on thy base, I come, I bring unto thee a Tet of gold, thou shalt rejoice therein. APPENDIX (From the Papyrus of Nebseni and the Papyrus of Nu) Rise up thou, O Osiris, thou hast thy backbaone, O Still-heart, thou hast thy neck vertebrae and thy back, O Still-heart! Place thou thyself on thy base. I put water beneath thee, and I bring unto thee a Tet of god that thou mayest rejoice therein.

RUBRIC (From the Papyrus of Nu): [This Chapter] shall be recited over a Tet of gold set in a stand made of sycamore wood which hath been steeped in a tincture of ankhamu flowers, and it shall be placed on the neck of the deceased on the day of the funeral. If this amulet be placed on his neck he shall become a perfect Khu in Khert-Neter, and at the festivals of the New Year he shall be like unto the Followers of Osiris continually and for ever.

RUBRIC (From the Turin Papyrus): [This Chapter] shall be said over a Tet of gold fashioned out of the trunk of a sycamore tree, and it shall be placed on the neck of the deceased. Then shall he enter in through the doors of the Tuat. His words whall be silenced. He shall place himself on the ground on New Year's Day among the Followers of Osiris.
If this Chapter be known by the deceased he shall live like a perfect Khu in Khert-Neter. He shall not be sent back from the doors of Amentet. There shall be given to him the shens cake, and a cup of wine, and the persen cake, and slices of meat on the altars of Ra, or as some read, Osiris Un-Nefer. And his word shall be truth before his enemies in Khert-Neter continually, and for ever and for ever.

THE CHAPTER OF A TET OF CARNELIAN. The Osiris Ani, whose word is truth, saith:- The blood of Isis, the spells of Isis, the magical powers of Isis, shall make this great one strong, and shall be an amulet of protection [against him] that would do to him the things which he abominateth.

APPENDIX RUBRIC (From the Papyrus of Nu): [This Chapter] shall be said over a Tet of carnelian, which hath been washed in a tincture of ankhamu flowers, and is fashioned out of the trunk of a sycamore tree. It shall be placed on the neck of the deceased on the day of the funeral. If this be done for him the magical powers of Isis will protect his members. Horus, the son of Isis, shall rejoice when he seeth him. [No] road shall be blocked to him. His hand shall be to heaven, his hand shall be to earth, for ever. Do not let anyone see him. Verily....

RUBRIC (From the Saite Recension): [This Chapter] shall be said over a Tet of carnelian, anointed with a tincture of ankhamu flowers, made from the trunk of a sycamore tree. It shall be placed on the neck of the Khu. If this book be done for him, the magical spells of Isis shall protect him, and Horus the son of Isis shall rejoice [when] he seeth him. No road shall be blocked to him. His hand shall be to heaven, his hand shall be to earth....... If this book be known by him he shall be in the following of Osiris Un-Nefer, and his word shall be truth in Khert- Neter. The doors in Khert-Neter shall be opened to him. Wheat and barley shall be given to him in Sekhet-Aanru. His name shall be like [the names of] the gods who are there, the Followers of Horus who reap.

THE CHAPTER OF A HEART OF SEHERT STONE. The Osiris Ani, whose word is truth, saith:I am the Benu bird, the Heart-soul of Ra, the guide of the gods to the Tuat. Their Heart-souls come forth upon earth to do what their KAU wish to do, and the Heart-soul of the Osiris Ani shall come forth to do what his Ka wisheth to do.

THE CHAPTER OF THE HEAD-REST, which is to be placed under the head of the Osiris Ani, whose word is truth. Awake out of thy sufferings, O thou who liest prostrate! Awake thou! Thy head is in the horizon. I lift thee up, O thou whose word is truth. Ptah hath overthrown thine enemies for thee. Thine enemies have fallen, and they shall never more exist, O Osiris.

APPENDIX (From the Papyrus of Nebseni, Sheet 21) THE CHAPTER OF THE HEAD-REST [OR PILLOW]. Awake out of thy sufferings, O thou who liest prostrate. They (the gods) keep watch over thy head in the horizon. Thou art lifted up, thy word is truth in respect of the things which have been done by thee. Ptah hath cast down headlong thine enemies. This work was ordered to be done for thee. Thou art Horus, the son of Hathor, Nesert, Nesertet, who giveth back the head after it hath been cut off. Thy head shall not be carried away from thee, after [it hath been cut off]; thy head shall be carried away from thee, never, never!

THE TEXTS IN THE FUNERAL CHAMBER SPEECH OF ISIS. Isis saith:- I have come to be a protector unto thee. I waft unto thee air for thy nostrils, and the north wind which cometh forth from the god Tem unto thy nose. I have made whole for thee thy windpipe. I make thee to live like a god. Thine enemies have fallen under thy feet. I have made thy word to be true before Nut, and thou art mighty before the gods. SPEECH OF NEPHTHYS. Nephthys saith unto the Osiris Ani, whose word is truth:- I go round about thee to protect thee, O brother Osiris. I have come to be a protector unto thee. [My strength shall be near thee, my strength shall be near thee, for ever. Ra hath heard thy cry, and the gods have made thy word to be truth. Thou art raised up. Thy word is truth in respect of what hath been done unto thee. Ptah hath overthrown thy foes, and thou art Horus, the son of Hathor.]

SPEECH OF THE TET. I have come quickly, and I have driven back the footsteps of thy god whose face is hidden. I have illumined his sanctuary. I stand near the god Tet on the day of repelling disaster. I watch to protect thee, O Osiris. SPEECH OF KESTA (Mesta). I am Kesta, thy son, O Osiris Ani, whose word is truth. I come to protect thee. I will make thy house to flourish, permanently, even as Ptah hath commanded me, and as Ra himself hath commanded.

SPEECH OF HAPI. I am Hapi, thy son, O Osiris Ani, whose word is truth. I come to protect thee. I bind together thy head and the members of thy body. I smite down for thee thine enemies under thee. I give unto thee thy head for ever and for ever, O Osiris Ani, whose word is truth, whose word is truth in peace. SPEECH OF TUAMUTEF. Tuamutef saith:- I am thy son Horus, who loveth thee. I come to avenge thee, O my father Osiris, upon him that did evil unto thee. I have set him under thy feet for ever and for ever, permanently, permanently, O Osiris Ani, whose word is truth, whose word is truth.

SPEECH OF QEBHSENUF. Qebsenuf saith:- I am thy son, O Osiris Ani, whose word is truth. I come to protect thee. I have collected thy bones and I have gathered together thy members. [I have brought thy heart, and I have placed it upon its throne within thy body. I make thy house to flourish after thee, O thou who livest for ever.] SPEECH OF THE FLAME. I protect thee with this flame. I drive him [the foe] away from the valley of the tomb. I cast the sand about [thy feet]. I embrace the Osiris Ani, whose word is truth, in peace. SPEECH OF THE FLAME. I come to hew in pieces. I have not been hewn in pieces, and I will not permit thee to be hewn in pieces. I come to do violence [to thy foe], but I will not permit violence to be done unto thee. I protect thee. A SOUL SAITH:- The Osiris Ani, whose is truth, praiseth Ra when he rolleth up into the sky in the eastern horizon of heaven. A SOUL SAITH:- The Osiris Ani, whose word is truth, in peace in Khert- Neter, praiseth Ra when he setteth in the western horizon of heaven, [and saith], "I am a perfect soul." SPEECH OF ANI. The Osiris Ani, whose word is truth, saith:- I am a perfect soul dwelling in the divine egg of the Abtu Fish. I am the Great Cat which dwelleth in the Seat of Truth, wherein the god Shu riseth. SPEECH OF THE USHABTI FIGURE [THE CHAPTER OF NOT DOING WORK IN KHERTNETER]. Illumine the Osiris Ani, whose word is truth. Hail, Shabti Figure! If the Osiris Ani be decreed to do any of the work which is to be done in Khert-Neter, let everything which standeth in the way be removed from him- whether it be to plough the fields, or to fill the channels with water, or to carry sand from [the East to the West]. The Shabti Figure replieth: I will do it, verily I am here [when] thou callest.

APPENDIX (From the Papyrus of Nu and the Papyrus of Nebseni) The Speech of Anpu: Anubis the dweller in the mummy chamber, Governor of the Divine House, layeth his hands upon the lord of life, the scribe, the draughtsman of Ptah, Nebseni, the lord of fealty, begotten of the scribe and mason Thena, born of the lady of the house Mut-rest, whose word is truth, and devoting himself to him as his guardian, saith:- Homage to thee, thou happy one, lord! Thou seest the Utchat. Ptah-Seker hath bound thee up. Anpu hath exalted thee. Shu hath raised thee up, O Beautiful Face, thou governor of eternity. Thou hast thine eye, O scribe Nebseni, lord of fealty, and it is beautiful. Thy right eye is like the Sektet Boat, thy left eye is like the Atet Boat. Thine eyebrows are fair to see in the presence of the Company of the Gods. Thy brow is under the protection of Anpu, and thy head and face, O beautiful one, are before the holy Hawk. Thy fingers have been stablished by thy scribe's craft in the presence of the Lord of Khemenu, Thoth, who hath bestowed upon thee the knowledge of the speech of the holy books. Thy beard is beautiful in the sight of Ptah-Seker, and thou, O scribe Nebseni, thou lord of fealty, art beautiful before the Great Company of the Gods. The Great God looketh upon thee, and he leadeth thee along the path of happiness. Sepulchral meals are bestowed upon thee, and he overthroweth for thee thine enemies, setting them under thy feet in the presence of the Great Company of the Gods who dwell in the House of the Great Aged One which is in Anu.

[HERE] BEGIN THE CHAPTERS OF SEKHET-HETEPET, AND THE CHAPTERS OF COMING FORTH BY DAY, OF ENTERING INTO AND COMING FORTH FROM KHERT-NETER, OF ARRIVING IN SEKHET-AANRU, AND OF LIVING IN PEACE IN THE GREAT CITY, THE LADY OF WINDS.

[The Osiris the scribe Ani, whose word is truth, saith:-] Let me be master there. Let me be a khu there. Let me plough there. Let me reap there. Let me eat there. Let me drink there. [Let me beget there]. Let me do there all the things which one doeth upon earth. The Osiris Ani, whose word is truth, saith:- Horus vanquished Set when [he] looked at the building of Sekhet-Hetepet. [He] spread air over the Divine Soul in its Egg, in its day. He delivered the interior of the body of Horus [from the Akeru Gods]. I have crowned him in the House of Shu. His house is the stars. Behold, I take up my place in its nomes. He hath guided the hearts of the Company of the Firstborn Gods. He hath reconciled the Two Fighters (Horus and Set), the guardians of life. He hath done what is fair, bringing an offering. He hath reconciled the Two Fighters with him that belongeth to them. He hath cut off the hairy scalp of the Two Fighters. He hath destroyed the revolts of [their] children.

I have done away all the evil which attacked their souls. I am master in [Sekhet-Hetepet]. I know it. I have sailed over its lakes that I might arrive at the cities thereof. I have made strong my mouth. The Spirit-souls are ready [to fight], but they shall not gain the mastery over me. I am equipped in thy Fields, O god Hetep. What thou wishest thou shalt do, [saith this god].

APPENDIX (From the Papyrus of Nebseni, Sheet 17) HERE BEGIN THE CHAPTERS OF SEKHET-HETEPET, AND THE CHAPTERS OF COMING FORTH BY DAY; OF GOING INTO AND OF COMING FORTH FROM KHERT-NETER; OF ARRIVAL IN SEKHET-AARU; OF LIVING IN SEKHET-HETEPET, THE MIGHTY CITY, THE LADY OF WINDS; OF HAVING POWER THEREIN; OF BECOMING A SPIRIT-SOUL THERE; OF PLOUGHING THERE; OF REAPING THERE; OF EATING THERE; OF DRINKING THERE; OF MAKING LOVE THERE; AND OF DOING EVERYTHING THERE EVEN AS A MAN DOETH UPON EARTH. NEBSENI, THE SCRIBE AND DRAUGHTSMAN OF PTAH, SAITH:-

Set vanguished Horus, who was looking at the building in Sekhet- Hetepet. I set free Horus from Set. Set opened the paths of the Two Eyes (the Sun and Moon) in the sky. Set ejected water with air upon the soul of his Eye, which dwelt in the town of Mert; he delivered the interior of the body of Horus from the hands of the Akeru Gods. Behold me! I paddle this great boat over the Lake of the god Hetep; I seized upon it in the mansion of Shu. The mansion of his stars reneweth youth, reneweth youth. I paddle over the Lakes thereof so that I may arrive at the towns thereof. I sail up to the town of the god Hetep....

Behold, I am at peace with his times, and with his guidance, and with his will, and with the Company of the Gods, who are his firstborn. He maketh the Two Fighters (Horus and Set) to be at peace [with each other], and to keep ward over the living whom he hath created in fair form, and he bringeth peace; he maketh the Two Fighters to be at peace with those who watch over them. He cutteth off the hair from their divine fighters, he driveth away storm from the children. He guardeth from attack the Spirits. I have gained power therein. I know it. I have sailed over its Lakes so that I might arrive at its towns. My mouth is strong. I am equipped against the Spirits. They shall not gain the mastery over me. I am rewarded [with] these thy Fields, O god Hetep. What thou wishest that do thou, O lord of the winds. I shall be a spirit therein. I shall eat therein. I shall drink therein. I shall plough therein. I shall reap the grain therein. I shall be strong therein.

I shall make love therein. My words shall be strong therein. I shall not be in subjection therein. I shall be a man of might therein. Thou hast made strong the mouth and throat. Hetep Qettbu is its name. [It is] stablished upon the pillars of Shu, and is linked with the pleasant things of Ra. He is the divider of years, the hidden of mouth; silent is his mouth, hidden is what he uttereth, he fulfilleth eternity, he taketh possession of everlastingness of existence as Hetep, Neb-Hetep. Horus maketh himself strong like unto a hawk which is one thousand cubits in length, and two thousand cubits in life. He that equipments with him, he journeyeth on, he cometh to the place where his heart would be, among the Lakes which are in its towns. He begetteth in the birth-chamber of the god of the town, he is satisfied with the food of the god of the town; he doeth what ought to be done there, in the Field of Smas-er-Khet..... everything of the birth-chamber of the god of the town.

Now [when he] setteth in the [land of] life like crystal he performeth everything therein, [which things are] like unto the things done in the Lake Neserser, wherein there is none that rejoiceth, and wherein are evil things of all kinds. The god Hetep goeth in and cometh out, and marcheth hither and thither in the Field of Smas-er-Khet, the Lady of the birth- chamber of the god of the town. [Let me] live with the god Hetep, clothed, and not despoiled by the Lords of the North, and may the Lord of things bring food unto me. May he make me to go forward. May I come forth. May he bring to me my Power there, may I receive it, and may I be rewarded by the god Hetep. May I be master of the great and mighty word in my body in this my place. Make me to remember it. Let me [not] forget it. Let me go forward, let me plough.

I am at peace with the god of the town. I know the water, the towns, the nomes, and the lakes which are in Sekhet-Hetepet. I live therein. I am strong therein. I shine therein. I eat therein. I..... therein. I reap the harvest therein. I plough therein. I beget children therein. I am at peace therein with the god Hetep. Behold I sow seed therein. I sail about on the lakes thereof, and I arrive at its towns, O god Hetep. Behold my mouth is equipped, it possesseth horns . Give unto me the abundance of the KAU (Doubles) and Spirit-souls. He who counteth me is Shu. I know him not. I come to its towns. I sail over its lakes. I walk about in Sekhet-Hetepet.

Behold, it is Ra who is in heaven. Behold, it is Hetep [who is] its double offering of peace. I have advanced to its territory. I have put on my apparel. I have come forth. I have given what it was upon me to give. I have made glad in [my] heart. I have conquered. I am strong. I have given directions to Hetep. [Hail], Unen-em-hetep, I have come to thee. My soul followeth me. The god Hu is on my hands. [Hail], Nebt-taui, in whom I remember and forget, I have become alive. I have attacked none, let none attack me. I have given, give thou to me gladness. Make thou me to be at peace, bind thou up my veins, let [me] receive air. [Hail], Unen-em-hetep, the Lord of Winds. I have come there. I have opened my head. Ra sleepeth. I watch not, [for] the goddess Hetemet is at the door of heaven by night. Obstacles have been put before, but I have collected his emissions. I am in my city. O Nut-urt (Great City),

I have come into thee. I have counted up my abundant stores. I advance on my way to Uakh. I am the Bull which is tied with a rope of lapis-lazuli, the lord of the Field of the Bull, the lord of the words of the god, the goddess Septet (Sothis) at her hours. O Uakh, I have come into thee. I have eaten my food. I am master of choice pieces of the flesh of oxen and of feathered fowl, and the birds of Shu have been given unto me. I follow the gods, and I come [after the Doubles]. O Tcheft, I have come into thee. I array myself in apparel, and I gird about myself the sat garment of Ra. Behold the Court of the sky, and the followers of Ra who dwell in heaven. O Un-em-hetep, the lord of the Two Lands, I have come into thee. I have plunged into the Lakes of Tchesert;

behold, impurity of every kind hath removed from me. The divine Great One flourisheth therein. Behold, I have found [him]. I have netted geese, and have fed full upon the finest of them. O Qenqentet, I have come into thee. I have seen the Osiris [my father]. I have saluted my mother. I have begotten children. I have snared the serpents, and I am delivered. I know the name of the god who is with the goddess Tchesert, and who hath straight hair, and is equipped with horns [ready to gore]. He reapeth, and I both plough and reap. O Hetemet, I have entered into thee. I have approached the lapis-lazuli. I have followed the winds of the Company of the Gods. The Great God hath given my head unto me. He who hath bound my head on my body for me is the Mighty One, with eyes of lapis-lazuli, namely, Ari-en-ab-f ("He doeth as he pleaseth").
O Usert, I have come into thee, to the house wherein food is brought unto me. O Smam, I have come into thee. My heart watcheth, my head is equipped with the White Crown. I act as the guide of the celestial beings. I make to flourish terrestrial beings. There is joy of heart for the Bull, and for the celestial beings, and for the Company of the Gods. I am the god, the Bull, the Lord of the gods, who maketh his way over the turquoise. O wheat and barley of the nome of the god, I have come into thee. I have come forward. I have lifted [you] up, following the best offerings of the Company of the Gods. I have moored my boat to the tying-up post in the lakes of the celestial beings. I have pulled up the typing-up post. I have recited words, and I have ascribed praises unto the gods who dwell in Sekhet-Hetepet.

THE CHAPTER OF PROVIDING THE DECEASED WITH MEAT, MILK, ETC.
The Osiris Ani, whose word is truth, saith:- Homage to thee, O Ra, the Lord of Truth, the Only One, the Lord of Eternity and Maker of Everlastingness. I have come before thee, O my Lord Ra. I would make to flourish the Seven Cows and their Bull. O ye who give cakes and ale to the Spirit-souls, grant ye that my soul may be with you. Let him be born on your thighs. Let him be like unto one of you for ever and for ever. Let the Osiris Ani, whose word is truth, have glorious power in the Beautiful Amentet. The Names of the Seven Holy Cows and their Bull: 1. Het-Kau Nebtertcher. 2. Akertkhentetasts. 3.

Khebitetsahneter. 4. Urmertusteshertshenti. 5. Khnemtemankhanuit. 6. Sekhmetrensemabats. 7. Shenatpetuthestneter. Bull: Kathaihemt.

ADDRESSES TO THE FOUR RUDDERS OF HEAVEN Hail, thou Beautiful Power, thou Beautiful Rudder of the Northern Heaven. Hail, thou who circlest, Guide of the Two Lands, Beautiful Rudder of the Western Heaven. Hail, Splendour, Dweller in the temple of the Ashemu gods, Beautiful Rudder of the Eastern Heaven. Hail, Dweller in the temple of the Red gods, Beautiful Rudder of the Southern Heaven.

ADDRESSES TO THE FOUR COMAPNIES OF THE GODS Hail, ye gods who are above the earth, ye Guides of the Tuat. Hail, ye Mother-goddesses, who are above the earth in Khert-Neter, in the House of Osiris. Hail, ye gods who guide Ta-tchesert, who are above the earth and are guides of the Tuat. Hail, ye Followers of Ra, who follow in the train of Osiris.

APPENDIX (From the Papyrus of Nu) RUBRIC: [These words] shall be said when Ra appeareth over [figures] of these gods written in colour upon a tablet, and thou shalt place offerings of tchefau food before them, cakes, ale, flesh, geese, and incense. They shall cause the deceased to enjoy the "offerings which come forth at the word [of command]" before Ra; and they shall give the deceased an abundance of food in Khert-Neter, and shall deliver him from every evil thing whatsoever. And thou shalt not recite this Book of Un- Nefer in the presence of anyone except thine own self. If this be done for the deceased Ra shall be a rudder for him, and shall be to him a strong protecting power, and he shall destroy all his enemies for him in Khert-Neter, and in heaven, and upon earth, and in every place whereinsoever he may enter, and he shall enjoy celestial food regularly and continually for ever.

(From the Saite Recension) THE BOOK OF MAKING PERFECT THE KHU in the heart of Ra, of making him to have the mastery before Tem, of magnifying him before Osiris, of making him mighty before Khent-Amentet, and of setting awe of him before the Company of the Gods. It shall be recited on the day of the New Moon, on the sixth day festival, on the fifteenth day festival, on the festival of Uak, on the festival of Thoth, on the Birthday of Osiris, on the festival of Menu, on the night of Heker, [during] the Mysteries of the Tuat, during the celebration of the Mysteries in Akertet, at the smiting of the emissions, at the passage of the Funerary Valley, [and] the Mysteries...... [The recital thereof] will make the heart of the Khu to flourish and will make long his strides, and will make him to advance, and will make his face bright, and will make it to penetrate to the God. Let no man witness [the recital] except the king and the Kherheb priest, but the servant who cometh to minister outside shall not see it.

Of the Khu for whom this Book shall be recited, his soul shall come forth by day with the living, he shall have power among the gods, and it will make him irresisitible for ever and ever. These gods shall go round about him, and shall acknowledge him. He shall be one of them. [This Book] shall make him to know how he came into being in the beginning. This Book is indeed a veritable mystery. Let no stranger anywhere have knowledge of it. Do not speak about it to any man. Do not repeat it. Let no [other] eye see it. Let no [other] ear hear it. Let no one see it except [thyself] and him who taught [it to thee]. Let not the multitude [know of it] except thyself and the beloved friend of thy heart. Thou shalt do this book in the seh chamber on a cloth painted with the stars in colour all over it. It is indeed a mystery. The dwellers in the swamps of the Delta nad everywhere there shall not know it. It shall provided the Khu with celestial food upon in Khert-Neter. It shall supply his Heart-soul with food upon earth. It shall make him to live for ever. No [evil] thing shall have the master over him.

THE ADDRESSES OF THE FOUR RUDDERS Hail, Power of Heaven, Opener of the Disk, thou Beautiful Rudder of the Northern Heaven. Hail, Ra, Guide of the Two Lands, thou Beautiful Rudder of the Western Heaven. Hail, Khu, Dweller in the House of the Akhemu gods, thou Beautiful Rudder of the Eastern Heaven. Hail, Governor, Dweller in the House of the Tesheru Gods, thou Beautiful Rudder of the Southern Heaven. Grant ye cakes, and ale and tchefau food to the Osiris Auf-ankh, whose word is truth. Hail, Father of the

Gods! Hail, Mother of teh Gods in Khert-Neter! Deliver ye the Osiris from every evil thing, from every evil obstruction, from every dire attack of an enemy, and from that deadly snarer with knife-like words, and from men, and gods, and Spirit-souls, and the damned, on this day, on this night, on this present festival of the fifteenth day, and in this year, and from the things of evil thereof.

HYMN TO OSIRIS KHENTI-AMENTI UN-NEFER The Osiris Ani, whose word is truth, praiseth Osiris Khenti-Amenti Un- Nefer, and saith:- Hail, my Lord, who dost hasten through eternity, whose existence is for ever, Lord of Lords, King of Kings, Sovereign, God of the Gods, who live in their shrines,.... gods.... men. Make thou for me a seat with those who are in Khert-Neter, who adore the forms of thy KA, and who traverse millions of millions of years....... May no delay arise for thee in Ta-mera. Let them come to thee, all of them, great as well as small. May this god give the power to enterin and to come forth from Khert-Neter, without repulse, at any door of the Tuat, to the KA of the Osiris Ani.

APPENDIX (From the Papyrus of Sutimes) SUTIMES, THE LIBATIONER AND PRESIDENT OF THE ALTAR CHAMBER OF THE APTS, DIRECTOR OF THE SCRIBES OF AMEN, WHOSE WORD IS TRUTH, PRAISETH OSIRIS, AND DOETH HOMAGE TO THE LORD OF ETERNITY, AND SATISFIETH THE WILL OF THE GOD, AND SPEAKETH TRUTH, THE LORD OF WHICH IS UNKNOWN, AND SAITH:

Homage to thee, O thou Holy God, thou mighty and beneficent being, thou Prince of Eternity, who dwellest in thy abode in the Sektet Boat, whose risings are manifold in the Atet Boat, unto whom praises are rendered in heaven and upon earth. Peoples and nations exalt thee, and the awe of thy terror is in the hearts of men, and Spirt-souls, and the dead. Thy soul dwelleth in Tetu, and the awe of thee is in Hensu. Thou settest the visible emblems of thyself in Anu, and the majesty of thy transformations in the holy place. I have come unto thee. Truth is in my heart, and in my breast there is neither craft nor guile. Grant thou that I may have my being among the living, and that I may sail up and down the river among those who are in thy following.

THE CHAPTER OF THE PRAISE OF HATHOR, LADY OF AMENTET

Hathor, Lady of Amentet, the Dweller in the Great Land, the Lady of Ta-Tchesert, the Eye of Ra, the Dweller in his breast, the Beautiful Face in the Boat of Millions of Years, the Seat of Peace of the doer of truth, Dweller in the Boat of the favoured ones.....

APPENDIX THE CHAPTER OF THE FOUR TORCHES (From the Papyrus of Nu, Sheets 26 and 27) THE CHAPTER OF THE FOUR LIGHTED LAMPS WHICH ARE MADE FOR THE SPIRITSOUL.

Behold, thou shalt make four rectangular troughs of clay wherein thou shalt scatter incense, and thou shalt fill them with the milk of a white cow, and by means of these thou shalt extinguish the lamps. The Osiris Nu, the steward of the overseer of the seal, whose word is truth, saith:- The fire cometh to thy KA, O Osiris Khenti-Amenti! The fire cometh to thy KA, O Osiris Nu, whose word is truth. The ordering of the night cometh after the day. [The fire cometh to thy KA, O Osiris, Governor of those who are in Amenti], and the two sisters of Ra come likewise. Behold it (the fire) riseth in Abtu, and it cometh; I cause it to come, the Eye of Horus. It is set in order upon thy brow, O Osiris Khenti-Amenti; it is set in thy shrine and riseth on thy brow; it is set on thy brow, O Osiris Nu, it is set on thy brow. The Eye of Horus protecteth thee, O Osiris Khenti-Amenti, and it keepeth thee in safety; it casteth down headlong all thine enemies for thee, and all thine enemies have fallen down headlong before thee. O Osiris Nu, the Eye of Horus protecteth thee, it keepeth thee in safety, and it casteth down headlong all thine enemies. Thine enemies have fallen down headlong before thy KA, O Osiris Khenti-Amenti. The Eye of Ra protecteth thee, it keepeth thee in safety, and it hath cast down headlong all thine enemies. Thine enemies have fallen down headlong before thy KA, O Osiris Nu, whose word is truth.

The Eye of Horus protecteth thee, it keepeth thee in safety, it hath cast down headlong for thee all thine enemies, and thine enemies have fallen down headlong before thee. The Eye of Horus cometh. It is sound and well, it sendeth forth light even as doth Ra in the horizon. It covereth the powers of Suti with darkness, it mastereth him, and it bringeth its flame against him by its own command. The Eye of Horus is sound and well, thou eatest the flesh thereof, thy body possesseth it. Thou acclaimest it. The Four Fires enter into thy KA, O Osiris Khenti-Amenti, the Four Fires enter into thy KA, O Osiris Nu, the steward of the overseer of the seal, whose word is truth.

Hail, ye sons of Horus, Kesta, Hapi, Tuamutef, and Qebhsenuf, ye have given your protection to your divine Father Osiris Khenti-Amenti, give ye your protection to the Osiris Nu, whose word is truth. Now therefore, inasmuch as ye have destroyed the Opponent of Osiris Khenti-Amenti, who liveth with the gods, having smitten Suti with his right hand and arm when dawn came upon the earth, and Horus hath become master [of Suti], and hath avenged his divine Father himself; and inasmuch as your divine Father hath been made to flourish through the union of the KA of Osiris Khenti-Amenti, which ye effected, and the Eye of Horus hath avenged him, and hath protected him, and hath cast down headlong for him all his enemies, and all his enemies have fallen down before him, even so do ye destroy the Opponent of the Osiris Nu, the steward of the overseer of the seal, whose word is truth.

Let him live with the gods, let him smite his enemy, let him destroy him, when light dawneth on the earth. Let Horus be master and avenge the Osiris Nu, and let the Osiris Nu flourish through his union with his KA which ye have effected. O Osiris Nu, the Eye of Horus hath avenged thee. It hath cast down headlong all thine enemies for thee, and all thine enemies have been cast down headlong before thee. Hail, Osiris Khenti-Amenti, grant thou light and fire to the perfect Heart-soul which is in Hensu. And [O ye Sons of Horus], grant ye power unto the living heart-soul of the Osiris Nu by means of his fire. Let him not be repulsed, and let him not be driven back at the doors of Amentet! Let his offerings of bread and of linen garments be brought unto him among the lords of funeral oblations. O offer ye praises, as unto a god to the Osiris Nu, the destroyer of his Opponent in his form of Truth, and in his attributes of a god of truth.

RUBRIC: [This Chapter] shall be recited over four torches of atma cloth, which hath been anointed with the finest Thehennu unguent, and the torches shall be placed in the hands of four men who shall have the names of the pillars of Horus written upon their shoulders, and they shall burn the torches in the beautiful light of Ra, and this shall confer power and might upon the Spirit-soul of the deceased among the stars which never set. If this Chapter be recited for him he shall never, never perish, and he shall become a living soul for ever.

These torches shall make the Spirit-soul to flourish like Osiris Khenti-Amenti, regularly and continually for ever. It is a struggle. Thou shalt not perform this ceremony before any human being except thine own self, or thy father, or thy son, because it is an exceedingly great mystery of the Amentet, and it is a type of the hidden things of the Tuat. When this ceremony hath been performed for the deceased, the gods, and the Spirit-souls, and the dead shall see him in the form of Khenti-Amenti, and he shall have power and dominion like this god. If thou shalt undertake to perform for the deceased that which is ordered in this "Chapter of the four blazing torches," each day, thou shalt cause the form of the deceased to come forth from every hall [in the Tuat], and from the Seven Halls of Osiris. And he shall live in the form of the God. He shall have power and dominion corresponding to those of the gods and the Spirit-souls for ever and ever.

He shall enter in through the secret pylons and shall not be turned back in the presence of Osiris. And it shall come to pass, provided that the following things be done for him, that he shall enter in and come forth. He shall not be turned back. No boundary shall be set to his goings, and the sentence of the doom shall not be passed upon him on the Day of the Weighing of Words before Osiris- never, never. And thou shalt perform whatsoever [is written in] this book on behalf of the deceased, who shall thereby become perfect and pure. And thou shalt "open his mouth" with the instrument of iron. And thou shalt write down these things in accordance with the instructions which are found in the books of Prince Herutataf, who discovered them in a secret coffer

(now they were in the handwriting of the god [Thoth] himself and had been deposited in the Temple of the goddess Unnut, the Lady of Unu) during a journey which he was making in order to inspect the temples, and the temple-estates, and the sanctuaries of the gods. And thou shalt perform these ceremonies secretly in the Tuat-chamber of the tomb, for they are mysteries of the Tuat, and they are symbolic of the things which are done in Khert-Neter. And thou shalt say: I have come, I have advanced hastily. I cast light upon his (the deceased's) footsteps. I am hidden, but I cast light upon his hidden place. I stand up close to the Tet. I stand up close to the Tet of Ra, I turn back the slaughter. I am protecting thee, O Osiris.
RUBRIC: This Chapter shall be recited over a Tet of crystal, which shall be set upon a brick made of crude mud, whereupon this Chapter hath been inscribed. Thou shalt make a cavity in the west wall [of the tomb], and having turned the front of the Tet towards the east, thou shalt wall up the cavity with mud which hath been mixed with extract of cedar. This Tet shall drive away the enemies of Osiris who would set themselves at the east wall [of the tomb].

And thou shalt say: I have driven back thy foes. I keep watch over thee. He that is upon his mountain (Anpu) keepeth watch over thee ready for the moment when thy foes shall attack thee, and he shall repulse them for thee. I will drive back the Crocodile at the moment when it attacketh thee, and I will protect thee, O Osiris Nu. RUBRIC: This Chapter shall be recited over a figure of Anpu made of crude mud mixed with incense. And the figure shall be set upon a brick made of crude mud, whereupon this Chapter hath been inscribed. Thou shalt make a cavity in the east wall, and having turned the face of the figure of Anpu towards the west wall [therein] thou shalt wall up the cavity. This figure shall repulse the enemies of Osiris, who would set themselves at the south wall. And thou shalt say; I am the belt of sand round about the hidden coffer. I turn back the force of the blazing fire of the funerary mountain. I traverse the roads, and I protect the Osiris Nu, the steward of the overseer of the seal, whose word is truth.

RUBRIC: This Chapter shall be recited over a brick made of crude mud whereon a copy of this Chapter hath been inscribed. And thou shalt place a reed in the middle thereof, and thou shalt smear it with pitch, and set light thereto. Then thou shalt make a cavity in the south wall, and, having turned the front of the brick towards the north, thou shalt wall the brick up inside it. [It shall repulse the enemies of the Osiris Nu] who would assemble at the north wall. And thou shalt say: O thou who comest to set fire [to the tomb or mummy], I will not let thee do it. O thou who comest to cast fire [herein], I will not let thee do it. I will burn thee, and I will cast fire upon thee. I protect the Osiris Nu, the steward of the overseer of the seal, whose word is truth.

RUBRIC: This Chapter shall be recited over a brick of crude mud, whereon a copy of this Chapter hath been inscribed. [And thou shalt set upon it] a figure of the deceased made of palm wood, seven fingers in height. And thou shalt perform on it the ceremony of "Opening the Mouth." Then thou shalt make a cavity in the north wall, and having [placed the brick and the figure inside it], and turned the face of the figure towards the south, thou shalt wall up the cavity. [It shall repulse the enemies of the Osiris Nu], who would assemble at the south wall. And behold, these things shall be done by a man who is washed clean, and is ceremonially pure, and who hath eaten neither meat nor fish, and who hath not [recently] had intercourse with women. And behold, thou shalt make offerings of cakes and ale to these gods, and shalt burn incense on their fires. Every Spirit-soul for whom these things shall be done shall become like a holy god in Khert-Neter, and he shall not be turned back at any gate in Amentet, and he shall be in the following of Osiris, whithersoever he goeth, regularly and continually.

I would like to thank God and my Ancestors for giving the opportunity to compile this very deep and inspiring spiritual manual. I would like to thank you too for reading it and please pass it on.......Vincent Happy Mnisi

Printed in Great Britain
by Amazon